Learning from Media

Arguments, Analysis, and Evidence

A volume in
Perspectives in Instructional Technology and Distance Learning
Series Editors: Charles Schlosser and Michael Simonson,
Nova Southeastern University

Library of Congress Cataloging-in-Publication Data

Clark, Richard E. (Richard Edward), 1940-
  Learning from media : arguments, analysis, and evidence / by Richard
E. Clark.
      p. cm. – (Perspectives in instructional technology and distance
learning ; 1)
Includes bibliographical references and index.

  1. Media programs (Education) I. Title. II. Series.
  LB1028.4 .C53 2001
  371.33–dc21
                                    2001004276

Printed in the United States of America

Learning from Media

Arguments, Analysis, and Evidence

Richard E. Clark
Editor

INFORMATION AGE
PUBLISHING

80 Mason Street
Greenwich, Connecticut 06830

This book is dedicated
with love
to Jason Patrick Clark

CONTENTS

PREFACE

This book presents a view of the historical development and current opinions in an ongoing debate about the role of instructional technology and media in learning and performance. The question driving the debate is whether media such as computers and television are able to influence the learning of anything, by anyone, anywhere. In the early 1980s, I joined the debate with an article that claimed that all available research best supported the conclusion that there are no learning benefits to be had from any medium used for any instructional purpose for any learners in any setting. My argument included the "grocery truck" analogy that has been quoted more often than any other part of the debate. I claimed that "The best current evidence is that media are mere vehicles that deliver instruction but do not influence student achievement any more that the truck that delivers our groceries causes changes in our nutrition" (Clark, 1983, p. 446). I made it clear that I believed that there were significant "economic" benefits to be had from media but that we could not justify instructional uses of media based on claims that they make any unique contribution to learning.

While others had made similar claims before me, I thought that the evidence justified the definite conclusion that "media do not cause learning" and I recommended that people stop asking research and evaluation questions about learning from media "unless a novel theory is suggested" (p. 457). The debate became much more interesting when Robert Kozma, then at the University of Michigan, published two major articles in which he disagreed with my views (Kozma, 1991, 1994). His articles are included in this book as are accounts of many other critics of the "media do not influence learning" position.

WHAT MOTIVATED THIS BOOK?

Many of the key articles representing the development of the arguments in the media and learning debate are no longer readily available. Nearly everyone involved with instructional uses of media has an opinion about their learning benefits and about this debate. Yet few people have had the opportunity to read and consider the arguments carefully—including some of those who have participated actively in the debate. Like many interesting issues in education, this one cannot be fully understood from an analogy or from oversimplified accounts of the arguments. Many of the key issues in the debate are connected to the very foundation of our reasoning about the scientific method, the design of experiments, and how we reason about what causes things to happen. Issues connected with these topics are often poorly understood.

Another reason for this book is that many universities now ask their instructional technology students to master the arguments in the debate. For example, the following web page describes a qualifying exam requirement at Indiana University: http://www.indiana.edu/~ist/programs/quals/readings.html. The discussion has spawned a large number of web sites that provide incomplete and often inaccurate copies of published and unpublished articles about the debate (See below for examples). In addition, nearly every new technology (or every novel use of an older technology) is accompanied by claims about "learning benefits." These claims are examined by researchers, journalists, and by those who must make decisions about the delivery of various types of instruction for very different people in a wide range of settings. This book is intended to make it easier for people with questions about the issues to get information and answers.

DESCRIPTION OF THE CHAPTERS AND
SUGGESTIONS FOR READERS

If you are trying to understand the media and learning debate arguments for a class assignment or for your own interest, I recommend that you read the chapters in this book in the following sequence: First, read chapter 1. The first chapter reproduces the beginning of my entry into the debate in 1983. The chapter is still very relevant and it is the basis for many of the subsequent arguments. I summarized that article and described published criticisms of the 1983 article over a seven-year period, in chapter 6. Then read Robert Kozma's two chapters (chapters 8 and 9). After you read Kozma, you might be interested in my reply to his arguments in chapters 11 and 12. In my view, Gary Morrison (chapter 10) has very accurately captured and criticized the exchanges between Kozma and me—and his brief analysis is well worth your time. Finally, chapter 17 is an attempt to bring the argument up to date as of late 2001.

Chapters 2 through 5 are attempts to present some of the many issues that are related to this argument. For example, chapter 2 is a critique of the meta-analytic studies of media effects on learning published by Robert and Chen-lin Kulik. Their analyses are a significant chunk of the evidence most people offer in support of the claim that media do influence learning. I reanalyzed the studies that form the heart of their argument, found a number of problems with their data, and reached a very different conclusion. Chapter 3 is a discussion of many wider issues about media and technology that was originally published as a chapter in the Handbook of Research on Teaching—co-authored with my mentor and friend, Gavriel Salomon.

Chapter 4 is a description of the argument for an international audience coauthored with Brenda Sugrue, an Irish colleague and friend, formerly a tenured professor of education at the University of Iowa and now head of her own dot com company, elearnia.com, located in Iowa City. Brenda was educated in both Europe and the United States. She understands the European context in both the research and the practical business issues connected to media questions. She and I recently co-authored a chapter on media selection for training in the American Psychological Association's new training handbook (Sugrue & Clark, 2000).

Chapter 5 is an attempt to extend the argument to multimedia research with Terry Craig, also a friend and a very successful consultant on training design and development in Los Angeles.

Chapters 13 to 16 describe my attempt to do what Gabi Salomon and I suggested fifteen years ago—to conduct research on media and technology "…in the context of, and with reference to, similar questions in the general cognitive sciences" (Clark & Salomon, 1986, p. 475). Chapters 13 and 14 were co-authored with a former student and my good friend, Fred Estes, formerly head of instructional design for the Hewlett Packard Company. Fred and I wanted to clarify the construct "technology," place it in an historical and scientific perspective, and suggest ways to enhance the development of science-based learning and performance technologies. Chapter 15 represents one of my latest enthusiasms, the study of automated mental processes that may interfere with learning from multimedia-delivered instruction. Chapters 16 and 17 attempt to apply the "media does not cause learning" argument to the evaluation of distance education programs. Chapter 17 was contributed by Gary Morrison of Wayne State University. Gary has continued to monitor the media and methods debate since it started (see chapter 10). His discussion of "equivalent evaluation" designs is a very positive way to think about media comparisons for distance learning programs.

Robert Kozma and I had an e-mail dialogue about his current views as background for chapter 18. He is taking an early, phased retirement and in general, stands by his earlier arguments. I have attempted to describe current views and how they have changed in chapter 18.

At the end of the book, you will find a biography (Appendix A) written by Mike Molenda, who is Professor of Instructional Systems Technology in the School of Education at Indiana University.

OTHER DOCUMENTS, IDEAS, AND PEOPLE INVOLVED IN THE DEBATE

Many people who have influenced this debate are not included in this book. Space limitations forced me to select only a few of the arguments and people who have made contributions. Many other ideas have been suggested.

ETR&D Special Issue. For example, the reader interested in going beyond this book might start with the excellent special issue on the debate presented in the *Educational Technology Research, and Development* journal (Vol. 42, 2, 1994) edited by Dr. Steve Ross of the University of Memphis. In that issue you will find very thoughtful articles by Sharon Shrock and Bob Reiser. The article by Gary Morrison is included in this book. I had difficulty connecting the other contributions in that issue to the media, methods, and learning issue.

NSD Media Comparison Archive. Perhaps the most extensive body of literature on media research has been developed over the years by Tom Russell who recently retired as director of Telecommunications at North Carolina State University. He has edited and sells a book that contains about 350 references of media comparison studies that resulted in NSD ("no significant differences"—check the following Web page, last accessed in August of 2001 http://teleeducation.nb.ca/nosignificantdifference/). His web page also invites researchers to submit new No Significant Difference reports of media comparison studies so that they are accessible on the web. My argument about published research in this area includes the perception that most journal editors and editorial consultants refuse to print reports of studies that contain "no significant differences." This seldom-discussed feature of academic research bias may distort our perception of the impact of media on learning. Since we only see published reports of learning advantages due to one medium or another (research that is most often confounded by poor design, in my judgement), the result is a bias that influences many people.

Web Sites Where the Debate is Discussed. There are a large number of Web pages devoted to this argument or where the issues are discussed and debated. Among them are: Steve Tripp in Japan http://itech1.coe.uga.edu/itforum/paper16/paper16.html; A paper by Tom Cobb at the Universite du Quebec a Montreal, in Montreal, Canada printed by the Educational Technology Research and Develoment journal: http://webfuse.cqu.edu.au/Information/Resources/Readings/No_Significant_Difference/; Terry Anderson at the University of Alberta commenting on implications for distance education: http://www.atl.ualberta.ca/articles/disted/alt_media.cfm; Earnest Joy at the Florida Institute for Technology and Frederico Garcia at the Center for Naval Analysis http://www.aln.org/alnweb/journal/Vol4_issue1/joygarcia.htm; Tom Reeves at the University of Georgia: http://www.doe.d5.ub.es/te/any97/gallego_force/; A South African site managing a web-based debate, includes comments from Tom Reeves and others: http://hagar.up.ac.za/rbo/construct/media.html I thought that the people who characterized my argument on this site had read it carefully. Yet this site conducted a vote on the outcome and my argument lost, 15 to 5; A discussion in French: http://www.upmf-grenoble.fr/sciedu/pdessus/Media99.PDF; and another discussion in Spanish: http://www.doe.d5.ub.es/te/any97/gallego_force/ and finally, a discussion site reacting to a posting on the debate from Gary Morrison http://www.fcae.nova.edu/WWWBOARD/fcae/si456/messages/9.html

ACKNOWLEDGMENTS

This book was suggested and enthusiastically supported by Mike Simonson, who serves as co-editor of the Information Age Publishing series *Perspectives in Instructional Technology and Distance Education.* Mike is Program Professor in the Fischler Graduate School of Education and Human Services at Nova Southeastern University in Ft. Lauderdale Florida. This book would not have been published without his encouragement and help.

I also want to thank the University of Southern California for their continued support of a generous sabbatical leave program for tenured faculty. The most focused and productive work I've done in my career has been as a direct result of the financial support I've received from USC for sabbatical research. In my view, the best research and theory is produced when distractions are removed for a significant amount of time.

No listing of acknowledgments would be complete without emphasizing the contributions of the many graduate students who have worked with me in the past thirty years. I could not hope to list them all, but I do want to acknowledge their help, support and ideas. Kay Ho, Ph.D., suggested the "generic drug" analogy and helped me shape the "grocery truck" analogy. Stuart Leonard, M.S. had a considerable influence on chapter 2 in this book. Terry Craig, Ph.D., and I co-authored chapter 5. Sydney Blake, Ph.D., collaborated on the research that supports chapter 6. And Fred Estes, Ed.D., has collaborated with me on a number of ideas, including co-authoring chapters 13 and 14.

A number of colleagues have also given strong support and helpful advice. Bob Heinich, former editor of *Audio Visual Communication Review* (the journal that became *Educational Technology Research and Development*) and a Professor in the Instructional Systems Technology program at Indiana University, gave me support and helpful advice beginning when I was a graduate student and continuing long after he had retired. Jim Knowlton, a professor at IU and one of my advisors, created and supported a questioning intellectual environment where he expected students to engage in critical thinking about basic issues. Richard Snow, professor of Education and Psychology at Stanford University and a visiting professor at Indiana University was also very supportive of my approach to media research.

Finally, and most important, I want to acknowledge the help and friendship of my teacher, mentor, and friend—Gabi Salomon. Gabi is now a senior professor and former dean of education at the University of Haifa in Israel, where he co-directs a center for peace education. In my view, since he first published his media research and theory articles in the 1970s, Gabi has been the most creative and influential media and technology researcher in the world. He is one of those rare teachers who combine brilliant analysis of problems, extraordinary expectations of his students and colleagues, and a very engaging, energetic, and supportive manner.

REFERENCES

Clark, R.E. (1983). Reconsidering research on learning from media. *Review of Educational Research, 53*(4), 445–459.

Clark, R.E., & Salomon, G. (1986) Media in teaching. In M. Wittrock (Ed.), *Handbook of research on teaching* (3rd ed., pp. 464–478). New York: Macmillan.

Kozma, R. (1991). Learning with media. *Review of Educational Research, 61*(2), 179–212.

Kozma, R.B. (1994). Will media influence learning? Reframing the debate. *Educational Technology Research, and Development, 42*(2), 7–19.

Sugrue, B.M., & Clark, R.E. (2000). Media selection for training. In S. Tobias & D. Fletcher (Eds.), *Training and retraining: A handbook for business, industry, government and the military* (pp. 208–236). New York: Macmillan.

CHAPTER 1

MEDIA ARE "MERE VEHICLES"

The Opening Argument

Richard E. Clark

Originally published as: Clark, R.E. (1983). Reconsidering research on learning from media. *Review of Educational Research, 53*(4), 445–459. Copyright 1983 by the American Educational Research Association, Reprinted by permission of the publisher.

ABSTRACT

Recent meta-analyses and other studies of media's influence on learning are reviewed. Consistent evidence is found for the generalization that there are no learning benefits to be gained from employing any specific medium to deliver instruction. Research showing performance or time-saving gains from one or another medium are shown to be vulnerable to compelling rival hypotheses concerning the uncontrolled effects of instructional method and novelty. Problems with current media attribute and symbol system theories are described and suggestions made for more promising research directions.

INTRODUCTION

Studies of the influence of media on learning have been a fixed feature of educational research since Thorndike (1912) recommended pictures as a labor-saving device in instruction. Most of this research is buttressed by the hope that learning will be enhanced with the proper mix of medium, student, subject matter content, and learning task. A typical study compares the relative achievement of groups who have received similar subject matter from different media. This research has led to so-called "media selection" schemes or models (e.g., Reiser & Gagne, 1982). These models generally promise to incorporate existing research and practice into procedures for selecting the best medium or mix of media to deliver instruction. Most of these models base many of their prescriptions on presumed learning benefits from media (Jamison, Suppes, & Welles, 1974).

However, this article will argue that most current summaries and meta-analyses of media comparison studies clearly suggest that media do not influence learning under any conditions. Even in the few cases where dramatic changes in achievement or ability have followed the introduction of a medium, as was the case with television in El Salvador (Schramm, 1977), it was not the medium that caused the change but rather a curricular reform that accompanied the change. The best current evidence is that media are mere vehicles that deliver instruction but do not influence student achievement any more than the truck that delivers our groceries causes changes in our nutrition. Basically, the choice of vehicle might influence the cost or extent of distributing instruction, but only the content of the vehicle can influence achievement. While research often shows a slight learning advantage for newer media over more conventional instructional vehicles, this advantage will be shown to be vulnerable to compelling rival hypotheses. Among these rival explanations is evidence of artifact and confounding in existing studies and biased editorial decisions which may favor research showing larger effect sizes for newer media.

MEDIA COMPARISON STUDIES

In the 1960s, Lumsdaine (1963) and others (e.g., Mielke, 1968) argued that gross media comparison and selection studies might not pay off. They implied that media, when viewed as collections of mechanical instruments, such as television and computers, were simple delivery devices. Nevertheless, earlier reviewers also held the door open to learning effects from media by attributing much of the lack of significance in prior research to poor design and lack of adequate models or theory.

Lumsdaine (1963) dealt primarily with adequate studies that had used defensible methodology, and had found significant differences between treatments. With the benefit of hindsight it is not surprising that most of the studies he selected for review employed media as simple vehicles for instructional methods, such as text organization, size of step in programming, cuing, repeated exposures, and prompting. These studies compared the effects of, for example, different step size in programmed instruction via television. It was step size (and other methods), not television (or other media), which were the focus of these studies. This is an example of what Salomon and Clark (1977) called research with media. In these studies media are mere conveyances for the treatments being examined and are not the focus of the study, though the results are often mistakenly interpreted as suggesting benefits for various media. An example of instructional research with media would be a study which contrasted a logically organized audio tutorial lesson on photosynthesis with a randomly sequenced presentation of the same frames (cf. Clark & Snow, 1975; Salomon & Clark, 1977, for a review of similar studies). Perhaps as a result of this confusion, Lumsdaine (1963) reached few conclusions beyond the suggestion that media might reduce the cost of instruction when many students are served because "the cost of perfecting it can be prorated in terms of a denominator representing thousands of students" (p. 670).

A decade later, Glaser and Cooley (1973) and Levie and Dickie (1973) were cautious about media comparison studies, which apparently were still being conducted in large numbers. Glaser and Cooley (1973) recommended using any acceptable medium as "a vehicle for making available to schools what psychologists have learned about learning" (p. 855). Levie and Dickie (1973) noted that most media comparison studies to that date had been fruitless and suggested that learning objectives can be attained through "instruction presented by any of a variety of different media" (p. 859). At the time, televised education was still a lively topic and studies of computerized instruction were just beginning to appear.

During the past decade, television research seems to have diminished considerably, but computer learning studies are now popular. This current research belongs to the familiar but generally fruitless media comparison approach or is concerned with different contents or methods being presented via different media (e.g., science teaching via computers). Generally, each new medium seems to attract its own set of advocates who make claims for improved learning and stimulate research questions which are similar to those asked about the previously popular medium. Most of the radio research approaches suggested in the 1940s (e.g., Hovland, Lumsdaine, & Sheffield, 1949) were very similar to those employed by the television movement of the 1960s (e.g., Schramm, 1977) and to the more recent reports of the computer-assisted instruction studies of the 1970s and 1980s (e.g., Dixon & Judd, 1977). It seems that similar research questions have resulted in similar and ambiguous data. Media comparison studies, regardless of the media employed, tend to result in "no significant difference" conclusions (Mielke, 1968). These findings were incorrectly offered as evidence that different media were "equally effective" as conventional means in promoting learning. No significant difference results simply suggest that changes in the outcome scores (e.g., learning) did not result from any systematic differences in the treatments compared.

Occasionally a study would find evidence for one or another medium. When this happens, Mielke (1968) has suggested that the active ingredient might be some uncontrolled aspect of the content or instructional strategy rather than the medium. When we investigate these positive studies, we find that the treatments are confounded. The evidence for this confounding may be found in the current meta-analyses of media comparison studies. The next section argues that it is the uncontrolled effects of novelty and instructional method which account for the existing evidence for the effects of various media on learning gains.

REVIEWS AND META-ANALYSES OF MEDIA RESEARCH

One of the most interesting trends in the past decade has been a significant increase in the number of excellent reviews and meta-analyses of research comparing the learning advantage of various media. The results of these overviews of past comparison studies seem to be reasonably unambiguous and unanimous. Taken together, they provide strong evidence that media comparison studies that find causal connections between media and achievement are confounded.

SIZE OF EFFECT OF MEDIA TREATMENTS

A recent series of meta-analyses of media comparison studies have been conducted by James Kulik and his colleagues at the University of Michigan (Cohen, Ebling, & Kulik, 1981; Kulik, Bangert, & Williams, 1983; Kulik, Kulik, & Cohen, 1980; Kulik, Kulik, & Cohen, 1979). These reviews employ the relatively new technology of meta-analysis (Glass, 1976), which provides more precise estimates of the effect size of various media treatments than were possible a few years ago. Previous reviews dealing primarily with "box score" sums of significant findings for media versus conventional instructional delivery were sometimes misleading. Effect size estimates often were expressed in portions of standard score advantages for one or another type of treatment. This discussion will express effects in one of two ways: (a) the number of standard deviations separating experimental and control groups, and (b) as improvements in percentile scores on a final examination.

Box Scores Versus Effect Size

An illustration of the advantage of meta-analytical effect size descriptions of past research over "box scores" is available in a recent review of Postlethwait's audio tutorial instruction studies (Kulik, Kulik, & Cohen, 1979). The authors found 42 adequate studies, of which 29 favored audio tutorial instruction and only 13 favored conventional instruction. Of those 42, only 15 reported significant differences, but 11 of the 15 favored audio tutorial and only 4 favored conventional instruction. This type of box score analysis would strongly favor the learning benefits of the audio tutorial approach over more conventional means, whereas effect size estimates of these data show only .2 standard deviations differences in the final exam scores of audio tutorial and conventional treatments. Kulik and his colleagues reported that this difference was equivalent to approximately1.6 points on a 100-point final examination. This small effect is not significant and could easily be due to confounding.

The most common sources of confounding in media research seem to be the uncontrolled effects of (a) instructional method or content differences between treatments that are compared, and (b) a novelty effect for newer media which tends to disappear over time.

UNCONTROLLED METHOD AND CONTENT EFFECTS

In effect size analyses, all adequate studies are surveyed. They involved a great variety of subject matter content, learning task types, and grade levels. The most common result of this type of survey is a small and positive effect for newer media over more conventional instructional delivery devices. However, when studies are subjected to meta-analysis, our first source of rival hypotheses, medium and method confusion, shows up.

The positive effect for media more or less disappears when the same instructor produces all treatments (Kulik, Kulik, & Cohen, 1980). Different teams of instructional designers or different teachers probably give different content and instructional methods to the treatments that are compared. If this is the case, we do not know whether to attribute the advantage to the medium or to the differences between content and method and the media being compared. However, if the effect for media tends to disappear when the same instructor or team designs contrasting treatments, we have reason to believe that the lack of difference is due to greater control of non-medium variables. It was Mielke (1968) who reminded us that when examining the effects of different media, only the media being compared can be different. All other aspects of the treatment, including the subject matter content and method of instruction, must be identical.

META-ANALYTICAL EVIDENCE FOR METHOD AND CONTENT CONFOUNDING

In meta-analyses of college-level computerized versus conventional courses, an effect size of .51 results when different faculty teach the compared course (Kulik, Kulik, & Cohen, 1980). This effect reduces to .13 when one instructor plans and teaches both experimental and control courses. Presumably, the weak but positive finding for college use of computers over conventional media is due to systematic but uncontrolled differences in content and/or method, contributed unintentionally by different teachers of designers.

Time Savings with Computers

Another instance of this artifact may be found in studies that demonstrate considerable time savings due to certain media. Comparisons of computer and conventional instruction often show 30 to 50 percent reductions in time to complete lessons for the computer groups (Kulik, Kulik, & Cohen, 1980; Kulik, Bangert, & Williams, 1983). A plausible rival hypothesis here is the possible effect of the greater effort invested in newer media programs than in conventional presentations of the same material. Comparing this increased effort invested in computer instruction to that afforded conventional instruction might be likened to sponsoring a race between a precision engineered racer and the family car. The difference in effort presumably involves more instructional design and development, which results in more effective instructional methods for the students in computer treatments. Presumably, the students in other treatments would fare as well if given the advantage of this additional design effort, which produces more effective presentations requiring less time to complete.

EXCHANGE METHOD FOR MEDIA IN
INSTRUCTIONAL RESEARCH

There is evidence in these meta-analyses that it is the method of instruction that leads more directly and powerfully to learning. Glaser (1976) defines instructional methods as "the conditions which can be implemented to foster the acquisition of competence" (p. 1). It seems not to be media but variables such as instructional methods that foster learning. For example, instructional programs such as the Keller (1968) personalized system of instruction (PSI) and programmed instruction (PI) contain methods which seek to add structure, shorter steps, reduced verbal loads, and self-pacing to lessons. Each, however, is typically associated with a different medium. The PSI (Keller plan) approach is usually presented by text, and PI is often the preferred approach of those who design computer-assisted instruction. When Studies of PI via text and via computer-assisted instruction are compared for their effect size they are similar. Both seem to show about a .2 standard deviation final examination advantage over conventional instruction (Kulik, Kulik, & Cohen, 1980). A compelling hypothesis to explain this similarity might be that most computerized instruction is merely the presentation of PI or PSI via a computer.

When computer and PI effects are compared with the use of visuals in televised or audio tutorial laboratories, the PI and computer studies show about a 30 percent larger effect size. The largest effect size however, is reserved for the PSI approach. The description of this instructional program tends to focus on its essential methods rather than on a medium. Perhaps as a result, it typically results in a .5 standard deviation effect size when compared with conventional, computer, PI or visual instruction (Kulik, Kulik, & Cohen, 1980). This would indicate that when we begin to separate method from medium we may begin to explain more significant amounts of learning variance.

UNCONTROLLED NOVELTY EFFECTS WITH NEWER MEDIA

A second, though probably less important source of confounding, is the increased effort and attention research subjects tend to give media that are novel to them. The increased attention paid by students sometimes results in increased effort or persistence, which yield achievement gains. If they are due to a novelty effect, these gains tend to diminish as students become more familiar with the new medium. This was the case in reviews of computer-assisted instruction at the secondary school level (grades 6 to 12) (Kulik, Bangert, & Williams, 1983). An average effect size of .32 (e.g., a rise in exam scores from the 50th to the 63rd percentile) for computer courses tended to dissipate significantly in longer duration studies. In studies lasting 4 weeks or less, computer effects were .56 standard deviations. This reduced to .3 in studies lasting 5 to 8 weeks and further reduced to the familiar .2 effect after 8 weeks of data collection. Cohen (1977) describes an effect size of .2 as "weak" and notes that it accounts for less than 1 percent of the variance in a comparison. Cohen, Ebling, and Kulik (1981) report a similar phenomenon in their review of visual-based instruction (e.g., film, television, pictures). Although the reduction in effect size for longer duration studies approached significance (about .065 alpha), there were a number of comparisons of methods mixed with different visual media, which makes interpretation difficult.

In their review of computer use in college, Kulik, Kulik, and Cohen (1980) did not find any evidence for this novelty effect. In their comparison of studies of 1 or 2 hours duration with those which held weekly sessions for an entire semester, the effect sizes were roughly the same. Computers are less novel experiences for college subjects than for secondary school students.

Editorial Decisions and Distortion of Effect Estimates

There is also some evidence for the hypothesis that journal editors typically select research that finds stronger effects for new media. Kulik, Bangert, and Williams (1983) reported .21 and .3 effect sizes for unpublished and dissertation studies respectively. Published studies have average effect sizes of .47 standard deviations, which is considerably larger. Kulik, Kulik, and Cohen (1979) found similar evidence in an analysis of audio tutorial instruction studies. Published studies showed a 3.8 percent final examination advantage for audio tutorial methods over conventional instruction (.31 standard deviations), but this reduced to a .6 percent advantage for the same method in unpublished studies.

A Research Caution

Based on this consistent evidence, it seems reasonable to advise strongly against future media comparison research. Five decades of research indicates that there are no learning benefits to be gained from employing different media in instruction, regardless of their obviously attractive features or advertised superiority. All existing surveys of this research indicate that confounding has contributed to the studies attributing learning benefits to one medium over another and that the great majority of these comparison studies clearly indicate no significant differences.

This situation is analogous to the problems encountered in research on teaching. In that area, the teacher was constantly confused with teaching. Improvements in research findings result when specific teaching behaviors compete to influence learning rather than different types of teachers (Rosenshine, 1971). Where learning benefits are at issue, therefore, it is the method, aptitude, and task variables of instruction that should be investigated. Studies comparing the relative achievement advantages of one medium over another will inevitably confound medium with method of instruction.

CONCLUSIONS

One might reasonably wonder why media are still advocated for their ability to increase learning when research clearly indicates that such benefits are not forthcoming. Of course such conclusions are disseminated slowly and must compete with the advertising budgets of the multimillion dollar industry which has a vested interest in selling these machines for instruction. In many ways the problem is analogous to one that occurs in the pharmaceutical industry. There we find arguments concerning the relative effectiveness of different media (tablets, capsules, liquid suspensions) and different brand names carrying the same generic drug to users.

An equal contributor to this disparity between research and practice is the high expectation we have for technology of all kinds. Other machine-based technologies similar to the newer electronic media have revolutionized industry and we have had understandable hopes that they would also benefit instruction. And, there is the fact that many educators and researchers are reserved about the effectiveness of our system of formal education. As environments for learning, media seem to offer alternative and more effective features than those available from the conventional teacher in the conventional classroom. Tobias (1982) for example, has provided evidence that we can help overcome student anxiety by allowing anxious students the chance to replay a recording of a lesson. This quality of "reviewability" is commonly thought to distinguish some of the newer media from the conventional teacher's lecture. It is important to note however, that teachers are entirely capable of reviewing material for anxious students (and probably do so often). It is what the teacher does—the teaching—that influences learning. Most of the methods carried by newer media can also be carried or performed by teachers. Dixon and Judd (1977), for example, compared teacher and computer use of "branching" rules in instruction and found no differences in student achievement attributable to these two media.

The point is made, therefore, that all current reviews of media comparison studies suggest that we will not find learning differences that can be unambiguously attributed to any medium of instruction. It seems that research is vulnerable to rival hypotheses concerning the uncontrolled effects of instructional method and novelty.

More recent evidence questions previous evidence for the media-based attempts to determine the components of effective instructional methods. These symbol system or media attribute theories seem to be useful for instructional design but of limited utility in explicating the necessary conditions that must be met by effective methods. Future research should therefore focus on necessary characteristics of instructional methods and other variables (task, learner aptitude, and attributions), which are more fruitful sources for understanding achievement increases. Recent studies dealing with learner attributions and beliefs about the instructional and entertainment qualities of different media seem particularly attractive as research directions. There are no media variables in attribution research, however. Independent variables are concerned with learner beliefs, and outcome measures are typically some measure of learner persistence at a task. It seems reasonable to recommend, therefore, that researchers refrain from producing additional studies exploring the relationship between media and learning unless a novel theory is suggested.

REFERENCES

Blake, T. (1977). Motion in instructional media: Some subject-display mode interactions. *Perceptual and Motor Skills, 44,* 975–985.

Bovy, R.A. (1983, April). *Defining the psychologically active features of instructional treatments designed to facilitate cue attendance.* Paper presented at the annual meeting of the American Educational Research Association, Montreal.

Clark, R.E. (1975). Constructing a taxonomy of media attributes for research purposes. *Audio Visual Communication Review, 23*(2), 197–215.

Clark, R.E. (1982). Antagonism between achievement and enjoyment in ATI studies. *The Educational Psychologist, 17*(2), 92–101.

Clark, R.E., & Snow, R.E. (1975). Alternative designs for instructional technology research. *Audio Visual Communication Review, 23*(4), 373–394.

Cohen, J. (1977). *Statistical power analysis for the behavioral sciences* (rev. ed.). New York: Academic Press.

Cohen P., Ebling, B., & Kulik, J. (1981). A meta-analysis of outcome studies of visual based instruction. *Education Communication and Technology Journal, 29*(1), 26–36.

Dixon, P., & Judd, W. (1977). A comparison of computer managed instruction and lecture mode for teaching basic statistics. *Journal of Computer Based Instruction, 4*(1), 22–25.

Glaser, R. (1976). Components of a psychology of instruction: Towards a science of design. *Review of Educational Research, 46*(1), 1–24.

Glaser, R., & Cooley, W.W. (1973). Instrumentation for teaching and instructional management. In R. Travers (Ed.), *Second handbook of research on teaching*. Chicago: Rand McNally College Publishing.

Glass, G.V. (1976). Primary, secondary and meta-analyses of research. *Educational Researcher, 5*(10), 3–8.

Hess, R., & Tenezakis, M. (1973). The computer as a socializing agent: Some socio-affective outcomes of CAI. *Audio Visual Communication Review, 21*(3), 311–325.

Hovland, C., Lumsdaine, A.A., & Sheffield, F. (1949). *Experiments on mass communication*. Princeton, NJ: Princeton University Press.

Jamison, D., Suppes, P., & Welles, S. (1974). The effectiveness of alternative instructional media: A survey. *Review of Educational Research, 44*, 1–68.

Keller, F. (1968). Good-bye teacher. *Journal of Applied Behavioral Analysis, 1*, 70–89.

Ksobiech, K. (1976). The importance of perceived task and type of presentation in student response to instructional television. *Audio Visual Communication Review, 24*(4), 401–411.

Kulik, C., Kulik, J., & Cohen, P. (1980). Instructional technology and college teaching. *Teaching of Psychology, 7*(4), 199–205.

Kulik, J., Bangert, R., & Williams, G. (1983). Effects of computer-based teaching on secondary school students. *Journal of Educational Psychology, 75*, 19–26.

Kulik, J., Kulik, C., & Cohen, P. (1979). Research on audio-tutorial instruction: A meta-analysis of comparative studies. *Research in Higher Education, 11*(4), 321–341.

Levie, W.H., & Dickie, K. (1973). The analysis and application of media. In R. Travers (Ed.), *The second handbook of research on teaching*. Chicago: Rand McNally.

Lumsdaine, A. (1963). Instruments and media of instruction. In N. Gage (Ed.), *Handbook of research on teaching*. Chicago: Rand McNally.

Machula, R. (1978–1979). Media and affect: A comparison of videotape, audiotape and print. *Journal of Educational Technology Systems, 7*(2), 167–185.

Mielke, K. (1968). Questioning the ETV research. *Educational Broadcasting Review, 2*, 6–15.

Mielke, K. (1980). Commentary. *Educational Communications and Technology Journal, 28*(1), 66–69.

Olson, D. (1972). On a theory of instruction: Why different forms of instruction result in similar knowledge. *Interchange, 3*(1), 9–24.

Olson, D., & Bruner, J. (1974). Learning through experience and learning through media. In D. Olson (Ed.), *Media and symbols: The forms of expression, communication, and education* (73rd Yearbook of the NSSE). Chicago: University of Chicago Press.

Reiser, R., & Gagne, R. (1982). Characteristics of media selection models. *Review of Educational Research, 52*(4), 499–512.

Rosenshine, B. (1971). *Teacher behaviors and student achievement*. London: National Foundation for Educational Research in England and Wales.

Salomon, G. (1974a). Internalization of filmic schematic operations in interaction with learners' aptitudes. *Journal of Educational Psychology, 66*, 499–511.

Salomon, G. (1974b). What is learned and how it is taught: The interaction between media, message, task and learner. In D. Olson (Ed.), *Media and symbols: The forms of expression, communication, and education* (73rd Yearbook of the NSSE). Chicago: University of Chicago Press, 1974.

Salomon, G. (1979). *Interaction of media, cognition and learning.* San Francisco: Jossey Bass.

Salomon, G. (1981). *Communication and education.* Beverly Hills, CA: Sage.

Salomon, G., & Clark, R.E. (1977). Reexamining the methodology of research on media and technology in education. *Review of Educational Research, 46,* 99–120.

Saracho, O.N. (1982). The effect of computer assisted instruction program on basic skills achievement and attitude toward instruction of Spanish speaking migrant children. *American Educational Research Journal, 19*(2), 201–219.

Schramm, W. (1977). *Big media little media.* Beverly Hills, CA: Sage.

Shuell, T.J. (1980). Learning theory, instructional theory and adoption. In R.E. Snow, P. Federico, & W. Montigue (Eds.), *Aptitude, learning and instruction* (Vol. 2). Hillsdale, NJ: Lawrence Erlbaum.

Stimmel, T., Connor, J., McCaskill, E., & Durrett, H.J. (1981). Teacher resistance to computer assisted instruction. *Behavior Research Methods and Instrumentation, 13*(2), 128–130.

Thorndike, E.L. (1912). *Education.* New York: Macmillan.

Tobias, S. (1982). When do instructional methods make a difference? *Educational Researcher, 11*(4), 4–9.

CHAPTER 2

QUESTIONING THE META-ANALYSES OF COMPUTER-BASED INSTRUCTION RESEARCH

Richard E. Clark

Originally published as: Clark, R.E. (1985). Evidence for confounding in computer-based instruction studies: Analyzing the meta-analyses. *Educational Communications and Technology Journal, 33*(4) 249–262. Reprinted by permission of the publisher, the Association for Educational Communications and Technology.

ABSTRACT

A 30 percent sample of the computer-based instruction (CBI) studies meta-analyzed by Kulik et al. was examined for evidence of confounding. The purpose of the analysis was to explore the validity of competing claims about the contribution of the computer to measured achievement gains found in CBI studies. Some of these claims propose that CBI effects are overestimated and others argue that CBI effects are underestimated. The result of the analysis strongly suggests that achievement gains found in these CBI studies are overestimated and are actually due to the uncontrolled but robust instructional methods embedded in CBI treatments. It is argued that these methods may be delivered by other media with achievement gains comparable to those reported for computers. Construct validity cautions are offered for those who wish to use meta-analytic results as evidence for implementing CBI in schools and for the design of future CBI research.

COMPUTER EFFECTS ON LEARNING

One of the major sources of support for the use of computers for instruction is the result of research studies that compare computer-based instruction (CBI) with more traditional teaching methods (e.g., Clark, 1983; Clark & Salomon, 1985; Kearsley, Hunter, & Sidel, 1983; Kulik, Bangert, & Williams, 1983; Reiser & Gagne, 1982; Sheingold, Kane, & Enderweit, 1983; Stimmel, Common, McCaskill, & Durett, 1981). Five years ago, Kulik and his colleagues located more than 500 studies in a search for classroom-based comparisons of CBI and conventional teaching (Kulik, Kulik, & Cohen, 1980). Those studies generally suggested that CBI results in more student achievement than do traditional means of instruction. It is safe to suggest that the number of locally supported research and evaluation studies that demonstrate the same CBI superiority is much greater today.

One solid indicator of our enthusiasm for computers may be found in the recent increase in the volume of research on the topic. For example, Clark (1984) noted that about 8 percent of the papers presented at the annual meeting of the American Educational Research Association examined computer use in education. It is now common for school districts to support local and costly CBI evaluations (e.g., Sheingold, Kane, & Enderweit, 1983).

META-ANALYTIC STUDIES

The most systematic attempts to review CBI research, meta-analytical surveys, report average gains of 4/10 of a standard deviation in CBI achievement scores over traditional instructional strategies (Clark, 1985). This averages to about a 15-point advantage for CBI students on a 100-point final examination. These findings are consistent for all levels of education including college (Kulik, Kulik, & Cohen, 1980), secondary schools (Kulik, Bangert, & Williams, 1983), and elementary schools (Kulik, Kulik, & Bangert-Drowns, 1984).

Yet there have been recent disputes about the validity of the CBI studies. One point of view notes evidence for the confounding of medium and method of instruction. The claim here is that methods such as the use of examples and matched non-examples, individualized pacing, corrective feedback after response, and a close correspondence between instruction and test items tend to be used in the design of CBI lessons but not by teachers in comparison treatments. The opposite interpretation suggest that confounding, when it exists, may diminish more powerful CBI effects. Here it is suggested that teachers compete with the computer, and their rivalry with a new technology masks the true effect of CBI on student achievement.

Disputes: The Instructional Method Interpretation of the "Same Teacher" Effect

Clark (1983, 1984, 1985) argues that many CBI studies are poorly designed and that variables such as instructional method, curriculum content, and/or novelty are seldom controlled. In support of the claim, Clark (1985) points to evidence that college CBI effect sizes reduce to insignificant levels when the same teacher designs *both* the CBI and the traditional treatments. He suggests that when only one designer produces both treatments, the opportunity for controlling all but the CBI aspects of the main treatment are greatest. In the "same teacher" studies therefore, the differences between CBI and traditional forms "wash out." He also points to evidence in both the college and secondary school CBI studies that the strongest effect sizes occur in the shorter term studies which suggests a novelty effect. If this hypothesis is accurate, the expensive adoption of computers by schools in order to provide compensatory enhancement of achievement may require more serious consideration.

Those who argue for the influence of instructional methods find some support in analysis of earlier media research. Freeman (1924, quoted in Saettler, 1968) challenges the simple "new versus old media" comparison study and recommended multivariate studies with more careful controls. Mielke (1968) described problems and solutions for the design of instructional television research which form the historical basis for the instructional method approach to CBI studies. He advised that when the learning benefits of newer media are being compared with the benefits of older media, only those elements which are the *fixed criterial or defining attributes of the media* can be allowed in the comparison. This means that if, for example, computers are being compared with television or teachers as instructional tools, all treatments must contain exactly the same instructional methods to present the same curriculum content. If different methods are employed to teach the same content, the results of such research would be confounded (i.e., we would not be able to distinguish the effects of a method from those of medium on subsequent changes in learning scores). In fact, a moment's reflection will establish that under these conditions there may be no reason to conduct such a study in the first place. There is little reason to believe that when all non-medium variables have been controlled, learning changes attributable to medium will occur.

Those who explain the "same teacher" data by pointing to instructional method confounding usually note the CBI research treatments employ very different levels of design effort and instructional method than contrasting or "traditional" treatments. The typical CBI treatment uses some form of drill and practice plus rule/example instructional methods to teach. These CBI programs are often the result of considerable instructional design and development effort. So-called "traditional" treatments, regardless of their delivery medium (e.g., teachers, booklets), usually take less effort and involve different (and often vaguely described) methods such as "teacher lecture plus discussion." We cannot attribute learning differences found in these comparisons to "CBI." The "same teacher" evidence in the meta-analytic reviews is, in this view, only one indication of the primacy of instructional methods over media in influencing student achievement.

Alternatives: The "John Henry" Interpretation of the "Same Teacher" Effect

There are, of course, other plausible explanations for the "same teacher" findings. It is possible that when the same teacher designs both CBI and "traditional" (usually classroom lecture) presentations, a "John Henry" (Heinich, 1970) or compensatory rivalry effect is the result (J. Kulik, personal communication). Here, the CBI teacher consciously or unconsciously reduces the learning impact of the new technology. Heinich (1984) has recently noted studies where teachers and other workers engage in such rivalry when their jobs are threatened. If this phenomenon is operating in these studies, there would be indications that the "same teacher" is producing a weak CBI presentation while enhancing the less threatening (to the teacher) "traditional" treatment. If this is the case, the actual effect size of CBI treatments should be *even greater* than the meta-analytical research reviews have suggested.

Advocates of the use of computers for instruction notice, for example, that: "The ways in which the labor movement tried to protect its members from the encroachment of technology are very similar to how teacher groups seek to maintain the labor intensive character of instruction" (Heinich, 1984, p. 78). The basic argument here is that teachers and/or curriculum specialists engage in at least two activities that lead to research confounding. First, when they develop and/or administer comparison treatments they *denigrate* the treatment(s) that are threatening. This is the opposite hypothesis to the "instructional method" explanation for the

Type of Confounding	Reason for Confounding	Impact of Confounding on Achievement Data
Instructional Methods	Methods not controlled. More robust methods used in CBI studies due to invest- ment of more design effort.	CBI Effect on Achieve- ment OVER estimated
John Henry	Teachers resist computer by denigrating CBI instruc- tion. Less robust methods used in CBI treatments.	CBI Effect on Achieve- ment UNDER estimated

Figure 1.   Summary of the instructional method and John Henry interpretations of the same teacher effect in CBI research meta-analyses.

"same teacher" CBI effect. The "John Henry" confounding occurs when teachers in the non-CBI control or comparison groups invest extraordinary effort to "defeat" the threatening technology. Examples of this phenome- non are noted by Cooley and Lohnes (1976) in their analysis of their review of large-scale evaluations of instructional programs. The source of confounding was common enough for them to recommend that future evaluations include measures of "opportunity to learn" from new instruc- tional approaches. This source of confounding was documented by Hein- ich (1970) who notes a series of studies of filmed and televised science courses such as the Wisconsin experiment on the Harvey White physics course. It is reasonable to suggest that the actual influence of CBI on learn- ing cannot be accurately estimated in the face of John Henry types of con- founding (refer to Figure 1 for a summary of the source and effect of both types of confounding).

Resolving the Disputes

One generally suspects that disputes like the one surrounding CBI will be resolved by finding "middle distance" solutions—in this case that some of the research is confounded and some is not. One obvious solution in this event would be to locate the unconfounded research and redo the meta-analysis. Yet, the problem here is that there is very little disagreement over *whether* the CBI research is confounded. The disagreement involves the *nature* of the confounding. If CBI effects are due to uncontrolled method, content, and/or novelty, then resources invested in that technol- ogy for instruction are not going to have *achievement* consequences. If the confounding is due to uncontrolled variables such as the "John Henry" effect, a correct identification of the source will allow educators to assess more realistically the potential of CBI for education. This report describes a reexamination of the studies which have formed the basis of the Kulik meta-analytic reviews to determine the source and the extent of the confounding. The discussion turns next to a closer examination of the arguments offered by both the "instructional method" and the "John Henry" advocates.

CONFOUNDING IN INSTRUCTIONAL RESEARCH

In confounded research, causes or effects cannot by unambiguously identified. When causes are confounded, it is still possible to determine the size of the effect of the treatment on the outcome measure. However, it is not possible to determine which of many uncontrolled—yet correlated—parts of the treatment contributed to the difference. In a review of problems similar to those which confront CBI analyses, Shaver (1983) concluded the "Statistical significance is not a meaningful criterion for judging whether teaching methods were adequately controlled" (p. 8). Actually, the problem is common to all research carried out in real-life settings in which clusters of correlated and uncontrolled variables operate in unison.

Those who conduct applied research are usually more concerned with effects than with causes. Cook and Campbell, in a useful discussion of the problem, explain that "...what one wants to see is evidence that the social problem being addressed is at least partially ameliorated ... Thus, great care goes into measuring outcomes ... It is our distinct impression that most applied experimental research is much more oriented toward high construct validity of effects than of causes" (1979, p. 63). Yet, attention to effects rather than causes is ultimately and paradoxically self-defeating. Since we do not know what causes the measured change, we cannot reliably repeat our successes or construct prescriptive theories. The emphasis is on *whether* things worked rather than why things worked. The result provides us with knowledge about the past applications but provides no useful predictions about ways to influence the problem in the future (Kerlinger, 1977) except to exactly replicate successful but confounded treatments.

CBI Construct Validity Benefits

The volume of research on CBI applications offers a number of potential advantages for enhancing future theory development and practice. On the one hand, there is the opportunity to increase the practical utility of CBI research by determining whether it is confounded with uncontrolled variables. While this is admittedly a negative activity, the results of such an analysis would contribute to the confidence level of those who purchase, program, and employ CBI for teaching tasks. On the other hand, an analysis of the construct validity of existing studies would also lend information about what "may have" caused the impressive achievement gains in these studies if the active ingredients were not the "computer" attributes. Such information lends itself to the generation of hypotheses and theoretical models to guide future research. As Cook and Campbell (1979) suggest, "The important point is that construct validity consists of more than merely assessing the fit between planned constructs and the operations that were tailored to these constructs. One can use the obtained pattern of data to edit one's thinking about both the cause and the effect constructs, and one can suggest, *after the fact*, other constructs that might fit the data better than those with which the experiments began" (p. 69). The goal of this research was to assess the construct validity of the CBI studies that made up the Kulik et al. meta-analyses. It is important to note that it has *not* been the goal of CBI studies to establish the construct validity of "CBI." However, the failure to attend to construct validity may have clouded our thinking about the utility of the many studies produced to date.

Meta-Analytic Studies

Recently developed technology of meta-analytic reviews of existing studies (Glass, 1976; Slavin, 1984) provides one method for gaining indicators of CBI confounding. These studies aggregate all acceptable research in an area and reduce their findings to a common metric. The purpose is to determine their "effect size" (the difference on a criterion measure between experimental and control groups, divided by the standard deviation of the control group). While the concern of these studies is internal validity, studies are coded by different design features. This allows us to estimate whether effect size might be related to design elements.

However, internal validity is a necessary (but not sufficient) prior condition for external validity. All too often, "box score" tallies of studies provided in research reviews are selected according to the reviewer's bias (Slavin, 1984). In the meta-analyses performed by Kulik and his colleagues (Kulik, Kulik, & Cohen, 1980; Kulik, Bangert, & Williams, 1983; Kulik, Kulik, & Bangert-Drowns, 1984) all available studies were surveyed and those analyzed were selected when: (a) they were methodologically sound (i.e., random subject selection, not teaching to the test in one treatment, no attrition problems); (b) studies measured outcomes of both CBI and control groups; and (c) the treatments were presented in a field (i.e., classroom/school) location. The results of these analyses indicate that the treatments used in these studies produced a robust and educationally significant gain in achievement. Therefore, these studies would be the first place to look for a determination of the active construct(s) which contributed to the gains.

In the case of the CBI meta-analyses, there are strong indications of confounding. The same teacher confounding was obvious in data reported by Kulik et al. (1980, refer to Table 1). Note that as the tendency for the same instructor to design both CBI *and* the traditional instructional treatments *increases* in the meta-analyzed studies, the effect size *decreases* (–.27). This significant correlation is one type of evidence found in the meta-analysis that provides a basis for competing claims (e.g., that the same instructor was designing the same teaching method into both CBI and control treatments which eliminated method as a source of confounding versus the same instructor was threatened by the CBI and purposely reduced its teaching effect).

Table 1.   Correlations of Selected CBI Study Features and Achievement from Kulik, Kulik, and Cohen (1980, p. 536)

Study Characteristics	Correlation with Effect
Use of Computer for Simulation	–.18
Use of Computer for Programming	–.14
Extent of use	.15
Control for Same Instructor Effect	–.27*
Duration of Treatment	–.08
Content Emphasis on "hard" discipline	–.18
Content Emphasis on "life" studies	.16

Note: *p < .05

Another type of evidence for the "same teacher" effect is represented in Table 2. Here the effect sizes are divided into those found for same teacher versus different teacher designed studies, divided by level of education. In the college sample (Kulik, Kulik, & Cohen, 1980) the contribution of CBI to achievement reduces from .51 to .13 standard deviations in same teacher studies. A similar phenomenon is obvious in the secondary school data (Kulik, Bangert, & Williams, 1983) where same teacher studies demonstrate a .07 standard deviation advantage, but different teacher studies yield a .12 advantage. The only exception to this pattern is in the more recent elementary school meta-analysis (Kulik, Kulik, & Bangert-Drowns, 1984) where the two types of studies both produced relatively high and equivalent effect sizes of .41 (for different teacher studies) and .44 (for same teachers studies).

Table 2.   Effect Size Estimates for CBI Studies Divided by Educational Level and Teacher Design Characteristic

Educational Level	Teacher Design of CBI	
	Same Teacher	Different Teacher
College (Kulik, Kulik, & Cohen, 1980)	.13	.51
Secondary (Kulik, Kulik, & Williams, 1982)	.07	.12
Elementary (Kulik, Kulik, & Bangert-Downs, 1984)	.44	.41

Since previous thinking about CBI research indicated the possibility of instructional method and compensatory rivalry problems, these are some of the main issues to be explored further. Kulik's data clearly indicate that control problems exist in many of the studies selected for analysis. If the same instructor designation is a proxy for studies where method and content are uncontrolled, one would want to know which methods are responsible for the impressive achievement gains from these studies. If teachers are purposely reducing the effects of CBI because of perceived threats, those who design instruction will benefit from the knowledge. Method confounding provides an opportunity to misinterpret the "active ingredient" of CBI as the computer when it is the choice of "instructional method" which influences learning gains. Unidentified compensatory rivalry problems lead to the assumption that CBI is less effective. Method confounding limits the *external validity* (the ability to generalize) of research whereas compensatory rivalry is a threat to *internal validity*. Since reports of CBI studies typically provide more extensive descriptions of research procedures, it is expected that they will give indications concerning the source of the confounding.

This study had three primary objectives: (a) to secure and review a representative sample of the studies that formed the basis of the meta-analyses of CBI influence on achievement; (b) to determine the type and extent of either method or compensatory rivalry confounding, perform new meta-analyses on subsets of these studies, and to note design problems with these studies if they exist; and (c) to summarize the results of the reanalysis of the studies in two forms:

1. Suggestions directed to those who develop and/or use CBI in education.
2. Suggestions directed to those who conduct research on CBI applications to teaching.

METHOD

Identification and Selection of Studies

Researchers selected a 30% random sample (n = 42) of the 128+ studies utilized by Kulik and his colleagues for their meta-analyses of college (Kulik, Kulik, & Cohen, 1980), secondary school (Kulik, Kulik, & Williams, 1983), and elementary school studies (Kulik, Kulik, & Bangert-Drowns, 1984).

Coding the Design Features of Studies

All studies were read by two experienced researchers who coded the manifest features of each study that was of interest following Clark's (1985) design. The reader should note that I was one of the two readers (and I am an advocate of the instructional method interpretation of these data). A colleague who was neutral served as the second reader.

The determination of confounding in research involves a two-stage process. First, one must determine which variables were operationalized in the treatments. This determination involves the listing of the critical defining features of each construct. Second, it is necessary to isolate and identify "cognate constructs" (Cook & Campbell, 1979). The first step is an attempt to determine whether some commonly understood and accepted version of CBI was manipulated. The second step involves a check to see if common (or uncommon) sources of threats to external validity were plausibly involved and active in the study. The only difficulty expected with the first determination is that in a number of studies, the computer is only used to test or "manage" instruction by record keeping or is used with a "no treatment" control group. These uses do not permit clear instructional comparisons between CBI and traditional forms of teaching.

It was the second determination, the identification of plausible rival hypotheses, that required the most intensive effort. Coding sheets were developed to allow reviewers to determine the robustness of many plausible external validity threats including: (a) surplus construct irrelevancies (e.g., standardizing of method and content between treatments), (b) inadequate preoperational explication of constructs (e.g., Was the CBI treatment based on what is commonly understood by that term?), (c) mono operational or mono method bias (i.e., Was more than one operational procedure examined?), (d) experimenter expectancies (i.e., Did the researcher deliver one or more treatments?), (e) a confounding of construct levels (i.e., Did one treatment exhibit more intensity or provide more opportunity to learn than another?), and (f) compensatory rivalry (i.e., Was there evidence that control teachers competed with CBI treatment?).

RESULTS AND DISCUSSION

Characteristics of the Study Sample

The two reviewers coded 40 features for each of the studies and agreed on 83% of the coding decisions—disputes were settled through discussion. It was determined that studies numbered 26 and 44 (study numbers correspond to the list at the end of the reference section) were uninterpretable and could not have been used in the meta-analyses—reports only provided mean differences between groups. Therefore, the final sample reported here totaled 40 studies. Table 3 presents the breakdown of the studies by source (dissertation, journal article, or special report), by level (primary, secondary, or college), and by expected and obtained frequencies. Since the expected frequency in each source/level cell matched the obtained frequency, we presumed that the sample was representative. Reviewers coded each study separately even though reports, 20, 34, and 40 gave details of multiple studies.

Table 3. Number of Observed and Expected Frequencies of Studies by Publication Type and Grade Level

Type	Grade			Total
	Elementary	Secondary	College	
Dissertation	4 (3)	9 (8.8)	4 (5.5)	17 (17.3)
Special Report	2 (3)	2 (1.5)	4 (4.8)	8 (9.3)
Journal	5 (5.8)	3 (2.8)	7 (6.4)	15 (15)
Total	11 (11.8)	14 (13.1)	15 (16.7)	40 (41.6)

Note: Expected study frequencies are in parentheses. Expected frequencies are the percent of the total studies in each grade/type cell.

Meta-analytic procedures applied to the 40 studies indicated that the average effect size estimate for CBI treatments was .49 standard deviations over comparison groups. This was comparable to the average of Kulik's effect size estimates (see Table 2). Other coded features of the studies also indicated that the sample was representative. The studies had a mean publication year of 1973 and a standard deviation of 3.7 years. The number of subjects participating varied from 18 to 5,000, but over 75 percent of the studies utilized 50 or more participants. A majority of the studies taught either mathematics (n = 18) or "hard" sciences (physics, chemistry, biology; n = 9) content. Over 70 percent of the studies utilized treatments which lasted over 10 hours with a time range of from 1 to 60 hours reported and a mean treatment time of 18.7 hours (sd = 13.6).

Study Design Quality

The reviewers agreed that only 10 studies in the sample were adequately designed (numbers 12, 13, 17, 18, 20, 21, 22, 23, 27, and 37). In fact, study number 17, reported by Green and Mink (1972) and conducted by the psychology faculty at Macalester College in Minnesota, was judged to be outstanding and could serve as a model for this type of investigation. The dissertation by Hatfield (1969) reported two studies (numbers 20 and 21) that were judged to be excellent examples of the way carefully conducted dissertation research evolves.

The reviewers also identified a great number of studies which seemed to have serious design flaws. For example, of the 40 studies which were interpretable, 18 provided CBI which was apparently *not* matched by non-computer delivered, control group instruction. In three other studies (numbers 19, 34, and 35) the computer group was forced to persist until an achievement criterion had been reached while subjects in the control treatments were allowed to quit instruction whenever they wished. In two other studies (numbers 1 and 7) there was obvious disproportional subject attrition from the CBI group (perhaps due to treatment difficulty). At least two studies (numbers 8 and 14) had obvious selection problems that may have resulted in more able experimental groups that control groups. In only 10 of the 40 studies were subjects randomly assigned to treatments.

Perhaps the most serious problem was that over half of the meta-analyzed studies used an untreated "traditional" control. That is, the CBI group received instruction, but the competing group(s) did not. We could hardly conclude that achievement advantages for the CBI group could be attributed to CBI advantages over traditional instruction when the comparison groups received no instruction in any form. In most cases where comparison groups were not instructed, the researchers were concerned about whether the computer could efficiently and non-reactively take over the delivery of drill and practice, thus freeing the classroom teacher. One of these studies (number 12) was particularly well designed. Yet, over half of the studies were *not* examining the *relative* learning benefits of CBI versus traditional instruction.

Confounding of Instructional Method

The most common form of CBI instructional method (n = 15 studies) was some form of "drill and practice" similar to that made popular by Suppes and Morningstar (1969). This was the method most often used for CBI subjects when no "competing" traditional treatment was used in the comparison (i.e., in numbers 9, 12, 15, 29, 38, 39, 40, 41, and 42). This control problem makes it impossible to conclude that the measured achievement gains were due to any aspect of the "computer" which was used to deliver the drill and practice. Achievement could have resulted from drill and practice delivered by nearly any medium, including teachers. Achievement gains my also have been due to student-generated learning strategies activated by simple exposure to the content. These possibilities were illustrated very dramatically in a series of CBI studies by Suppes and Morningstar (1969). They used computers to deliver additional mathematics drill and practice to elementary students. Both experimental and control groups got the same instructional methods and content, but the CBI group received an additional 5 to 8 minutes per day of computerized drill. They outperformed the control groups in all but one instance. In that school, the control group achievement was the highest of any group in this very large and well-managed study. Upon investigation, Suppes and Morningstar (1969) found that in one of the control schools the principal had become alarmed at the pretest mathematics score levels of his students and had, on his own initiative, ordered 25 minutes of teacher-provided drill and practice in mathematics a day—without the computer. We concur with Suppes and Morningstar's (1969) conclusion that the computer was not the important ingredient in the achievement gains. What was important was that "…the computerized drill and practice program required no extra time from the teacher and the student lost only 5 to 8 minutes from non-mathematical subjects" (p. 346).

The Same-Instructor Effect

There is considerable evidence in these studies (see Table 4) that when the same teacher taught both experimental (CBI) and control treatments (n = 15 studies), the opportunity for control of both instructional methods and curriculum content were *significantly greater* (Chi square value = 3.55, df = 1,39, p < .05). Perhaps more important was the finding that when meta-analysis techniques were applied to this set of same teacher studies *the effect size of CBI treatments was .09*. It was also obvious that method and content were not controlled in *all* of the "same instructor" studies, which may

Table 4.   Chi Square Analysis of Teacher And Method/Content Control Features of Study Sample

		Same Teacher?	
		Yes	No
Both method and content controlled?	Yes	8	6
	No	7	19

Note: Chi square = 3.55; df 1,39; p < .05.

be why the average effect size for the CBI treatments does not reduce to zero when these studies are separately considered in meta-analyses.

Even more important was the result of our meta-analysis of studies in our sample where instructional methods were controlled between treatments. As Table 5 illustrates, when adequate method and content controls were applied, significantly fewer outcomes in these studies favored CBI (Chi square = 4.95, df = 1,39, p < .05). *Our meta analysis of the studies in our sample where method was controlled produced an insignificant effect size of −.01.*

In only 2 of 15 studies (numbers 21 and 27) where method and content were controlled, were there significant effects for CBI. It is interesting to note that both of these well-controlled studies found differences favoring CBI only after reanalyses of delayed post tests focused on the performance of students at different ability levels. In each case (Hatfield, 1969; Lang, 1976) high ability students profited from computer programming of math or physics principles whereas low ability students had their learning depressed by the computer programming activity. In Hatfield (1969), the non-CBI treatment required performance of the same activity without the computer. In Lang (1976), the CBI instruction was an additional drill and practice exercise not matched by control group instruction. The type of task used by Hatfield requires a systematic procedural plan for using a principle to solve a problem (e.g., setting up a "lab exercise" to practice a physics principle). The plan can be developed without using a computer. In the Hatfield study, the lower ability students presumably had difficulty mastering the computer *and* the procedural planning. The computer programming task may have given the higher ability students the opportunity to employ their skills more idiosyncratically which seems generally to result in greater learning for them (e.g., Cronbach & Snow, 1977). However, even here the best hypothesis for the advantage of the high aptitude students may be in the fact that they were challenged by the difficulty of the CBI *learning task,* not by the computer per se (cf. the discussion by Clark & Salomon, 1985).

Table 5. Chi Square Analysis of Statistical Difference Results of Group Comparisons by Method/Content Control Features in Study Sample

		Statistical Differences	
		Favor CBI	NSD or Favor Control
Both methods and contents controlled?	Yes	2	12
	No	13	13

Note: Chi square = 4.95, df 1,39; p < = .05; NDS = No significant difference

Evidence for Compensatory Rivalry

It is difficult to determine whether control group teachers exerted extraordinary effort to compete with the "new" computer instruction. However, there were 10 studies in this sample where significant differences were found *favoring the control groups* (numbers 2, 3, 4, 11, 12, 22, 33, 40, 41, and 42). In these studies, live teachers outperformed computers. This seems a promising place to look for the "John Henry Effect."

Of the 10 studies where control group advantages were found, three (numbers 2, 4, and 33) were "same teacher" studies. Reviewers assumed that rivalry would be most likely where the same teacher designs both treatments. However, in two of the same teacher studies that favored the control group, there were also significant differences favoring the CBI treatments (numbers 4 and 33). Reviewers judged such mixes unlikely sources for compensatory rivalry. It is improbable that a teacher would purposely "lose" to the computer after "rigging" the competition in favor of him or herself. In two of the remaining seven studies (numbers 12 and 22), reviewers felt that both the content and methods were uncontrolled between groups, and so they were eliminated from consideration. In one of the remaining studies (number 11) the computer was used only to test students, and no instruction was provided. There was no indication of rivalry. In another of the remaining studies (number 3), there was clear evidence that the subjects simply found the CBI treatment too difficult in the time allotted.

The three remaining studies (numbers 40, 41, and 42) were all reported by Suppes and Morningstar (1969). In these studies, matched control schools had only pre- and post test measures taken. It is possible that in the control schools the pretest sensitized teachers to greater efforts and/or that there was contaminating information that control schools were competing with "computer" schools. The example (discussed above) in which one control group school principal instigated additional, non-computer drill after viewing the pretest math scores for his school is a compelling instance. Yet, three studies out of 40 do not provide strong evidence for a "John Henry Effect" interpretation of the meta-analytic reviews. Of course, it is still possible that rivalry influenced results in some of these studies, but it is impossible to determine from published reports.

SUMMARY AND CONCLUSIONS

A number of tentative conclusions can be drawn from this reanalysis of a sample of the Kulik et al. studies:

1.   The meta-analysis of our sample produced an effect size estimate of .49 which was similar to Kulik's. Yet, 75 percent of the studies used in the meta-analyses gave evidence of serious design flaws.
2.   In over 50 percent of the studies, there were obvious failures to control the amount of instruction received in the experimental and control groups. CBI groups received more instruction which may have been a major factor in producing the effect size estimates of the meta-analyses.
3.   In about 40 percent of the studies, the same teacher taught both CBI and control groups. These "same teacher" studies had significantly better teaching method and content controls than other studies. In these studies, the revised effect size of CBI was .09.
4.   Instructional method was controlled in only half of the 30 studies analyzed. The revised CBI effect size in these more adequately-controlled studies was an insignificant −.01.
5.   In only 2 of the 15 studies where instructional methods were controlled were there significant differences favoring the CBI groups. In both of these studies, significant differences were found only after delayed analyses examined the performance of students at different ability levels. This finding implies that only 5 percent of the meta-analytic studies have important achievement data favoring CBI instruction. Even here there are rival hypotheses that suggest the achievement differences are due to student trait and task interactions, not to the "computer."
6.   There is meager but compelling evidence for the "John Henry Effect" (compensatory rivalry). One study clearly indicated that a control school had been sensitized by pretest scores and, after extra non-computer drill and practice exercises, outperformed the CBI

schools. This evidence tends to support the instructional method claim of overestimation of CBI effects.

Suggestions for Research

Researchers who design CBI studies are urged to avoid gross comparisons of the relative *achievement* available from CBI and "traditional instruction." There seems to be ample evidence in existing studies that no theoretical reason exists to ask such a question. Whenever adequately designed studies have asked the question, no differences in achievement have been found that may be unambiguously attributed to "computers." Instead, researchers are encouraged to investigate the relative efficiency and cost of CBI versus traditional instruction. It is possible that computers and other new technologies for delivering information (e.g., video disk) will significantly influence the cost, management, availability, and/or the efficiency of instructional delivery to diverse student populations. In these efficiency studies, researchers are cautioned to control instructional method and content.

Suggestions for Practice

Practitioners interested in CBI are cautioned that the achievement gains attributed to the computer mode of delivery are probably due instead to the instructional methods employed in their "software." These methods could probably be delivered by a teacher. The contribution of the computer (and other new delivery technologies) may be to make instruction more efficient (free the teacher, reach more students with less per-student cost). Educators are urged to avoid rationalizing computer purchases by referencing the achievement gains in the meta-analytic studies. Computers make no more contribution to learning that the truck which delivers groceries to the market contributes to improved nutrition in a community. Purchasing a truck will not improve nutrition just as purchasing a computer will not improve student achievement. Nutrition gains come from getting the correct "groceries" to the people who need them. Similarly, achievement gains result from matching the correct teaching method to the student who needs it.

POSTSCRIPT

Since this article was written, Dr. James Kulik and his colleagues at the University of Michigan have had an opportunity to read this argument and have revised their original claims. They recently received a grant from the Exxon Education Foundation to conduct an updated analysis of the CBI research. They ignored a number of poorly designed studies from earlier analyses and included new studies which have appeared since those publications. A brief description of their new data (Kulik, Kulik, & Bangert-Drowns, in press) will be published in the *Journal of Educational Computing Research.* In a prepublication draft of that article they note that all of their more recent meta-analyses of CBI studies continue to show the "same teacher" effect. The effects are weaker in current studies but, as they state "...the direction of the difference,... is consistent with Clark's notions." (p. 9). They speculate that the lower effect size for same teacher studies is due to "...diffusion of the innovative treatment to the control condition. Involvement of a teacher in an innovated approach to instruction may have a general effect on the quality of the instructor's teaching. Outlining objectives, constructing lessons, preparing evaluation materials and working with computer materials—requirements in CBI—may help a teacher to do a better job in a conventional teaching assignment. If this is the case, two instructor studies provide the better basis for estimating the size of an experimental effect" (p. 10).

REFERENCES

Clark, R.E. (1983). Reconsidering research on learning from media. *Review of Educational Research, 53*(4), 445–460.

Clark, R.E. (1984, April). *Learning from computers: Theoretical problems.* Paper presented at the annual meeting of the American Educational Research Association, New Orleans, LA.

Clark, R.E. (1985). Confounding in educational computing research. *Journal of Educational Computing Research, 1*(2), 137–148.

Clark, R.E., & Salomon, G. (1985). *Media in teaching.* In M. Wittrock (Ed.), *Handbook of research on teaching* (Vol. III). New York: Macmillan.

Cook, T.D., & Campbell, D.T. (1979). *Quasi-experimentation.* Chicago: Rand McNally.

Cooley, W.W., & Lohnes, P.R. (1976). *Evaluation research in education.* New York: Irvington.

Cooper, H.M. (1982). Scientific guidelines for conducting integrative research reviews. *Review of Educational Research, 52*(2), 291–302.

Cronbach, L.J., & Snow, R.E. (1977). *Aptitudes and instructional method.* New York: Irvington.

Glass, G.V. (1976). Primary, secondary and meta-analysis of research. *Review of Educational Research, 5*, 3–8.

Green, C., & Mink, W. (1973). *Evaluation of computer simulation of experiments in teaching scientific methodology.* St. Paul, MN: Macalester College, ERIC No. 082475.

Hatfield, L.L. (1969). *Computer assisted mathematics: An investigation of the effectiveness of the computer used as a tool to learn mathematics.* Unpublished doctoral dissertation from the University of Minnesota, University Microfilms No. 70-5569.

Heinich, R. (1970). *Technology and the management of instruction.* Washington, DC: Association for Educational Communications and Technology.

Heinich, R. (1984). The proper study of instructional technology. *Educational Communication and Technology Journal, 32*(2), 67–68.

Jamison, D., Suppes, P., & Welles, S. (1974). The effectiveness of alternative instructional media: A survey. *Review of Educational Research, 44*, 1–68.

Kearsley, G., Hunter, B., & Sidell, R. J. (1983). Two decades of computer based instruction: What have we learned? *Technological Horizons of Education Journal, 10*, 88–96.

Kerlinger, F.N. (1977, September). The influence of research on educational practice. *Educational Researcher,* pp. 5–12.

Kulik, C., Kulik, J., & Bangert-Drowns, R. (1984). *Effects of computer based education on secondary school pupils.* Paper presented at the annual meeting of the American Educational Research Association, New Orleans, LA.

Kulik, J., Kulik, C., & Bangert-Drowns, R. (in press). The importance of Outcome Studies: A Reply to Clark. *Journal of Educational Computing Research.*

Kulik, J., Kulik, C., & Williams, G. (1983). Effects of computer-based teaching on secondary school students. *Journal of Educational Psychology, 75*(1), 19–26.

Kulik, J., Kulik, C., & Cohen, P. (1980). Effectiveness of computer-based college teaching: A meta-analysis of findings. *Review of Educational Research, 50*, 525–544.

Lang, C.R. (1976). *Computer graphic simulations in high school physics.* Unpublished doctoral dissertation, Kansas State University. University Microfilms No. 72-32, 153.

Merrill, M.D. (1983). Component display theory. In C. Reigeluth (Ed.), *Instructional design theories and models.* Hillsdale, NJ: Lawrence Erlbaum Associates.

Mielke, K.W. (1968). Questioning the questions of ETV research. *Educational Broadcasting Review, 2*, 6–15.

Papert, S. (1980). *Mindstorms: Children, computers and powerful ideas.* New York: Basic Books.

Reiser, R., & Gagne, R. (1982). Characteristics of media selection models. *Review of Educational Research, 52*(4), 499–512.

Saettler, P.A. (1968). *A history of instructional technology.* New York: McGraw Hill.

Salomon, G. (1979). *Interaction of media, cognition and learning.* San Francisco: Jossey Bass.

Sheingold, K., Kane, J. H., & Enderweit, M.E. (1983). Microcomputer use in schools: Developing a research agenda. *Harvard Education Review, 53*, 412–432.

Shaver, J.P. (1983, October). The verification of independent variables in teaching methods research. *Educational Researcher,* pp. 3–9.

Slavin, R.E. (1984, October). Meta-analysis in education: How has it been used? *Educational Researcher,* pp. 6–16.

Stimmel, T., Common, J., McCaskill, B., & Durrett, H.J. (1981). Teacher resistance to computer assisted instruction. *Behavior Research Methods and Instrumentation, 13,* 128–130.

Suppes, P., & Morningstar, M. (October, 1969). Computer-assisted instruction. *Science, 166,* 343–350.

APPENDIX A

Randomly selected and reviewed studies. Numbers in the left margin correspond to those used in the text. There were no studies assigned to numbers 10 and 32.

01   Alderman, D.L. (1978). *Evaluation of the TICCIT computer-assisted instructional system in the community college.* (ETS PR 78-10). Princeton, NJ: Educational Testing Service.

02   Axeen, M.E. (1971). *Teaching library use to undergraduates—comparison of computer-based instruction and the conventional lecture.* Urbana: University of Illinois. ERIC Document No. ED 014316.

03   Boyd, A.L. (1973). Computer aided mathematics instruction for low-achieving students. *Dissertation abstracts international, 33,* 553A. University Microfilms No. 73-17, 131.

04   Broh, C.A. (1975). *Achievement and attitude with computer related instruction: A field experiment.* Paper presented at the annual meeting of the American Political Science Association, San Francisco. ERIC No. ED 110 399.

05   Cox, S. (1974). Computer assisted instruction and student performance in macro-economic principles. *The Journal of Economic Education, 6*(1), 29–37.

06   Chiang, A., Stauffer, C., & Cannara, A. (1978). *Demonstration of the use of computer-assisted instruction with handicapped children. Final Report.* (Report No. 446-AH-60076A), Arlington, VA: RMC Research Corp. ERIC No. ED 166 913.

07   Confer, R.W. (1971). The effect of one style of computer-assisted instruction on the achievement of students who are repeating general mathematics. *Dissertation Abstracts International,* 32, 2399A. University Microfilms No. 71–29, 729.

08   Coffman, W.E., & Olsen, S.A. (1980). *The first two years of PLAN: An evaluation of program impact.* Iowa City, IA: Iowa Testing Programs. ERIC No. ED 190 674.

09   Crawford, A.N. (1970). A pilot study of computer assisted drill and practice in seventh grade remedial mathematics. *California Journal of Educational Research, 21,* 170–174.

11   Davies, T.P. (1972). An evaluation of computer assisted instruction using a drill and practice program. *Dissertation Abstracts International,* 32, 6970B. University Microfilms No. 72-18, 627.

12   Delon, F.G. (1970). A field test of computer assisted instruction in first grade mathematics. *Educational Leadership, 28,* 170–180.

13   Deloach, S.J. (1977). *A comparative study of use of computer programming activities in an introductory college mathematics course for disadvantaged students.* Unpublished doctoral dissertation, Indiana University. University Microfilms No. 78-5629.

14   Denton, J.J. (1973). A methodological study of a computer-managed instructional program in high school physics. *Dissertation Abstracts International, 33,* 4966A. University Microfilms No. 73-7023.

15   Fejfar, F.L. (1969). ISU lab school fourth graders learn through CAI. *Contemporary Education, 40,* 296–297.

16   Gershman, J., & Sakamoto, E. (1981). Computer-assisted remediation and evaluation: A CAI project for Ontario secondary schools. *Educational Technology, 21,* 40–43.

17   Green, C., & Mink, W. (1973). *Evaluation of computer simulation of experiments in teaching scientific methodology.* St. Paul, MN: Macalester College. ERIC No. 082 475.

18   Gallagher, P.D. (1970). *An investigation of instructional treatments and learner characteristics in a computer managed instruction course.* Unpublished doctoral dissertation, Florida State University. University Microfilms No. 71-7013.

19   Haberman, E.L. (1977). *Effectiveness of computer assisted instruction with socially/ emotionally disturbed children.* Unpublished doctoral dissertation from the University of Pittsburgh. University Microfilms No. 77-21, 221.

20   Hatfield, L.L. (1970). *Computer assisted mathematics: An investigation of the effectiveness of the computer used as a tool to learn mathematics.* Unpublished doctoral dissertation from the University of Minnesota. First Study; conducted in 1969. University Microfilms No. 71-18, 720.

21   Hatfield, L.L. (1970). Note: Same report as 20 but this is the second study, conducted in 1970.

22   Johnson, R.E. (1971). *The effect of activity oriented lessons on the achievement and attitudes of seventh grade students in mathematics.* Dissertation Abstracts International, 32, 304A. University Microfilms No. 73-3897.

23   Jones, J.E. (1974). *Computer simulated experiments in high school physics and chemistry.* Unpublished doctoral dissertation, University of Iowa. University Microfilms No. 71-18, 720.

24   Jones, L.A., & Sorlie, W.E. (1976). Increasing medical student performance with an interactive, computer assisted appraisal system. *Journal of Computer Based Instruction, 2*(3), 57–62.

25   Kelly, A.C. (1972). TIPS and technical change in classroom instruction. *American Economic Review, 62,* 422–428.

26   Krunhout, O.M., Edwards, S., & Schwarz, G.A. (1969). A computer guided general education physics course. *American Journal of Physics, 37*(10), 995–1001.

27   Lang, C.R. (1976). *Computer graphic simulations in high school physics.* Unpublished doctoral dissertation, Kansas State University. University Microfilms No. 68-17, 690.

28   Lee, A.L. (1974). *A comparison of computer assisted instruction and traditional laboratory instruction in an undergraduate geology course.* Unpublished doctoral dissertation, the University of Texas. University Microfilms No. 73-26, 036.

29   Litman, G. (1977). *Relation between computer-assisted instruction and reading achievement among fourth, fifth and sixth grade students.* Unpublished doctoral dissertation, Northern Illinois University. University Microfilms No. 77-20, 883.

30   Mandelbaum, J. (1974). *A study of the effects on achievement and attitude, on the use of the computer as a problem solving tool with low performing tenth grade students.* Unpublished doctoral dissertation, Temple University. University Microfilms No. 74-1809.

31   McEwen, N., & Robinson, A. (1976). *Computer assisted instruction in secondary school French. Final Report.* Edmonton: Alberta University. ERIC No. ED 150 846.

33   Paden, J.S. (1970). *An experimental study of the individualized instruction in high school physics using the computer to prescribe activities as a function of selected ideographic factors.* Unpublished doctoral dissertation, the University of Missouri at Columbia. University Microfilms No. 71-8373.

34   Paden, D.W., Dalgaard, B.R., & Barr, M.D. (1977). A decade of computer-assisted instruction. *The Journal of Economic Education, 9*(1), 14–20. [Note: Study 1, 178 subjects.]

35   Paden, D.W. et al. [Note: Same as 34 above, Study 2, 382 subjects.]

36   Paden, D.W. et al. [Note: Same as 34 above, Study 3, 63 subjects.]

37   Skavril, R.V. (1974). Computer based instruction of introductory statistics. *Journal of Computer Based Instruction, 1*(1), 32–40.

38   Skavril, R.V., Birdy, J. Jr., Dahrkopf, R.E., & Knight, J.A. (1976). The use of CAI to provide problems for students in introductory genetics. *Journal of Computer Based Instruction, 3*(1), 13–20.

39   Smith, E.S. (1980). *The effect of computer-assisted instruction on academic achievement, school daily attendance and school library usage at Margaret Murray Washington Career Center.* Unpublished doctoral dissertation from George Washington University. University Microfilms No. 80-26, 342.

40   Suppes, P., & Morningstar, M. Computer-assisted instruction. *Science, 166,* 343–350. [Note: 1966–67 study with 880 subjects.]

41   Suppes, P., & Morningstar, M. [Note: Same as 40 above, 1967–68 study with 1800 subjects.]

42   Suppes, P., & Morningstar, M. [Note: Same report as 40 above, 1967–68 Mississippi study with 1900 subjects.]

43 Weiss, E. (1971). *An investigation of the relative effectiveness of two techniques of teaching a transitional course in physics on the college level.* Unpublished doctoral dissertation, New York University. University Microfilms No. 71-28, 569.

44 Wilson, P.M. (1982). *Computer based education and proficiency testing: A model of cost-effectiveness.* Paper presented at the July SALT Conference on training effectiveness and evaluation.

CHAPTER 3

WHY SHOULD WE EXPECT MEDIA TO TEACH ANYONE ANYTHING?

Richard E. Clark and Gavriel Salomon

Originally published as: Clark, R.E. & Salomon, G. (1986). Media in teaching. In M. Wittrock (Ed.), *Handbook of research on teaching* (pp. 464–478, 3rd ed.). New York: Macmillan. Reprinted by permission of the Gale Group.

Research on media in teaching has become conceptually distinguished from "instructional technology" in the past 15 years. The Commission on Instructional Technology (Tickton, 1970) defined instructional technology as "a systematic way of designing, carrying out and evaluating the total process of learning and teaching in terms of specific objectives, based on a combination of human and nonhuman resources to bring about more effective instruction" (p. 12). Thus, instructional technology has been separated from the more traditional research on media in teaching.

All technologies are applications of research and experience to solve some practical problem. "Instructional technology" encompasses *all* instructional problems and thus is the technology *of* instruction. It should not be confused with the focus of this chapter which is the study of media *in* teaching. Media are part of instructional technology. They are the replicable "means," forms or vehicles by which instruction is formatted, stored, and delivered to the learner (Schwen, 1977). Thus, this chapter is concerned with the study of media when it serves instructional functions.

The need for a chapter on media in teaching springs partly from our own curiosity about its effects on children. Statistics concerning the use of various electronic media for entertainment purposes by children have alarmed many parents and educators. The basis of their concerns becomes apparent considering that the average 9-month-old child is watching an hour-and-a-half of TV a day (Holenbeck & Slaby, 1979). Children 3–4-years-old average 4 hours a day (Singer, 1983), and by the end of high school, the total amount of television-viewing time exceeds the time spent being taught in school (Morrisett, 1984). These statistics are coupled with an increased concern with the effects of the new computerized video games and the rapid addition of microcomputers to school curricula and home use (Sheingold, Kane, & Enderweit, 1983). This concern with the effects of media on young learners is not a recent phenomenon. Plato apparently expressed concern about the influence of the written delivery of instruction and recommended oral teaching instead (Saettler, 1968).

Another reason to study media in teaching is that there is a historically recurring expectation that student motivation and performance may be enhanced by them. At least since Thorndike suggested the use of pictures as labor-saving devices at the turn of the century, each new medium has created a wave of interest and positive enthusiasm on the part of educators. More recent media are widely used in classroom teaching. More than half of the school teachers in the United States use television material in class, particularly for teaching science and social sciences; 75 percent report using audiotapes and radio; and 62 percent use computers (Riccobono, 1984).

In this light, it becomes important to examine the research in the field for at least two reasons. First, we must discover what we know about the utility and effectiveness of media for instructional purposes. What in the media exerts what kinds of influence on whom and in what situational and instructional contexts? Second, the recent explosion of interest in the computer as an instructional tool requires that we examine the lessons learned from more veteran media and apply them to the study of new ones (Clark, in press; Salomon & Gardner, 1984).

The reader is cautioned that space prevents a comprehensive review of the great quantity of published material in this area. Excellent reviews and position papers are easily available. A number of articles and books exist that offer a more thorough treatment of problems than will be given here (Clark, 1983; Clark & Snow, 1975; Fleming & Levie, 1978; Heidt, 1978; Jamison, Suppes, & Welles, 1974; Kearsley, Hunter, & Seidel, 1983; Leifer, 1976; Lesgold & Reif, 1983; Salomon & Clark, 1977; Salomon & Gardner, 1984; Schramm, 1977; Sheingold et al., 1983; Suppes, 1979; Wilkinson, 1980).

Our goal is to acknowledge and examine some of the difficulties that the field of research on media in instruction faces. We will analyze the results of past research and describe current significant changes in those questions. We will then discuss the way lessons of past media research impinge on future directions.

REVIEW: WHO IS THE FAIREST OF THEM ALL?

Any profession concerned with the improvement of human life, as Glaser (1982, p. 292) points out, bases its activities on beliefs about human nature. The field of media in instruction is no exception. Media research began during the behaviorist era in education, so early researchers assumed learners to be reactive, responding to external stimuli which were designed to control their behavior. Many early researchers operated on the belief that media in instruction offered great advantages in increased control of learning behaviors. Skinner's teaching machines fit this model very well, as did the early hopes voiced by audio-visual advocates (Saettler, 1968). Divergent views urging cognitive interactive questions by early researchers such as Freeman (1924, quoted by Saettler, 1968) were largely ignored.

The perceptions of learners as reactive and under stimulus control led to an intensive search for the "one best medium," a search stimulated by the great excitement that each new medium aroused and the many hopes this excitement cultivated (Clark, 1975). This early research was long on the enthusiastic advocacy of media comparison questions and short on the development of theories concerning the way media might be made to influence learning (Wartella & Reeves, 1983).

MEDIA COMPARISON STUDIES

In the 1960s, Lumsdaine (1963) and others (e.g., Mielke, 1968) argued that gross comparisons of the influence of different media on learning might not be useful. They implied that media, when viewed as no more than collections of electro-mechanical devices such as television and movies, were simple delivery instruments and that when *everything else* was held constant, they would not be found to influence learning directly in and of themselves. And while it has been the case that subsequent research has borne out their suspicion, many researchers continued to search for overall learning benefits from media. But, as has become evident, learning from instruction is a much more complicated process that often involves interactions between specific tasks, particular learner traits, and various components of medium and method. In this mix, the effects of gross, undifferentiated "medium" variables could not be productive. Part of the reason for the continued reliance on media comparisons was that earlier reviewers held the door open to media influences on learning by blaming much of the lack of systematic findings in prior research on poor research design and on a lack of adequate theory.

As a result, Lumsdaine (1963), writing in the first *Handbook of Research on Teaching,* dealt primarily with adequate studies which had utilized defensible methodology, and in which significant differences were found between media treatments. With the benefit of hindsight, it is not surprising that in most of the studies he reviewed media were employed as simple vehicles for the delivery of instructional materials, and researchers manipulated such variables as text organization, size of step in programed instruction, cueing, or repeated exposures and prompting. None of these variables were generic to the media that the researchers purported to study. This is an example of what Salomon and Clark (1977) have called research *with* media, which they distinguished from research *on* media. Only in research *on* media are generic media variables examined. In the former type, media are used as mere conveyances for the treatments being examined. Although media often were not the focus of study, the results were erroneously interpreted as suggesting that learning benefits had been derived from various media.

An example of instructional research *with* media would be a study that contrasts a logically versus a randomly organized slide-tape presentation on photosynthesis (cf. Kulik, Kulik, & Cohen, 1979 for a review of a number of similar studies). Such a comparison could be carried out by any medium, thus failing to single out for study any distinguishable or unique attribute of a medium that could be expected to contribute to achievement gains.

A decade later, chapters in the *Second Handbook of Research on Teaching* by Glaser and Cooley (1973) and Levie and Dickie (1973) were cautious about the media comparison studies that were still being conducted in apparently large numbers. Levie and Dickie (1973) noted that most overall media comparison studies to that date had been fruitless and suggested that most learning objectives could be attained through "instruction presented by any of a variety of different media" (p. 859). This observation was echoed by Schramm (1977), according to whom "learning seems to be affected more by what is delivered than by the delivery system" (p. 273). At that time, televised education was still a lively topic and studies of computerized instruction were just beginning to appear. In the intervening decade, more effort has been made to analyze and refocus the results of existing comparison studies.

REVIEWS AND META-ANALYSIS OF MEDIA STUDIES

A comprehensive and often cited review by Jamison et al. (1974) surveyed comparisons of traditional instruction with instruction via computers, television, and radio. Their survey utilized a "box score" tally of existing studies, evaluations, and reviews of research. They concluded that a small number of studies reported advantages for media and others indicated more achievement with traditional instruction, but the most typical outcome was "no significant difference" between the two. As they explained, "when highly stringent controls are imposed on a study, the nature of the controls tends to force the methods of presentation into such similar formats that one can only expect the 'no significant differences' which are found" (p. 38). However, there have been criticisms of the box score method of summarizing past media research (e.g., Clark & Snow, 1975). Many of these criticisms have been accommodated by newer "meta-analytic" methods of teasing generalizations from past research (Glass, 1976). A recent series of meta-analyses of media research was conducted by James Kulik and his colleagues at the University of Michigan (Cohen, Ebling, & Kulik, 1981; Kulik, Bangert, & Williams, 1983; Kulik et al., 1979; Kulik, Kulik, & Cohen, 1980). Such meta-analyses allow for a more precise estimate of treatment effect sizes than was possible a few years ago. Meta-analytic procedures yield effect size estimates which are converted to percentage of standard deviation gains on final examination scores due to the more powerful treatment, if any. Most of the meta-analytic surveys of media research demonstrated a typical learning advantage for "newer" media of about .5 standard deviations on final examination performance, compared with "conventional" treatments. In the case of computer-based instruction studies in college environments, for example, this advantage translated to an increase from the 50th to the 66th percentile in final examinations in a variety of courses (Kulik et al., 1980). This is an impressive accomplishment if one accepts it at face value.

Confounding in Media Comparison Studies

Clark (1983) has reviewed existing meta-analysis of media research. His conclusion was that while most analyses showed positive learning effects for newer media over more conventional treatments, there was compelling evidence for confounding in the reviewed research. Two illustrations from Clark's (1983) discussion will provide an example of these two types of confounding. The sizeable effect of .5 standard deviations on final exams that has been attributed to computers in the college setting has been used to justify computer-based instruction (CBI) for teaching. However, this effect reduced to .13 standard deviations in those studies wherein one teacher planned and presented both the computer and the conventional courses. Clark (1983) claimed that this was compelling evidence that the larger effects were due to systematic but uncontrolled differences in content, novelty, and/or teaching method between conventional and media treatments but not to CBI per se. Even when the same teacher designs both treatments it is possible that slightly different and more productive presentations of content or method could be included in the computer condition which accounted for the .13 advantage. But this slight learning advantage could have been produced by any of a variety of media.

Another source of confounding, novelty, was evidenced by a decrease in the differences between media and conventional treatments over time. Clark and Snow (1975) reported that most media treatments in published studies at that time averaged about 20 minutes with a very small standard deviation. Kulik et al. (1983) reported that when computer treatments lasted less than 4 weeks, average effects were .56 standard deviations over conventional treatments. This diminished to .3 standard deviations after 5 to 8 weeks and further to .2 standard deviations after 8 weeks of student work with CBI. It is plausible to hypothesize a novelty effect in these studies and to suggest that students are becoming more familiar with the medium and expend less effort in learning from it over time. Clark (1983) has also argued that similar confounding could account for reports of reductions in study time for computers or other media.

A Conclusion About Media Comparisons

General media comparisons and studies pertaining to their overall instructional impact have yielded little that warrants optimism. Even in the few cases where dramatic changes in achievement or ability were found to result from the introduction of a medium such as television, as was the case in El Salvador (Schramm, 1977), it was not the medium per se that caused the change but rather the curricular reform that its introduction enabled. This in itself is an important observation, for the introduction of a new medium often allows the production of high-quality materials and novel experiences, or leads to organizational and practice changes not otherwise afforded.

One would need to distinguish here between the potential effects of a medium's generic *attributes* (e.g., ways to shape information that cultivate cognitive skills), and the effects of the medium's *introduction*. Gross media comparisons were often intended as studies of media attributes, but failing to identify and carefully manipulate specific attributes, they fell short of their goal (Clark, 1978, 1983; Clark & Snow, 1975; Levie & Dickie, 1973;

Salomon, 1979; Salomon & Clark, 1977). Nor did they illuminate the process and effects of media introduction, for they focused on direct learning outcomes, not on the consequences of curricular or organizational changes in the schools.

The study of media's effects on learning precludes their treatment as unitary tools such as "television," "radio," or "computer." The common denominator of all televison instances, transcending differences of content, task, method of presentation, instructional context, symbolic and formal features used, and the like, is much too narrow. It does not warrant "computer-based instruction" with an equally undifferentiated alternative. This is certainly the case with computers—whose variety of forms, usages, contents, and the activities they allow, exceeds anything known before.

The shortcomings of overall media comparisons do not render such studies useless for all purposes. The evaluation of particular products, the weighting of a medium's overall cost effectiveness, and the close monitoring of a medium's employment in practice can all benefit from one or another kind of media comparison. However, such gross comparisons have little utility for the study of those specific media attributes that may make a difference in learning for some learners on specific tasks. This lesson appears to be of special importance when applied to research on computers for, unlike TV, their instructional potential is still largely unexplored.

Cognizant of these and similar considerations, researchers shifted their attention to other types of questions. These newer approaches were based more on cognitive than behavioral approaches to learning. They were addressed at specific media attributes assumed to be inherent to the medium under study and of potential relevance to learning-related cognition. Hypotheses typically dealt with the interactions of particular media attributes, teaching methods, tasks, and learner traits, and focused on the cognitive consequences of different combinations for different students. While the historical vestiges of this type of question date back at least to the 1920s (e.g., Freeman, 1924, quoted by Saettler, 1968), most of the research activity has taken place in the last decade. However, as we will see, the shift to a cognitive approach has led the field away from practical research on media as it was formerly conceptualized.

The Shift of Focus: Cognitive Aspects of Media Attributes

The media comparison questions were discarded at the same time that instructional psychology was replacing behaviorist with more cognitively oriented views. In the cognitive approach, more attention is devoted to the way various media attributes, such as the visualization and imagery-evoking properties of stimuli (see review by Winn, 1981, 1982), interact with cognitive processes to influence learning. Thus, it became necessary to examine how specific elements of an instructional message might effect or activate particular cognition for certain learners under specific task conditions. No wonder, therefore, that aptitude-treatment interaction (ATI) research has been welcomed by media researchers who expected it not only to suggest which specific media attributes were most effective for whom (e.g., Clark, 1975; Clark & Snow, 1975; Schramm, 1977), but also to indicated the kinds of cognition that are or may become involved in the processing of differently packaged and coded materials (Salomon, 1971, 1979).

Related Questions Concerning Information Processing

There is also a growing body of research on developmental cognitive processes which are relevant to the understanding of media attributes. That research ranges from the study of reading acquisition (e.g., Resnick & Weaver, 1979) to the comprehension of stories (e.g., Stein & Glen, 1979); and from the study of how children learn to process artistic depictions (Gardner, 1980), to the study of how one learns to process narration (e.g., Collins, 1981; Jaglom & Gardner, 1981) and handle computers (e.g., Turkle, 1984).

Other literature of increasing volume is concerned with neuropsychology and the psychobiology of processing symbolic information. Unfortunately, although this research opens up a new area of interest, it still yields many contradicting interpretations, particularly in the area of hemispheric dominance or brain lateralization (Gardner, 1982). As it turns out, popular claims about an instructionally important division of labor between the two brain hemispheres are not clearly supported by research (Hellige, 1980). It is apparently the case that the left hemisphere has momentary advantage in dealing with the basic building clocks of simple, familiar, digital elements and in such logical processes as classifications. The right hemisphere is the initial processor of unfamiliar, pictorial, and spatial material. Yet the right hemisphere turns out to play a role in the comprehension of stories, metaphors, puns, jokes, and other linguistic material that require paralinguistic "scaffolding" for comprehension (Gardner, 1982). So prevailing speculations that there may be a clear hemispheric specialization for different media attributes appear to be premature.

Unlike previous research concerned with the instructional utility of media, the more current research into the way different modes of information presentation are processed and how these processing capabilities develop appear to yield important implications for instruction. Thus, for example, Anderson and Lorch (1983) have found that children attend to televised material that is comprehensible to them, implying that comprehensibility determines attention rather than the other way around. This finding suggests that instructional production techniques should be oriented to conveying comprehensible information rather than attracting attention. Newer media literary programs are attempting to draw on this research and apply it to instructing children on how to get more selective knowledge out of mediated instruction (e.g., Dorr, Graves, & Phelps, 1980; Singer, Zuckerman, & Singer, 1980).

By and large, there were at least two results of the shift in focus in media research. First, there was the need to identify critical attributes of media which not only distinguish between media in meaningful ways but which also affect learning-relevant cognition. This then was expected to lead to clearer distinctions between the *means* of information delivery and manipulation (e.g., radio, computers, television, books) and other components of media, notably their intrinsic modes of information presentation and the kinds of mental operations they afford. The second result was the long-overdue development of theories. The chapter turns next to a brief description of three of these theories which have evolved in the last decade and to the disputes they have generated.

Goodman's Symbol System Theory

The idea that media attributes or the modes of information presentation in instruction are crucial to learning has been around for some time. However, it was not until Gardner, Howard, and Perkins (1974) introduced Goodman's (1968) theory of symbol systems that the constructs of "modes of presentation" could be systematically examined.

Following Goodman (1968), Gardner et al. (1974) explained that a *symbol is anything that can be used in a referential way,* and that can be organized into systems. They offered a number of semantic and syntactic conditions to distinguish among symbol systems—including the way they are structured and the way they map upon their respective fields of reference. They offered specific dimensions of symbol systems to illustrate the way they differ.

One of the structural characteristics of symbol systems is notationality. This is the extent to which a symbol system can be unambiguously mapped onto a frame of reference. Here, for each of the system's characters there must be one, and only one, equally differentiated element in the field of reference. The system of musical notations is a prime example of notationality. Symbol systems differ in notationality. For example, verbal systems are more notational than pictorial ones, a distinction that leads to specific psychological and educational implications. Less notational symbol systems (e.g., pictures) are neither easier nor more difficult to comprehend or learn, as there is nothing inherent in these systems that makes them "easy."

Nor does any system necessarily "resemble" its referents more than another. Rather, symbol systems, and hence the media of communication and tools of information manipulation that carry them, exhibit differential information biases (e.g., Meringoff, 1980) and activity biases (Salomon & Gardner, 1984). Thus, TV tends to highlight action properties of a narrative while print versions of the same material highlight figurative language. Each such presentation bias is correlated with an information pickup bias—televiewers place the narrative in a spatial imagery framework and storybook listeners place it in a temporal-descriptive one.

The introduction of a formal theory of symbol systems could potentially offer a bridge between research on media and research on cognition and symbolic behavior. Indeed, this development led to the creation of new theories and research questions by media researchers. Those theories are briefly described next. However, these new theories led away from the study of media as complex communication systems characterized by television, books, and other means of delivering messages. Current research based on symbol system theories is no longer focused on media in instruction, for as Gardner (1982) pointed out, there is no necessary one-to-one correspondence between media and symbol systems. We will return to this issue later on.

Olson's Theory of Instructional Means

Olson bases his theory on Bruner's (1964) contention that the introduction of technologies and techniques is accompanied by the development of relevant cognitive skills, and on McLuhan's interest in the forms and structures of information media. Olson (1976; Olson & Bruner, 1974) argues that any account of human activity must begin with an understanding of the activities whereby information is picked up from the environment, mentally transformed, and stored. Different kinds of activities yield not only different aspects of the world but also engage and develop different mental skills. Olson thus distinguished between the knowledge one acquires and the skills that are involved in and are developed during the process. From observing a picture, argued Olson, one acquires knowledge about the depicted object as well as developing cognitive skills related to observation.

Olson (1976) offered a theory of instructional means. The theory attempts to show "how in … instruction, the content of the medium [is] related to the knowledge acquired, while the means employed (the code in which the message is represented) is related to the skills, strategies and heuristics that are called upon and developed" (1976, p. 26). Each of these elements may result in a different kind of transfer of learning: the content component results in transfer of rules and principles (a set of features that is invariant across different activities), whereas the codes or the means of instruction may result in the transfer of skills "assumed or developed in the course of relying upon that means" (1976, p. 23). These skills are the mental operations that are invariant across different contents. Each system of codes, symbols, or methods requires a different set of activities. While all such instructional means may ultimately map upon the same knowledge structure, they differ with respect to the cognitive processes they activate and cultivate (Olson & Bruner, 1974). Thus, Olson suggested (1974) that perhaps the function of media that present new symbol systems is not so much to convey old knowledge in new forms but rather to cultivate new skills for exploration and internal representation.

One important extension of Olson's theory is his distinction between "utterance" and "text" (Olson, 1977). According to Olson (1977), oral language "is a flexible, unspecialized, all purpose instrument with a low degree of conventionalization" in which the meanings of sentences must be "negotiated in terms of the social relations, the context and the prior world knowledge of the participants" (p. 10). On the other hand, written language, "by virtue of its demands for explicitness of meaning, its permanence ... and its realignment of social and logical function, serves the intellect in several ways" (Olson, 1977, p. 11). It serves the cultivation and maintenance of analytic, scientific, and philosophical knowledge (as contrasted with commonplace knowledge). In school, "intelligence" is skill in the medium of text. This Olson (1977) calls the "literacy bias."

Olson's distinction between cultures of utterance and text, and between similar developmental phases in a child's schooling, is of particular relevance to hypotheses concerning the cognitive effects of computer programing. Programing is a highly structured and analytic activity in a rigidly constrained symbol system (Pea & Kurland, 1985). It may—if sufficiently intense and continuous—lead to new "literacy biases" exceeding the ones attributed by Olson to texts.

Salomon's Media Attributes Theory

Extending the work of Olson and Gardner, Salomon (1979) offered a theory based on the assumptions that (a) both the media and the human mind employ symbols to represent, store, and manipulate information; and (b) that some of the symbol systems employed in cognition are acquired from the symbol systems employed by media. Salomon conceptualized technologies that allow the development of unique symbol systems and combinations thereof, just as the development of the technologies of maps, films, or computers led to the development of cartography, cinematics, and programing languages. The more distinctive or contrived the symbol system used to represent information, the more distinctive the mental skills that are required and called upon. Hence, Salomon (1974a) distinguished, for example, between televised instruction that only employs the technology of television without much emphasis on the medium's unique symbolic potentialities, and televised instruction that does utilize these features fully. Only the latter might make a difference in the kind of knowledge acquired and the meanings derived from instruction as it calls upon different sets of mental skills (Salomon & Cohen, 1977).

There are a number of instructionally relevant features to the Salomon theory. He hypothesized (1979) that an instructional presentation can be "closer to" or "more distant from" the way a learner tends mentally to represent the information presented under given task requirements. The closer the match between the communicational symbol system and the content and task-specific mental representations, the easier the instructional message is to recode and comprehend. Certain symbolic modes of representation can thus "save" the learner taxing mental transformations from communicational to mental symbolic forms depending on their aptitudes, the task, and the subject matter to be learned.

A second feature of the Salomon theory is his contention that some of the symbolic features of instruction, under some conditions, can be internalized by learners and henceforth serve as "tools of mental representation." He presented evidence (Salomon, 1974a) that students deficient in cue attending are able to internalize the "zooming" of a camera lends into a stimulus field and thus increase their cue-attending skill. Another possibility here is that these same features may merely activate and strengthen partly mastered cognitive skills for other students, and in some instances such features may actually inhibit learning by preventing the use of previously acquired but more efficient skills that serve the same ends. Research following the theory has provided evidence that skill cultivation and inhibition, though limited in scope, take place under natural conditions such as exposure to a new medium like television. Salomon (1979) reported such effects on Israeli children exposed to "Sesame Street" and Schramm (1977) found similar effects on the nonverbal skills of El Salvadorean children exposed to instructional television for the first time. However, it should be remembered that Salomon's research demonstrates that symbolic features of media *can be made* to cultivate cognitive effects, not that those effects necessarily occur naturally as a result of uninvolved exposure to a medium. The occurrence of cognitive effects depends on a number of factors including the effort invested, depth of processing, and special aptitudes of individual learners (Salomon, 1983a).

Other Symbol System Theories

The development of the three related theories briefly described above was paralleled by other, more symbol-system or domain-specific theories: theories pertaining to the processing of words and pictures (e.g., Fleming, 1979; Pressley, 1977), televiewing and listening (Meringoff, 1980), artistic depiction (Gardner, 1980), diagrams (Winn, 1982), and more. Common to these undertakings was a growing concern with the cognitive processing of differently coded materials. Questions of instructional effectiveness were generally abandoned.

Issues Related to Symbol System Theories

Most of these newer theories have at least one important assumption in common: that cognitive representations and processing are carried out in *various* symbolic modes that are *influenced* by the symbol systems employed by media, that some of these cognitions are *unique* counterparts of communicational symbol systems, and thus can be cultivated by symbol systems. This general assumption has been challenged by critics who suggested that the type of symbolic mode employed in instructional representations may not serve any unique function in cognition and learning. Clark (1983, in press), for example, has argued that many of the different symbolic representational modes used in instruction may serve the *same basic function* in cognitive processing. If this turns out to be the case, the choice of symbol system may be less important for instruction and learning than the symbol system theories imply. Instructional designers and curriculum planners could then choose the less expensive or more convenient medium for instruction, provided that its symbolic modes were *sufficient* to yield the necessary cognitive transformations required by the learning task and learner. This issue is similar to one currently being discussed in the larger arena of cognitive science, that is, the concern about whether images or propositions are the more "basic" representational modes for information in cognition.

Imagery and Propositions in Thought

A particularly important topic and ongoing theoretical debate in cognition was, and continues to be, concerned with the nature and foundations of images or "analogous" mental representations as contrasted with "propositions" (e.g., Anderson, 1983; Olson & Bialystock, 1983). An example of the difference between the two would be a trace image of an object in memory (an analogous representation) versus a description of the critical attributes of the object (a proposition).

The image-versus-proposition argument to some extend replaces earlier dual trace arguments concerning whether information is stored in memory as words, pictures, or both (e.g., Paivio, 1977). It is part of the general search for a deeper understanding of information processing, a topic of special relevance to research on media in teaching since different theory and practice implications appear to follow from the two approaches. Space limitations allow only a brief description of the two approaches and their related implications.

The Dual-modality Approach

Kosslyn (1981), Kosslyn and Pomerantz (1977), Paivio (1977), and Shepard (1978) have claimed that images constitute a distinct class of cognitive representation, parallel and equal in importance to semantic propositions. Shepard (1978) argued that the perception of a mental image is a process that is analogous to the perception of actual objects. Kosslyn (1981), basing his approach on computer simulation models, argues that images have both "surface representation" and "deep representation" components. Surface representations occur in a spatial mode and are a visual depiction of objects. This underlies the experience of mental imagery. The deep structure component entails a literal representation (some encoding of appearance) and a propositional element (a description of the object). The deep representation is a long-term memory trace. The trace is used spontaneously when people retrieve information about incidentally learned objects, when required to allude to physical properties of objects and when subtle comparisons are to be made. Less subtle comparisons are likely to be handled "propositionally" (Kosslyn, 1981).

The dual-modality side of this argument bears a general resemblance to media attribute theories. If images bear a direct resemblance to externally depicted objects, the acquisition of communicationally provided images of events and processes should enrich a learner's store of cognitive images and operations. Salomon's (1979) theory of the internalization of symbolic forms and Olson and Bruner's (1974) claim that intelligence is skill in a medium appear to be related to the dual-modality argument.

The Propositional Approach

Pylyshyn (1973) denied a central role for imagery components in cognition by describing them as "epiphenomena." He relegated their alleged role in cognitive representation and processing to "abstract descriptions accessed by computationally primitive semantic interpretation functions"

(Hampson & Morris, 1978). More recently, however, Pylyshyn (1981) has narrowed the debate to the question of whether images are or are not similar to what goes on when people observe corresponding events actually happening. "Similarity," he argues, is an illusory and unclear construct that is based on our commonsense knowledge. More specifically, the argument was that images are not *intrinsic* properties of the mind which are "wired in," such that they cause it to behave as it does. Rather, images are "cognitively penetrable." They are governed by conceptual, rational knowledge— by propositions—rather than exclusively by the actual features of the objects perceived. Therefore, the images we form of external reality are not determined by our direct perceptions of the features of the objects (or their pictorial representation) but by "a tacit physical theory which is good enough to predict most ordinary natural events correctly most of the time" (Pylyshyn, 1981, p. 41).

Research evidence for the propositional argument includes the finding that children who are blind from birth perform as well as sighted children on tasks that seem to require imagery (e.g., Zimler & Keenan, 1983). These findings and others challenge the dual-modality/imagery theories and suggest that the mental representations used by both the blind and the sighted take a semantic, propositional form. Additionally, one should take into account recent evidence provided by Kyllonen, Lohman, and Snow (1984), who imply that spatial thought and strategies are most useful for solving only simple problems. As problem solving (including spatial problems) becomes more difficult, learners tend to switch to the more semantic-analytical strategies.

Implications of These Approaches

The dual- (or multiple-) modality approaches lead to implications similar to the ones developed earlier by Olson, Bruner, and Salomon. The propositional approach leads to different hypotheses, implying that the particular surface-symbolic appearance of a message may be relatively less consequential in learning, as it is going to be handled propositionally anyway during deeper processing. Thus, all images used in cognition may be "constructed" following propositional "rules." Imagery knowledge, and thus the symbol-system-specific cognitive skills cultivated from symbolic attributes, may only serve in the *decoding* of instruction delivered via different media.

Salomon (1983b) has recently proposed that the symbolic carriers of information mainly affect the early phases of decoding but not subsequent phases of mental elaboration of the already recoded and mentally represented material. The latter phases, he argued, include such operations as inference generation and are symbol system independent. Indeed, Salomon and Ben-Moshe have recently found that when sixth graders are taught to view television more mindfully and invest more effort in processing televised instruction, their reading comprehension scores increase significantly. This suggests that the operations involved in the deeper processing of television and print material may share a number of important procedural or strategic components.

More generally, it follows that if most basic cognitive operations rest in propositional structures, then the issue of symbol system and medium diversity in instruction may not be as important in learning as was initially assumed by the symbol system theories. We should entertain the possibility that symbol systems affect differently only initial decoding. For it is quite possible that information presented in some symbolic form is more easily recoded into (internal) propositions than when presented in another form. It is also possible that as each symbolic form offers a different information bias (highlighting selected aspects of the information), each such form may lead to different kinds of internal propositions. Thus, according to this view, media's symbolic forms may not call upon and cultivate different skills; still, they may result in easier or more difficult learning. They may also result in more or less stereotypic or varied sets of internal propositions that complement each other (Olson & Bialystock, 1983).

Another issue concerns the conditions that surround the cultivation and transfer of cognitive skills. We turn next to a brief discussion of these issues and how they might influence our understanding of media symbol system theories.

Skill Cultivation: Questions of Uniqueness and of Transfer

Salomon (1979), and more recently Greenfield (1984), have reviewed research where symbolic features of mediated experiences and instruction were shown to affect differentially the skills activated in the service of knowledge acquisition and on the mastery of these skills. Such research was inspired by Bruner's (1964) argument that internal representations and operations partly depend on learning "precisely the techniques that serve to amplify our acts, perceptions and our ratiocinative activities" (p. 2).

Such a Vygotskian view implies that unique coding or structural elements of the media (e.g., filmic causal sequences) or uniquely afforded activities (e.g., programing) may have unique effects on related mental skills. Thus, the employment of a coding element such as a close-up, or the allowance for students' manipulation of input data (e.g., Lesgold & Reif, 1983), may activate specific mental operations that facilitate the acquisition of knowledge as well as their improved mastery.

But the possibility of skill activation and cultivation from specific media attributes also raises new conceptual and empirical questions. If media's symbolic modes of information presentation can activate, even cultivate mental operations and skills, are these skills *unique?* What is their utility? *How far do they transfer, if at all?* These questions are of particular interest with Pea and Kurland, 1985; Tilomirov, 1974, for many computer-afforded activities are rationalized in terms of their unique effects on transferable skills. Writes Papert (1980, p. 27): "By providing [a] very concrete, down-to-earth model of a particular style of thinking, work with the computer can [foster] … a 'style of thinking' … that is to say learning to think articulately about thinking."

It is very difficult to provide evidence to support the uniqueness argument since it might always be claimed that substitutions are or could be made available. More importantly, one could question the assumption implied in this approach that there is a one-to-one correspondence between coding elements and afforded activities, on the one hand, and specific modes of mental representation and operation, on the other. Wittrock's (1978) generative model of instruction suggests that when, for example, learners fails to generate relevant relationships, they should be made explicit for the learners in any means or medium available. This assumes functional equivalence between various devices for delivering instruction and various symbolic modes for representing information.

Indeed, it is possible that nominally different modes of instructional presentation (including symbolic attributes) accomplish the same function in learning, and thus activate the same operations and therefore serve instruction equally well. Blake (1977) taught chess moves to high- and low-visual-ability undergraduates using still pictures, animated arrows within pictures, or a motion film plus a narration. While all three conditions worked equally well for the higher ability learners, low visualizers learned the chess moves equally well from the arrow and motion which were significantly more effective than the static pictures. Blake's poor visualizers profited from two different operational definitions of the necessary model, animated arrows and moving chess pieces. It seems that the necessary process for learning chess moves was the visualization of the entire move allowed each piece. It could be operationalized in any of a variety of equally sufficient conditions for successful performance.

The possibility that alternative coding and structural elements, within and across symbol systems, may be functionally equivalent suggest two things. First, it suggests that research ought not to seek the unique cognitive *effects* of one or another discrete media element but rather focus on the cognitive *functions* accomplished. Filmic zooms can visually supplant part-whole relations, but so can other elements as well. And the acquisition of some sequential logic, although facilitated by computer programming, may be similarly facilitated by direct tutoring. Second, it may well be that media selection decisions (e.g., Reiser & Gagne, 1982) ought not be based on their different surface capacities to influence achievement, for a focus on surface appearance differences overlooks the possibility that whatever we think goes on is not necessarily what goes on, cognitively.

The other important issue concerns the transferability of the skills wrested from a medium's symbol system or exercised during a computer-afforded activity. One would need to distinguish between, say, the acquisition of a particular image or operation, on the one hand, and the cultivation of imagery *ability* or generalized *skill*, on the other. It is one thing if children learn from televiewing only how to become better televiewers or from programing Logo how to be better Logo programmers; it is another if they show skill cultivation that transfers beyond the boundaries of that medium or activity. Work by Scribner and Cole (1981) concerning the effects of acquiring basic literacy skills in non-school settings serves as a warning against unwarranted optimism here. Contrary to earlier claims they found no evidence to show that literacy affected abstract thinking or, for that matter, any other generalizable ability. The Vai may have been denied what Olson (1977) has called a "culture of literacy" that may amplify the effects of basic literacy into transferable skills. For such participation would enable the literate individuals to apply the initially specific operations in a variety of complex tasks and situations, thus to allow the generalizability of these into skills.

Salomon and Perkins (1984) have recently suggested that the acquisition of knowledge and skill can potentially lead to their transfer if either one of two roads is taken: (a) the acquired skill or knowledge is mindfully and deliberately decontextualized, that is, recoded in a representational code that affords abstraction; or (b) it is practiced to the point of automatically in a large variety of instances demanding good performance. Exposure to, say, television's codes, or extensive exploratory activity with Logo geometry could, according to this view, lead to the cultivation of transferable skills provided either one of the roads is taken. But this is not easily achieved because the first (mindful) road demands the motivated expenditure of effort, and the second (automatic) demands more and more varied practice than usually afforded in schools. Neither road was taken by the Vai tribesman studies by Scribner and Cole, hence yielding no transfer effects from their new "literacy" to other cognitive tasks. The poor transfer effects of children's (usually limited) experience with Logo (Pea & Kurland, 1984) may be explained in the same way (Clark & Voogel, in press).

The road from possible to actual transfer is fraught with difficulties. It is certainly not a matter of one-shot, brief experiences and encounters, except in the unlikely event that such mental effort is expended in reaching transferable conclusions, formulating rules, or generating guiding

metacognitions. Transfer is somewhat more likely as a consequence of prolonged, continuous, and intensive application of newly developed skill and
knowledge, as may be the case after years of televiewing or prolonged
focused computer activity.

In all, it appears that media's symbolic forms and computers' afforded
activities may have skill-cultivating effects, but that these are not necessarily
unique nor easily transferable. Future research, particularly that concerned with computer-afforded learning activities will do well to ask not
just whether particular skills are acquired but also how else they could be
developed, and under what instructional, contextual, and psychological
conditions they can be made to transfer.

A Paradigm for Future Developments

Thus far, research on media in instruction, much like all research on
teaching, has centered on the *means* of instruction as independent variables and on learning outcomes in the form of knowledge or skill acquisition as dependent variables. In this respect, the basic paradigm which
originates from the behavioristic assumptions about human learning has
not changed even though cognitive processes have been introduced as
mediators between stimuli and responses. Yet, once cognitions are seriously considered, one cannot escape examining them, not only as mediators but also as partial determiners of the way learners experience the
stimulus.

The basic assumption here is that learners often affect the way they
experience the so-called stimulus through their previously acquired attributions, personal and socially shared expectations and beliefs, personal
interests, and the like. As Shulman (1980) pointed out, "The teacher's pedagogical actions merely set the task environment for pupil learning, which
task environment predictably is transformed by the pupil into his or her
own problem space" (p. 7).

Acknowledgment of these phenomenological inputs as factors that
affect the way stimuli are experienced, thus handled, reflects the current
shift of paradigms for it ascribes the learner a far more active and less
externally controlled role. It examines the process of learning as an ongoing transaction or reciprocal interaction between learners and their phe-
nomenologically perceived environment (e.g., Bandura, 1978; Olweus,
1977; Salomon, 1981; Shulman, 1980; Wittrock, 1978).

Media are thus perceived as external devices which, along with other
factors, set the stage for some cognitive activities precisely because they are
part of a learner's a priori anticipations. What the student thinks or
believes to be the case about a particular mediated presentation or class of

media can come therefore to exert at least as much influence over learning as the medium itself. This may include beliefs about the medium's difficulty level, its entertainment potential, the type of information usually presented, and typical instructional demands. Some of these anticipations are socially generated and shared. Shulman (1981), while reviewing the literature on how students invent incorrect problem-solving procedures, pointed out the role of perceived social context in influencing the way problems are treated by students: "The social context of the classroom changes the meaning of instructional tasks in significant ways. Thus, a problem-to-be-solved and an assignment-to-be-completed are psychologically quite distinct, even if the specific exercise and its attendant solutions are identical in both instances" (p. 19).

Research that uses the reciprocal paradigm is relatively new, but it carries with it a good measure of theoretical and application potential. Only a brief review, suggestive of the types of questions asked, will be attempted here because of space limitations.

Attitudes Toward Media

Hess and Tenezakis (1972) explored the affective responses of predominantly Mexican-American, low-SES seventh, eighth, and ninth graders to remedial mathematics presented either by computer or teacher. Among a number of interesting findings was an unanticipated attribution of more fairness to the computer than to the teachers. The students reported that the computer treated them more equitably (kept promises, did not make decisions based on stereotypes) than some of the teachers. Students consistently trusted the computer more but found it to be less "flexible," as well as unresponsive to student desires to change the course of content of the instruction. Similarly, Stimmel, Common, McCaskill, and Durrett (1981) found a strong negative affect toward computers and computerized instruction among a large group of pre-service teachers. These same teacher trainees had similar reactions to mathematics and science teaching and may have associated computers with these disciplines. It would be interesting to study how the perceptions and attitudes of computer users guide their strategies for learning from computers, how these different strategies influence learning, and how work with computers changes or maintains these perceptions reciprocally.

Perceived Learning Demands from Different Media

Presumable, differences in the qualities attributed to different media may influence learning-related behaviors of students. Ksobiech (1976) and Salomon (1981) have reported studies wherein student beliefs about the different demands placed on them by different media influenced their approach to learning tasks. Ksobiech (1976) told 60 undergraduates variously that televised and book lessons were to be evaluated by them, were to be entertaining, or were to be the subject of a test. The test group performed best on a subsequent examination with the evaluation group next best, and the students who expected to be entertained showing the poorest exam performance. Some subjects were allowed to push a button and receive more video or more narrative content from the televised treatments. The test group consistently chose more narrative (verbal) information, presumably because they believed that it was a surer route to the factual information they needed to succeed at the test. Also, the subjects who believed that a test awaited them persisted longer than the other groups.

Salomon (1981) has recently suggested a model for conceptualizing these differences in mental effort expenditure that result from different attributions to the media.

According to Salomon's model, the amount of mental effort invested in nonautomatic elaboration of material (i.e., the extent of mindful processing) depends primarily on two factors: the learners' perception of the learning-relevant characteristics of the medium and task, and their own perceived self-efficacy in elaborating the information they will receive. In a series of studies (see Salomon, 1983a for summary) he found that television is perceived to be mentally less demanding than print material of comparable content and that learners report investing less mental effort in television. This, in turn, led the more able students to generate fewer inferences from such material. Manipulating the learners' perceived task demands positively affected the amount of effort they invested and the amount of inferential learning they achieved from television. Students also came to mobilize their abilities more readily, thus moving the more able students ahead of their less able peers.

Merrill (1984) tried to affect learners' control over content, pace, display, and other input variables through the careful design of TICCIT computer-assisted instruction. None of the manipulated control variables accounted for learning differences. The only variable that did account for learning differences was an estimate of the amount of effort invested provided by the learners themselves on a posttreatment questionnaire. These findings can be taken to support the claim that learners' choices of effort investment strategies affect learning quite independently of the manipulation of instructional program features. The Merrill data suggest that effort investment, an important facilitator of nonautomatic processing of material, is very much "cognitive penetrable" and *not* totally subject to the "objective" attributes of media.

Student Choice of Media and Method

Another area that provides consistent evidence for the perceived learning demands of media is the recent literature on student choice of instructional conditions. Saracho (1982), Machula (1978–1979), and Clark (1982) reported studies wherein student enjoyment of instructional media and their subsequent achievement were negatively correlated. The results of these studies suggest that allowing students to choose the medium or method they prefer may not always result in maximum learning outcomes.

In a year long study involving over 250 third to sixth grade students, Saracho (1982) found that those assigned to computer-assisted instruction in basic skills liked the computer less but learned more than from other media. Similarly, Machula (1978–1979) gave instruction to over 100 undergraduates via television, voice recording, and printed text. Students liked the television less but learned more from it than from the voice recording, which they liked more.

Clark (1982) has reviewed similar studies and has suggested that students use erroneous a priori rules to choose media or methods which often result in less learning than when their aptitudes are used to assign them to instructional conditions. Students incorrectly assess the extent to which the instructional methods associated with the medium will allow them the most efficient use of their effort. Strong interactions with general ability are often found in this research. Higher ability students seem to like methods and media that they perceive as better structured and more directive because they think these demand less effort to achieve success. However, more structured methods prevent these higher ability students from employing their own considerable skills and therefore yield poorer achievement than methods that require them to structure their own learning activities. Lower ability students, on the other hand, seem to like the less structured and more discovery-oriented methods and media. They seem to want to avoid investing the effort required by the more structured approaches, which they may expect to result in failure. Since investing more effort to achieve the same disappointing result is less attractive, they prefer the unstructured approaches whereby they can control the effort they invest and remain relatively anonymous in the process. These lower ability students, however, need more structure and so they tend to achieve less with the instructional methods they prefer more.

The change we anticipate in the basic paradigm on media and technology is not from an instructionally centered ("situational") approach to a learner-centered ("personological") one. Rather, it is a shift from a unidirectional view to a reciprocal view. The instructional powers do not reside solely in the media, for the way one perceives media influences the way one treats them. Nor, however, are learners the sole power brokers, for their perceptions are founded on the kinds of media they actually encounter and the activities they are actually afforded. Research in this domain, if it is to follow a reciprocal paradigm, may benefit from the recent advances made in other fields—such as personality research (e.g., Mischel, 1984), spatial cognition (e.g., Olson & Bialystock, 1983), aptitude processes (Kyllonen et al., 1984), and person-environment interaction (Magnusson, 1981)—where such a paradigm is used.

SUMMARY AND CONCLUSION

The history of our experience with media in teaching has been characterized by ambivalent expectations. One the one hand, each new medium has raised our hopes for benefits to instruction and learning similar to those achieved in the entertainment, communication, and information-handling arenas. These hopes are encouraged by large industries who hope to sell newer electronic media to schools. The extraordinary development of the computer and video disc technologies in the past decade has been the most recent source of this expectation.

One the other hand, there has been a historical concern on the part of parents and educators over the impact of increased exposure to newer media. This concern carries with it a fear that children might be somehow harmed or misdirected if they spend too much time with newer mediums such as video games or television.

These expectations and fears have stimulated a great deal of research interest in the past decade and a number of attempts to build models and theories. Perhaps the most positive outcome of this effort has been a shift in the focus of research questions about media. Earlier studies, initially generated during the behavioral emphasis on external events in instruction, emphasized gross, undifferentiated comparisons of the learning impact of newer media such as television with more "traditional" media such as classroom instruction. Recent studies have exchanged the behaviorally based comparison between media with more cognitively oriented questions. We moved from asking which medium was a better teacher to a concern with which "attributes" of media might combine with learner traits under different task conditions and performance demands to produce different kinds of learning. So, for example, these newer questions ask about the possible cognitive effects of explicit filmic supplantation of cognitive operations on students' mastery of related skills; or about the relative effectiveness of animating actual object movement in teaching allowable moves in chess.

Most important during the past decade was the development of long-overdue theories and models. The theories that have attracted the most attention are those concerned with the cognitive processes activated and cultivated as a result of instruction based in media attributes. These "symbol system" theories have led to a number of engaging hypotheses such as Olson's (1977) claim that "intelligence is skill in a medium," and Salomon's (1979) expectation that student comprehension will be aided when symbolic modes of instruction more closely match student cognitive representations.

They symbol system theories have generated controversy as might be expected when the focus of a field shifts. It is interesting to note that the disputes surrounding the symbol system theories have close parallels with questions that are currently being debated in the general cognitive sciences. For example, one implicit claim of early symbol system theory inspired by Bruner (1964) was that different symbolic modes might result in the cultivation of *unique* cognitive skills. This expectation provided impetus for a now-considerable body of research. To date, the results of that research have suggested that different symbolic attributes of media can, under special conditions, cultivate cognitive skills. However, the issue of whether these skills are the unique products of media attributes or symbolic modes and whether the attributes serve *functionally* different cognitive operations is still being discussed.

The research evidence seems very similar to what has been found in the dispute between dual encoding and proposition proponents in the general cognitive literature (e.g., Kosslyn, 1981; Pylyshyn, 1981). Dual encoding research provides evidence that different types of images can have unique influences on learning and memory. Other data are offered to support an alternative view that images are coded into abstract, semantic propositions for storage and later recalled to "construct" or "reconstruct" specific images. Here a logical extension of existing arguments would suggest that many different images could be coded in the same proposition and that the form of an instructional representation has less of an effect than initially assumed.

Generally, it appears that media do not affect learning in and of themselves. Rather, some particular qualities of media may affect particular cognitions that are relevant for the learning of the knowledge or skill required by students with specific aptitude levels when learning some tasks. These cognitive effects are not necessarily unique to one or another medium or attribute of a medium. The same cognitive effect may often be obtained by other means, which suggests a measure of "functional equivalence." This implies that there may be "families" of functionally equivalent but nominally different instructional presentation forms.

It is also important to note that uniqueness is not an all-or-nothing concept. Some "families" may be relatively small and many of these functionally equivalent groups will contain forms that are more difficult or expensive to duplicate than others. For example, the kind of cognitive effects that Papert expects the programing activities "Logo" to produce could, in principle, be replicated by direct teaching of logic. However, in actuality, this functional equivalence would be extremely difficult to obtain in most classrooms given current curricular realities. Moreover, direct instruction may be functionally equivalent to programming in one respect (e.g., facilitation of procedural logic) but not in others (e.g., addressing some learners' need for control).

Lessons for Future Research

As we suggested in the beginning of this chapter, there are lessons to be discerned from past research that may inform future research questions addressed at new media. It is to these lessons that we turn at last.

There is an already rapidly growing body of studies comparing computer-based instruction with more conventional means (e.g., Kulik et al., 1980 have identified over 500 such studies reminiscent of the old TV-versus-traditional-instruction question). There is also a growing interest in the cognitive effects of media-related activities such as inductive thinking skills affected by computer games (e.g., Greenfield, 1984), which is a renewal of similar questions asked in reference to television. It seems that as each new medium comes along, researchers select questions previously addressed to older media (Clark, in press; Gardner, 1982; Wartella & Reeves, 1983). Some of these questions seem, on the basis of past experience, to be more useful than others. Our summary of some of the most important lessons and questions follows:

1. *Past research on media has shown quite clearly that no medium enhances learning more than any other medium regardless of learning task, learner traits, symbolic elements, curriculum content, or setting.*

Gross comparisons of computers or video disc technologies versus more conventional media for instruction are not likely to prove to be more useful in the future than they have been in the past. All such research to date is subject to compelling rival hypotheses concerning uncontrolled effects of instructional content, method, and novelty. We do not expect that any known or to-be-developed media will alter this expectation. However, *evaluations* of developed and developing media-based programs might usefully compare alternative forms of delivering and shaping instruction on the basis of cost efficiency, and appeal to students without making inferences about "learning" or "performance" advantages due to the medium selected. This would also suggest that future media selection schemes (e.g., Reiser & Gagne, 1982) should be based on appeal and efficiency *rather* than presumed learning benefits.

   2.   *Any new technology is likely to teach better than its predecessors because it generally provides better prepared instructional materials and its novelty engages learners.*

While media are not causal factors in learning, they often provide the focus for curricular reform. As each new medium is developed and gradually introduced to educational settings, it provides the opportunity for trying out novel and often engaging instructional design strategies. This is particularly true if the new medium is held in as much awe as computers.

So, as each new medium is put into educational use, researchers might consider a number of different questions. For example, we might ask about the impact of a medium's introduction on the setting (e.g., organizational climate, interactions between provider and user groups, allocation of resources), and the changes the setting undergoes (e.g., Sheingold et al., 1983). It would be useful to have more investigation of two aspects of the problem: first, the way that such innovations *naturally* influence educational settings and resources, and ways that such introductions might be *made to influence* desirable outcomes. This latter type of question is particularly important in the case of computers since their available modes of use and their actual influence on education are still far from their potential.

Aside from organizational and resource changes, newer media also *afford* convenient and often novel ways to shape instructional presentations. Of course, there is evidence from past symbol system and general cognitive science research that many different symbolic representations, such as those resulting from exposure to different media attributes, sometimes serve the same or similar functions in cognitive processing. Yet, we should notice that newer media such as computers *allow* for flexible and local construction of the conditions that facilitate skill cultivation, even though these materials might also be constructed in other ways. In this fashion, newer media serve as a *proxy* for the causal variables that influence learning and performance. Here the researcher is relatively unconcerned with the way that media attributes *naturally* influence learning. As in the case of organizational change, the concern is with the way that media attributes and the instructional presentations they afford *can be directed* in the most efficient and effective way to achieve learning goals.

Finally, researchers might wish to follow up on the issue of the "functional equivalence" between nominally different media attributes. It appears that there are "families" of attributes that may have similar cognitive consequences when they are used in instruction. It would be interesting to learn whether there are ways to predict such family "memberships" and whether these families vary in uniqueness, size, and impact. For example, does functional equivalence follow from structural similarity? Or, is structural similarity irrelevant?

Researchers should also note that few, if any, profound cognitive effects of the kind often expected from computer-afforded learning activities can be expected from *brief* exposures and occasional engagements. If, for example, essay writing on word processors is to effect essay-writing *ability* (e.g., Kane, 1983), then no short-term, out-of-context experience with the tool is likely to show much of an effect. The activity must be central, continuous, consequential, and mindfully carried out in order to render observable effects.

3. *Future research on media should be conducted in the context of and with reference to similar questions in the general cognitive sciences.*

One of the truly important changes to take place in media research in the past decade is the change from an externally oriented, behavioral approach to a more cognitive, interactive, reciprocal focus. Current views suggest that instructional efficacy does not reside in either external or internal events alone, but that complex interactions between events in each domain will characterize the most productive hypotheses. These newer questions, particularly those associated with the symbol system theories, bear a strong resemblance to those in various domains of cognitive sciences such as artificial intelligence, information processing, attribution theory, dual coding, and imagery, and studies of the antecedents of various kinds of transfer of learning and training. While different perspectives on the same problems have a strong and productive history in most sciences, George Mandler's (1984) recent caution is that we might find it "useful to learn more about the achievements and disasters of other scientific enterprises, lest the blinding insights that you discover at regular intervals turn out to be somebody else's old saws" (p. 314).

4. *In the future, researchers might ask not only how and why a medium operates in instruction and learning, but also why it should be used at all.*

The final ethical question raised by the history of media use in teaching is the pattern of its use by educators. In the past there has been a pattern of adoption by schools in response to external pressures from commercial and community special interests rather than as a result of an identified and expressed need. Most new media are not developed with educational applications as their foremost goal. Consequently, decisions to adopt them occur before there is clear evidence about their efficacy or the availability of superior materials. This was certainly the case with television and is as clearly the case with microcomputers. While the enthusiasms that surround the introduction of a new medium lend a certain currency and legitimacy to schools, they also take scarce resources away from already identified priorities. Not everything that is available for empirical study is, when seen in perspective, also desirable to study.

This is not to imply, however, that the very availability of TV or computers is in itself a poor justification for their demands on the educational system. The conscientious researcher may, on occasion, recommend that schools postpone their entry into a "higher tech" era before a number of basic questions have been addressed. For example, we need to know how media might be made to support instructional objectives and other roles it takes on, what the teachers' role will be when children receive most of their instruction from computers, and how already overburdened schools will accommodate the special demands of newer media. The study and development of media in education are aimed at the improvement of the education, not the glorification of the media. This, then, suggests a new class of questions to be asked: not only what technology, for whom, and so forth, but *why this technology now?* The lesson was best expressed by Seymour Sarason (1984), who pointed out that "Because something can be studied or developed is, in itself, an insufficient base for doing it however wondrous it appears to be in regard to understanding and controlling our world" (p. 480).

REFERENCES

Allen, W.H., (1971). Instructional media research: Past, present and future. *AV Communication Review, 19,* 5–18.

Anderson, D.R., & Lorch, E.P. (1983). Looking at television: Action or reaction. In J. Bryant & D.R. Anderson (Eds.), *Watching TV, understanding TV.* New York: Academic Press.

Anderson, J.R. (1983). *Architecture of cognition.* Cambridge, MA: Harvard University Press.

Association for Educational Communications and Technology. (1977). *Educational technology: A glossary of terms* (Vol. 1). Washington, DC: AECT.

Bandura, A. (1978). The self system in reciprocal determinism. *American Psychologist, 33,* 344–358.

Blake, T. (1977). Motion in instructional media: Some subject-display mode inter-actions. *Perceptual and Motor Skills, 44,* 975–985.

Bolter, J.D. (1983). Computers for composing. In R. Case (Ed.), *Chameleon in the classroom: Developing roles for computers* (Tech. Rep. No. 22). New York: Bank Street College.

Bransford, J.D. (1979). *Human cognition.* Belmont, CA: Wadsworth.

Brown, J.W., & Van Lehn, K. (1981). Toward a generative theory of bugs in proce-dural skills. In T. Romberg, T. Carpenter, & J. Moses (Eds.), *Addition and sub-traction: Developmental perspectives.* Hillsdale, NJ: Lawrence Erlbaum.

Bruner, J.S. (1964). The course of cognitive growth. *American Psychologist, 19,* 1–15.

Card, S.K., Moran, T.P., & Newell, A. (1980). Computer text-editing: An informa-tion Processing analysis of a routine cognitive skill. *Cognitive Psychology, 12,* 32–34.

Clark, R.E. (1975). Constructing a taxonomy of media attributes for research pur-poses. *AV Communication Review, 23*(2), 197–215.

Clark, R.E. (1978). Doctoral research training in educational technology. *Educa-tional Communication and Technology Journal, 26*(2), 165–173.

Clark, R.E. (1982). Antagonism between achievement and enjoyment in ATI stud-ies. *Educational Psychologist, 17*(2), 92–101.

Clark, R.E. (1983). Reconsidering research on learning from media. *Review of Edu-cational Research, 53*(4), 445–460.

Clark, R.E. (in press). Confounding in educational computing research. *Journal of Educational Computing Research.*

Clark, R.E., & Snow, R.E. (1975). Alternative designs for instructional technology research. *AV Communication Review, 23*(4), 373–394.

Clark, R.E., & Voogel, A. (in press). Transfer of training principles for instructional design. *Educational Communication and Technology Journal, 33*(2).

Cohen, P., Ebling, B., & Kulik, J. (1981). A meta-analysis of outcome studies of visual based instruction. *Educational Communication and Technology Journal, 29*(1), 26–36.

Collins, A. (1981). Schemata for understanding television. In H. Kelly & H. Gard-ner (Eds.), *Viewing children through television.* San Francisco: Jossey-Bass.

Dixon, P., & Judd, W. (1977). A comparison of computer managed instruction and lecture modes for teaching basic statistics. *Journal of Computer Based Instruction, 41*(1), 22–25.

Dorr, A., Graves, S.B., & Phelps, E. (1980). Television literacy for young children. *Journal of Communication, 30,* 71–83.

Dweck, C.S., & Bemechat, J. (1983). Children's theories of intelligence: Conse-quences for learning. In S.G. Paris, G.M. Olson, & H.W. Stevenson (Eds.), *Learning and motivation in the classroom.* Hillsdale, NJ: Lawrence Erlbaum.

Fleming, M.L. (1979). On pictures in educational research. *Instructional Science, 8,* 235–251.

Fleming, M.L., & Levie, H. (1978). *Instructional message design.* Englewood Cliffs, NJ: Educational Technology Publications.

Foreman, G.E., & Edwards, C.P. (1982). *The use of stopped-action video replay to heighten theory testing in young children solving balancing tasks* (Final report). Amherst: University of Massachusetts.

Gardner, H. (1977). Senses, symbols, operations: An organization of artistry. In D. Perkins & B. Leondar (Eds.), *The arts and cognition*. Baltimore, MD: Johns Hopkins University Press.

Gardner, H. (1980). *Artful scribbles.* New York: Basic Books.

Gardner, H. (1982). *Art, mind and brain: A cognitive approach to creativity.* New York: Basic Books.

Gardner, H., Howard, V.A., & Perkins, D. (1974). Symbol systems: A philosophical, psychological and educational investigation. In D. Olson (Ed.), *Media and symbols: The forms of expression, communication and education* (73rd annual yearbook of the National Society for the Study of Education). Chicago: University of Chicago Press.

Glaser, R. (1976). Components of a psychology of instruction: Towards a science of design. *Review of Educational Research, 46*(1) 1–24.

Glaser, R. (1982). Instructional psychology: Past, present and future. *American Psychologist, 37,* 292–305.

Glaser, R., & Cooley, W.W. (1973). Instrumentation for teaching and instructional management. In R.M.W. Travers (Ed.), *Second handbook of research on teaching* (pp. 832–857). Chicago: Rand McNally College Publishing.

Glass, G.V. (1976). Primary, secondary and meta-analysis of research. *Review of Educational Research, 5,* 3–8.

Goodman, N. (1968). *Languages of art.* Indianapolis, IN: Hackett.

Greenfield, P. (1984). *Mind and media: The effects of television, video games, and computers.* Cambridge, MA: Harvard University Press.

Hampson, P.J., & Morris, P.E. (1978). Unfulfilled expectations: A criticism of Neisser's theory of imagery. *Cognition, 6,* 79–85.

Heidt, E. U. (1977). *Instructional media and the individual learner.* New York: Nichols Publishing.

Hellige, J.E. (1980). Cerebral hemisphere asymmetry: Methods, issues and impressions. *Educational Communication and Technology Journal, 28*(2), 83–98.

Herminghouse, E. (1957). Large group instruction by television. *School Review, 65,* 119–133.

Hess, R., & Tenezakis, M. (1972). The computer as a socializing agent: Some socioaffective outcomes of CAI. *AV Communication Review, 21*(3), 311–325.

Hollenbeck, A.R., & Slaby, R.G. (1979). Infant visual and vocal responses to television. *Child Development, 50,* 41–45.

Jaglom, L.M., & Gardner, H. (1981). The preschool television viewer as anthropologist. In H. Kelly & H. Gardner (Eds.), *Viewing children through television.* San Francisco: Jossey-Bass.

Jamison, D., Suppes, P., & Wells, S. (1974). The effectiveness of alternative instructional media: A survey. *Review of Educational Research, 44,* 1–68.

Kane, J.H. (1983). Computers for composing. In R. Case (Ed.), *Chameleon in the classroom: Developing roles for computers* (Tech. Rep. No. 22). New York: Bank Street College.

Kearsley, G., Hunter, B., & Seidel, R.J. (1983). Two decades of computer based instruction: What have we learned? *T.H.E. Journal, 10,* 88–96.

Kolers, P.A. (1977). Reading pictures and reading text. In D. Perkins & B. Leondar (Eds.), *The arts and cognition.* Baltimore, MD: Johns Hopkins University Press.

Kosslyn, S.M. (1981). The medium and the message in mental imagery: A theory. *Psychological Review, 88*, 46–66.

Kosslyn, S.M., & Pomerantz, J.R. (1977). Imagery, propositions and the form of internal representations. *Cognitive Psychology, 9*, 52–76.

Ksobiech, K. (1976). The importance of perceived task and type of presentation in student response to instructional television. *AV Communication Review, 24*(4), 401–411.

Kulik, C., Kulik, J., & Cohen, P. (1980). Instructional technology and college teaching. *Teaching of Psychology, 7*(4), 199–205.

Kulik, J., Bangert, R., & Williams, G. (1983). Effects of computer-based teaching on secondary school students. *Journal of Educational Psychology, 75*(1), 19–26.

Kulik, J., Kulik, C., & Cohen, P. (1979). Research on audio-tutorial instruction: A meta-analysis of comparative studies. *Research in Higher Education, 11*(4), 321–341.

Kyllonen, P.C., Lohman, D.F., & Snow, R.E. (1984). Effects of aptitudes, strategy training, and task facets on spatial task performance. *Journal of Educational Psychology, 76*(1), 130–145.

Leifer, A.D. (1976). Teaching with television and film. In N.L. Gage (Ed.), *The psychology of teaching methods*. Chicago: University of Chicago Press.

Lesgold, A.M., & Reif, F. (1983). *Computers in education: Realizing the potential* (Report of a research conference). Philadelphia, PA: American Society of Educators.

Levie, W.H., & Dickie, K. (1973). The analysis and application of media. In R.M.W. Travers (Ed.), *Second handbook of research on teaching*. Chicago: Rand McNally.

Lumsdaine, A. (1963). Instruments and media of instruction. In N.L. Gage (Ed.), *Handbook of research on teaching*. Chicago: Rand McNally.

Machula, R. (1978–1979). Media and affect: A comparison of videotape, audiotape and print. *Journal of Educational Technology Systems, 7*(2), 167–185.

Magnusson, D. (Ed.). (1981). *Toward a psychology of situations: An interactional perspective*. Hillsdale, NJ: Lawrence Erlbaum.

Mandler, G. (1984). Cohabitation in the cognitive sciences. In W. Kintsch, J. Miller, & P. Polson (Eds.), *Methods and tactics in cognitive science*. Hillsdale, NJ: Lawrence Erlbaum.

Meringoff, L.K. (1980). Influence of the medium of children's story apprehension. *Journal of Educational Psychology, 72*, 240–249.

Merrill, M.D. (1984). Learner control and computer based learning. In B.K. Bass & C.R. Dills (Eds.), *Instructional development: The state of the art II*. Dubuque, IA: Kendall/Hunt.

Mielke, K. (1968). Questioning the questions of ETV research. *Educational Broadcasting Review, 2*, 6–15.

Mischel, W. (1984). Convergences and challenges in the search for consistency. *American Psychologist, 39*, 351–364.

Morrisett, L. (1984). Forward. In J. Murray & G. Salomon (Eds.), *The future of children's television*. Boys Town, NE: Boys Town Center.

Olson, D. (1972). On a theory of instruction: Why different forms of instruction result in similar knowledge. *Interchange, 3*(1), 9–24.

Olson, D. (1974). Introduction. In D. Olson (Ed.), *Media and symbols: The forms of expression, communication, and education* (73rd yearbook of the National Society for the Study of Education). Chicago: University of Chicago Press.

Olson, D. (1976). Towards a theory of instructional means. *Educational Psychologist, 12*, 14–35.

Olson, D. (1977). Oral and written communication and the cognitive processing of children. *Journal of Communication, 27*, 10–26.

Olson, D., & Bialystock, E. (1983). *Spatial cognition*. Hillsdale, NJ: Lawrence Erlbaum.

Olson, D., & Bruner, J. (1974). Learning through experience and learning through media. In D. Olson (Ed.), *Media and symbols: The forms of expression, communication, and education* (73rd yearbook of the National Society for the Study of Education). Chicago: University of Chicago Press.

Olweus, D. (1977). A critical analysis of the "modern" interactionist position. In D. Magnusson & N.S. Endler (Eds.), *Personality at the crossroads*. Hillsdale, NJ: Lawrence Erlbaum.

Paivio, A.U. (1971). *Imagery and verbal process*. New York: Holt, Rinehart & Winston.

Paivio, A.U. (1977). Images, propositions and knowledge. In J.M. Nicholas (Ed.), *Images, perceptions and knowledge*. Dordrecht, The Netherlands: Reidel.

Papert, S. (1980). *Mindstorms: Children, computers and powerful ideas*. New York: Basic Books.

Pea, R., & Kurland, M. (1985). On the cognitive effects of learning computer programming. *New Ideas in Psychology*.

Pressley, M. (1977). Imagery and children's learning: Putting the picture in developmental perspective. *Review of Educational Research, 47*, 585–622.

Pylyshyn, Z.W. (1973). What the mind's eye tells the mind's brain: A critique of mental imagery. *Psychological Bulletin, 80*, 1024.

Pylyshyn, Z.W. (1981). The imagery debate: Analogue media versus tacit knowledge. *Psychological Review, 88*, 16–45.

Reigeluth, C. (1983). *Instructional-design theories and models*. Hillsdale, NJ: Lawrence Erlbaum.

Reiser, R., & Gagne, R. (1982). Characteristics of media selection models. *Review of Educational Research, 52*(4), 499–512.

Resnick, L.B., & Weaver, P.A. (Eds.). (1979). *Theory and practice of early reading*. Hillsdale, NJ: Lawrence Erlbaum.

Riccobono, J.A. (1984). *Availability, use and support of instructional media, 1982–83: Corporation for Public Broadcasting*. Washington, DC: National Center for Educational Statistics.

Rice, T., Huston, A.G., & Wright, J.C. (1982). *The forms and codes of television: Effects on childrens' attention, comprehension and social behavior* (National Institute of Mental Health Update of the 1972 Report of the Surgeon General's Scientific Advisory Committee on Television and Social Behavior). Washington, DC: Surgeon General's Office.

Rumelhart, D.E., & Norman, D.A. (1981). Analogical processes in learning. In J.R. Anderson (Ed.), *Cognitive skills and their acquisition*. Hillsdale, NJ: Lawrence Erlbaum.

Saettler, P.A. (1968). *A history of instructional technology*. New York: McGraw-Hill.

Salomon, G. (1971). Heuristic models for the generation of aptitude-treatment interaction hypotheses. *Review of Educational Research, 42,* 327–343.

Salomon, G. (1974a). Internalization of filmic schematic operations in interaction with learners' aptitudes. *Journal of Educational Psychology, 66,* 499–511.

Salomon, G. (1974b). What is learned and how it is taught: The interaction between media, message, task and learner. In D. Olson (Ed.), *Media and symbols: The forms of expression, communication and education* (73rd yearbook of the National Society for the Study of Education). Chicago: University of Chicago Press.

Salomon, G. (1979). *Interaction of media, cognition and learning.* San Francisco: Jossey-Bass.

Salomon, G. (1981). *Communication and education: Social and psychological interactions.* Beverly Hills, CA: Sage.

Salomon, G. (1983a). The differential investment of mental effort in learning from different sources. *Educational Psychologist, 18,* 42–50.

Salomon, G. (1983b). Television literacy and television vs. literacy. In B.W. Bailey & R.M. Fosheim (Eds.), *Literacy for life: The demand for reading and writing.* New York: Modern Language Association of America.

Salomon, G., & Clark, R.E. (1977). Reexamining the methodology of research on media and technology in education. *Review of Educational Research, 47*(1), 99–120.

Salomon, G., & Cohen, A.A. (1977). Television formats, mastery of mental skills, and the acquisition of knowledge. *Journal of Educational Psychology, 69*(5), 612–619.

Salomon, G., & Gardner, H. (1984). *The computer as educator: Lessons from television research.* Cambridge, MA: Harvard University, Graduate School of Education.

Salomon, G., & Perkins, D. (1984, August). *The rocky road to transfer: Rethinking mechanisms of a neglected phenomenon.* Paper presented at the Harvard Conference on Thinking, Cambridge, MA.

Saracho, O.N. (1982). The effect of a computer-assisted instruction program on basic skills achievement and attitude toward instruction of Spanish speaking migrant children. *American Educational Research Journal, 19*(2), 201–219.

Sarason, S.B. (1984). If it can be studied or developed, should it be? *American Psychologist, 39,* 477–485.

Schramm, W. (1977). *Big media, little media.* Beverly Hills, CA: Sage.

Schwarts, J. (1983). Tyranny, discipline, freedom and license: Some thoughts on educational ideology and computers. In *Education in the electronic age.* New York: WNET Media.

Schwen, T. (1977). Professional scholarship in educational technology: Criteria for inquiry. *AV Communication Review, 25,* 35–79.

Scribner, S. & Cole, M. (1981). *The psychology of literacy.* Cambridge, MA: Harvard University Press.

Sheingold, K., Kane, J.H., & Enderweit, M.E. (1983). Microcomputer use in schools: Developing a research agenda. *Harvard Education Review, 53,* 412–432.

Shepard, R.N. (1978). The mental image. *American Psychologist, 33,* 125–137.

Shulman, L.S. (1980). *Reflections on individual differences and the study of teaching.* Paper presented at the American Educational Research Association, Boston.

Shulman, L.S. (1981). *Educational psychology returns to school* (G. Stanley Hall Series). Paper presented at the annual meeting of the American Psychological Association, Los Angeles.

Singer, D.G. (1983). A time to reexamine the role of television in our lives. *American Psychologist, 38,* 815–816.

Singer, D.G., Zuckerman, D.M., & Singer, J.L. (1980). Helping elementary school children learn about T.V. *Journal of Communication, 30,* 84–93.

Snow, R.E., Tiffen, J., & Siebert, W.F. (1965). Individual differences and instructional film effects. *Journal of Educational Psychology, 56*(6), 315–326.

Stein, J.L., & Glen, C.G. (1979). A analysis of story comprehension in elementary school children. In R. Freedle (Ed.), *New directions in discourse comprehension.* Norwood, NJ: Ablex.

Stimmel, T., Common, J., McCaskill, B., & Durrett, H.J. (1981). Teacher resistance to computer assisted instruction. *Behavior Research Methods and Instrumentation, 13*(2), 128–130.

Suppes, P. (1979). Current trends in computer-assisted instruction. *Advances in Computers, 18,* 173–229.

Tickton, S.G. (Ed.). (1970). *To improve learning: An evaluation of instructional technology.* New York: Bowker.

Tikomirov, O.K. (1974). Man and computer: The impact of computer technology on the development of psychological process. In D. Olson (Ed.), *Media and symbols: The forms of expression, communication, and education* (73rd yearbook of the National Society for the Study of Education). Chicago: University of Chicago Press.

Tobias, S. (1982). When do instructional methods make a difference? *Educational Researcher, 11*(4), 4–9.

Turkle, S. (1984). *The second self: Computers and the human spirit.* New York: Simon and Schuster.

Wartella, A., & Reeves, B. (1983). Recurring issues in research on children and media. *Educational Technology, 23,* 5–9.

Weizenbaum, J. (1976). *Computer power and human reason.* New York: Freeman.

Wilkinson, G. (1980). *Media in instruction: Sixty years of research.* Washington, DC: Association for Educational Communications and Technology.

Winn, W. (1981). Effect of attribute highlighting and diagrammatic organization on identification and classification. *Journal of Research in Science Teaching, 18*(1), 23–32.

Winn, W. (1982). Visualization in learning and instruction. *Educational Communication and Technology Journal, 30*(1), 3–25.

Wittrock, M.C. (1978). The cognitive movement in instruction. *Educational Psychologist, 13,* 15–31.

Wolf, T. (1977). Reading reconsidered. *Harvard Educational Review, 47,* 411–429.

Zillman, D., Williams, B.R., Bryant, J., Boyton, K.R., & Wolf, M.A. (1980). Acquisition of information from educational television programs as a function of differently paced humourous inserts. *Journal of Educational Psychology, 72,* 170–180.

Zimler, J., & Keenan, J.M. (1983). Imagery in the congenitally blind: How visual are visual images? *Journal of Experimental Psychology: Learning, Memory and Cognition, 9,* 269–282.

CHAPTER 4

INTERNATIONAL VIEWS OF THE MEDIA DEBATE

Richard E. Clark and Brenda M. Sugrue

Reprinted from the *International Journal of Educational Research, 14*(6), 485–579. Clark, R.E. & Sugrue, B.M., North American Disputes about Research on Learning from Media. Copyright 1990, with permission from Elsevier Science.

ABSTRACT

In North America, some of the more important media disputes focus on: (1) the effects of different media on learning; (2) whether media play any essential role in the cultivation of or transfer of cognitive skills; (3) the motivating properties of media; and (4) the economic benefits of different media. This review suggests that American media researchers tend to belong to either a "strong" or a "weak" media theory group. Evidence for each of the two extreme theory positions is examined and it is concluded that sufficient evidence has not been advanced to support a "strong" theory of media effects on learning, motivation or cost.

INTRODUCTION:
WEAK AND STRONG THEORIES OF MEDIA

There are four main types of disputes among North American researchers who investigate the effects of media on learning. They are disputes about:

1. Which media are superior for academic achievement;
2. The cognitive skills cultivated by particular media;
3. The motivational effects of different media; and
4. The economic benefits of various media.

This paper will discuss the main arguments and relevant research relating to each of these four disputes. Before we begin a discussion of each type of dispute however, a brief comment on the arguments is in order.

It is our impression that these four arguments have one origin—they all stem from conflicts over the intuitive belief by one group of researchers that each medium makes *unique* contributions to learning and motivation. For example, many researchers believe that instructional uses of television contribute something unique to academic achievement which is not possible with computers or textbooks—or that computers foster unique cognitive skills that are not available from television or teachers. This "strong" media theory view holds that certain media produce unique cognitive skills and therefore more of some types of learning for certain students and subject matter. The other side in the argument, the "weak" media theory approach, claims that media do not have any psychological influence over learning but that media may influence the "economics" (speed and cost) of learning. At the center of North American arguments are issues of research design—such as the debate that surrounds the media comparison studies. This article will explore both the "strong" and the "weak" media theory evidence and will conclude that there is not sufficient evidence to support the "strong" theory.

MEDIA COMPARISONS

Until recently, a typical study by the "strong" media theorists compared the relative achievement of groups who received similar subject matter from different media (e.g., Mielke, 1968). The goal of such studies was to find out which medium was "superior." With the advent of each new instructional medium, a new crop of such studies has emerged, comparing the new medium with an older one. During the past decade, television research has diminished considerably, being replaced by computer assisted learning studies. Each new medium seems to attract its own set of "strong media" theory advocates who make claims for improved learning and stimulate research questions which are similar to those asked about the previously popular medium. It seems that similar research questions have resulted in similar and ambiguous data. Media comparison studies emphasized comparisons of the learning impact of newer media such as television with more "traditional" media such as classroom instruction. Evidence from these studies usually favored newer media. Thus, during the early days of the motion picture, studies tended to favor movies over teachers. Later, similarly designed studies favored television over teachers, movies or textbooks. As a result of these studies, conducted largely in the quarter century between 1950 and 1975, the media movement grew and prospered.

Recent Reviews of Research

More recent analyses indicate that media comparison studies, regardless of the media employed, tend to result in "no significant difference" conclusions (Clark, 1983). The active ingredient, in studies which find one medium superior to another, is usually some uncontrolled aspect of the instructional method (e.g., programmed instruction) rather than the medium. In the 1970s, skepticism about media comparison studies, still being conducted in apparently large numbers, began to grow. The evidence began to favor "weak media" theory. A number of comprehensive reviews concluded that there was no good evidence that any medium produced more learning or motivation than any other medium. Levie and Dickie (1973) noted that most overall media comparison studies to date had been fruitless and suggested that most learning objectives could be attained through "instruction presented by any of a variety of different media" (p. 859). This observation was echoed by Schramm (1977), according to whom "learning seems to be affected more by what is delivered than by the delivery system" (p. 273).

Meta-analytic Studies of Media
During the past decade, more effort has been made to analyze and refocus the results of existing comparison studies. The statistical technique called meta-analysis has proved to be a most useful approach to summarizing instructional media (and other kinds of educational) research. The current meta-analyses of media comparison studies provide evidence that any reported significant differences in performance have been due to confounding in the treatments employed in the studies. A recent series of meta-analyses of media research was conducted by James Kulik and his colleagues at the University of Michigan (Clark, 1985, contains citations for most of these meta-analyses). Generally, meta-analyses allow for a more

precise estimate of treatment effect sizes than was possible a few years ago. Meta-analytic procedures yield effect size estimates that are converted to percentage of standard deviation gains on final examination scores due to the more powerful treatment, if any. Most of the meta-analytic surveys of media research demonstrate a typical learning advantage for "newer" media of about one-half a standard deviation on final examination performance, compared with "conventional" (i.e., teacher presented) treatments. In the case of computer-based instruction studies in college environments, for example, this advantage translates as an increase from the 50th to the 66th percentile on final examinations in a variety of courses. This is an impressive accomplishment if one accepts it at face value. Closer inspection of these reviews, however, reveals that most of the large effect sizes attributed to computers in these studies are actually due to poorly designed studies and confounding (Clark, 1983, 1985). These weak effect sizes seem to support the "weak" media theory.

Media Research Design Problems

According to Clark (1983), the most common sources of confounding in media research seem to be the uncontrolled effects of (a) instructional method or content differences between treatments that are compared, and (b) a novelty effect for newer media, which tends to disappear over time. Evidence for each of these controlled effects can be found in the meta-analyses. The positive effect for newer media more or less disappears when the same instructor produces all treatments in a study (Clark, 1985). Different teams of instructional designers or different teachers probably give different content and instructional methods to the treatments that are compared. If this is the case, we do not know whether to attribute the advantage to the medium or to the differences between content and method being compared. However, if the effect for media tends to disappear when the same instructor or team designs contrasting treatments, we have reason to believe that the lack of difference is due to greater control of non-medium variables. Clark and Salomon (1986) cited a number of researchers in the past who have reminded us that when examining the effects of different media, only the media being compared can be different. All other aspects of the mediated treatments, including the subject matter content and method of instruction, must be identical in the two or more media being compared. In meta-analyses of college level computerized versus conventional courses, an effect size of one-half a standard deviation results when different faculty teach the compared course. Clark (1983) found that this effect reduces to about one-tenth of a standard deviation advantage when one considers only studies in which one instructor plans and teaches both experimental and control courses.

Novelty in Media Experiments

A second, though probably less important source of confounding in media comparison studies, is the increased effort and attention research subjects tend to give to media that are novel to them. The increased attention paid by students sometimes results in increased effort or persistence which yields achievement gains. If they are due to a novelty effect, these gains tend to diminish as students become more familiar with the new medium. This was the case in reviews of computer-assisted instruction at the secondary school level (grades 6 to 12). An average computer effect size of three-tenths of a standard deviation (i.e., a rise in examination scores from the 50th to the 63rd percentile) for computer courses tended to dissipate significantly in longer duration studies. In studies lasting four weeks or less, computer effects were one-half a standard deviation. This reduced to three-tenths of a standard deviation in studies lasting five to eight weeks and further reduced to the familiar and weak two-tenths of a standard deviation computer effect after eight weeks of data collection. Effects of two-tenths or less account for less than 1 percent of the variance in a comparison. The Kuliks (cf. Clark, 1983, 1985 for citations) report a similar phenomenon in their review of visual-based instruction (e.g., film, television, pictures). Although the reduction in effect size for longer duration studies approached significance (about .065 alpha), there were a number of comparisons of methods mixed with different visual media, which makes interpretation difficult (cf. Clark & Salomon, 1986). In their review of computer use in college, the Kuliks did not find any evidence for this novelty effect. In their comparison of studies of one or two hours duration with those which held weekly sessions for an entire semester, the effect sizes were roughly the same. It is possible that computers are less novel experiences for college subjects than for secondary school students.

Weak Theory Support

In the face of consistent evidence indicating that any learning benefits in media comparison studies can be attributed to media-independent variables, it is becoming less and less valid to ask the question "Which medium promotes greater learning?" Existing comparison study evidence seems to provide much more support for the "weak" media theory.

CULTIVATION OF COGNITIVE SKILL

A second class of disputes about research on learning from media concerns the identification of specific elements or attributes of an instructional medium which might activate or cultivate particular cognitive skills in learners. On one side of the dispute are the "strong media" researchers who claim that there are unique attributes of particular media which influence the way that information is processed in learning. On the other side of the dispute are "weak media" researchers who claim that the cognitive processing induced by the identified "unique attributes" can also be induced by other media or media attributes; and, indeed, that such processing may not even be sufficient for learning and transfer.

Unique Media Attributes?

Studies of the "attributes" of media and their influence on the way that information is processed in learning were popular in the 1970s. In this approach, many media were thought to possess unique attributes such as the capacity to slow the motion of objects or "zoom" into details of a stimulus field or to "unwrap" a three-dimensional object into its two-dimensional form. These attributes were thought to cultivate cognitive skills when modeled by learners, so that, for example, a child with low cue attending ability might learn the cognitive skill of "zooming" into stimulus details (Salomon, 1974a), or novice chess players might increase their skills in recognizing potential moves and configurations of chess pieces through animated modeling of moves and patterns. Because this type of question dealt with the way that information is selected and transformed in the acquisition of generalizable cognitive skills, many believed that the possibility of a coherent "strong" theory dealing with media attributes was forthcoming. In addition, it was exciting to imagine that these media attributes might result in unique cognitive skills because they promised to teach mental transformations which had not heretofore been experienced.

Media Attribute Theory Hypotheses

The promise of the "strong" theory media attributes approach was based on at least three expectations: (a) that media attributes were an integral part of media and would provide a connection between instructional uses of media and learning; (b) that attributes would provide for the cultivation of cognitive skills for learners who needed them; and (c) that identified attributes would provide unique independent variables for instructional theories that specified causal relationships between attribute modeling and learning. The final point (c) is most important because it represents a renewed search for evidence of a "strong" connection between media (or media attributes in this instance) and learning. The media attribute research review that follows is an attempt to explore the evidence for each of the three expectations listed above.

Symbol System Theory

The first expectation was that media attributes would somehow represent the psychologically relevant aspects of media. However, few of the originators of the media attribute construct (Salomon, 1974b) claimed that they were more than "correlated" with different media, that is, that any one media attribute was available from more than one (and often many) media. Since they are not exclusive to any specific media and were only associated with them by habit or convenience, "media" attributes are not media variables any more certainly than the specific subject matter content, format, organization or layout of a book is part of the definition of a "book." In fact, the early discussions of media attributes most often referred to "symbol systems" or symbolic "elements" of instruction. All instructional messages were coded in some symbolic representational system, the argument went, and symbols vary in the cognitive transformation they allow us to perform on the information we select from our environment. Some symbolic elements (animated arrows, zooming) permit us to cultivate cognitive skills. However, many different media can present a given attribute so there is no necessary correspondence between attributes and media. Media are mere vehicles for attributes, so the term "media attributes" is misleading.

The Cultivation of Cognitive Skills

The second expectation of the attribute approach was that attributes would provide for the cultivation of cognitive skills for learners who needed them. Salomon (1979), and more recently Greenfield (1984), have reviewed research where symbolic features of mediated experiences and instruction were shown to differentially affect the skills activated in the service of knowledge acquisition and on the mastery of these skills. Such research was inspired, in part, by Jerome Bruner's (1964) argument that internal representations and operations partly depend on learning "precisely the techniques that serve to amplify our acts, perceptions and our ratiocinative activities" (p. 2). Such a view characterizes the essence of the "strong" media theory—it implies that unique coding or structural elements of a given medium (e.g., filmic causal sequences) or uniquely afforded activities (e.g., computer programming) may have unique effects on related mental skills. Thus, the employment of a coding element such as a close-up, or the allowance for students' manipulation of input data may activate specific mental operations that facilitate the acquisition of knowledge as well as improved mastery.

Salomon's Research on Media Attributes

In one study (Salomon, 1974a), students who had difficulty attending to cues in a visual field learned the skill by seeing it modeled in a film where they saw a camera "zoom" from a wide field to close-up shots of many different details. An analysis of the task suggested that effective cue attending required an attention-directing strategy which began with a view of the entire stimulus and then narrowed the stimulus field until a single, identifiable cue remained. For those students with low cue-attending skill (the requisite cognitive skill to perform the task), Salomon (1974b) reasoned that the required instructional method would be modeling. In this case, the construction of the model followed an analysis of the symbol systems, which allowed this particular method to be coded for delivery to the students. While the zooming treatment used was available in many media (e.g., film, television, video disc), the students seemed to model the zooming and used it as a cognitive skill which allowed them to attend to cues.

Replications of Salomon's Research

The results of Salomon's zooming studies have not always held up when they have been replicated. In a partial replication of the Salomon (1974a) "zooming" study, Bovy (1983) found that a treatment which used an "irising" attribute to provide practice in cue-attending was as effective as Salomon's zooming in cultivating the skill during practice. Irising consisted of slowly enclosing cues in a circular, gradually enlarging, darkened border similar to the effect created by an iris which regulates the amount of light permitted through a camera lens. When details were highlighted by the iris, cue attending skill was cultivated as effectively as with "zooming." More important, however, was Bovy's finding that a treatment that merely isolated cues with a static close-up of the same details singled out by the zooming and irising, was even more effective in cultivating cue attending skill than either zooming or irising. It may be that only the efficient isolation of relevant cues is necessary for this task. In a similar study, Blake (see Clark, 1983) taught chess moves to high or low visual ability undergraduates through a standard narration and (a) still pictures, (b) animated arrows with the pictures, or (c) a motion film from which the still pictures were taken. While all three conditions worked for the higher ability students, low visualizers learned the chess moves equally well from the arrow and the motion treatments which were significantly better for them than the static pictures. Here, as in the Salomon (1974a) study, we presume that the modeled chess moves compensated for the low ability students' lack of spatial visualization. Unlike Salomon's experimental subjects, Blake's subjects profited from two different operational definitions of the necessary model, animated arrows and moving chess pieces. Different stimulus arrangements resulted in similar performances but, we might expect, led to nominally different cognitive processes being modeled. The necessary process for learning chess moves, the visualizing of the entire move allowed each piece, could therefore be operationalized in a variety of ways. Each of those manifestly different visualizations provided a psychologically sufficient condition for the successful cultivation of skill in imagining chess piece moves. The cognitive feature in the chess study was the simulation of beginning and ending points of the moves of the various chess pieces. In the cue-attending studies by Salomon and Bovy, the cognitive features were probably the isolation of relevant cues. It is the external modeling of these features in any symbol system understood by the student that yields the required performance. When a chosen symbol system is shaped to represent the critical features of the task and other things are equal, learning will occur. When a medium delivers a symbol system containing this necessary arrangement of features, learning will occur also but will not be due to either the medium or the symbol system.

Transfer of Learning from Media

The possibility of cognitive skill activation and cultivation from specific media attributes raises new conceptual and empirical questions. If media's symbolic modes of information presentation can activate, even cultivate mental operations and skills, are these skills unique? What is their utility? How far do they transfer, if at all? These questions are of particular interest with respect to the use of computers in instruction for many computer-afforded activities are rationalized in terms of their unique effects on transferable skills. One would need to distinguish between, say, the acquisition of a particular image or operation, on the one hand, and the cultivation of imagery ability or generalized skill, on the other. It is one thing if children learn from televiewing only how to become better televiewers or from programming in Logo how to be better Logo programmers; it is another if they show skill cultivation that transfers beyond the boundaries of that medium or activity.

Logo Experiments

The Logo programming environment has generally failed to cultivate cognitive skills of planning and problem solving which would transfer beyond the context of the Logo environment (Salomon & Perkins, 1987). A few studies have reported transfer of cognitive skills from Logo to other contexts (e.g., Clements & Gullo, 1984). However, there is no evidence to support the "strong" theory or to suggest that such transfer cannot be achieved by other media apart from the computer and the Logo activity.

Conclusions about Attribute Theories

In all, it appears that media's symbolic forms and computers' afforded activities may have skill-cultivating effects, but that these are not necessarily unique nor easily transferable. Future research, particularly that concerned with computer-afforded learning activities, will do well to ask not just whether particular skills are acquired, but also how else they could be developed, and under what instructional, contextual, and psychological conditions they can be made to transfer. The problem lies not in the fact that symbol systems can be made to cultivate skills but in whether these symbolic elements or attributes are *unique, exclusive to any particular medium, or necessary for learning.* If the attributes identified to date are useful in instruction, they are valuable. However, theory development depends on the discovery of more basic or necessary processes of instruction and learning.

ARGUMENTS ABOUT THE
MOTIVATIONAL EFFECTS OF MEDIA

In recent years there has been a great deal of interest in the effects of student and teacher values, attitudes and beliefs towards media. This section briefly reviews that research. Before presenting a model for understanding these studies however, it must be noted that the "strong" media theory suggests that certain media are more "motivating" than other media. Presumably, the positive reactions by students and teachers to some media cause increases in the amount of attention and effort they will spend to learn from media. The "weak" media theory suggests that the independent variable in motivation studies is *not* media, but is our beliefs or values related to media. Therefore, if there are learning or motivation benefits uncovered in studies, those benefits may not be attributed to media. Attitude variables are learner variables and learning gains must be attributed to "individual differences" or "learner traits."

Attitude research has a long history and critics of the area have noted a number of serious flaws in study design and have disputed the utility of research results for the development of instructional prescriptions. Recently however, there has been a promising series of developments that have resulted from the growth of cognitive theories of learning. While space does not permit a detailed account of these developments, a brief summary of them follows.

In general, it is thought that our attitudes, beliefs and values influence our *motivation* to learn. Motivation is typically measured by either our willingness to engage in a task (i.e., to choose one task over a number of things which compete for our attention) and/or to invest effort in a task we have selected to perform. Effort investments can range from very shallow (i.e., when we perform automatically, mindlessly, and without much thought) to very deep (i.e., when we give all our attention and intelligence to a task). Motivation is one of the necessary components of learning. One may have all the necessary ability for learning without the motivation to invest effort. Similarly, one may have motivation and lack ability. One might think of the difference between motivation and intelligence as analogous to the difference between gasoline and the engine of an automobile. While the analogy fails in a number of areas, the best engine will not run on an empty tank and the highest octane gas will not cause a car to run when the engine has a mechanical problem. If learning is enhanced when values, beliefs or attitudes change it is because the learner gains motivation to engage in a task or invest the required level of effort—the engine gets gas. If an increase in motivation does not increase learning, the problem may have been a lack of ability—the engine malfunctions.

Attitude research has resulted in some very confusing results. While our expectation of a positive relationship between attitude and learning is generally borne out in the research literature, we find a number of studies where the reverse is true. There is a significant group of well-designed studies where more positive attitudes towards a medium result in *less* learning and other studies where negative attitudes results in *more* learning. Clark and Salomon (1986) reviewed a number of specific studies where one finds these conflicting and counterintuitive results. The outcome of an analysis of these studies suggests that the relationship between attitude (and our resulting motivation to learn) on the one hand and learning on the other is not direct or monotonic.

Current Cognitive Theory of Motivation to Learn from Media

One of the most interesting new North American cognitive "self efficacy" theories of motivation (Bandura, 1979; Salomon, 1981) suggests that the relationship between attitude toward media and learning is best conceptualized as an "inverted U." This theory suggests that students invest effort on the basis of their beliefs about, or attitude towards, two factors: (1) the requirements of a task; and (2) the student's assessment of his or her own skills related to task requirements. Salomon calls these two factors "perceived demand characteristics" (PDC—for task requirements) and "perceived self efficacy" (PSE—for self assessment of required skills). Drawing on Bandura's theory, Salomon hypothesizes that as students' perception of the difficulty of a medium increases from low to moderate, the effort they will invest in learning from that medium increases from very low to its maximum level. The same result occurs when a student's perception of his or her own skills increases from low to moderate. However, when a student's perception of the difficulty of a medium reaches a very high level or his or her judgment about his or her own skills at learning from a medium is very high, his or her effort investment falls to very low levels. It is moderate levels of PDC and/or PSE that result in the greatest level of motivation. In addition, there may be large national and cultural differences in PDC and PSE judgments. Salomon (1984) for example, notes that North American students generally believe that television is an easy medium while books are difficult. While there is nothing essentially more difficult about books, students will generally invest more effort in learning from them than from a televised presentation. Salomon notes that Israeli children, who have a different perception of the demands of televised instruction, do not make the same distinctions.

Counterintuitive Research Findings Explained

This new motivation theory may go some distance in explaining the often counterintuitive research findings in previous research on attitudes, values and beliefs about media such as those described by Salomon (1981,1984) and Clark (1983). For example, studies which have shown increases in motivation (or learning) with *decreases* in attitude toward a specific medium are now predictable given self efficacy theory.

One of the areas not adequately addressed by attitude theory is the construct of "value". One may value a medium and prefer to learn from it simply because it is liked, not because it represents an "easier" way to learn or because the learner perceives him or herself as more or less capable with it. There is currently very little research on values for learning from one or another medium. There is a budding interest in values however in current cognitive theories of learning. Researchers interested in this area might consult studies by Dweck and Bernechat (1983) for direction. Generally, we suspect that a student's values will influence his or her decision to engage in learning from a specific medium (or a learning task) but not the amount of effort they invest (recall the distinction made earlier between engagement and effort in motivation theory). One may have ability and an attitude which would allow for effort to be spent at a medium but simply value some other medium so much more that one refuses to choose to learn from the medium employed for instruction. This may have been the case in attitude studies reported by Saracho (1982) and Machula (1978–79). These and other studies (Clark, 1982) suggest that student values toward or against certain media may change radically over a brief span of time within the same instructional module. One indication of these changes is the extent to which student "attention" and "engagement" in tasks wanders on and off task as they choose to "think about" things other than the instructional task. Indications that values change in a brief span of time suggest that the design of studies in this area contain measurement techniques that are sensitive to such changes.

Conclusions about Motivation Research With Media

Cognitive theories of motivation may have brought a measure of clarity to research on attitudes, values and beliefs about media. Previous research results which seemed conflicting and counterintuitive are now more understandable. Generally, attitude research is better conceptualized as part of motivation theory and media researchers interested in attitudes or values are urged to master the growing literature on cognitive theories of motivation—particularly the work which has resulted from Bandura's Self Efficacy theory and the extensions of that theory by Salomon (1981, 1984). Basically, the cognitive theories seem also to support the "weak" media theory. Evidence suggests that all motivation results from the answer to three largely implicit questions learners ask themselves: (1) Do I like this medium (or learning task)?; (2) What skills are required to learn from this medium (or learning task)?; and (3) Do I have the skills that it takes to learn from this medium (or learning task)? The answer to the first question leads learners to choose to learn from one or another valued medium. The answers to the second two questions influence the amount of effort one invests in learning from any given medium. Researchers in this area are urged to focus on a careful measurement of engagement, level of effort, values and related constructs such as "perceived demand characteristics" and "perceived self-efficacy." In addition, researchers are urged to separate learning from motivational issues in studies. This can be accomplished by insuring that motivation studies are not confounded by ability or prior knowledge differences on the part of subjects. In this way, the motivational influences on achievement will be separated from the contribution of general and specific abilities.

One final suggestion is in order. We suspect that these new cognitive theories of motivation imply some changes in our understanding of research on *feedback* during mediated instruction. This is particularly important in the design of research on the "interactivity" advantages of computer-based instruction (CBI). Many CBI studies are designed to investigate different forms of interaction between learner and computer courseware. The "feedback" given by the computer may be conceptualized in many ways but, if researchers think of it as answering one or more of the three "motivation" questions (in addition to other questions), the literature in this area may become more productive. In other words, feedback might be about values, media demands on the learner or the learner's capabilities to learn from one or more media—depending on whether the researcher wanted to manipulate engagement with a medium or the amount of effort invested in learning from a given medium.

DISPUTES ABOUT THE ECONOMIC BENEFITS OF MEDIA

Disputes surrounding research on the economic benefits of media center on an issue similar to that involved in media comparison studies where achievement was the measure of success.

On the "strong" media theory side of the dispute about the economic benefits of media are researchers or enthusiastic practitioners who assume that a particular medium will be less expensive for more or less all instructional situations. On the "weak" media theory side of the dispute are those who maintain that it is other medium-independent factors that determine which medium will be most cost effective to deliver a particular instructional program.

Computer Cost-Effectiveness Research

While there have been many recent studies of the economic benefits and pitfalls of media, one of the most thorough and important is the recent, yet unpublished, review by Henry Levin at Stanford University (1987). He has reanalyzed a number of recent, comprehensive CBI cost-effectiveness studies. His conclusions, presented only briefly here, note that CBI cost-effectiveness (C/E) is relatively poor in most evaluation studies. For example, a series of studies by Levin, Glass, and Meister (1984, 1987) found that CBI was less cost-effective than peer tutoring for increasing reading and mathematics achievement at the primary level.

Levin's analysis of recent cost-effectiveness studies revealed that, when sites make a determined effort to promote *full utilization* of computers and software, C/E increases by a factor of 50 percent. Most important for media managers is Levin's finding that there are dramatic C/E differences for the same CBT programs *between implementation sites.* That is, when the same CBT program is implemented in different schools or cities, the C/E ratio changes by as much as 400 percent! This strongly suggests the importance of management systems for implementing and directing the use of CBT systems. Levin's study also provides many important cautions for the researcher and the practitioner communities. To date he has located about 80 large-scale CBT evaluation studies where costs and time were assessed. Yet, his attempt to include only adequate studies in his analyses excluded all but eight from his final analysis. It seems that we should be wary of basing research or implementation decisions on any arbitrarily selected subset of this flawed literature. Levin's description of what he calls the CBT "implementation" issue should be required reading for all media researchers. He notes, for example, that elementary school computer systems tend to be more fully utilized than those in secondary or college settings—which may account for the typically larger achievement effect sizes found at elementary school level in the meta-analyses by Kulik and others.

More Economic Studies Needed

One of the least obvious, yet most compelling, aspects of the media research conducted during the last decade is the robustness of economic questions *and* the scarcity of economic studies. There is a growing consensus that past media comparison, media attribute and motivation studies indicate that media do not influence whether someone learns from instruction. Learning seems to be due to factors such as task differences, instructional methods and learner traits (including attitudes) but not the choice of media for instruction. Another way to state this conclusion is that media do not influence the psychological elements of learning and have no place as independent variables in attempts to predict learning outcomes. Yet, it seems that there is equally dramatic evidence that *media do influence the economic elements of learning.* That is, under certain conditions media can dramatically influence the *cost* of learning. Here, "cost" can be defined in any of a variety of ways—as the amount of *time* it takes a learner to reach an achievement criterion or a development team to develop, revise and/or present instructional programs; as the *cost* in resources (such as dollars, committed facilities, or the drain on an organization); and/or as the cost of access to instruction by different types of learners (in dollars, effort or time). For example, comparisons of computer and conventional instruction often show a 30 to 50 percent reduction in time to complete lessons for the computer groups (Clark & Salomon, 1986). While some of this dramatic economic advantage of computers may be due to a novelty effect that disappears over time, not all time savings are attributable to research design errors. We hope that the level of research on the economics of instructional media will increase in the next few years. While school systems in the United States are not forced to rationalize their plans in terms of cost-effectiveness yet, we seem to be moving in that general direction. We may find that some media make certain instructional methods cheap enough for broad implementation. For example, computers and video disk media may provide the constant interaction that individualized instruction requires but which has only been previously available from expensive live teachers. In this case it would not be necessary to claim that computers made a unique contribution to learning in order to rationalize their use in education. It would be sufficient to provide evidence that a medium made some necessary instructional method cheap enough to be "affordable" within current levels of support.

CONCLUSION

Most of the disputes surrounding the research on learning from media have resulted from a confusion about which technology was serving what purpose. Technology is best interpreted as the "application of a science" to solving practical problems rather than a collection of machines. In our field we too often mean "machine" when we use the term "media technology." Actually, the machines we call media are the result of communication technology, that is, they are the consequence of the sciences dedicated to describing the transportation of information. One of the oldest and closest scientific relatives of communication science is economics. One resulting technology called media solves problems related to the *efficiency* of transporting or "delivering" information. However, delivery technology does not solve psychological problems. The social "science" of psychology and social psychology is applied in the technology of instructional design. Here we deal with issues of, for example, the psychological consequences of different task, individual difference and instructional method variables. When we confuse the two technologies and, by extension, their underlying sciences—we design confounded research, such as media comparison studies.

There is currently relatively little dispute among researchers as to the validity of media comparison studies. Most of the North American media researchers who have examined the evidence seem to support the "weak" media theory in reference to the comparison studies. However there is still a very active dispute between strong and weak theory proponents about whether or not particular media attributes or computer-based activities cultivate transferable cognitive skills. The conclusion of the present authors is that the primary advantages of using new electronic media such as computers, television and video disks for teaching may be *economic* and not psychological, that is, under some conditions they make learning faster and/or cheaper but no one medium contributes unique learning benefits that cannot be obtained from another medium. We suspect that the experimental evidence from well-designed studies will continue to support the "weak" media theory. Those seeking to influence learning and motivation will have to look beyond media for causal variables.

REFERENCES

Anderson, D.R., & Lorch, E.P. (1983). Looking at television: Action or reaction. In J. Bryant & D.R. Anderson (Eds.), *Watching TV, understanding TV*. New York: Academic Press.

Bandura, A. (1978). The self system in reciprocal determinism. *American Psychologist, 33*, 344–358.

Bovy, R.A. (1983, April). *Defining the psychologically active features of instructional treatments designed to facilitate cue attendance*. Paper presented at the annual meeting of the American Educational Research Association, Montreal, Canada.

Bruner, J.S. (1964). The course of cognitive growth. *American Psychologist, 19*, 1–15.

Clark, R.E. (1983). Reconsidering research on learning from media. *Review of Educational Research, 53*(4), 445–460.

Clark, R.E. (1985). Confounding in educational computing research. *Journal of Educational Computing Research, 1*(2), 28–42.

Clark, R.E., & Salomon, G. (1986), Media in teaching. In M. Wittrock (Ed.), *Handbook of research on teaching* (3rd ed.). New York: Macmillan.

Clark, R.E., & Snow, R.E. (1975), Alternative designs for instructional technology research. *Audio Visual Communication Review, 23*(4), 373–394.

Clements, D.H., & Gullo, D.F. (1984). Effects of computer programming on young children's cognition. *Journal of Educational Psychology, 76*, 1051–1058.

Dorr, A., Graves, S.B., & Phelps, E. (1980). Television literacy for young children. *Journal of Communication, 30*, 71–83.

Dweck, C.S., & Bernechat, J. (1983). Children's theories of intelligence: Consequences for learning. In S.G. Paris, G.M. Olson, & H.W. Stevenson (Eds.), *Learning and motivation in the classroom*. Hillsdale, NJ: Lawrence Erlbaum.

Greenfield, P. (1984). *Mind and media: The effects of television, video games and computers*. Cambridge, MA: Harvard University Press.

Jamison, D., Suppes, P., & Wells, S. (1974). The effectiveness of alternative instructional media: A survey. *Review of Educational Research, 44*, 1–68.

Levie, W.H., & Dickie, K. (1973), The analysis and application of media. In R.M.W. Travers (Ed.), *Second handbook of research on teaching*. Chicago: Rand McNally.

Levin, H.M. (1986). *Cost-effectiveness of computer-assisted instruction: Some insights*. Report No. 86. Stanford, CA: Stanford Education Policy Institute, School of Education, Stanford University.

Levin, H.M., & Meister, G.R. (1985). *Educational technology and computers: Promises, promises, always promises*. Report No. 85-A13. Stanford, CA: Center for Educational Research at Stanford, School of Education, Stanford University.

Machula, R. (1978–79). Media and affect: A comparison of videotape, audiotape and print. *Journal of Educational Technology Systems, 7*(2), 167–185.

Mielke, K.W. (1968). Questioning the questions of ETV research. *Educational Broadcasting, 2,* 6–15.

Salomon, G. (1974a). Internalization of filmic schematic operations in interaction with learners' aptitudes. *Journal of Educational Psychology, 66,* 499–511.

Salomon, G. (1974b). What is learned and how is it taught: The interaction between media, message, task and learner. In D. Olson (Ed.), *Media and symbols: The form of expression, communication and education* (The 73rd yearbook of the N.S.S.E.). Chicago: University of Chicago Press.

Salomon, G. (1979). *Interaction of media, cognition and learning.* San Francisco: Jossey Bass.

Salomon, G. (1981). *Communication and education: Social and psychological interactions.* Beverly Hills, CA: Sage.

Salomon, G. (1984). Television is easy and print is "tough": The differential investment of mental effort in learning as a function of perceptions and attributions. *Journal of Educational Psychology, 76*(4), 647–658.

Saracho, O.N. (1982). The effect of a computer-assisted instruction program on basic skills achievement and attitude toward instruction of Spanish speaking migrant children. *American Educational Research Journal, 19*(2), 201–219.

Schramm, W. (1977). *Big media, little media.* Beverly Hills, CA: Sage.

CHAPTER 5

WHAT ABOUT MULTIMEDIA EFFECTS ON LEARNING?

Richard E. Clark and Terrance G. Craig

Originally published as: Clark, R.E., & Craig, T.G. (1992). Research on multimedia learning effects. In M. Giardina (Ed.), *Interactive multimedia learning environments*. New York: Springer Verlag. Reprinted by permission of the publisher, Springer Verlag.

ABSTRACT

A survey of available multimedia and interactive videodisc research, reviews of research and relevant theory is presented. Conclusions are offered that: (1) multiple media, including videodisc technology, are *not* the factors that influence learning; (2) the measured learning gains in studies of the instructional uses of multiple media are most likely due to instructional methods (such as interactivity) that can be used with a variety of single and multiple media; (3) the aspects of dual coding theory which formed the basis for early multimedia studies have not been supported by subsequent research; and (4) future multimedia and interactive videodisc research should focus on the *economic* benefits (cost and learning time advantages) of new technology.

INTRODUCTION

Two tacit assumptions, the *additive* assumption and the *multiplicative* assumption, seem to govern past and present enthusiasms for the use of multiple media in instruction and training:

1. *The Additive Assumption:* Instructional media, if used properly, make valuable contributions to learning and therefore instruction presented in two or more media produce more learning than instruction presented by only one medium because the learning benefits of each of the combined media are additive;
2. *The Multiplicative Assumption:* Multimedia benefits are sometimes multiplicative, that is, greater than the sum of the benefits of individual media.

These two assumptions have a good bit of face validity and represent the intuitive beliefs of many instructional media specialists. Yet there are many instances in the history of education where controlled research studies produced evidence for counterintuitive conclusions. The goal of this paper is to examine the research evidence for each of these two tacit and intuitive assumptions and any theories that support the use of multiple media in instruction. While there have been a number of recent research reviews that examine research on the first assumption (e.g., Clark, 1983, 1985; Clark & Salomon, 1986; Clark & Sugrue, 1989; Levie & Dickie, 1972; Mielke, 1968; Schramm, 1977) there have been few systematic research attempts to examine the second assumption and no dominant theory to guide research that multimedia combinations provide valuable learning benefits.

Research Support for Instructional Use of Multimedia

The discussion begins with an examination of the first tacit assumption.

Does available research support the claim of additive learning benefits from different media?

It is important to explain at the beginning of this discussion that if we have evidence for unique learning benefits from any media, then we could have additive learning benefits from a number of combined media. However, if existing research does not indicate that different media provide different learning benefits, then we could not assume that combinations of media would produce additive benefit. Therefore, the best place to start a review of the additive assumption is in the research that compares the relative learning benefits of different media.

After at least seventy years of empirical research on the media comparison question in a number of nations, it is still not possible to report agreement among all researchers on the answer. Many of the arguments about summary conclusions from the media comparison studies seem to have one primary origin—they stem from conflicts over the intuitive belief by a few researchers and many professional educators that each teaching medium makes *unique* contributions to learning. For example, some researchers expect that instructional uses of computers contribute something unique to academic achievement which is not possible with television, teachers or textbooks—or that video disk instruction may foster unique cognitive skills that are not available from television or books. These advocates of a "strong" media theory suggest that certain media produce unique cognitive effects when used for instruction and therefore some media produce more of some types of learning for certain students and subject matter. The extension of this argument—that combinations of media produce benefits to learning that are the sum of their separate benefits—is the basis of the additive assumption held by those who promote the use of multiple media. Advocates of a "weak" media theory, on the other hand, claim that media do not have any psychological influence over learning but that media may positively influence the "economics" (speed and cost) of learning. At the center of the conflict between these two approaches to media use in education are issues of research design. This is the case in the debate that surrounds media comparison studies.

Additive Media Comparison Studies

In the 1970s, skepticism about media comparison studies, still being conducted in apparently large numbers, began to grow. At that time, the evidence began to favor a "weak media" theory. A number of comprehensive reviews concluded that there was no good evidence that any medium produced more learning or motivation than any other medium. Levie and Dickie (1973) noted that most overall media comparison studies to date had been fruitless and suggested that most learning objectives could be attained through "instruction presented by any of a variety of different media" (p. 859). This observation was echoed by Schramm (1977), according to whom "learning seems to be affected more by what is delivered than by the delivery system" (p. 273). More recent analyses indicate that media comparison studies, regardless of the media employed, tend to result in "no significant difference" conclusions (Clark & Salomon, 1986). Clark (1983, 1985) has claimed that the active ingredient in studies which find one medium superior to another, is usually some uncontrolled aspect of the instructional method (e.g., programmed instruction) rather than the medium.

Meta-analytic Studies of Media Comparisons

During the past decade, more effort has been made to analyze and refocus the results of existing comparison studies. The statistical technique called meta-analysis has proved to be a most useful approach to summarizing instructional media (and other kinds of educational) research. The current meta-analyses of media comparison studies provide evidence that any reported significant differences in performance have been due to confounding in the treatments employed in the studies. A recent series of meta-analyses of media research was conducted by James Kulik and his colleagues at the University of Michigan (Clark, 1985, contains citations for most of these meta-analyses). Generally, meta-analyses allow for a more precise estimate of treatment effect sizes than was possible a few years ago. Meta-analytic procedures yield effect size estimates that are converted to percentage of standard deviation gains on final examination scores due to the more powerful treatment, if any. Most of the meta-analytic surveys of media research demonstrate a typical learning advantage for "newer" media of about one-half a standard deviation on final examination performance, compared with "conventional" (i.e., teacher presented) treatments. In the case of computer-based instruction studies in college environments, for example, this advantage translates as an increase from the 50th to the 66th percentile on final examinations in a variety of courses. This is an impressive accomplishment if one accepts it at face value. Closer inspection of these reviews, however, reveals that most of the large effect sizes attributed to computers in these studies are actually due to poorly designed studies and confounding (Clark, 1983, 1985). These weak effect sizes seem to support the "weak" media theory.

Additive Media Research Design Problems

According to Clark (1983), the most common sources of confounding in media research seem to be the uncontrolled effects of (a) instructional method or content differences between treatments that are compared, and (b) a novelty effect for newer media, which tends to disappear over time. Evidence for each of these controlled effects can be found in the meta-analyses. The positive effect for newer media more or less disappears when the same instructor produces all treatments in a study (Clark, 1985). Different teams of instructional designers or different teachers probably give different content and instructional methods to the treatments that are compared. If this is the case, we do not know whether to attribute the advantage to the medium or to the differences between content and method being compared. However, if the effect for media tends to disappear when the same instructor or team designs contrasting treatments, we have reason to believe that the lack of difference is due to greater control of non-medium variables. Clark and Salomon (1986) cited a number of researchers in the past who have reminded us that when examining the effects of different media, only the media being compared can be different. All other aspects of the mediated treatments, including the subject matter content and method of instruction, must be identical in the two or more media being compared. In meta-analyses of college level computerized versus conventional courses, an effect size of one-half a standard deviation results when different faculty design the compared course. Clark (1983) found that this effect reduces to about one-tenth of a standard deviation advantage when one considers only studies in which one instructor plans and teaches both experimental and control courses.

Novelty in Additive Media Experiments

A second, though probably less important source of confounding in media comparison studies, is the increased effort and attention research subjects tend to give to media that are novel to them. The increased attention paid by students sometimes results in increased effort or persistence which yields achievement gains. If they are due to a novelty effect, these gains tend to diminish as students become more familiar with the new medium. This was the case in reviews of computer-assisted instruction at the secondary school level (grades 6 to 12). An average computer effect size of three-tenths of a standard deviation (i.e., a rise in examination scores from the 50th to the 63rd percentile) for computer courses tended to dissipate significantly in longer duration studies. In studies lasting four weeks or less, computer effects were one-half a standard deviation. This reduced to three-tenths of a standard deviation in studies lasting five to eight weeks and further reduced to the familiar and weak two-tenths of a standard deviation computer effect after eight weeks of data collection. Effects of two-tenths or less account for less than 1 percent of the variance in a comparison. The Kuliks (cf. Clark, 1983, 1985 for citations) report a similar phenomenon in their review of visual-based instruction (e.g., film, television, pictures). Although the reduction in effect size for longer duration studies approached significance (about .065 alpha), there were a number of comparisons of methods mixed with different visual media, which makes interpretation difficult (cf. Clark & Salomon, 1986). In their review of computer use in college, the Kuliks did not find any evidence for this novelty effect. In their comparison of studies of one or two hours duration with those which held weekly sessions for an entire semester, the effect sizes were roughly the same. It is possible that computers are less novel experiences for college subjects than for secondary school students.

Conclusions About Additive Research Evidence for Different Learning Benefits from Different Media

So, to repeat the question that began this first part of the discussion, "does available research support the claim of different learning benefits from different media?", the answer seems to be—not yet. There is compelling research evidence that learning benefits found in media comparison research over the past seventy years may *not* be attributed to media per se. One of the problems with research is that it tends to be most clear about those things that fail to produce learning and less intelligible about what actually does cause measured learning gains. As a result of more recent studies it is becoming less and less valid to suggest that any given medium provides a learning benefit that is in any essential way different than those potentially available from another medium. While there is not complete agreement among researchers on this conclusion, the burden of future research evidence seems to be placed on the strong media theories. As a consequence of the lack of evidence for specific effects from specific media, there seems to be little support available in this area for the additive use of multiple media. Thus, the discussion moves on to the second question, the multiplicative assumption.

The Multiplicative Assumption

> *Does available research support the claim that when two or more media are combined, their learning benefits are greater than (multiples of) any of the combined media used alone?*

Implicit in the multiplicative research assumption is the expectation that media in combination may produce learning benefits that are not possible from any of the separate media. This finding is common in science. Even in educational research we sometimes find that individual variables, by themselves, have little impact on learning. However when separate variables are combined, they sometimes *interact* to produce strong and important effects. This is, for example, the basis for the entire area of "aptitude-treatment interaction" research (refer to Clark, 1982). Thus, we must also examine the possibility that multiple media combinations may be more than the sum of their separate media.

While there are many studies that compare the learning advantage of one medium versus another medium, few studies have compared the multiplicative effects of many media in combination versus any of the combined media used alone to teach the same subject matter.

Interactive Videodisc Studies as Examples of Multiplicative Research

The only current example of multiplicative studies is to be found in the experiments that have been conducted on interactive videodisc (computer control of videodisc access) compared with either computers alone or other single media. Bosco (1986) reviewed 28 of these comparison studies and found results that are similar to those reported by Clark (1983, 1985) for single media comparison studies. When learning was assessed as an outcome, results of were mixed. Some studies showed advantages for the multimedia interactive video, some for the single comparison media (most often computers or television) and some comparisons resulted in "no significant differences." One suspects the familiar lack of control of instructional method and curriculum content (Clark, 1983) between the different media. A similar conclusion was reached by Hannafin (1985) in his reviews of a number of studies of computer-controlled interactive video. He suggests that learning is influenced by the cognitive effects of instructional methods, not by the choice of media. He implies that the same teaching method can be used in a number of "specific instructional technologies" (media). He states:

> While interactive video technology itself may offer interesting potential, it seems unlikely that interactive video differs from allied technology from either learning or cognitive perspectives. Technologically-independent research in learning and processing provides empirically-based techniques and methods likely to facilitate learning. Similarly, studies designed to examine the ways in which the mental activities of the learner are supported to improve learning offer insights into effective lesson design and activity independent of specific instructional technologies. It seems improbable that these principles will be redefined as a consequence of interactive video technology. (p. 236)

Also similar to the results reported in the single media comparisons, the interactive video studies show "attitude" and training time advantages under some conditions. Subjects seem to report liking the interactive video better than the single media comparison conditions. However, this attitude advantage might be an example of the novelty effect described by Clark (1983, 1985) since most of these studies represents a relatively brief exposure to the multi media condition.

Another problem with these studies tends to be a lack of control of the informational content of the lessons presented in the different treatments (Clark, 1985). What sometimes happens is that the research team attempts to duplicate an existing, single-medium instructional program on a multimedia system. During the duplication process, information required by the test and available in the original lesson is, by accident, not transferred to the multimedia version. In this case, we would expect to find evidence that the more complete single-media version results in greater learning. Examples of studies where this control problem can be found are described by Clark (1985) and Clark and Salomon (1986).

Conclusions About the Learning Benefits of Multiple Versus Single Media

Available research does *not* support the claim that when two or more media are combined, their learning benefits are greater than when they are used alone. While there are relatively fewer studies in this area, their results seem to follow the same pattern as the single media comparison studies.

Why have the media comparison studies resulted in such negative and ambiguous results? The primary difficulty with the studies may stem from a lack of control of the instructional method or technique used to teach the tested learning content. So, for example, in a study on the use of interactive video disk versus a non-interactive televised presentation of the lesson, the superior learning from videodisc will be attributed to its "multiple" media capacity. Yet, it would be difficult to rule out the strong possibility that the variable which produced a learning gain was not media, but the method variable many of us refer to as "interactivity."

Interactivity: A Medium or A Method Variable?

Interactivity is variously defined (refer to Hannifin, 1985) but common to most definitions are the qualities of providing corrective and informational feedback based on student responses during instruction. Floyd defines interactivity as an instructional context where "...the sequence and selection of messages are determined by the user's response to the material" (1982, p. 2). While practitioners might argue that these qualities are the inherent features of the interactive video disk technology, it is possible to provide interactivity in other media. For example, all of these instructional variables could be presented by computer-based instruction and by live instructors. Hannifin (1985) describes experiments where interactivity was successfully presented to learners by various, single media. These experiments provide evidence for the claim that instructional methods such as interactivity can be provided with a variety of single and multiple media to produce similar learning benefits.

When studies that do not control instructional methods are reported, they tend to show evidence in favor of the multimedia treatment when the results are actually due to powerful instructional methods that are *only* used in the multimedia condition. This is most likely the case with the recent large scale meta-analysis of forty-seven North American interactive videodisc studies reported by Fletcher (1990). In the introduction to the report, Fletcher acknowledges the validity of Clark's (1983) argument in a statement that media such as videodisc "...do not guarantee [learning] impact, but the functionalities they support and their applications do" (p. II-1). Functionalities is a construct that is similar to instructional methods.

Interactivity is a "functionality" of instruction with videodisc *and* other media, including human beings. Nevertheless, Fletcher, in his summary of the review permits the reader to slip back into the strong media argument when he concludes that "Interactive videodisc instruction was more effective than conventional approaches to instruction … and … computer-based instruction … but there was little in the reviewed studies to indicate how interactive videodisc instruction achieves its success" (pp. IV-1, 4). Since meta-analytic reviews seldom examine experimental control for methods or functionalities, the conclusions they reach tend to be as confounded as the studies they review. Well-designed studies that control for methods by having the same method available in all media treatments, generally show "no significant differences" on learning outcomes (Clark & Salomon, 1986).

Conclusions About Interactivity and Other Methods

While it is impossible to reach a definitive conclusion, the best evidence seems to support the claim that various instructional methods (such as interactivity) are responsible for the measured achievement gains when multiple media treatments are compared with more "conventional" single media treatments. This result has been found with each successive wave of new media and technology for at least the past seven decades of educational research. Why then do we continue to repeat the same conceptual and design error? It is likely that part of the problem is our tendency to base research questions on problems that have financial or popular support but no theoretical justification.

The Theoretical Origins of Multimedia Research

Aside from obvious research design problems, the main obstacle to multimedia and learning studies is that they are conducted without the benefit of any theory about *why* one would expect differences in the first place. Perhaps the only theoretical basis for the interest in multimedia instruction stems from the Dual Coding Theory (DCT) suggested by Paivio over two decades ago (see Paivio, 1985). The first mention of the multimedia concept is reputed to be found in the popular media text by Brown, Lewis, and Harcleroad (1959, 1972). Jim Brown, the fist author of the text, reported (Brown, Personal Communication, 1980) that his idea of using many media at the same time for instruction stemmed, in large part, from the Pavio theory. In the 1960s Pavio and others noticed that when learners in memory experiments were exposed to both words and pictures of items to be remembered, they often obtained significantly higher recall scores than if they received only words or only pictures. Brown and others generalized this finding and reasoned that instruction using both word media and picture media together would enhance learning more than instruction using either word or picture media alone.

The exact connection between the Dual Coding Theory (DCT) and multi media is not as clear as we might prefer. One might think, for example, that a single medium such as a book or television program would have the capacity to present both words and pictures—and therefore achieve the benefit without the complication of multiple media. Nevertheless, it is useful to briefly examine the current status of the theory since its history parallels the development of the multimedia movement.

Dual Coding Theory and Multimedia Instruction

Dual Coding Theory proposes that there are at least two separate cognitive coding functions that specialize in the organization and transformation of visual and verbal information (see Pavio, 1986). According to DCT, visual information is organized such that different parts of an imagined object are simultaneously available for further processing. Any remembered scene may be mentally scanned from a "fixation point" according to the remembered relative position of objects in a mental image. In contrast, verbal information seems to be recalled, processed, and used sequentially. Verbal information can, therefore, only be mentally reorganized in sequence—by, for example, changing word order or inserting word strings in remembered sequences. Visual images, on the other hand, can be modified in a great variety of spatial and sensory dimensions (e.g., by rotation, size, and color). We could, for example, imagine a movie running backwards (because visual information is free of sequential constraints) but we would have difficulty remembering the sentences in a novel backwards.

If DCT is correct, it is reasonable to assume that when we learn information in visual and verbal forms, each form is stored in a separate cognitive system. Early on, DCT proponents claimed that two storage systems for the same information accounted for the superior recall of information taken in by words and pictures. Since recall required that we locate some item in memory, items with two processing locations might be remembered better than items with one location.

Evidence for the Dual Coding Theory

After more than two decades of research, many elements of DCT are still controversial. However, there does seem to be general agreement that the theory does *not* support the use of words and pictures for instruction. Whatever produced the early memory advantage of the word plus picture conditions, it was most likely not the words and pictures. Space limitations prevent a thorough discussion of this literature but see Anderson (1985) for a succinct treatment of the issues. As of now, most researchers in this area accept that early memory gains in word and picture conditions were due to features such as the concreteness and familiarity of the items presented in the experiments. There is also evidence that multiple codings of words and pictures resulted in more contexts for remembering. However, it seems that the visual and verbal forms of the instruction did not influence eventual memory activation. The "visualness" or "verbalness" of information mostly likely does not significantly influence its cognitive processing. A popular current theory suggests that cognitive processing may favor a distinction between *spatial* (not visual) and *sequential* (not verbal) information in any modality or medium (Anderson, 1985). Thus, when words, or pictures, or sounds are placed in some relative position to each other in some space, they are processed differently than when they are ordered sequentially. Thus, there appears to be no compelling evidence in the DCT research record to support the use of multiple media or different benefits for words and pictures in instruction.

FUTURE DIRECTIONS

The long history of research on the media comparison question, including recent interest in interactive multimedia learning environments suggest a number of future directions:

1. Do not continue multimedia research and application based on expected *learning* benefits.

There is a lack of evidence for the dual coding basis for multimedia theory and questionable results from empirical studies. This conclusion suggests that we should cease investing in multimedia studies and applications based on presumed *learning* gains. Future research in this area should not be supported unless there is a clear theoretical reason to expect learning gains due to any characteristic exclusive to a certain mix of media. When interactive videodisc instruction programs are produced and evaluated, Reeves's (1986) evaluation models may prove useful for examining the confounding found in past studies and teasing out important effects.

2. Focus "learning from instruction" research resources and studies on the effects of instructional *methods* for different types of students.

There is clear but often ignored evidence that the positive learning results attributed to interactive videodisc technology is, in fact, due to the learning benefits of *interactivity* rather than the technology that provided the interactivity (Fletcher, 1990). There is also tantalizing evidence that this benefit is greater for some students than for others (Sugrue, 1990) and that inter-activity may result in decreased learning for yet other students (Clark, 1982). Most likely the number of instructional methods available to support learning from instruction will be found to be as large as the number of distinct cognitive processes that underlie the learning process. Other such methods are implicit in all recent discussions of "metacognitive processes" such as the *monitoring* of learning progress; the *connecting* of new with familiar information in memory; and the *selecting* of important elements in instructional materials while ignoring less important elements (Clark, 1990; Corno & Mandinach, 1983). Once we have located a cognitive process that must be supported for certain students, we can cast around for the least expensive and most convenient medium (or mix of media) to present it to students.

3.   Focus multimedia research on *economic* questions such as the cost of delivering instruction and the speed with which media permit the achievement of preset learning or performance standards.

Fletcher's (1990) meta analysis of interactive videodisc studies found some solid evidence for cost and speed of learning gains in some situations. Some of these gains were likely to be due to interactivity, some to the videodisc technology and some to a combination of both. One possible problem with these studies is that they tend to be designed and conducted by people who have a vested interest in finding economic benefits to justify large financial investments in costly training technology. Clark and Sugrue (1989) have suggested that the strategies and reviews of Levin (1986) and Levin and Meister (1985) are models for future economic research in this area. Learning benefits are most likely to be found in instructional methods that support the cognitive processing necessary for achievement. But the cost of delivering those methods in various media and the time it takes learners to achieve specified achievement levels may be determined, in large part, by the choice of delivery media and the management of those media.

REFERENCES

Anderson, J.R. (1985). *Cognitive psychology and its implications* (2nd ed.). New York: W.H. Freeman.

Bosco, J. (1986). An analysis of the evaluations of interactive video. *Educational Technology, 26*(5), 7–17.

Brown, J.W., Lewis, L.B., & Harcleroad, F.F (1959). *Instructional media and methods.* New York: McGraw Hill.

Clark, R.E. (1982). Antagonism between achievement and enjoyment in ATI studies. *Educational Psychologist, 17*(2).

Clark, R.E. (1983). Reconsidering research on learning from media. *Review of Educational Research, 53*(4), 445–460.

Clark, R.E. (1985). Confounding in educational computing research. *Journal of Educational Computing Research, 1*(2), 28–42.

Clark, R.E., & Salomon, G. (1986). Media in teaching. In M. Wittrock (Ed.), *Handbook of research on teaching* (3rd ed.). New York: Macmillan.

Clark, R.E., & Sugrue, B.M. (1989, September). *North American disputes about research on learning from media.* Paper read at the Biannual meeting of the European Association for Research on Learning and Instruction in Madrid, Spain.

Corno, L., & Mandinach, E.B. (1983). The role of cognitive engagement in classroom learning and motivation. *Educational Psychologist, 18*(2), 88–108.

Fletcher, J.D. (1990). *Effectiveness and cost of interactive videodisc instruction in defense training and education.* (Report No. 81-1502). Alexandria, VA: Institute for Defense Analyses.

Hosie, P. (1987). Adopting interactive videodisc technology for education. *Educational Technology, 27*(7), 5–10.

Hannafin, M.J. (1985). Empirical issues in the study of computer-assisted interactive video. *Educational Communications and Technology Journal, 33*(4), 235–247.

Levie, W.H., & Dickie, K. (1973). The analysis and application of media. In R.M.W. Travers (Ed.), *Second handbook of research on teaching.* Chicago: Rand McNally.

Levin, H.M. (1986). *Cost-effectiveness of computer-assisted instruction: Some insights.* Report No. 86. Stanford, CA: Stanford Education Policy Institute, School of Education, Stanford University.

Levin, H.M., & Meister, G.R. (1985). *Educational technology and computers: Promises, promises, always promises.* Report No. 85-A13. Stanford, CA: Center for Educational Research at Stanford. School of Education, Stanford University.

Mielke, K.W. (1968). Questioning the questions of ETV research. *Educational Broadcasting, 2,* 6–15.

Paivio, A. (1985). *Mental representations: A dual approach.* New Oxford University Press.

Reeves, T.C. (1986). Research and evaluation models for the study of interactive video. *Journal of Computer-Based Instruction, 13*(4), 102–106.

Schramm, W. (1977). *Big media, little media.* Beverly Hills, CA: Sage.

Sugrue, B.M. (1990). *A cognitive media selection model applied to the instructional use of computers.* Paper presented at the annual meeting of the American Educational Research Association, Boston.

CHAPTER 6

DO MEDIA AID CRITICAL THINKING, PROBLEM SOLVING, OR "LEARNING TO LEARN"?

Richard E. Clark

Originally published as: Clark, R.E. (1992). Facilitating domain-general problem solving: Computers, cognitive processes and instruction. In E. DeCorte, M.C. Linn, H. Mandl, & L. Verschaffel (Eds.), *Computer-based learning environments and problem solving* (pp. 265–285). New York: Springer-Verlag. Reprinted by permission of the publisher, Springer Verlag.

ABSTRACT

Research on the transfer of problem solving between knowledge domains is reviewed. The point is made that evidence does not support the role of computers and/or instruction in computer programming in either specific or general transfer. Instead, it is recommended that studies focus on the cognitive processes that are required for farther transfer and how these processes can be supported by instruction for students who fail to transfer. Two types of processes are discussed: (1) The *selecting* of structural features of problem representations and the *connecting* of features in two or more domains during transfer. Two types of connections are hypothesized: First, *horizontal* connections in knowledge structures in the form of analogies, and (2) *vertical* connections in the form of rule-example chains. It is expected that errors during the selecting process are primarily responsible for "negative" transfer and that positive transfer is encouraged by instruction that highlights the similar structural or criterial features of relevant information in source and target schemas; vertical rule-example connections promote the "tuning" of knowledge structures and result in near transfer; horizontal analogical connections can be used either for tuning and near transfer or for domain-general transfer, and that analogies which promote domain-general transfer do so because their horizontal cognitive connections extend beyond source domain boundaries and induce rules that enlarge and extend the pathways between knowledge schemas. Based on this research, a number of instructional prescriptions are offered to support the design of instruction intended to facilitate domain-general problem solving.

INTRODUCTION

The basis for our interest in problem solving ability is the expectation that it can be taught and, once learned, transferred to novel problems. The goal of this discussion is to discourage certain hypotheses and to encourage others for future research on the design of instruction which seeks the domain-general transfer of problem solving skills. On the one hand, hypotheses suggesting any necessary connection between computers or computer programming skill and the acquisition or domain-general transfer of problem solving ability will be discouraged. On the other hand, hypotheses which draw on recent cognitive research on the metacognitive components of transfer will be recommended and the use of computers as tools for future problem solving research and instructional delivery will be supported. Evidence from transfer experiments based on the metacognitive selecting and connecting model will be presented.

COMPUTERS AND PROBLEM SOLVING

Given the many difficulties and conflicts in the research on the transfer of problem solving skills, it appears that there is no clear or immediate solution available. Yet, there seems to be general agreement that the problem lies at the core of current efforts to develop cognitive theories of learning and instruction (Estes, 1988; Glaser & Bassok, 1989; Phye & Andre, 1986; Resnick, 1989). A number of solution paths have been developed in the service of understanding the cognitive mechanisms which support transfer. One of the main branches has been occupied by those who hoped that newer electronic media could be adapted to gain theoretical insight and, eventually, instructional environments for teaching generalizable problem solving skills. At this point it is difficult to point to unambiguously positive conclusions. However, a number of those who have reviewed progress on the computer path suggest that we should now put up a "dead end" sign and choose one of the other routes because there is little evidence that computer use facilitates knowledge transfer.

History

There is a historical tendency to search for psychological and educational advantages for newer media (Cuban, 1986). The proclivity is strong and has been repeated often in the history of education and psychology. Television, originally an entertainment medium, was quickly adapted for instructional use despite the evidence that it brought no identifiable learning benefits over less expensive media (Salomon & Gardner, 1984). The computer has been adopted for instructional purposes even more enthusiastically than television. This fact is due, in part, to the perceived necessity to make the operation of computers part of a contemporary school curriculum in many European nations and in North America (Sugrue, 1990). Poorly designed studies provided support for the expectations that the use of computers for instruction would increase learning and transfer (Clark, 1983, 1985, Clark & Sugrue, 1989). Original expectations that programming would be a necessary skill in the twenty-first century led to a commitment to teach programming languages. Early experience with computer programming instruction led some to reason that exposure to the computer or skill in programming might cultivate generalizable cognitive skills.

It takes considerable enthusiasm to overlook the strong evidence for the hypothesis that the use of computers (or other media) for instruction does *not* make any necessary psychological contribution to learning, motivation to learn or the transfer of what is learned from instruction (Clark, 1985; De Corte, Verschaffel, & Schrooten, 1990; Levie & Dickie, 1973; Palumbo, 1990; Salomon, 1984). The evidence in these reviews of research gives good support to the claim that whatever learning or motivation advantage one can accomplish with computers can also be accomplished with other instructional delivery media and settings. The advantage of computers appears to be economic, not psychological. In ideal situations, computer-delivered and managed treatments permit us to exercise greater control and reliability over many more instructional variables at less cost and with greater convenience than more traditional alternatives. Continued research on the psychological contributions of the computer to the learning and transfer of problem solving skills might reasonably be characterized as a triumph of enthusiasm over substance.

Computer Programming and Transfer

More reasonable than expecting transfer from the use of computers for problem solving, was to hypothesize that the learning of computer programming languages and debugging skills might transfer to new and different problem solving applications. Yet when we review progress to date on these studies, evidence of even limited "domain specific" learning and transfer is rare. One important line of research in this area explores the hypothesis that adequate instruction in one computer language often will make it easier or quicker to learn yet another computer language (e.g., Kurland, Pea, Clement, & Mawby, 1989; Linn & Dalbey, 1989; Mayer, Dyck, & Vilberg, 1989). As Palumbo concludes in his recent review, "research that specifically addresses thinking skills that closely parallel the programming environment yields the most conclusive result" (1990, p. 75), others (Clark & Sugrue, 1989; Salomon & Perkins, 1987) are even less optimistic.

Thus it would be very surprising indeed to find compelling evidence of "domain-general" transfer *which is attributable to computer programming expertise* (Ginther & Williamson, 1985). To date, the best evidence supports the conclusion that whenever "domain general" problem solving or learning to learn skills are acquired, neither computers nor computer programming skills were necessary aspects of the responsible treatments (Clark, 1985; Palumbo, 1990). Given the weight of negative evidence, the best advice one might derive from a survey of the programming and transfer research is that we should reduce our investment of scarce research funds in transfer studies of programming. It appears that computer programming is no more related to domain-general transfer than the learning of any other analytic problem solving activity (Salomon & Perkins, 1987).

THE REIFICATION OF A METAPHOR

The origin of the confusion over computer use, computer programming skills and the learning of transferrable thinking skills may be found, in part, in the pervasive and sometimes inappropriate use of a metaphor used to understand human cognition. A number of metaphors have served psychology in the past. The mind has been compared to a wax tablet and to the muscular system. Former theories of transfer which resulted from those metaphors were also unproductive. For example, the classical theory of transfer fixed on a muscular metaphor and recommended that generalizable problem solving and reasoning skills would be developed through the "exercise" of the mind while learning classical subjects such as Latin and Greek.

Norman (1986) argues that the computer metaphor for cognition is more difficult to limit than previous metaphors because the architecture of the digital computer was influenced by its designers' tacit theories of cognition. Thus he suggests that we now have a tendency to turn the metaphor around and assume that there is isomorphism between both physical structures and programming processes in the computer and psychological structures and processes. Lohman (1989) notes that some go so far as to argue that "similar principles govern the functioning of any system that processes information" (p. 336). For those who advocate a strong computer analogy for cognitive processing, the mind is a mechanism for symbol manipulation (e.g., Fodor, 1981). Thus, in this view, the structural and process differences between the computer and the mind are irrelevant. Some of the more ardent advocates of this model have taken to calling cognitive skills "mindware." In this perspective it is reasonable to assume that writing programs for the computer would not only help the computer to reason but would also "program the programmer." While few would dispute the value of computer models of cognitive processes, it is the inappropriate reification of the models which seems to be at the root of the problem. Miller (1981) reminds us that computer models of thought are similar to computer models of the weather yet few of us would expect that a model of violent weather would damage the computer center. Notwithstanding, the value of a model is, in part, its capacity to suggest productive hypotheses about cognitive processing. The reified computer model of domain-general transfer of problem solving may be an inefficient diversion rather than a positive influence.

For those who have conducted computer-based transfer studies, there is consolation in the knowledge that researchers in many other areas have achieved nearly identical results. For example, Eylon and Linn (1988) reached a distressing conclusion about the current results of science instruction research, which they characterized as in a "sorry state." They summarized their concerns in a series of questions such as: "Why do learners stop short of creating well integrated, self-consistent knowledge structures? Why instead do they acquire larger amounts of isolated, context-dependent, and domain-specific knowledge?" (p. 291). The best evidence to date is that when domain-general transfer of problem solving skills are acquired, the antecedents are instructional methods which teach and compensate for the cognitive processes which are required for domain-general transfer (De Corte, Verschaffel, & Schrooten, 1990). Insights about transfer will be found in a direct study of the cognitive processes required for domain-general transfer.

WHAT FACILITATES DOMAIN-GENERAL TRANSFER OF PROBLEM SOLVING?

The study of transfer has recently focused on task domains such as analogical problem solving (e.g., Gick & Holyoak, 1980, 1983, 1987; Spencer & Weisberg, 1986), artificial intelligence (e.g., Hayes-Roth & McDermott, 1978), concept learning (Bransford, Nitsch, & Franks, 1977) and science (Mayer, 1989). Along with Gardner (1985) we find it useful to characterize current learning and transfer theories not by the tasks they investigate but by the methodologies they employ. In this regard, transfer research can be categorized into two main approaches; an inductive (or bottom-up) approach and a deductive (or top-down) approach. It appears that each approach directs attention at different aspects of transfer *and* that only one of the approaches directly investigates domain-general transfer. Characteristics of these two main approaches closely parallel those that engaged Judd (1908) and Thorndike (1903) in their arguments about transfer at the turn of the century.

Inductive Theories

In transfer, bottom-up or inductive theories (e.g., Anderson, 1983; Newell & Simon, 1972) are more Thorndikian and seem often to emphasize *how*, rather than *what* knowledge is used during learning and transfer. Inductive theorists focus on the automated learning of experts and the nature and expression of expertise (e.g., Chase & Simon, 1973; Chi, Glaser, & Rees, 1982; Greeno, 1978; Simon & Simon, 1978). Although robust, inductive theories emphasize the relatively "near" transfer of automated knowledge, that is, sequences of linked productions that form automated, goal-directed steps within specific domains. Research indicates that over time, expertise may produce higher order procedures (e.g., Anderson, 1983, 1985), however, these superordinate procedures promote generalization of knowledge *within* but probably not *between* knowledge domains (e.g., Anderson, 1983, 1985).

While few studies have explored the extent to which expert procedures transfer outside of knowledge domains, the research on expert problem solving offers some evidence that procedural knowledge is domain specific (Anderson, 1985; Chi, Feltovich, & Glaser, 1981; Chi, Glaser, & Rees, 1982). Expert learning and problem solving procedures have been classified as "specific performance routines" (Brown, 1978) or "patterns" that are specific to a domain (Anderson, 1985). These domain-specific knowledge structures are not expected to facilitate the domain-general transfer that is required for the successful solution to a novel problem in a domain where no expertise exists.

Deductive Theories

Top down theorists (e.g., Gagne & White, 1978; Gick & Holyoak, 1980; 1983; Holyoak, 1985) are more associated with Judd's (1908) argument in favor of domain-general transfer. The focus of their investigation is the "farther" transfer of knowledge. These theorists emphasize domain general transfer and direct their attention more to *what* transfers but are less specific about *how* transfer occurs. The deductive approaches to transfer theory therefore tend to be weaker than the inductive approaches because of the lack of explicitness about the transfer processes. Nevertheless, it is the more deductive approaches that have explored the types of knowledge that are involved in transfer to novel problems and insight. For example, some deductive theorists have examined declarative knowledge and produced promising evidence of transfer between domains (e.g., Gray, 1983; Gick & Holyoak, 1980, 1983; Spencer & Weisberg, 1986). Additional evidence can be found in the research on analogies and metacognition.

The Role of Analogies

Rumelhart and Norman (1981, 1989) suggest that the knowledge hierarchies which characterize schema could be duplicated by analogy to form new schema and that "...learning by analogy, [involves] taking one schema and creating another one identical to it except in specified ways" (1981, p. 344). They offer the example of the familiar "slice-of-pie" analogy used by many mathematics teachers as they move students from an understanding of whole numbers to fractions. Presumably, every child's schema for food contains both procedural and declarative knowledge about the definition, utility and (perhaps) even the addition and subtraction of fractions of food. Suggesting that fractions are "like" the pieces of a whole pie implicitly invites students to "copy" the more familiar schema into an "empty" space in cognition and make it available for "editing." The pie and fraction analogy is a good example of domain-general transfer. Knowledge from one schema is transferred to create another and therefore the old knowledge crosses a domain boundary. Within this relatively simple slice-of-pie analogy are at least two implicit hypotheses about the types of knowledge used and the cognitive processes that are engaged when domain-general transfer occurs.

Selecting Salient Features. First, it seems that analogies require a judgment that essential "similarities" exist between declarative knowledge in the source and declarative knowledge in the "target." Successful similarity judgments require that learners are able to identify or *select* the most important criteria or structural features that are shared by the source and target schema (Gick & Holyoak, 1980, 1983, 1987). In the case of the slice-of-pie analogy, the teacher presumably makes the selection by presenting key concepts and principles in the slicing of pies that are nearly identical to those required for the learning of fractions.

The Connecting Process

The second hypothesis implicit in the slice-of-pie analogy is that an analogy is essentially an association or *connection* between a familiar schema or chunk of declarative knowledge and some problem or knowledge to be learned. Familiar declarative knowledge from a source schema within one domain is "mapped" onto similar information in another domain or copied into an "empty" space to form a new domain. An explication of the cognitive processes and consequences involved in selecting salient structural features of knowledge and making analogical connections is important in understanding how domain-general transfer occurs.

Metacognitive Activity During General Transfer
One predictor of selecting and connecting skills may be measures of general ability. Gick and Holyoak (1983) reported that in problem solving studies using the Dunker (1945) radiation problems, only students with the highest general ability level spontaneously noticed analogical connections between the problem and solution. Snow (1986) has suggested that fluid ability (Horn, 1983) which presumably represents aptitude for solving novel problems is associated in domain-general transfer of knowledge. There is evidence that learners with higher levels of fluid ability are able to select the critical features of a learning task without assistance (Gray, 1983; Snow & Lohman, 1984) but that those with middle level aptitudes may require prompts (Gick & Holyoak, 1983; Spencer & Weisberg, 1986) and that those with very low aptitude levels may require full compensatory models or simulations of the selecting process (Corno & Mandinach, 1983; Snow & Lohman, 1984). In addition, Gray (1983) found evidence for cognitive grouping, reorganization and elaboration activities in higher ability students. Analysis of student notes and "teach back" exercises demonstrated that higher aptitude students will often translate text into their own idiosyncratic words and include personal references and elaborations. Lower aptitude students recorded direct quotes without inference. They simply rehearsed information that was presented to them. In short, aptitude differences showed through in the organizational assembly and control activities learners use to adapt to new instruction.

Bransford and others (e.g., DiVesta & Peverly, 1984; Gick & Holyoak, 1983) have found that when similar examples or limited analogies are used to teach concepts, all subjects seem to have difficulty with domain-general transfer of the concept (Bransford, Nitsch, & Franks, 1977). DiVesta and Peverly (1984) proposed that when concept learning involved the presentation of homogenous examples (encoding constancy) the result was learning which was context dependent. Their research suggests that practice with examples from the same context encourages the use of context as an "orientating" guide which emphasizes certain attributes and relations in the task to be learned. As a result, these attributes and relations become cue-dependent on the context. On the other hand, encoding variability contributes to learning that is more decontextualized and therefore more applicable to novel domains (domain-general transfer). It is possible that students with higher fluid scores would find it more difficult to exercise their skill at domain-general transfer when instruction provides near transfer practice.

Selecting and connecting appear to be high level cognitive processes that seem important in facilitating transfer. Since domain-general transfer is hypothesized to extend beyond the borders of knowledge domains and therefore beyond the influence of expertise, these processes are best conceptualized as "metacognitive" (Flavell, 1981). Both selecting and connecting were described by Corno and Mandinach (1983) in their discussion of the development of "self-regulated learning." They related both metacognitive skills to the "transformational" information processing theory originally suggested by Anderson and Bower (1973). Transformation is a general term which refers to cognitive activity that reorganizes and/or extends knowledge structures to accommodate external learning demands.

Similarity Judgments

Domain-general transfer requires an awareness of the *similarities* between information located in one area of long term memory (called the "source") and some other bit of information in another area of long term memory (called the "target"). The exact choice of the features of the source which are judged similar to the target are critical in transfer. For example, to judge the formal similarities of "smoke" and "fog," we must know that the criterial features of smoke are that it is "particulate matter resulting from combustion which is suspended in air." In addition, smoke also has odor, color, shape, density, direction, volume and other characteristics which are not criterial to its definition. Assume that fog is defined as "water molecules suspended in air." To judge that smoke and fog are similar, one must notice that their defining attributes are similar, that is, that both involve matter suspended in air. It is the judgment of such similarities that seems to underlie that part of metacognitive selecting which supports transfer. In order to successfully transfer information, one must select information in the source and target that have the required similarities.

Attention to similarity judgments have been associated with transfer research since Thorndike (1903) described the "theory of identical elements." At the core of the theory was the notion that events which share common stimulus properties will be recognized as similar and that the learned response to one event will therefore generalize to the other event. This theory was the origin of our understanding of "near" transfer. It also formed the basis of Osgood's (1949) transfer surface theory which was an attempt to explain the role of similarity in both positive and negative transfer.

Studies of the role of similarity judgments in domain-general transfer are aided by the seminal studies of human judgment by Kahneman and Tversky (1973). They have explored the way we use judgment heuristics to make similarity judgments when confronted with a great deal of uncertainty. They suggest that we look both at the obvious similarities and that we also "decompose" items being compared into their most abstract and criterial shared features. Decomposition is related to what transfer researchers have called "decontextualization" (Royer, 1979). Kahneman and Tversky note our increasing predisposition to judge things as similar when they share a large number of perceptual and familiar features. In these instances, shared criterial features tend to be de-emphasized. For example, we tend to judge robins and sparrows as more alike than robins and penguins. The problem is that when one must choose examples of the concept "bird," robins, sparrows *and* penguins are all members of the category, even though penguins have many obvious but irrelevant features that differ from the other two instances. Kahneman and Tversky's theory would suggest that for most of us, robins and sparrows are more "representative" of birds than are penguins.

Negative Transfer

The tendency of human beings to make similarity judgments using the representativeness heuristic causes many transfer errors. Effective domain-general transfer requires that we decompose information in both the source and target domain into their most criterial or structural features. It is these features alone which determine their "similarity" for formal purposes. Birds, for example, all have feathers and bear their young in eggs. Many birds fly but this feature is not criterial, although it is a very "representative" trait and is therefore often assumed to be a criterial feature of birds. Whenever the representativeness heuristic leads us to add features that are salient but non-criterial, negative transfer will occur, i.e., the exclusion of the penguin from the category "bird."

Concept Learning and Transfer

Much of the existing research on the learning of categories and concepts is very relevant to our understanding of the typical errors involved in making similarity judgments. For example, the literature on prototype versus best example use in concept identification, makes some of the same predictions of errors in judgment as does the representativeness literature (e.g., Glass & Holyoak, 1986). The research on transfer contains many examples of problems caused by similarity judgments. In some cases, research problems are caused by the way that subtle differences in the description of transfer tasks are described. A small difference in the order or wording of concepts which are presented for similarity judgments can greatly affect the outcome of studies (Tversky & Gati, 1978). This fact might also account for a number of the current disputes in the transfer literature that is focused on problem solving (e.g., Gick & Holyoak, 1983; Spencer & Weisberg, 1986). In problem solving tasks, one must choose solutions that correspond to the conditions imposed by the "goal state" (Anderson, 1985). Goal states contain the structural features of a problem category (Gick & Holyoak, 1980, 1983). Structural features include the goal (reason for action), the resources (or enabling conditions), and the constraints (or obstacles). Wording of the goal states in training tasks can affect the similarity judgments made between the training and target problem. If the wording is incomplete, i.e., missing a most criterial feature, such as an important constraint, a more salient but noncriterial feature, that is, environmental context, may cause transfer errors. Examples of these errors are found in studies by Spencer and Weisberg (1986), Glaser and Bassok (1989).

Similarity judgments are crucial because they support the next step in the transfer process, the connecting of source and target information. Presumably, one first reaches the judgment that two chunks of information are similar enough to connect and then proceeds to select the type of connection which will be made. The discussion turns next to a description of the nature of the cognitive connections that underlie different amounts of transfer.

Transfer requires that an association or connection be formed between a source and target information. In near transfer the connection is within a domain where knowledge is structured hierarchically. Domain-general transfer requires that a connection be formed between information in a usually more familiar source schema located in one domain and information in a different and less familiar "target" domain. When connections are made, a pathway between source and target is opened. All features and existing associative pathways in the source are made available through spreading activation to the target. It appears that there are at least two different types of cognitive connections that promote transfer—connections by example and by analogy.

Vertical Connection by Example

As we learn and use concepts and principles, examples and their related "rules" are one of the important units of knowledge hierarchies (Anderson, 1985). It is most likely that we form the rules or definitions of concepts through experience where we select obvious similarities between instances (Gagne, 1985; Glass & Holyoak, 1986). We transfer these superordinate rules when we make the decision that a new experience is an "instance" of a more general category. Since hierarchies of knowledge may contain a number of levels of rule-example chains (Collins & Quillian, 1969), this type of connection can be made at a fairly abstract level. This is the type of connection that one would make when confronted with an ostrich for the first time. It has feathers and bears its young in eggs but it does not fly and it is considerably larger than most birds. Successful transfer would require that a learner note that the ostrich has all of the criterial features of birds and that the "unrepresentative" qualities of size and flight are not important. More important is that a successful connection at this point would most certainly be "near"—within a knowledge domain and close to the original information about birds. We have concluded that the reason for this near transfer application of rule-example chains is that they are always "vertical" connections in knowledge hierarchies. Examples are always subordinate to rules which are always superordinate to examples. The vertical nature of this type of connection ties it to the context of the schema or domain in which it resides. If houses were domains of knowledge and stairways between floors were connections, one would not expect to easily use the stairs to get to another house. We hypothesize that rule-example connections primarily support learning within but not between domains.

Horizontal Connection by Analogy

Analogies have received a great deal of attention in the current transfer literature (e.g., Cormier & Hagman, 1988; Keane, 1988). Many researchers have offered evidence that analogies promote creative problem solving (e.g., Gick & Holyoak, 1987), insight (Gick, 1989), mindful learning (Salomon & Globerson, 1987), an understanding of human brain functions (Pribram, 1986), and scientific reasoning (Mayer, 1989). Much of the underlying reason for the recent focus on analogies in higher order cognitive operations, we suggest, is the nature of the cognitive connection they support. Analogies can be defined as *horizontal* connections between two similar chunks of information at the same level of *abstraction.*

Unlike rule-example chains which connect between different levels in knowledge hierarchies, analogies connect two items at the *same level of abstraction* in a hierarchy. As horizontal connections they may occur between concrete example pairs within a domain (i.e., when we suggest that a robin is like an ostrich) or between domains (i.e., when we suggest that a pressure dial is like a clock face). Horizontal connections by analogy may also be more abstract although they occur within a domain. For example, we can say that the addition of whole numbers and the addition of fractions is analogous. For our purposes, one important aspect of analogies is their capacity to build a bridge between domains of knowledge. Analogical connections prompt the noticing of basic similarities between two domains. When they are provided to students during instruction, analogies prompt the copying of the contents of one schema into an "empty" space within a domain. As a result, new schemas are developed.

An important feature of analogies is that they seem to support "decontextualization" of the information they connect by inducing us to produce a list of their shared attributes. For example, when we suggest that the robin and ostrich are analogous, we imply that they share the same criterial attributes and implicitly invite the *subtraction* of all unlike attributes. Since robins and ostriches are more unlike than robins and sparrows, the resulting set of shared criterial attributes are closer to the formal list that defines the category "bird." When robins and sparrows are connected, the resulting list of shared attributes includes things such as their similar size and capacity for flight which do not formally define birds. One would expect therefore, that instruction which uses very divergent examples of the same category would produce a more accurate impression of the criterial attributes of the category than the use of examples that share more non relevant attributes. Divergent examples would also be expected to produce domain-general transfer of the concept than more familiar examples, even though the transfer was within a domain.

One advantage of specifying the type of connection promoted by examples and analogies is to clarify ambiguities in transfer research studies. Treatments which provide examples sometimes promote vertical connections, sometimes horizontal connections within domains and occasionally horizontal connections between domains. In our system, only instances which promote vertical connections are examples. Analogies may have decontextualization consequences which cover the full range from very near to very far. Evidence for transfer qualities of treatments labeled "examples" can be found in the research of Bransford (Bransford, Nitsch, & Franks, 1977). He has offered evidence that when successive examples of concepts from the same domain are presented, the resulting learning primarily serves nearer transfer. When subjects received examples of a concept selected from successively different domains, the concept more readily transferred farther.

The decontextualization effect of analogies becomes very important when a connection is made *between* knowledge domains. Simple examples can be found in the common analogies made between the heart and a water pump, the structure of the atom and the solar system or fractions and slices of pie. The strength of horizontal connections between domains is that they commonly induce a general rule made up of the most abstract elements of the common components of the source and target—and therefore more easily promote domain-general transfer.

How Might Instruction Facilitate Farther Transfer?

The discussion of domain-general transfer research has thus far been guided by a question, "What cognitive processes occur as transfer distance increases?". The rationale for the question was the expectation that domain-general transfer learning goals could be achieved only if instruction supported those necessary cognitive processes. Since few students achieve spontaneous domain-general transfer, some instructional support seems necessary. Disputes and important unanswered questions remain in the existing research. However, for those interested in designing instructional systems which support domain-general transfer, the growing body of research offers a few useful insights. The remainder of this discussion is an attempt to summarize tentative advice for the design of instructional systems. The suggestions are organized according to the system suggested by Clark (1990), that instructional design theories should focus on three classes of variables; (1) learning task variables; (2) the individual difference variables which moderate the task and suggest; (3) instructional methods which will meet instructional goals for individual learners. If the current results of descriptive studies were to be organized into those three categories, tentative advice for instructional designers might look something like the following.

Learning Task Considerations in Instruction

1.   Limit learning tasks to declarative knowledge.

There are a number of different ways to conceptualize the representations and actions which define declarative knowledge and no agreement on which way is best for instruction (e.g., Rumelhart & Norman, 1988). However, the best evidence supports the claim that composed and automated procedures do not transfer beyond the boundaries of knowledge domains. It is possible that some of the higher level declarative productions which yield procedures may be available for farther transfer during interdomain problem solving. Second generation task analysis systems may contain promising ways to represent and instruct farther transfer tasks.

2. Generate specific learning goal statements.

This is familiar advice for experienced instructional designers but it appears vital for enhancing a number of aspects of farther transfer research. For example, goals seem to influence both individual learner actions during mapping and the choice of representational system the designer chooses. For example, some systems for conceptualizing declarative knowledge seem best for representing the processing of textual material, others for mathematical procedures (e.g., Anderson, 1983), and still others for learning the operation of technological devices (e.g., Mayer, 1989) and scientific theory. There is also evidence that transfer problems are often influenced by student misunderstanding of goals (Bassok, 1990). Thus, it seems particularly vital in far transfer instruction, very early on in the instructional design process, to follow traditional advice to make a clear statement of the goals and objectives of learning and communicate them to students. In addition to communicating task goals to students, they should be explicitly told that the learning task requires farther transfer.

3. Carefully identify and define the attributes and relations to be taught.

In a number of cases, farther transfer failed because learners fixed on superficial characteristics of the knowledge being transferred. In some instances the wrong attributes or relations were stressed during instruction (e.g., Brown, 1989). In other cases, individuals had learned inappropriate definitions or uses for existing knowledge (e.g., Bassok, 1990). In either case, clear definitions of concepts and principles to be taught will allow for accurate presentations and/or remedial correction of existing declarative knowledge.

4. Only a small percentage of the most motivated and intelligent students will achieve spontaneous far transfer.

Snow (1981, 1989) offers three uses of individual differences research for practical application: (1) to *select* people who can perform some task or set of tasks without training; (2) to *compensate* for inaptitude through training; and (3) to *develop* aptitude through training. One must be clear which of these three different educational goals are sought. If selection is the issue, we should note that existing studies of spontaneous solutions to novel and moderately difficult problems indicate that only about 5 percent of the most capable students succeed without direct instructional support (e.g., Gick & Holyoak, 1980, 1983).

5.   Far transfer aptitude deficits can be reduced by instructional methods which support necessary cognitive processing.

The number of solvers of far transfer problems increase to about 10 percent with a compensating hint or suggestion that familiar knowledge is analogous to a problem being solved (Spencer & Weisberg, 1986) and to between 20 to 30 percent when various types of fully compensated transfer aids are provided.

6.   Individual differences in specific prior learning of "conceptual entities" which are relevant to the transfer task, will influence transfer distance.

Bassok's (1990) study gives important indications of variations in subjects' prior experience of categories may prevent them from "recognizing the structural equivalence" between domains. She speculates that the problem is most difficult when intensive categories (defined by relations between two entities) are mixed with extensive categories (defined by one entity). It seems that different subjects are drawn to familiar "conceptual entities" and have difficulties with unusual combinations of extensive categories. She reports a very high rate of far transfer for problems where barriers to structural equivalence are eliminated. This implies that very specific types of "expertise" or prior knowledge differences between students influence farther transfer and may have to be considered in instructional design.

7.   Individual differences in *selecting* and *connecting* the structural features of declarative knowledge required for any given transfer task influence the mapping process required for farther transfer.

Bassok (1990) found that up to 80 percent of her subjects solved business to algebra transfer problems when instruction was compatible with their prior knowledge of the structural features of categories. This compatibility presumably supported the selection of structural features required for the connections made during mapping. Blake (1989) provided evidence that support for selecting during far transfer problem solving indirectly increased the number of solvers by enhancing schema development. Selecting structural elements for schemas may have facilitated the connecting process. Any instructional presentation from which succeeds in helping students separate structural from superficial elements of knowledge will suffice. Examples are the *highlighting* of key concepts (Mayer, 1989) or *underlining* structural elements.

Connecting involves the "linking" of information rich domains or schemas to distant schemas which are either information rich or poor. Evidence for the usefulness of connecting support can be found in most studies where farther transfer increases as a result of hints, multiple and varied examples and analogies. As with selecting, the presentation form of the help may be less important than whether it achieves its cognitive function. Unlike selecting, successful instructional methods seem to be specific to the amount of information in the domains being connected (Keane, 1988). Common examples of connecting forms are: (1) for transfer between two information-rich domains—*multiple and varied examples;* and, (2) for transfer from an information-rich to an information-poor domain—analogies. It is also likely that similar connecting functions are served by some forms of illustrated models (Mayer, 1989) and simulations.

SUMMARY AND CONCLUSION

With the benefit of hindsight, a number of researchers have noted that studies of the transfer consequences of computer programming are reminiscent of other failed theories of learning and transfer. At least three theories which come to mind quickly also hypothesized domain-general transfer generalizability of "languages" or communication devices. The ancient "classical transfer theory" suggested that the learning of Greek and Latin exercised the mind and promoted thinking and problem solving skills. More recently there were assumptions that the use of certain electronic media (e.g., television) or "symbol systems" based on the display capabilities of media (such as the capacity to "rotate" objects or "unfold" them from three to two dimensions) had different learning and transfer consequences than more traditional media or symbol systems (Clark & Salomon, 1986). Experiments which tested these theories have failed to provide compelling positive evidence. It appears that whenever classical curricula or newer media or media attributes are found to result in more learning or farther transfer, studies have failed to control for important variables (Clark & Sugrue, 1989). While any of these linguistic, media or symbol systems can be used as convenient task contexts in studies of transfer, they should not be classed as independent variables. When classical languages, media, or computer programming are the presumed antecedents of learning and far transfer experiments, the "tail wags the dog" and we learn very little.

Thus, the meager contributions of the research on programming, problem solving and transfer simply do not warrant future investment until a new theory is proposed. In the future, studies of domain general (far) transfer should focus more on *how* familiar knowledge is used to solve new problems or support the development of new domains. An emphasis on the way that instructional examples and analogies promote metacognitive connections seems particularly fruitful. It appears that two examples support transfer only within knowledge domains but that analogies foster both near and far transfer, depending on the way they are constructed and presented. At least two types of metacognitive processes, selecting and connecting, are supported by analogies. In order to achieve transfer, it is hypothesized that one must select different sets of declarative knowledge that have similar structural or criterial features and permit the connecting of at least two different knowledge structures in working memory.

It is proposed that domain-general transfer of problem solving (or any type of skill) is facilitated by a great variety of cognitive skills but that key roles are played by at least two types of metacognitive processes: (1) the *selecting* of similar structural or criterial features of declarative knowledge structures in different knowledge domains; and (2) the associating or *connecting* of knowledge between at least two different knowledge domains in working memory. Two types of connections will be discussed: (1) *horizontal* connections in knowledge structures in the form of analogies, and (2) *vertical* connections in the form of rule-example chains. Hypotheses will be offered that: (1) errors during the selecting process are primarily responsible for "negative" transfer; (2) positive transfer is encouraged by instruction that highlights the similar structural or criterial features of relevant information in source and target schemas; (3) vertical rule-example connections promote the "tuning" of knowledge structures and result in near transfer; (4) horizontal analogical connections can be used either for tuning and near transfer or for domain-general transfer, and (5) that analogies which promote domain-general transfer do so because their horizontal cognitive connections extend beyond source domain boundaries and induce rules that enlarge and extend the pathways between knowledge schemas.

REFERENCES

Anderson, J.R. (1983). *The architecture of cognition.* Cambridge, MA: Harvard University Press.

Anderson, J.R. (1985). *Cognitive psychology and its implications.* New York: W. H. Freeman and Company.

Anderson, J.R., & Bower, G.H. (1973). *Human associative memory.* Washington, DC: Winston.

Bassok, M., Transfer of domain-specific problem solving procedures. *Journal of Experimental Psychology: Learning, Memory, and Cognition, 16*(3): 522–533.

Bransford, J.D., Nitsch, K., & Franks, J. (1977). Schooling and the facilitation of knowledge. In R.C. Anderson, R. Spiro, & W. Montague (Eds.), *Schooling and the acquisition of knowledge.* Hillsdale, NJ: Lawrence Erlbaum Associates.

Blake, S.B. (1989). The effect of metacognitive selecting on far transfer in analog problem solving tasks. Unpublished doctoral dissertation. School of Education. University of Southern California, Los Angeles, CA 90089-0031.

Brown, A. (1978). Knowing when, where, and how to remember: A problem of metacognition. In R. Glaser (Ed.), *Advances in instructional psychology* (Vol. 1). Hillsdale, NJ: Lawrence Erlbaum Associates.

Chase, W.G., & Simon, H.A. (1973). Perception in chess. *Cognitive Psychology,* pp. 55–81.

Chi, M.T.H., Glaser, R., & Rees, E. (1982). Expertise in problem solving. In R. Sternberg (Ed.), *Advances in the psychology of human intelligence.* Hillsdale, NJ: Lawrence Erlbaum Associates.

Chi, M.T.H., Feltovich, P.J., & Glaser, R. (1981). Categorization and representation of physics problems by experts and novices. *Cognitive Science, 5,* 121–152.

Clark, R.E. (1983). Reconsidering research on learning from media. *Review of Educational Research, 53*(4), 445–459.

Clark, R.E. (1985). Confounding in educational computing research. *Journal of Educational Computing Research, 1*(2), 445–460.

Clark, R.E. (April, 1990) A cognitive theory of instructional design. Paper read at the national convention of the American Educational Research Association, Boston, MA.

Clark, R.E., & Sugrue, B.M. (1989). Research on instructional media, 1978–1988. In D. Ely (Ed.), *Educational media yearbook 1987–88.* Littletown, CO: Libraries Unlimited.

Clark, R.E., & Voogel, A. (1985). Transfer of training for instructional design. *Educational Communications and Technology Journal, 32*(2), 113–123.

Cormier, S.M., & Hagman, J.D. (1987). *Transfer of learning: Contemporary research and applications.* New York: Academic Press.

Corno, L., & Mandinach, E. (1983). The role of cognitive engagement in classroom learning and motivation. *Educational Psychologist, 33,* 88–108.

Corno, L., & Snow, R.E. (1986). Adapting teaching to individual differences among learners. In M. Wittrock (Ed.), *Handbook of research on teaching* (3rd ed.). New York: Macmillan Publishing Company.

Cuban, L. (1986). *A history of instructional technology.* New York: Teachers College Press.

De Corte, E. (1990). Towards powerful learning environments for the acquisition of problem-solving skills. *European Journal of Education, 5*(1), 5–19.

De Corte, E., Verschaffel, L., & Schrooten, H. (1990, March 20–22). *Cognitive effects of computer oriented learning.* Paper presented at the Seventh International Conference on Technology and Education, Brussels.

DiVesta, F.J., & Peverly, S.T. (1984). The effects of encoding variability, processing activity and rule example sequences on the transfer of conceptual rules. *Journal of Educational Psychology, 76,* 108–119.

Duncker, K. (1945). On problem solving. *Psychological Monographs, 58.*

Estes, W.K. (1988). Human learning and memory. In R.C. Atkinson, R.J. Herrnstein, G. Londzey, & R. D. Luce (Eds.), *Steven's handbook of experimental psychology* (2nd ed., Vol. II., pp. 351–415).

Flavell, J. H. (1981). Cognitive monitoring. In W.P. Dickson (Ed.), *Children's oral communication skills.* New York: Academic Press.

Fodor, J.A. (1981). *Representations: Philosophical essays on the foundations of cognitive science.* Cambridge, MA: MIT Press.

Gagne, R.M., & White, R.T. (1978). Memory structures and learning outcomes. *Review of Educational Research, 48,* 187–222.

Gardner, H. (1985). *The mind's new science: A history of the cognitive revolution.* New York: Basic Books, Inc.

Gick, M.L., & Patterson, K. (1989). *Contrasting examples, schema acquisition, and problem solving transfer.* Unpublished manuscript.

Gick, M.L., & Holyoak, K.J. (1980). Analogical problem solving. *Cognitive Psychology, 12,* 306–355.

Gick, M.L., & Holyoak, K.J. (1983). Schema induction and analogical transfer. *Cognitive Psychology, 15,* 1–38.

Gick, M.L., & Holyoak, K.J. (1987). The cognitive basis of knowledge transfer. In S.M. Cormier & J.D. Hagman (Eds.), *Transfer of learning.* New York: Academic Press.

Glaser, R., & Bassok, M. (1989). Learning theory and the study of instruction. In M.R. Rosenwig & L.W. Porter (Eds.), *Annual review of psychology* (Vol. 40, pp. 631–666). Palo Alto, CA: Annual Reviews Inc.

Glass, A.L., & Holyoak, K.J. (1986). *Cognition.* New York: Random House.

Gray, L.E. (1983). *Aptitude constructs, learning processes, and achievement.* Unpublished dissertation, Stanford University.

Greeno, J.G. (1978). Nature of problem solving abilities. In W.K. Estes (Ed.), *Handbook of learning and cognitive processes* (Vol. 5). Hillsdale, NJ: Lawrence Erlbaum Associates.

Hayes-Roth, R., & McDermott, J. (1978). An interface matching technique for inducing abstractions. *Communications of the ACM, 21,* 401–410.

Holyoak, K.J., (1985). The pragmatics of analogical transfer. In G.H. Bower (Ed.), *The psychology of learning and motivation* (Vol. 19). New York: Academic Press.

Horn, J.L. (1976). Human abilities: A review of research and theory in the early 1970s. *Annual Review of Psychology, 27,* 437–485.

James, W. (1908). *Principles of psychology* (Vol. 1). New York: Holt.

Judd, C.H. (1908). The relation of special training to intelligence. *Educational Review, 36,* 28–42.

Kahneman, D., & Tversky, A. (1973). On the psychology of prediction. *Psychological Review, 80,* 237–251.

Keane, M.T. (1988). *Analogical problem solving* New York: Halsted Press.

Klauer, K.J. (1989) Teaching for analogical transfer as a means of improving problem-solving, thinking and learning. *Instructional Science, 18,* 179–192.

Kurland, D.M., Pea, R.D., Clement, C., & Mawby, R. (1989). A study of the development of programming ability and thinking skills in high school students.

Levie, W.H., & Dickie, K. (1973). The analysis and application of media. In R.M. Travers (Ed.), *Second handbook of research on teaching.* Chicago: Rand McNally.

Linn, M.C., & Dalbey, J. (1989). Cognitive consequences of programming instruction. In E. Stolway & R.D. Spohrer (Eds.), *Studying the novice programmer* (pp. 57–81). Hillsdale, NJ: Erlbaum.

Lohman, D.F. (1989). Human intelligence: An introduction to advances in theory and research. *Review of Educational Research, 59*(4), 333–373.

Mayer, R.E. (1989). *Models for understanding.* Unpublished Manuscript in Progress.

Mayer, R., Dyck, J.L., & Vilberg, W. (1989). Learning to program and learning to think: What's the connection? In E. Stolway & R.D. Spohrer (Eds.), *Studying the novice programmer* (pp. 83–111). Hillsdale, NJ: Erlbaum.

Newell, A., & Simon, H. (1972). *Human problem solving.* Englewood Cliffs, NJ: Prentice-Hall.

Norman, D.A. (1986). Reflections on cognition and parallel distributed processing. In D.E. Rumelhart, J.L. McCelland, & the PDP Research Group (Eds.), *Parallel distributed processing: Vol. 2 Psychological and biological models* (p. 531–546). Cambridge, MA: MIT Press.

Osgood, C.E. (1949). The similarity paradox in human learning: A resolution. *Psychological Review, 56,* 132–143.

Palumbo, D.B. (1990). Programming language/problem solving research: A review of relevant issues. *Review of Educational Research, 60*(1), 65–89.

Phye, G.B., & Andre, T. (1986). *Cognitive classroom education: Understanding, thinking and problem solving.* New York: Academic Press.

Pribram, K.H. (1986). The role of analogy in transcending limits in the brain sciences. *Journal of Educational Psychology, 75,* 450–459.

Resnick, L.B. (1989). Introduction. In L.B. Resnick (Ed.), *Knowing, learning and instruction: Essays in honor of Robert Glaser.* Hillsdale, NJ: Erlbaum.

Royer, J.M. (1979). Theories of the transfer of learning. *Educational Psychologist, 14,* 53–69.

Rumelhart, D.E., & Norman, D.A. (1981). Analogical processes in learning. In J.R. Anderson (Ed.), *Cognitive skills and acquisition.* Hillsdale, NJ: Lawrence Erlbaum Associates.

Rumelhart, D.E., & Norman, D.A. (1988). Representation in memory. In R.C. Atkinson, R.J. Herrnstein, G. Lindzey, & R.D. Luce (Eds.), *Steven's handbook of experimental psychology, Learning and cognition* (2nd ed.). New York: Wiley.

Salomon, G. (1984). Television is easy and print is "tough": The differential investment of mental effort in learning as a function of perceptions and attributions. *Journal of Educational Psychology, 76*(4), 647–658.

Salomon, G., & Gardner, H. (1984). The computer as educator: Lessons from television research. *Educational Researchers.*

Salomon, G., & Perkins, D.N. (1987). Transfer of cognitive skills from programming: When and how? *Journal of Educational Computing Research, 3,* 149–170.

Schramm, W. (1977). *Big media, little media.* Beverly Hills, CA: Sage.

Simon, D.P., & Simon, H.A. (1978). Individual differences in solving physics problems. In R. Siegler (Ed.), *Children's thinking: What develops?* Hillsdale, NJ: Lawrence Erlbaum Associates.

Snow, R.E. (1986). Individual differences and the design of instructional programs. *American Psychologist, 41,* 1029–1039.

Snow, R.E., & Lohman, D.F. (1984). Toward a theory of aptitude for learning from instruction. *Journal of Educational Psychology, 76,* 347–378.

Spencer, R.M., & Weisberg, R.W. (1986). Context-dependent effects on analogical transfer. *Memory & Cognition, 14,* 442–449.

Sugrue, B.M. (1990). A comparative review of European and American approaches to computer-based instruction in schools. In T. Schlechter (Ed.), *Problems and promises of computer-based training.* Norwood, NJ: Ablex.

Thorndike, E.L. (1903). *Educational psychology.* New York: Lemcke & Buechner.

Tversky, A. (1977). Features of similarity. *Psychological Review, 84,* 327–352.

Tversky, A., & Gati, I. (1978). Studies in similarity. In E. Rosch & B.B. Lloyd (Eds.), *Cognition and categorization.* Hillsdale, NJ: Lawrence Erlbaum Associates.

Vygotsky, L.S. (1962) *Thought and language.* Cambridge, MA: MIT Press.

CHAPTER 7

A SUMMARY OF THE DISAGREEMENTS WITH THE "MERE VEHICLES" ARGUMENT

Richard E. Clark

Originally published as: Clark, R.E. (1991). When researchers swim upstream: Reflections on an unpopular argument about learning from media. *Educational Technology, 31*(2), 34–40. Reprinted by permission of Educational Technology Magazine.

At the Editor's invitation, this article is an informal report of my experience of the many disagreements caused by the controversial claim that media do not influence learning or motivation (Clark, 1983, 1985a). Before I go on to briefly describe the current status of the argument and my reactions, it's important for the reader to know that the claim of "no learning benefits" from media has been made and substantiated many times in the past. My articles are only the most recent publications to suggest that media have economic but not psychological benefits. For example, Keith Mielke (the former chair of Telecommunications at Indiana University and now with Children's Television Workshop in New York) was eloquent on the topic in an article he wrote for the now-defunct *Educational Broadcasting Review* (Mielke, 1968) titled "Questioning the Questions of ETV Research." Another example of the argument came from this century's most prolific media research reviewer, Wilbur Schramm, who claimed (Schramm, 1977) that learning is influenced more by the content and instructional strategy in a medium than by the type of medium. Howard Levie (recently deceased professor of Instructional Systems Technology at Indiana University) made the same point about the same time as Schramm in his chapter on media and technology research in the second *Handbook of Research on Teaching.*

It is therefore a mystery to me why my most recent restatement of the claim got so much attention. I suspect that there are two reasons. My initial article (Clark, 1983) was published during the time when our field was accepting and integrating the new cognitive models of learning and instruction. Every environmental event that might influence learning was suspect, including media. The second reason for the fuss may be that other authors have put the claim in very tentative terms (as befits our training as researchers) and left the door open to media effects on learning. I made the explicit and clear claim that there were *no* learning benefits possible and urged that we not continue to waste effort on the question until a "new theory" as developed. I intended to stimulate discussion, and I was not disappointed. Before I describe the fuss, however, the discussion turns next to a brief review of the argument.

THE LEARNING-FROM-MEDIA ARGUMENT

My early articles claimed, in part, that media are "mere vehicles that deliver instruction but do not influence student achievement any more than the truck that delivers our groceries causes changes in our nutrition" (1983, p. 445). The articles presented evidence in support of the hypothesis that instructional methods have been confounded with media and that methods are what influence learning. Further, I claimed that any necessary teaching method could be designed into a variety of media presentations.

The analogy I offered was that different media were similar to the different ways pharmacists have developed to provide us with the active ingredient in a medicine. Those "media" include a variety of tablets, liquid suspensions, suppositories, or injections. All of these different media serve to deliver the same "active" chemical ingredient with different levels of efficiency, but with equal effects on our physical symptoms.

I also disagreed with Gabi Salomon about the unique contributions of media attributes. Salomon has claimed that it is not the medium that influences learning but instead certain attributes of media that can be modeled by learners and shape the development of unique "cognitive processes." Examples of media attributes are the capacity of television and movies to "zoom" into detail or to "unwrap" three-dimensional objects into two dimensions. My problem with the media attribute argument is that there is strong evidence that many very different media attributes accomplish the same learning goal (i.e., there are a variety of equally effective ways to high-light details other than "zooming") and so no one media attribute has a unique cognitive effect. If different attributes have the same cognitive effect, they are each "proxies" of some deeper process—probably of what I am calling an instructional method.

WHAT IS A METHOD, AND HOW DOES IT DIFFER FROM A MEDIUM?

An instructional method is any way to shape information that compensates for or supplants the cognitive processes necessary for achievement or motivation. For example, students often need an example to connect new information in a learning task with information in their prior experience. If students cannot (or will not) give themselves an adequate example, an instructional presentation must be provided for them. All students require learning goals and information in order to learn. Not all will require instructional methods. Instructional technology engineers both the information and the instructional methods required for the necessary psychological support of students as they learn. Delivery technology packages and gives students access to necessary information and methods.

A CONFUSION OF TECHNOLOGIES

In a presentation for AECT at their 1987 Atlanta convention, I attributed our media research and practice problem to a "confusion of technologies" (Clark, 1987). Instructional or training design technologies draw on the psychological and social-psychological research to select necessary information and objectives (as a result of task analysis), and to design instructional methods and environments that enhance achievement. A very different technology—delivery technology—is necessary to provide efficient and timely *access* to those methods and environments. Both technologies make vital but very different contributions to education. Design technologies influence student achievement. In my view, there is a long history of basic confusion between these two technologies that strangles our study of the contributions of media.

MOTIVATION WITH MEDIA

Finally, I claimed that media not only fail to influence learning, they are also not directly responsible for motivation. Here I agreed wholeheartedly with the views of Gabi Salomon (1984) and others who draw on the new cognitive theories and attribute motivation to learners' beliefs and expectations about their reactions to external events—not to external events alone. There is compelling research evidence that students' beliefs about their chances to learn from any given media are different for different students and for the same students at different times.

THE ORIGINS OF THE IDEAS

The arguments I have just summarized are counterintuitive and generally unpopular. In 1980, when I began the two years of focused reading of media research which resulted in the original publication, I was taking a challenge from Bob Heinich (the former editor of *Audio Visual Communication Review*) to develop a specific taxonomy of media and learning outcomes. I was also working with Gabi Salomon on what became our *Handbook of Research on Teaching* review of media studies (Clark & Salomon, 1986). In those days before electronic mail, we were sending each other ten or more single-spaced letters of detail and argument as our manuscript developed. I began with the expectation that media were a significant element in any educational reform which sought achievement gains. The problem was that as I reviewed the evidence it seemed clear that it did not support my expectations or my intuition.

WHAT WERE THE REACTIONS TO THE ARGUMENT?

To admit that the claim (that there are no learning benefits to be had from media) caused a stir would be an understatement. For the first three years after its publication, I received a large volume of phone calls and written correspondence from media enthusiasts, researchers, and educators. Many were angry and most had not read (or at least did not understand) the argument. I was, for example, accused of "taking food away from my kids" by two different people whose media jobs were eliminated (though neither writer claimed that my article was directly responsible for their loss of employment).

A few writers who had carefully read the arguments understood them and sent interesting counter-arguments. For about five years, a few people wrote and published engaging and intelligent rebuttals. There were a smaller number of the congratulatory notes and calls. One example of the positive reactions was contact from the staff of the president of Harvard University. President Bok took the conclusions of my article and made them an important part of his 1985 annual report to the faculty and trustees of Harvard. The next day he gave the grocery truck analogy to a writer for *The New York Times*, who reported it verbatim, and attributed it to Bok. Other positive reactions came from graduate students and from a number of faculty who teach media research courses. I have been contacted by students or faculty at eight different universities where graduate students were required to prepare opposing views for a "debate" of the issues—usually pitting the media confounding argument against McLuhan, or focusing more narrowly on Salomon's media attribute argument.

Generally, reports of the argument have appeared in *Newsweek*, *Time*, *The Chronicle of Higher Education*, *Psychology Today*, in a great number of newspapers, and in radio and television news reports. My university kept a clipping file on the reports for a few years but abandoned the practice after budget cuts.

What follows is my attempt to answer editor Lawrence Lipsitz's questions and give my view of the upshot of the important arguments that followed, a report of how my views and my feelings have changed, and (at the editor's request) my impression of how our field treats unpopular arguments.

WHAT ARE THE COUNTER ARGUMENTS?

While there were a great variety of counter arguments, I categorize them into four types of rebuttals to the basic arguments: (1) reasoning based on the usual uses of a medium; (2) the meta-analysis evidence; (3) problems with empiricism and logical positivism; and (4) a lingering hope for media attributes.

1. *Usual Uses.* The majority of informal letters that I received took Marshall McLuhan's view that media and method were identical and inseparable. I think of it as the usual uses argument. It seems to develop because media specialists generate beliefs about the "best" contents and methods for each medium. So, for example, television is usually thought to convey "realistic" visual, real-time documentary information. Computers most often give semantically dense simulations of complex phenomena as well as drill and practice. Textbooks have tended to focus on the development of encyclopedic knowledge with illustrated examples and heavy verbal content. Many writers seemed to suggest that these "methods" were somehow intrinsic to a given medium. My argument is that the usual uses of a medium

do not limit the methods or content it is capable of presenting. Computers can present "realistic" visual, real-time documentary information, and televison can present semantically dense simulations. The method is the simulation or the real-time depiction. A good example of this point was uncovered in one of the earliest and largest (and best designed) studies of computers by Pat Suppes (Stanford University) during the 1960s. In a study of computers versus teachers using drill and practice in mathematics, Pat's researchers found that one of his control school districts had messed up the data collection by delivering more drill and practice in mathematics than was permitted by the study—using teachers and not computers. The result was that in the control school district, mathematics achievement increased at exactly the same rate as it did in districts where computers were giving drill and practice. Suppes concluded that it was not the medium but the drill and practice method that influenced achievement. However, he noted that the cost of the intervention might have been less with computers.

2.   *What Is the Matta with Meta-analyses?*   Jim and Chen-Lin Kulik, the couple who published all of those *meta-analyses* of media research, argued that their reviews suggest strong evidence for the positive effects of computers (for example) on achievement. Their analyses (including one published with Bob Bangert-Drowns, who is at SUNY Albany) show an approximate 20 percent increase in final exam scores in computer-based instruction (CBI) when CBI is compared to "traditional" forms (generally "live instruction").

After a number of arguments, Jim agreed with me that it is not the computer but the teaching method built into CBI that accounts for the learning gains in those studies. More importantly, he agreed that the methods used in CBI can be and are used by teachers in live instruction (cf. Clark, 1985b). In fact, I reanalyzed a 30 percent sample of the studies he used and found that when the same instructional design group produces CBI and presents the live instruction with which it is compared in many studies, there is no achievement difference between CBI and live conditions (Clark, 1985c).

To characterize the fact that these powerful methods can be and are used in a variety of media, Jim coined the catchy phrase "...diffusion of the innovative treatment to the control condition." This turn of phrase more or less acknowledges that most of the studies which are grist for the meta-analytic mill are confounded because the teaching method is not controlled (if it were controlled it could not "diffuse" anywhere). Thus, in my view, one of those things that Stan Pogrow (University of Arizona) complained is "the matta with meta" is that meta-analytic reviews of media studies have a serious GIGO (Garbage In, Garbage Out) problem. The Kuliks continue to publish meta-analyses of media studies and continue to find advantages for a range of electronic media over "traditional" forms of instruction. Since the "same teacher" control is not obvious in most of these studies, the confounding is perpetuated.

3. *Empiricism Envy.* Don Cunningham (Indiana University) in an *ECTJ* article did not dispute my argument that media made no difference to learning or motivation, but argued against my empirically-based claims that instructional methods were responsible for achievement gains. Don is well trained as a quantitative researcher, but is increasingly attracted to qualitative research and not to empirical method or logical positivism. I think his argument was with the unreconstructed empiricism of my argument rather than with the theoretical claims. I agreed with Don's contention that my claim (that it is instructional methods that account for learning gains) is a hypothesis, not a conclusion (Clark, 1986).

4. *Necessary Media Attributes.*   Two separate groups of researchers have argued with my rejection of the notion of unique contributions of what Gabi Salomon calls "media attributes." Remember that the capacity of movies to "zoom" into detail or to "unwrap" three-dimensional objects had led some to claim that new media have attributes that make unique cognitive representations available. A few go so far as to claim that new "intelligence" might be possible as a result of exposure to these attributes. I found good evidence that many very different media attributes could accomplish the same learning goal (i.e., there were a variety of equally effective ways to highlight details other than "zooming") and so no one media attribute has a unique cognitive effect.

In another *ECTJ* article, Petkovitch and Tennyson (1985) took me to task with an argument which I still do not completely understand. They seemed to agree that media comparison studies are useless but claimed that certain media attributes make necessary contributions to learning. The evidence they offered was a study where a computer simulation was used to teach students some skills required to fly a plane. I responded that people learned to fly planes before computers were developed and therefore the media attributes required to learn were obviously not exclusive to computers nor necessary for learning to fly.

A similar and more extensive argument has been made by Robert Kozma (in press) at the University of Michigan. Bob makes an interesting argument about my use of the word "necessary." It is a subtle argument which I do not completely understand and the issue is definitely not settled between us.

My problem with the media attribute argument is that some of my students have replicated a number of the original media attribute studies (the zooming study was replicated twice) and got very distressing results. Wherever media attribute like zooming or unfolding influences problem solving or some other achievement outcome, a range of completely different attributes from different media have similar effects (see citations in Clark & Sugrue, 1989).

HAVE MY VIEWS CHANGED?

I feel even more confident about some of the arguments than when they were developed nine years ago—and less confident about others. *The evidence is overwhelming that media do not influence achievement.* It is a proxy variable in studies. I am also more convinced about the interchangeable and arbitrary nature of the so-called media attributes. Yet I now think that motivation is likely to be an interaction between media and student perception. At least it is possible to vary motivation by varying media—though not in the same way for every student and not for very long (the motivational effects are very transitory because students' beliefs change with experience).

I originally claimed that published research was afflicted with gatekeeping by journal editors—that editors tended to publish studies where newer media influence learning and not studies which show n.s.d.'s, that is, "no significant differences." Jim Kulik has convinced me that there is no solid evidence for this claim. My problem is that I have been a critic or editor for most of the journals that publish this research, and I have many personal experiences of well-designed but n.s.d. studies which were not published. Since any well-designed study that controls for method and content when two or more media presentations are compared will have n.s.d. results, this is an important issue.

Many of the n.s.d. studies presumably joined the fugitive literature in ERIC or are buried in the file cabinets. Jim has studied the fugitive literature extensively and finds no effect size differences in unpublished studies—with one exception. Dissertations regularly show lower effect sizes for media in comparison studies. This may happen because graduate students are less experienced researchers—or because dissertation studies are supervised and there is a more conservative estimate of the effects (unsupervised researchers may make more liberal and self-serving interpretations of their data). The two hypotheses (supervised conservatism and unsupervised liberalism) are not mutually exclusive and the evidence available does not unambiguously support either one.

WHO IS PERSUADED?

It's difficult to make an objective assessment of whether the argument that media have no effect on achievement is widely accepted among researchers. With the exception of Kozma, they seem to agree when we talk but, of course, I do not talk to everyone. Bill Winn, in a recent chapter on media research in which he discusses the argument, concludes that I have "persuaded a large number of scholars" (1990, p. 53). Winn is kind since many researchers know that the argument (and much of the evidence) has been around for many years and were not persuaded by me or my recent restatement of the arguments. Winn, Tennyson, Kulik, and I were the members of a symposium panel of researchers who accepted an invitation by Mike Simonson of Iowa State to debate the issues at the 1987 AECT convention in Atlanta (cf. Clark, 1987). All of the people who offered rebuttals during that symposium accept the basic argument in different forms. Most of them were persuaded not by my arguments but by those of Mielke, Schramm, and others.

On the other hand, I suspect that the evidence either has not been read or is resisted by the majority of practitioners who produce educational media programs and by some of the new computer research crowd—particularly those who are enthused about the potential of computer programs like LOGO or the development of higher-order thinking skills from learning computer programming or video games. And, as you might expect, those who manufacture and sell media seem generally not to have been persuaded.

The comfort for all of us interested in media is that the same confounding is found in all areas of educational research and practice. Nevertheless, the computer enthusiasts seem to be well on the road to repeating the same mistakes as the television people, with similar results. Many of them think that the use of computers or the learning of computer programming will develop higher-order thinking skills. Whatever it is that develops such skill, computers are not part of the active ingredients.

The origin of the confusion over computer use, computer programming skills, and the learning of transferrable thinking skills may be found, in part, in the pervasive and sometimes inappropriate use of a metaphor used to understand human cognition. A number of metaphors have served psychology in the past. The mind has been compared to a wax tablet and to the muscular system. Former theories of transfer that resulted from those metaphors were also unproductive. For example, the classical theory of transfer fixed on a muscular metaphor and recommended that generalizable problem solving and reasoning skills would be developed through the "exercise" of the mind while learning classical subjects such as Latin and Greek.

Don Norman argues that the computer metaphor for cognition is more difficult to limit than previous media metaphors because the architecture of the digital computer was influenced by its designers' tacit theories of cognition. Thus, he suggests that we now have a tendency to turn the metaphor around and assume that there is isomorphism between both physical structures and programming processes in the computer and psychological structures and processes in the human mind. Dave Lohman notes that some go so far as to argue that "similar principles govern the functioning of any system that processes information." For those who advocate a strong computer analogy for cognitive processing, the mind is a mechanism for symbol manipulation. Thus, in this view, the structural and process differences between the computer and the mind are irrelevant. Some of the more ardent advocates of this model have taken to calling cognitive skills "mindware." In this perspective it is reasonable to assume that writing programs for the computer would not only help the computer to reason but would also "program the programmer."

While few would dispute the value of computer models of cognitive processes, it is the inappropriate reification of the models which seems to be at the root of the problem. George Miller reminds us that computer models of thought are similar to computer models of the weather, yet few of us would expect that a model of violent weather would damage the computer center. The value of a model is, in part, its capacity to suggest productive hypotheses about cognitive processing. The reified computer model of the development of higher-order thinking skills is simply the latest edition of the media attribute argument rather than a positive influence.

HOW DO I FEEL ABOUT THE EXPERIENCE?

Like most researchers I enjoy the give-and-take in an argument based on evidence. One of the problems with empirical research is that it can provide good evidence about what does not work, but it is less effective as a technology for confirming or drawing positive conclusions. A couple of my closest colleagues have given me the advice that I should "back off" from the argument and go in a more positive direction. For example, they suggest that I stress the economic advantages of media.

I have learned a great deal from the discussions and most everyone who has participated in the argument has been fair-minded and supportive. Unexpected support for the argument has come from European colleagues. Many European educational faculty have a long tradition of "didactics," which dates back to the early Gestaltists in Germany and the Netherlands. The root argument in didactics is very similar to my "method" argument, and European researchers seem to more easily separate medium and method. In fact, some of the Europeans think that the North American researchers are a bit balmy over the media issue and seem to think of the more fervent media advocates (particularly the new computer enthusiasts) as "snake oil salesmen" (as a Belgian colleague who likes American western movies put it to me recently).

The exceptions are understandable. One cannot expect participation or enthusiastic support from organizations or individuals whose support depends on popular enthusiasms for media. Yet, in the United States and Europe, the greatest support comes from organizations (primarily companies and government agencies) who design training for their employees. I have seen a number of large organizations postpone their plans to purchase sophisticated media for training after exposure to the argument.

Note that the operative word in the previous sentence is "postpone" and not "cancel." A number or organizations now want to conduct cost-benefit and cost-effectiveness analysis before making major purchases of new media. Unlike our formal schooling system, companies and government agencies need to rationalize their expenditures and contain costs while still achieving goals. The more that organizations insist on cost-effectiveness studies, the more they will begin to separate the different technologies that are involved in training.

CONCLUSION

I'll end the discussion by thanking Lawrence Lipsitz for my few minutes on the soapbox. He removed all the usual constraints of a "scholarly" piece and so encouraged me to be personal and candid. He asked me to close with a summary of the experience—and it runs something like the following.

The media research question is only one of a number of similar confoundings in educational research that seem difficult to rectify, even though adequate research exists to refute invalid but intuitively appealing beliefs. Part of the problem, in my view, is that we tend to encourage students (and faculty) to begin with educational and instructional *solutions* and search for problems that can be solved by those solutions. Thus, we begin with an enthusiasm for media, or individualized instruction, or deschooling and search for a visible context in which to establish evidence for our solution. Counter-evidence is suspect and we are predisposed to believe that it is flawed. Positive evidence is accepted easily.

We need greater appreciation for negative evidence and to begin with a focus on problems (the need to increase achievement, or access to instruction, or to address the labor intensiveness of instruction) and then search relevant research literatures for robust, research-based theories about the variety of solutions to those problems. If we begin by implicitly and explicitly attempting to validate a belief about the solutions to largely unexamined problems, we are less open to evidence that our intuitions might be very far off the mark.

REFERENCES

Clark, R.E. (1983). Reconsidering research on learning from media. *Review of Educational Research, 53*(4), 445–459.
Clark, R.E. (1985a). Confounding in educational computing research. *Journal of Educational Computing Research, 1*(2), 445–460.
Clark, R.E. (1985b). The importance of treatment explication in computer-based instruction research. *Journal of Educational Computing Research, 1*(3), 389–394.
Clark, R.E. (1985c). Evidence for confounding in computer-based instruction studies: Analyzing the meta analyses. *Educational Communications and Technology Journal, 33*(4).
Clark, R.E. (1986). Absolutes and angst in educational technology research: A reply to Don Cunningham. *Educational Communications and Technology Journal, 34*(1), 8–10.
Clark, R.E. (1987). *Which technology for what purpose?* Paper presented at an invited symposium for the annual meeting of the Association for Educational Communications and Technology, Atlanta, GA.
Clark, R.E., & Salomon, G. (1986). Media in teaching. In M. Wittrock (Ed.), *Handbook of research on teaching* (3rd ed.). New York: Macmillan.
Clark, R.E., & Sugrue, B.M. (1989). Research on instructional media, 1978–1988. In D. Ely (Ed.), *Educational media yearbook 1987–88*. Littletown, CO: Libraries Unlimited.
Kozma, R.B. (In press, Summer). Learning with media. *Review of Educational Research.*
Mielke, K.W. (1968). Questioning the questions of ETV research. *Educational Broadcasting, 2,* 6–15.
Petkovitch, M.D., & Tennyson, R.D. (1985). Clark's "Learning from media": A critique. *Educational Communications and Technology Journal, 32,* 233–241.
Salomon, G. (1984). Television is easy and print is "tough": The differential investment of mental effort in learning as a function of perceptions and attributions. *Journal of Educational Psychology, 76*(4), 647–658.
Schramm, W. (1977). *Big media, little media.* Beverly Hills, CA: Sage.
Winn, W. (1990). Media and instructional methods. In D.R. Garrison & D. Shale (Eds.), *Education at a distance: From issues to practice.* Malabar, FL: Krieger.

CHAPTER 8

ROBERT KOZMA'S COUNTERPOINT THEORY OF "LEARNING WITH MEDIA"

Robert B. Kozma

Originally published as: Kozma, R. (1991). Learning with media. *Review of Educational Research, 61*(2), 179–212. Copyright 1991 by the American Educational Research Association. Reprinted with permission of the publisher and the author.

ABSTRACT

This article describes learning with media as a complementary process within which representations are constructed and procedures performed, sometimes by the learner and sometimes by the medium. It reviews research on learning with books, television, computers, and multimedia environments. These media are distinguished by cognitively relevant characteristics of their technologies, symbol systems, and processing capabilities. Studies are examined that illustrate how these characteristics, and instructional designs that employ them, interact with learner and task characteristics to influence the structure of mental representations and cognitive processes. Of specific interest is the effect of media characteristics on the structure, formation, and modification of mental models. Implications for research and practice are discussed.

INTRODUCTION

Do media influence learning? The research reviewed in this article suggests that capabilities of a particular medium, in conjunction with methods that take advantage of these, interact with and influence the ways learners represent and process information, and may result in more or different learning when one medium is used compared to another, for certain learners and tasks.

This paper is in response to a challenge by Clark (1983) that, "...researchers refrain from producing additional studies exploring the relationship between media and learning unless a novel theory is suggested" (p. 457). He extended this challenge after reviewing the existing comparative research on media and concluding that, "...media do not influence learning under any conditions." Rather, "...media are mere vehicles that deliver instruction but do not influence student achievement any more than the truck that delivers our groceries causes changes in our nutrition" (p. 445). The theoretical framework supported by the current review presents an image of the learner actively collaborating with the medium to construct knowledge. It stands in vivid contrast to an image in which learning occurs as the result of instruction being "delivered" by some (or any) medium. The framework is meant to provide the novel approach required by Clark before research on media and learning can progress.

In this theoretical framework learning is viewed as an active, constructive process whereby the learner strategically manages the available cognitive resources to create new knowledge by extracting information from the environment and integrating it with information already stored in memory. This process is constrained by such cognitive factors as the duration and amount of information in short-term memory, the task-relevant information that is available in long-term memory, how this information is structured, the procedures that are activated to operate on it, and so on. Consequently, the process is sensitive to characteristics of the external environment, such as the availability of specific information at a given moment, the duration of that availability, the way in which it is structured, the ease with which it can be searched, and so on.

The sub domain of the external environment examined in this paper is "mediated information," not only that which is intentionally educational (such as a computer-based lesson) but other information embedded in books, television programs, etc. Not directly addressed by this review is information embedded in what are sometimes called "authentic situations" (Brown, Collins, & Duguid, 1989), though the thesis developed in this paper complements learning in such situations. Nor does the article examine the larger social environment within which mediated interactions occur (Perkins, 1985). Ultimately, it may be these contexts, and the ways media are integrated into them, that have the greatest impact on how people think and learn. While these broader contexts will be referenced from time to time, the primary focus of this paper is finer grained: specific episodes within which a learner interacts with mediated information to influence learning.

In support of the thesis stated above, this article will provide a definition of media and use it to examine the theoretical and research literature on learning from books, television, computers, and multimedia environments. Each section will examine how the complementary construction of representations, and operations performed on them, is influenced by characteristics of the medium, designs that take advantage of these, and the characteristics of learners and tasks. The intent is to demonstrate the relative cognitive effects of learning with different media, particularly effects related to the structure, formation, and modification of mental models.

MEDIA DEFINED

Media can be defined by their technology, their symbol systems, and their processing capabilities. The most obvious characteristic of a medium is its technology, the mechanical and electronic aspects that determine its function and to some extent its shape and other physical features. These are the characteristics that are commonly used to classify a medium as a "television," a "radio," and so on. The cognitive effects of these characteristics, if any, are usually indirect. Characteristics such as size, shape, and weight makes it more likely that a student will learn with a book while on a bus but not a computer, though of course this is changing as computers get smaller, lighter, and cheaper. On the other hand, some cognitive effects of technology are more direct. For example, the size and resolution of many computer screens is such that reading text may be more difficult than it is with books (Haas, 1989).

However, the primary effect of a medium's technology is to enable and constrain its other two capabilities: the symbol systems it can employ and the processes that can be performed with it. For example, a computer with a graphics board or a speech synthesis board can use different symbols in its presentations than those without. Computers with enough memory to run LISP and expert systems can process information in different ways than those without. Symbol systems and processing capabilities have a number of implications for learning.

Salomon (1974, 1979) describes the relationship between a medium's symbol systems and mental representations. Symbol systems are "modes of appearance" (Goodman, 1976), or sets of elements (such as words, picture components, etc.) that are interrelated within each system by syntax and are used in specifiable ways in relation to fields of reference (such that words and sentences in a text may represent people, objects, and activities and be structured in a way that forms a story). A medium can be described and perhaps distinguished from others by its capabilities to employ certain symbol systems. Thus, television can be thought of as a medium that is capable of employing representational (i.e., pictorial) and audio-linguistic symbol systems (among others). Such characterizations can also be used to specify a certain overlap or equivalence of media. Thus video and motion film can be thought of as equivalent in this regard, while they can be distinguished from radio which can employ only a subset of these symbol systems.

Salomon (1974, 1979) suggests that these characteristics should be used to define, distinguish, and analyze media since they are relevant to the way learners represent and process information from a medium. He contends that certain symbol systems may be better at representing certain tasks and that information presented in different symbol systems may be represented differently in memory and may require different mental skills to process. The research reviewed here supports and elaborates on this contention. For example, studies will be examined that illustrate how symbol systems characteristic of certain media can connect mental representations to the real world in a way that learners with little prior knowledge have trouble doing on their own, without the representation of information in these symbol systems.

But, as will be demonstrated, symbol systems alone are not sufficient to describe a medium and its cognitive effects. Information is not only represented in memory, it is processed. Media can also be described and distinguished by characteristic capabilities that can be used to process or operate on the available symbol systems. Thus, information can be searched or its pace of progression changed with videodisc in a way that is not possible with broadcast video. Including processing attributes in the definition of media can create useful distinctions between videodisc and broadcast video, even though they both have access to the same symbol systems. Computers are of course especially distinguished by their extensive processing capabilities, rather than by their access to a particularly unique set of symbol systems.

The processing capabilities of a medium can complement those of the learner; they may facilitate operations the learner is capable of performing or perform those that the learner cannot. As Salomon (1988) points out, if such processes are explicit and fall within what Vygotsky (1978) calls the "zone of proximal development," the learner may come to incorporate them into his or her own repertoire of cognitive processes. This review will examine research which illustrates how the processing capabilities of certain media can modify and refine the dynamic properties of learners' mental models.

However, it is important to remember that while a medium can be defined and distinguished by a characteristic cluster, or profile, of symbol systems and processing capabilities, some of these capabilities may not be used in a particular learning episode (Salomon & Clark, 1977). For example, a particular video presentation may use few or no representational symbols (e.g., a "talking head" presentation). Or, a viewer may allow a videodisc presentation to play straight through and not use the available search capabilities. In these cases a "virtual medium" is created that consists of the profile of symbol systems and processing capabilities that were actually used during the session: a television becomes, in effect, a radio; a videodisc player becomes broadcast television. It is only the capabilities of the virtual medium that can be expected to have an effect on learning processes and outcomes.

Whether or not a medium's capabilities make a difference in learning depends on how they correspond to the particular learning situation—the tasks and learners involved—and the way the medium's capabilities are used by the instructional design. Tasks vary in their situational characteristics and the demands they place on the learner to create mental representations of certain information and operate on that information in certain ways. Learners vary in their processing capabilities, the information and procedures that they have stored in long-term memory, their motivations and purposes for learning, and their metacognitive knowledge of when and how to use these procedures and information.

Many learners, perhaps most, can and frequently do supply useful representations and operations for themselves from the information externally available, regardless of medium used. On the other hand, learners will benefit most from the use of a particular medium with certain capabilities (as compared to the use of a medium without these), if the capabilities are employed by the instructional method to provide certain representations or perform or model certain cognitive operations that are salient to the task and situation, and which the learners can not or do not perform or provide for themselves. These representations and operations, in turn, influence problem solving and the ability to generate and use representations in subsequently encountered situations. This view of learning with media as a continuous, reciprocal interaction between person and situation—between learner and mediated information—is compatible with evolving aptitude-treatment interaction theory (Snow, 1989).

Learning with Books

The most common medium encountered in school learning is the book. As a medium, books can be characterized by the symbol systems they can employ: text and pictures. The following sections of the review will examine the cognitive processes used in processing text and text along with pictures. They will discuss how a distinctive characteristic of this technology—its stability—influences the processing of these symbol systems to construct knowledge representations and how these, in turn, are influenced by individual differences of learners, primarily differences in their prior domain-knowledge. The summary will describe how these processes and structures can be supported by the author when designing a book.

The Reading Processes and the Stability of the Printed Page

The primary symbol system used in books consists of orthographic symbols which, in Western culture, are words composed of phonemic graphemes, horizontally arrayed from left to right. That this arrangement is stable distinguishes text in books from other technologies that use the same symbol system, for example the marquee on Times Square. This stability also has important implications for how learners process information from books. Specifically, the stability of text aids in constructing a meaning of the text.

Learning with text involves the construction of two interconnected mental representations: a textbase and a situation model (Kintsch, 1988, 1989). The textbase is a mental representation derived directly from the text, both at the level of micro and macrostructure; it is a propositional representation of the meaning of the text. While progressing through the text, the reader assembles the propositions and integrates them with ones previously constructed. As memory limits are reached, the most recent and most frequently encountered propositions are retained in short-term memory and held together by repetition or the embedding of arguments (Kintsch & van Dijk, 1978). The reader generalizes from these local propositions to form macropropositions, or summary-like statements that represent the gist of the text. Integrating the information from the text in this way increases the likelihood that it will survive in short-term memory and be fixed in long-term memory.

The situation model is a mental representation of the situation described by the text (Kintsch, 1988, 1989). While the textbase is propositional, the situation model can be constructed from propositions or spatial information. The situation model is connected to and constructed from information in the textbase and from knowledge structures evoked from long-term memory by information appearing early in the text or that activated by the reader's purpose. These structures, called variously schemata (Anderson, Spiro, & Anderson, 1978), frames (Minsky, 1975) and scripts (Schank & Abelson, 1977), can be characterized as a framework with a set of labeled slots in which values are inserted for particular situations. These structures serve two related purposes: they provide a "scaffold" upon which the situation model is constructed from the textbase, and they provide default values so that the reader can make inferences about the local situation that were not explicitly mentioned in the text. Learning from text involves the integration of these representations into the comprehender's knowledge system by updating the schemata currently in long-term memory or by constructing a new schema for an unfamiliar situation.

But, what does any of this have to do with media? How does this symbol system influence mental representations and cognitive processes in distinctive ways? And why would learning processes and outcomes be any different for books, which store orthographic symbols in a fixed, stable way, and another medium, say audiotape or lecture, which may convey the same linguistic information but in a different symbol system and in a transient way (i.e., speech)?

In many situations for fluent readers, reading progresses along the text in a forward direction at a regular rate and the information could just as well be presented in another, more transient medium. But on occasion, reading processes interact with prior knowledge and skill in a way that relies heavily on the stability of text to aid comprehension and learning.

In the obvious case, the effort required of poor readers to decode the text draws on cognitive resources that would otherwise be used for comprehension, thus increasing the risk of comprehension or learning failure (LaBerge & Samuels, 1974). But even fluent readers may have difficulty with longer or novel words, such as technical terms in an unfamiliar domain. In both of these cases, readers will use the stability of text to recover from comprehension failure. When encountering difficulty, a reader will slow their rate, making more or longer eye fixations (Just & Carpenter, 1987) or they may regress their eyes, going back to review a word as an aid to retrieving a meaning for it from memory (Bayle, 1942). Alternatively, a reader may retrieve several meanings for a word and may make longer or additional fixations, or may regress over a phrase, a clause, or even a sentence to determine which is appropriate for a given context (Bayle, 1942; Just & Carpenter, 1987). Such difficulties might arise from unusual syntactic structures (e.g., "The thief stood before the black robed judge entered the courtroom.") or difficulties in interpreting combinations of words to construct local propositions. Readers will slow their rate for a passage on a difficult or novel topic (Buswell, 1937), when encountering information within a passage that is particularly important to the meaning of the text (Shebilske & Fisher, 1983), or when they must integrate less well organized sentences into macropropositions (Shebilske & Reid, 1979).

All of these are examples of how readers use the stability of the symbol system in books to slow their rate of progression or even to regress over text in a way that would seem difficult or impossible to do with audiotape's ever-advancing presentation of information. However, this distinction is likely to be crucial only in certain situations. For example, readers in the Shebilske and Reid (1979) study reduced their rate from 302 words per minute to 286. While statistically significant, this difference may not have practical significance with regard to media use since the typical audiotape presentation rate of 110–120 words per minute would seem to be slow enough to accommodate these comprehension difficulties. Even the apparent inability to regress over speech might be accommodated by the two second duration of information in acoustic memory (Baddeley, 1981) that would allow a listener to "recover" the three or four most recently spoken words and achieve the same affect as regression over text. The clearest advantage to the use of the stability of text to aid comprehension is when the reader must regress over segments of information larger than a phrase.

Perhaps more important than the use of the stability of text to recover from local comprehension failure in novel or difficult situations is its use in conjunction with highly-developed reading skills (such as those described by Brown, 1980) and elaborated memory structures to strategically process large amounts of text within very familiar domains. This is most dramatically illustrated in a study by Bazerman (1985), who interviewed seven professional physicists and observed them reading professional material in their field. These readers read very selectively, making decisions based on highly developed schemata that extended beyond extensive knowledge of accepted facts and theories in the field to include knowledge about the current state of the discipline and projections of its future development, as well as personal knowledge and judgments about the work of colleagues. Readers used this domain knowledge to serve their reading purposes. Most often their interests were to find information that might contribute to their immediate research goals or to expand their background knowledge of the field, and they made their selections based on these purposes.

Bringing schemata and purposes to bear, these subjects would typically read by scanning rapidly over tables of contents, using certain words to trigger their attention and question a particular title more actively. If a particular term attracted their attention, they would look at other words in the title with the result that about two-thirds of the titles more closely examined were subsequently rejected based on this additional information. If even more information was needed to make further selections, they would turn to the abstract.

Having identified an article of interest, they would read parts of it selectively and non-sequentially, jumping back and forth, perhaps reading conclusions then introductions, perhaps scanning figures, and reading those sections more carefully that fit their purpose. If an article did not readily fit with their comprehension schemata, the readers would weigh the cost of working through the difficulty against the potential gain relative to their purposes. If they chose to read through a difficult article or portion, they would occasionally pause at length to work through the implications of what had been read, or read it through several times. They might also look up background material in reference works and textbooks.

The studies above show the range of ways that readers take advantage of the stable structure of text to aid comprehension. In the Bazerman (1985) study, strategic readers with considerable domain knowledge would sometimes progress through the text at a rapid rate, using a single word to skip a vast amount of information. Other times, they would slow considerably, moving back and forth within a text and across texts, to add to their understanding of the field. In other studies (Bayle, 1942; Shebilske & Reid, 1979), readers encountering difficulties with unfamiliar words, syntactic structures, or ideas used the stability of the printed page to slow their rate and regress over passages. None of these processing strategies are available with the transient, linguistic information presented in audio tape or lectures.

Multiple Symbol Systems: Learning with Text and Pictures

Orthographic symbols are, of course, not the only ones available to books. Pictures and diagrams are used in books from primers to college textbooks to technical manuals. But, how do readers use pictures? What is the cognitive effect of pictures in combination with text? And, how does the stability of these symbols, as presented in books, influence this process compared to another medium, say television, which presents linguistic and pictorial symbols in a transient way? This last, comparative issue will be directly addressed in the subsequent section on learning with television. The following section examines the cognitive effects of pictures and text.

There is a large body of comparative research on learning from text with and without pictures. Almost all of the studies examine only the impact on cued recall and use traditional experimental designs, of the type criticized by Clark (1983). However, there is consensus among the reviews of this research that pictures have positive effects under certain conditions. Pressley (1977), Schallert (1980), and Levie and Lentz (1982) generally concur that the use of pictures with text increases recall, particularly for poor readers, if the pictures illustrate information central to the text, and when they represent new content that is important to the overall message, or when they depict structural relationships mentioned in the text. The problem with this type of research is that it does not reveal the mechanism by which pictures and text influence the learning process.

The four studies below examine processes of comprehension and learning with text and pictures. In brief, it appears that the use of both symbol systems facilitates the construction of the textbase and the mapping of it onto the mental model of the situation. This is particularly facilitative for learners who have little prior knowledge of the domain.

A study by Rusted and Coltheart (1979) examined the way good and poor fourth grade readers used pictured text to learn about physical features, behavior, and habitat of unfamiliar animals. Including pictures of animals in their environments along with the text resulted in better retention by both good and poor readers, over the use of text alone. It facilitated retention of all information by good readers, but only pictured information (i.e., recall of physical features) for poor readers. Observations of good readers showed that they spent time initially looking at the pictures and rarely looked at them once they started reading. Poor readers, on the other hand, frequently moved back and forth between text and pictures. While the process data are not detailed enough to be definitive, they suggest that good readers may be using the pictures to evoke an "animal schema" that guided their reading and aided comprehension. On the other hand, poor readers frequently moved back and forth between text and pictures, maybe to facilitate the decoding of particular words and perhaps to aid in building a mental model of these unfamiliar animals and their habitats.

Stone and Glock (1981) obtained similar findings, using more precise measures, when they examined the reading of second and third year college students. Subjects used either text without pictures, pictures without text, or pictured text to learn how to assemble a toy push-cart. The text-only group made significantly more assembly errors, particularly errors of orientation, while the text and picture group was most accurate in their constructions, making only 18 percent of the errors of the text-only group. Eye-tracking data indicated two patterns of picture use. Readers would typically spend the first few seconds examining the picture. Subsequently they would look from text to picture as they progressed through the passage, spending an average of more than 80 percent of their time looking at text rather than pictures. As in the Rusted and Coltheart study, the data suggest that readers initially use the pictures to evoke a schema that serves as a preliminary mental model of the situation. Subsequently, it seems that the text carries the primary semantic message, while the pictures are used to map this information on to this preliminary mental model, elaborating on the components of the push cart and their relative arrangement.

The usefulness of pictures seems to interact with specialized ability or domain knowledge. In a study by Hegarty and Just (1989) college students were tested on mechanical ability and assigned to either a "short text" or a "long text" describing a pulley system. The short text merely named the components of the system and described how it operated. The long text also elaborated on the arrangement and structure of the components in the system. All texts were accompanied by a schematic diagram of the pulley system. Precise eye-fixations measured the number and duration of movements back-and-forth between particular words in the text and specific locations in the diagram. There was a non-significant interaction such that low ability students spent more time than high ability students looking at the diagram when it accompanied the longer text which described the relationship among the components of the system. The high ability students spent more time examining the diagram with the shorter text. The results suggest that people low in mechanical ability have difficulty forming mental models of mechanical systems from text and use diagrams to help them construct this representation. People with high mechanical ability seem to construct this model from prior knowledge and information from text, without need to refer to the picture. On the other hand, these high ability students are better able to encode new information from a diagram when the text does not describe all the information relevant to understanding a mechanical system.

In a study by Kuntz et al. (1989), university students majoring in either geography or social science read passages that contained concepts and rules on meteorology. They received text either with or without two types of supplements: (1) representational pictures depicting spatial arrangement, appearance, and configuration of clouds, and (2) a tree diagram that provided an overview of the main concepts, constituting the macrostructure of the text. Students were divided on prior domain knowledge. For students with a higher prior knowledge, the examination of representational pictures did not correlate with post-task comprehension and the use of the tree diagram correlated negatively with performance. In contrast, subjects with low prior knowledge did better if they both inspected the representational picture very often and spent some time examining the tree diagram. These data suggest that students with little prior knowledge benefit most from the pictures and the tree diagram. On the other hand, students with sufficient prior domain knowledge can rely instead on their own, well-developed mental models to aid comprehension. Indeed, the tree diagram used in this study may have conflicted with the idiosyncratic way these students have domain knowledge structured and it may have actually interfered with their comprehension.

These studies may also explain the conclusion of Pressley (1977) in his review of studies of text and imaging. He found that learners who do not receive pictures but are instead instructed to generate images during the processing of story prose, recall as much as those who receive pictures, and more than those who neither receive pictures nor are instructed to generate images. However, there were developmental differences such that children of eight years and older could gainfully generate and use images during text processing, while those under the age of six appeared unable to generate useful images in response to text, even when directed to do so. In these studies, age may be a surrogate measure for accumulated world knowledge that allows older children to generate mental models which supplement the text and aid comprehension and recall. Younger children may not have sufficient world knowledge to generate such mental models and they benefit most from pictures to aid this process.

Greeno (1989) elaborates on the "situation model" in a way that can be useful in analyzing the relationship between text, pictures, cognitive structures, and processes. Greeno proposes a theoretical framework that defines knowledge as a relationship between an individual and a social or physical situation, rather than as a property of an individual only. It extends the information processing paradigm, which focuses primarily on internal structures and process, to include structures and processes external to the learner. This relativistic notion of knowledge depends heavily on a model of the situation and has considerable implications for learning with media.

In this framework, objects and events organized in relation to human activities (such as hitting a ball or buying and selling merchandise), as well as related abstractions (such as "force" or "profit margin"), are expressed within our culture in various symbolic notations and structures (verbal descriptions, diagrams, graphs etc.). Mental representations, or mental models, are derived from the symbolic structures and correspond to real world situations—objects, events, and their abstractions.[1] These mental models consist of symbolic objects, or mental entities, that may have properties associated with the symbol systems from which they were derived (e.g., arrows representing force vectors), as well as properties of objects in situations that the symbolic structures represent (e.g., balls moving through space and time along certain trajectories). Greeno contends that people can reason in this mental space to solve problems by operating on these symbolic objects in ways that correspond to operations in real situations.

However too often in school learning, these mental objects and operations have little correspondence to real world objects, events, and their abstractions and instead map only onto the symbolic domains from which they were derived. The research above suggests that for some learners, the use of pictures, in addition to text, may provide information needed to map mental representations derived from the text onto mental representations of the real world, perhaps because pictorial symbol systems share more properties with this domain.

Summary and Implications

We now have a picture of learning with books that illustrates the relationship between human information processes and the characteristic stability and symbol systems of the medium. Readers move along a line of text constructing a representation of the textbase. They build a mental model of the situation described with information from the textbase and schemata activated in long-term memory. They slow down to comprehend difficult or important points, stop or regress to retrieve the meaning of an unfamiliar word or a confusing clause or sentence. They may also use their knowledge of the domain along with highly developed strategies to read very selectively in service of a particular purpose they bring to the task. They use titles and abstracts to skip sections or entire articles, or to focus in on sections of interest. They read summaries, then overviews, reread portions, and move back and forth between texts.

If a picture is available, they may refer to it to supplement the text. An initial look at the picture will evoke domain knowledge, for those that have it. In a less familiar domain, readers will move back and forth frequently between text and picture to clarify the meaning of a word or construct or elaborate on a model of the situation. All of these strategies and their resulting mental representations are influenced by the knowledge and purpose the reader brings to the task, the symbol systems and stability of code that characterizes the book.

An author can use these capabilities in a way that complements the learner's skills and deficiencies. Text authors can use the stability of text and pictures in books and knowledge of comprehension processes to design structures within their texts that support and facilitate learning. Such structures may include titles (Brandsford & Johnson, 1972), postquestions (Wixson, 1984), explicitly stated behavioral objectives (Mayer, 1984), cohesive text elements (Halliday & Hasan, 1976), signals (Mayer 1984; Meyer, 1975), and so on. For example, in the Bransford and Johnson (1973) study, one group of students had considerable difficulty comprehending a paragraph even though it was linguistically simple and contained no difficult words, constructions, or complex concepts. A second group was presented the same paragraph, but this time the paragraph was preceded by a title. In this second condition, the subjects rated the paragraph as more comprehensible and they recalled it better. Presumably, the title evoked an appropriate schema that allowed the readers to supply information not explicit in the paragraph but was important for its comprehension. Other text strategies might evoke different reading processes, such as conducting backward reviews to facilitate retention (Wixson, 1984), or focus attention on certain types of information, or build internal connections among concepts in the text (Mayer, 1984). Such devices designed into the text can reduce the need for the regressive strategies observed in the Bayle (1942) and Shebilske and Reid (1979) studies, and support the purpose and schema-driven strategies evident in the Bazerman (1985) study, at least for students with sufficient prior knowledge.

An understanding of the cognitive function of pictures can also inform instructional practice. This can provide text authors with information that can be applied heuristically to identify situations where pictures would be useful, as well as how they might be usefully designed to accommodate particular learners and tasks (Winn, 1989). Such guidelines may suggest the positioning of pictures in the text, the degree of realism, the use of arrows and other highlighting mechanisms, and so on. For example, the research above suggests that for knowledgeable readers, pictures should be placed early in the text if they are used at all. On the other hand, a less knowledgeable readership would benefit from interspersed pictures, juxtaposed with their corresponding text. Winn (1989) reviews research that suggests that the use of arrows to highlight critical attributes of objects can facilitate subsequent identification, while the inclusion of details in an illustration can actually interfere with the learning of an object's structure or function.

Learning with Television

Television differs in several ways from books that may affect cognitive structures and processes. As with books, television can employ pictures, diagrams, and other representational symbol systems but in TV these symbols are transient and able to depict motion. While linguistic information in television can be orthographic, more often it is oral and, as with audiotape and radio, transient. Because in television, linguistic and pictorial symbol systems are transient and because they are presented simultaneously, it is possible that viewers process this information in a very different way than the back-and-forth serial processing of linguistic and representational information in books. It is also possible that the symbol systems used and their transient nature affects the mental representations created with television.

Television's Window of Cognitive Engagement

While popular notions of TV viewing portray children as staring zombie-like at the screen, reality is much different. When alternative activities are available, children generally look at and away from the TV between one and two hundred times an hour (Anderson & Field, 1983). Visual attention increases from very low levels during infancy to a maximum during the late elementary school years, declining somewhat during adulthood (Anderson et al., 1986). Although the median look duration is usually only several seconds, extended episodes as long as a minute are not rare. Looks as long as ten minutes are exceptional. This discontinuous, periodic attention to a medium whose information streams by ceaselessly has important implications for comprehension and learning.

Research indicates that visual attention is influenced by several factors. One set of factors, termed "formal features" by Huston and Wright (1983), includes the use of different types of voices (e.g., children, adult male, female), laughing, sound effects, music of different types, animation, cuts, zooms, pans, etc. While children's moment-to-moment visual attention may wander from the set, evidence suggests that they continually monitor the presentation at a superficial level, such that their visual attention is recaptured by certain audio cues. Features that are associated with the onset of visual attention are women's and children's voices, laughter, peculiar voices, sound effects, auditory changes, and visual movement (Anderson et al., 1979). Features associated with continued viewing are special visual effects, pans, and high physical activity. The offset of visual attention among children frequently corresponds to the use of men's voices, long zooms, and inactivity.

While this image of visual attention seems bottom-up and data-driven, other evidence suggests that these formal features come to be seen by children as corresponding to the presentation of more or less meaningful content and it is this second factor, the meaningfulness or comprehensibility of the presentation, that guides visual attention. For example, Anderson et al. (1981) found that visual attention to segments of *Sesame St.* was greater for normal segments than for the same visual presentation for which comprehensibility was experimentally reduced by using backward speech or a foreign language. Anderson and Lorch (1983) hypothesize that through extensive viewing experience, children come to acquire knowledge about the associations between the typical use of various formal features and the likelihood that the corresponding content will be meaningful and interesting. For example, men's voices may be perceived as generally corresponding to adult-oriented content which is less comprehensible and less interesting to children, and thus male voices do not recruit their visual attention.

Huston and Wright contend that this comprehensibility influences attention in an inverted-U relationship, such that content which is very simple or very difficult to comprehend maintains attention less well than content in an intermediate range of difficulty. This creates a window of cognitive engagement, one that is perhaps different for each viewer. Yet within this window, Huston and Wright (1983) conclude that visual attention is necessary though not sufficient for comprehension; the depth of comprehension varies.

Salomon (1983) introduces the construct of "amount of invested mental effort," or AIME, to account for the difference between what is viewed and the depth of comprehension. AIME distinguishes the "deep," effortful, nonautomatic elaboration of encountered material from the "mindless" or "shallow" processing of information that results in less learning. AIME is in turn influenced by several factors: One is the attitude people have about the amount of effort required to process a medium's messages; the other is the purpose that people bring to the task.

Salomon (1984) found that a sample of sixth graders rated TV as an "easier" medium from which to learn than books. When assigned to view comparable stories from television or print, the effort spent on learning reported by the reading group was significantly greater than that reported by the group that viewed the television program. While both groups scored the same on a test of factual recognition, the print group scored higher on a test of inferences based on the story.

Krendl and Watkins (1983) exposed fifth-grade children to a 15-minute educational television program. They manipulated the purpose of viewing by telling half of the students to watch it for entertainment purposes; the other half were told that it was an educational program and they should watch it in order to answer questions. While recall of the storyline was the same for both groups (i.e., number of recalled actions, facts, scenes, etc.), the group instructed to view the program for educational purposes responded to the content with a deeper level of understanding; that is, they reported more story and character elements and included more inferential statements about the meaning of the show.

These studies suggest that the perceptions students have about a medium and the purposes they have for viewing influenced the amount of effort that they put into the processing of the message and, consequently, the depth of their understanding of the story. The following sections elaborate on the cognitive mechanisms involved in effortful learning with television, and examine the interaction of these processes with the characteristics of the medium. Three issues related to the processing of televised information are examined: the relationship between simultaneously presented auditory and visual information, the processing pace of transient information, and the use of such transient presentations to inform the transformation functions of mental models. For the first of these issues, there is now a considerable amount of cognitive research available; however, there remains little research on the other two issues.

The Simultaneous Processing of Two Symbol Systems

An important attribute of video is its use of both auditory and visual symbol systems. Within the window of cognitive engagement, how do these symbol systems work, independently and together, to influence comprehension and learning with television? Can either symbol system convey the meaning of a presentation? Does the presentation of both at the same time inhibit or facilitate learning?

Baggett (1979) found that either pictorial or linguistic symbol systems alone can carry semantic information, such as a story line. In this study, college students were presented with either a dialogless movie, *The Red Balloon*, or an experimentally derived, structurally equivalent audio version. They wrote summaries of episodes within the story either immediately after the presentation or after a week delay. An analysis of the summaries by trained raters found that those written immediately after viewing the dialogless movie were structurally equivalent to those written immediately after listening to the story. While subjects could construct a semantic macrostructure (i.e., summary) from either medium, information obtained visually was more memorable. Summaries written a week after viewing the movie were judged to be more complete than those written a week after listening to the audio version.

While meaning can be conveyed by either symbol system, Baggett (1989) concludes that information presented visually and linguistically are represented differently in memory. She contends that visual representations contain more information and are "bushier." Whereas the statement "red leaf" contains only the name of an object and a modifier, a mental representation of a "red leaf" obtained from a picture carries with it information about size, color, shape, etc. Also, the visual representation has more "pegs" which can be used to associate it with information already in long-term memory. These additional associations also make it more memorable.

But, it is a significant attribute of video that the auditory and visual symbol systems are presented *simultaneously*. How does a viewer process information from both of these sources? Two basic hypotheses exist. One possibility is that the simultaneous presentation of audio and visual information competes for limited cognitive resources and this competition actually reduces comprehension. Another possibility is that information presented with these two symbol systems may work together in some way to increase comprehension.

A number of studies have compared a video program with its decomposed audio and visual presentations to determine the role of these two sources of information, individually and together (Baggett & Ehrenfeucht, 1982, 1983; Beagles-Roos & Gat, 1983; Gibbons et al., 1986; Hayes & Kelly, 1984; Hayes, Kelly, & Mandel, 1986; Meringoff, 1982; Nugent, 1982; Pezdek & Hartman, 1983; Pezdek, Lehrer, & Simon, 1984; Pezdek & Stevens, 1984). In none of these studies did the combination of audio and visual information result in lower recall than recall from either source alone. In most of these studies, the combined use of visual and auditory symbol systems resulted in more recall than visual-only and audio-only presentations. This compels the rejection of the hypothesis that simultaneous presentation of audio and visual information necessarily compete for cognitive resources at the expense of comprehension.

Several of these studies used multiple measures of recall to trace the symbol system source of different kinds of knowledge. In a 1982 study, Meringoff asked 9- and 10-year-old children to draw and talk about their imagery and to make and substantiate inferences about a story, *The Fisherman and His Wife*. Compared to those who heard the story, the children who saw the video drew more details and their pictures were more accurate. Children in the audio groups based their inferences about details on previous knowledge and personal experiences (more like those of children in the control group unexposed to the story) and they were frequently in error relative to the verbal descriptions. Beagles-Roos and Gat (1983) compared animated and audio-tape presentations of two stories to groups of 1st and 4th grade children. These researchers found that the explicit story content was learned equally well by both treatment groups. The visual groups recalled more details from the story, did better at a picture sequencing task, and based their inferences on depicted actions. The audio groups more frequently retold the stories using expressive language, and based their inferences on verbal sources and prior knowledge.

While people can construct a mental representation of the semantic meaning of a story from either audio or visual information alone, it appears that when presented together each source provides additional, complementary information that retains some of the characteristics of the symbol system of origin. Children recall sounds and expressive language from the audio track and visual details from the visual track. It also appears that the "bushier" nature of representations derived from the visual symbol systems are better for building mental models of the situation than are representations based on audio-linguistic information. Students listening to an audiotape are more likely to get information for this model from memory. While audio may be sufficient for those knowledgeable of a domain, visual symbol systems supply important situational information for those less knowledgeable.

These results parallel those for text and pictures. However, the processing of text appears to be driven by the construction of a representation of the linguistic information. Comprehension of video appears to be driven by the processing of visual information. This is apparent from a study by Baggett (1984), who varied the temporal order of audio and visual information within a video presentation on the names and functions of pieces of an assembly kit. In this study, the narration was presented in synchrony, or 21, 14, or 7 seconds ahead of or behind the visual presentation. College students performed best on immediate and 7 day delayed tests of recall in the synchrony and the 7-second visual-then-audio group. The worst performance was by groups with the audio presented first. This suggests that in a video presentation, the visual symbol system serves as the primary source of information and the audio symbol system is used to elaborate it.

The Processing of Transient Information

Another important characteristic of television is that the information it presents can be, and usually is, transient. Comprehension is affected by the pace of this presentation and by its continuity. Wright et al. (1984) used sixteen, 15 minute long children's television programs that varied in pace and continuity. Pace was defined by these researchers as the rate of scene and character change. Low-continuity programs were those whose successive scenes were independent and unconnected (i.e., magazine formats). High-continuity programs where those with connected scenes (i.e., stories). These programs were shown to groups of elementary school children whose recall was measured using seriation tasks of still pictures from the shows. The children who viewed slow paced and on high-continuity programs performed better on these tasks. The effect was additive for younger children.

While surprisingly little research has been done on the effect of pace on comprehension, this is a potentially crucial variable which distinguishes the process of learning with television, and other transient media, from learning with stable media, such as text. Wright et al. (1984) defined pace as a characteristic of the presentation—the amount of information *presented* per unit time (i.e., scene and character changes). But from a cognitive perspective, the critical consideration is cognitive pace, the amount of information *processed* per unit time. From this perspective, the hypothetical unit of information is the "chunk." The chunk is a semi-elastic unit whose size depends on the familiarity and meaningfulness of the information (Miller, 1956; Simon, 1974). A single word may be a chunk in the following list of words: Lincoln, calculus, criminal, address, differential, lawyer, Gettysburg. As rearranged into Lincoln, Gettysburg, address, criminal, lawyer, differential, calculus; the chunk might be larger than a word (e.g., "Lincoln's Gettysburg address"), but only if this phrase had some meaning in long-term memory. Simon (1974) examines the results of several experiments to conclude that the capacity of short-term memory is five to seven chunks. He also concludes that it takes between five to ten seconds to fixate each chunk in long-term memory. Thus, while the amount of time it takes to process information is relatively constant (i.e., one chunk per 5 to 10 seconds), the number of words processed per unit time depends on the size of the chunk. This, in turn, is dependent on relevant prior knowledge in long-term memory.

With books, the reader creates chunks of variable word size to effect a reading pace (i.e., words per unit time) that accommodates the cognitive requirements of comprehension. With television, the pace of presentation (i.e., words or visual elements per unit of time) is not sensitive to the cognitive constraints of the learner; it progresses whether or not comprehension is achieved. The television viewer may be familiar enough with the information to process it at the pace presented, even if it is "fast." That is, the viewer's chunks may be large enough so that the cognitive pace of processing words and ideas keeps abreast with the pace at which they are presented. Even if attention wavers and information is missed, knowledge of a familiar domain can be used to fill in the gaps by supplying information from long-term memory. If the viewer has little domain knowledge, the chunk size will be smaller and the cognitive pace will drop, perhaps below the pace at which ideas are presented. Also, there is less information from long-term memory to compensate for the information that might be missed. Because the information is transient, the viewer can not regress over it to refresh short-term memory. This situation may result in cascading comprehension failure mentioned by Anderson and Collins (1988). However, for lack of research, these contentions remain speculative and empirical work in this area is needed.

The discussion above concentrates on the potential problems created by the transient nature of video information. On the other hand, this transience may have some advantages in the development of dynamic mental models. As mentioned, Greeno (1989) contends that people use mental models to reason through the solution of problems. This is possible because a mental model is considered to be composed of a connected, "runnable" set of objects, or mental entities (Williams, Hollan, & Stevens, 1983). Each of these has an associated representation of its state, a set of parameters, a set of procedures which modify its parameters, and a set of relationships that connect it with other objects. The model is "run" by means of propagating a change of state in one object over time to those of connected objects, using the associated procedures and relationships to modify their parameters. Thus, the representation is transformed from the current state to some future state. This information is used to make inferences and solve problems (Holland et al., 1986).

For example, mental models in physics typically include entities that correspond to physical objects that are encountered in the situation, such as "blocks," "springs," "pulleys," etc. (Larkin, 1983). People operate on the mental entities as they would in real time and make inferences about "what would happen to them next" in order to solve physics problems.

Holland et al. (1986) contend that learning a representation of the transition function is the critical goal in the construction of a mental model. The prospect exists that the transient, time-based character of video information could be used to inform the dynamic properties of mental models, such as those in physics. The observation of objects moving along paths, for example, could provide learners with information needed to make estimates of changes in state. This information would not be available with static information, such as that in text. Whereas learners familiar with the domain might be able to supply such dynamic information from memory or use their prior knowledge to infer dynamic properties from static pictures, those novice to a domain may not be able to supply such constructions and might benefit from the dynamic character of televised information. However, as will be discussed in the subsequent section on learning with computers, this information may not be sufficient to overcome misconceptions that novices frequently bring to tasks, such as those involving the motion of objects (Clement, 1983; di Sessa, 1982; McCloskey,

1983). Again, for lack of research in this area, these contentions remain speculative.

Summary and Implications

This research paints a picture of television viewers who monitor a presentation at a low level of engagement, their moment to moment visual attention periodically attracted by salient audio cues, and maintained by the meaningfulness of the material. This creates a window of cognitive engagement. Within this window their processing is sometimes effortless, resulting in the construction of shallow, unelaborated representations of the information presented. However, when viewing with a purpose, people will attend more thoughtfully, constructing more detailed, elaborated representations and drawing more inferences from them.

The visual component of the presentation is particularly memorable and the representations constructed with it are especially good for carrying information about situations. The auditory symbol systems carry information about sounds and expressive language and help in interpreting the visual information. Auditory symbol systems alone draw primarily on prior knowledge for a construction of the situation model and this may be problematic for those with little prior knowledge.

Viewers use their prior domain knowledge to process information at the pace presented and supplement information that they may have missed. The transient information in the presentation may be useful in building the dynamic properties of mental models, so that inferences can be made about the phenomena they represent. However, if the topic is unfamiliar, little information exists in long-term memory to supplement viewing, the pace of the presentation may exceed their capacity to process it, and comprehension failure may result.

This knowledge can be used by instructional designers to make media-related decisions. For example, people who are very knowledgeable about a particular domain can process information at a much faster rate and more strategically with text than they can with audiotape or video, suggesting that text would suffice for these learners. However, people who are novice to a domain are likely to benefit from the ability to slow the rate of information processing, regress over text, and move back and forth between text and pictures, as they are presented in books. These same people are more likely to fail at comprehending some portion of a video presentation because their pace of processing information may fall below the pace at which it is presented. For learners moderately familiar with a topic, television's symbol systems can supply complementary information, particularly useful in constructing a situation model, and its pace will accommodate comprehension. In such productions, the linguistic information should be presented simultaneous to or just following the visual information.

Learning with Computers

So far, media have been described and distinguished from each other by their characteristic symbol systems. Some media are more usefully distinguished by what they can *do* with information—that is, their capability to *process* symbols. This is particularly the case for computers, the prototypic information processor. For example, computers can juxtapose, or transform, information in one symbol system to that in another (Dickson, 1985). A learner can type in printed text and a computer with a voice synthesizer can transform it into speech. The computer can take equations and numerical values or analog signals and transform them into graphs. Research is reviewed below which shows how the computer can be used to aid students in constructing links between symbolic domains, such as graphs, and the real world phenomena they represent. The research shows that it is the transformation capabilities of the computer, rather than its symbol systems, that are crucial in this regard.

The computer is also capable of "proceduralizing" information. That is, it can operate on symbols according to specified rules, such that a graphic object on the screen can move according to the laws of physics, for example. Research is reviewed below which illustrates the role that this capability can play in aiding learners to elaborate their mental models and correct their misconceptions with the use of microworlds.

Connecting the Real World to Symbols with MBL

An important part of school learning is acquiring an understanding of the relationship between various symbol systems and the real world they represent. Yet, students are frequently unable to connect their symbolic learning in school to real world situations (Resnick, 1988). The transformational capabilities of the computer can be used to make this connection.

Graphs provide an example of this. Mokros and Tinker (1987) found frequent errors among seventh and eighth grade students in the interpretation of graphs. Two patterns were identified. First, there was a strong graph-as-picture confusion. Half of the students drawing a graph of a bicyclist's speed uphill, downhill, and on level stretches drew graphs representing the hills and valleys rather than speed. In a less striking pattern, 75 percent of the students responded incorrectly when asked to specify maximum warming or cooling on a graph. About half of these selected the highest (or lowest) point on the graph as that showing the most rapid change.

Mokros and Tinker went on to use a microcomputer-based lab (MBL) with 125 seventh and eighth graders for three months. MBL involves the use of various sensors (temperature probes, microphone, motion sensors, etc.) connected to the computer to collect analog data. The computer transforms these data and displays them in real time on the screen as a graph. In a typical unit, the user can turn a heater on for a fixed period, thereby delivering a fixed quantity of thermal energy to a liquid. Using temperature probes interfaced to the computer, the increase and decrease of temperature is instantaneously graphed over time. Mokros and Tinker found a significant increase from pre to posttests on the interpretation of graphs (from $m = 8.3$ to $m = 10.8$ on a 16-item test). Of particular importance was the fact that students made the greatest gains on items sensitive to the graph-as-picture error.

In a similar study, Brasell (1987) used MBL with high school Physics students. One group of students spent a class session collecting and observing MBL data in real time (the Standard-MBL group). A second group used the MBL equipment to collect data but it was displayed after a 20-second delay. One control group plotted data with pencil and paper and another control group engaged in testing only. Brasell found that the posttest scores from the Standard-MBL treatment were significantly higher than scores from all other treatments. The analysis indicated that real-time transformation of data (i.e., the difference between Standard-MBL and Delayed-MBL) accounted for nearly 90 percent of the improvement relative to the control. Brasell suggests that unsuccessful students lack appropriate techniques for referring to previous events or experience and they fail to make explicit links between physical events and the graphed data, even when they are displayed after only a 20-second delay. The transformation capabilities of the computer made the connection between symbols and the real world immediate and direct.

Building Mental Models with Microworlds

Experts in a domain are distinguished from novices, in part, by the nature of their mental models and how they use them to solve problems. The processing capabilities of the computer can help novices build and refine mental models so that they are more like those of experts.

In physics, a series of studies (Chi, Feltovich, & Glaser, 1981; Hegarty, Just, & Morrison, 1988; Larkin, 1983; Larkin et al., 1980) has established that experts have extensive domain knowledge organized into large, meaningful schemata, or chunks, which are structured around the principles or laws of physics. These schemata not only contain information about the laws of physics, but information on how and under which conditions they apply. That is, they contain both declarative and procedural knowledge.

When encountering a text book physics problem, experts use the objects (e.g., springs, blocks, pulleys, etc.) and features mentioned in the problem statement to cue the retrieval of one or more relevant schemata (e.g., "force-mass" or "work-energy"). They construct a mental model, which contains both information that has been explicitly provided by the situation, as well as information supplied from memory. These mental models include mental entities that correspond to physical objects that are mentioned in the problem, such as "blocks," "pulleys," etc. (Larkin, 1983; Larkin et al., 1980), as well as entities which correspond to the formal constructs of physics that have no direct, concrete referent in the real world, such things as "force," "vectors," "friction," and "velocity." The relationships among these entities correspond to the laws of physics. Experts reason with this model to test the appropriateness of potential quantitative solutions. It is only after this qualitative analysis is complete that the expert will use an equation to derive a quantitative solution to the problem.

Novices represent and use information in this domain in a very different way. Not only do they have less knowledge about physics than do experts, but their knowledge is organized quite differently. For some novices, their physics-related knowledge is composed of a set of fragments or "phenomenological primitives," that are not connected by formal relationships but based on real world objects and actions. They evoke these fragments to construct a representation of a particular problem (di Sessa, 1988). Other novices may have coherent and consistent, though erroneous "theories," or misconceptions of the phenomenon (Clement, 1983; McCloskey, 1983). These may represent procedural relationships that are contrary to established laws of physics, such as "an object remains in motion only as long as it is in contact with a mover" or "an object should always move in the direction that it is kicked."

Confronted by a text book problem, novices will use the same surface cues as experts to evoke this information from memory. However, unlike those of experts, the mental models that novices construct with this information are composed primarily of entities that correspond to the familiar, visible objects mentioned in the problem statement (Larkin, 1983). These representations do not contain entities that represent formal physical constructs, such as "force" or "friction." Nor do they contain information on physical laws and principles, or this information is inaccurate or incomplete. Thus, the models are insufficient to determine a solution or the solution that is specified is incorrect.

How do people modify such incomplete and inaccurate mental models to form more accurate, expert-like models? First of all, this process is not automatic. Indeed, such misconceptions can be held into adulthood and after taking courses in the domain (McCloskey, 1983). Rather, modification of a mental model is triggered by certain conditions, such as the failure of a model to adequately predict or account for phenomena when it is used to achieve some desired goal (Holland et al., 1986). In such cases, a person can drop the current mental model in favor of another, maintain the model but lower confidence in its ability to reliably predict, or modify the model. The latter is most often the goal in school learning. One way a model is modified is by elaborating its situational components. These are the criteria used to evoke and select the appropriate model in response to a particular problem. Another way to modify a model is by changing the transformation rules associated with the situation. Which of these various changes ultimately occurs depends on the accumulated previous success with the model (a model which has been used successfully many times is more likely to be modified rather than replaced), the perceptual elements of the situation that might allow for differentiation (the existence of salient perceptual elements will be used to refine the selection criteria so that it is used in a somewhat different set of situations), and the future success of alternate models and rules when they compete to explain subsequent situations (modifications in the model that successfully predict subsequent situations are more likely to be retained). Expertise is developed through a series of such differentiations and elaborations as a result of extensive experience within a domain—both successful and unsuccessful.

Now, how might the processing capabilities of computers be used by novices to aid them in building more expert-like models? First, an important attribute of the computer is its ability to symbolically represent entities in ways that might inform mental models. Not only can they graphically represent concrete objects, such as carts and springs, but also formal, abstract entities (such as the forces, velocities, etc.), entities that novices do not normally include in their models. Second, the computer has the important capability of being able to "proceduralize" the relationships among these symbols. While abstract concepts can be represented in text by symbolic expressions, such as $f = ma$, or denoted in diagrams by arrows, Greeno (1989) points out that such symbols do not "behave" like forces and accelerations. With computer models, arrows and other symbols can behave in ways that are like the behavior of forces, velocities, and other abstract concepts. For example, a velocity arrow can become longer or shorter, depending on the direction of acceleration. Furthermore, learners can manipulate these symbols and observe the consequences, successful or otherwise, of their decisions. By using their mental models to manipulate these entities governed by the laws of physics, novices may become aware of the inadequacies and inaccuracies of the models. Through a series of such experiences, they can progressively move from initial fragmented, inconsistent, and inaccurate understanding to more elaborate, integrated, and accurate mental models of the phenomena.

This is illustrated in several studies by White (1984, 1989), who examined students as they learned principles of Newtonian dynamics within computer-based microworlds. She extended the work of di Sessa (1982), who created a computer-based Logo environment, called *Dynaturtle*, in which the task was to hit a target through a series of directional "kicks" imparted to the turtle. Di Sessa observed that physics-naive, elementary school students in his study commonly operated with an "Aristotelian" model of force and motion, expressed as, "if you impart a force on a moving object, then it will go in the direction last pushed." This Aristotelian notion of force can be contrasted with the Newtonian principle that the motion of an object is the vectorial sum of the forces that have acted on it. An Aristotelian strategy universally used by these students was to wait until the moving turtle was at the same height as the target and give it a 90% kick directly toward the target. The result in this Newtonian environment would be a compromised motion of 45% that would miss the target.[2]

White (1984) analyzed the correct, Newtonian strategy, decomposing it into component principles (i.e., the scalar sum of forces, the vectorial sum of forces, etc.), and created a series of games that progressively incorporated these component strategies. Each game instantiated both observable objects (e.g., a space ship) and formal physical objects (e.g., a force, represented by a key press). These objects were governed by one of the component Newtonian principles (e.g., combining two forces to increase speed in one direction). The series led up to the target game used by di Sessa. White found that the group of high school physics students who used these games for less than an hour, not only used the Newtonian strategies in the target game, but they showed significant improvement on transfer verbal force and motion problems. They also performed significantly better on these problems than did a control group of students who attended a physics class but were unexposed to the games.

White and Frederiksen (1987) present a paradigm for the development of a progression of computer models that support conceptual change. The progression leads the learner from advanced to simple models, increasing in their number of rules, qualifiers, and constraints taken into account, and in the range of problems they accommodate. The models allow students to make predictions, explain system function and purpose, solve problems and receive feedback and explanations. Each is designed to build upon and facilitate transformation from the previous model.

White (1989) applied this progressive paradigm to develop a two-month curriculum in Newtonian mechanics. This version contained significant improvements in the design. Additional formal constructs from physics were represented by dynamic symbols. For example, a history of the object's speed was represented by a "wake," and the vectorial components of forces acting on the object were represented by a "datacross." As the learner applied more force to the object he or she saw not only the resulting effect on the object as it moved, but a dynamic decomposition of the force into its orthogonal vectors (i.e., the datacross) and a dynamic representation of the change in velocity (i.e., its wake). The students were also provided with additional structure, such as a set of possible "laws" to test within the microworld, and set of real world transfer problems. Additional forces, such as friction and gravity, could be introduced into the system. Two classes of sixth graders were assigned to this curriculum for forty-five minutes a day, instead of their regular science course. At the end of the period, the groups using the microworld scored significantly better on a range of real world transfer problems than did two classes of sixth graders attending the regular science class. They also scored significantly better on these items than did four classes of high school physics students, including two classes that had just spent two and a half months studying Newtonian mechanics.

Summary

The studies above examined the processing capabilities of the computer and showed how they can influence the mental representations and cognitive processes of learners. The transformation capabilities of the computer connected the symbolic expressions of graphs to the real world phenomena they represent. Computers also have the capability of creating dynamic, symbolic representations of non-concrete, formal constructs that are frequently missing in the mental models of novices. More importantly, they are able to proceduralize the relationships between these objects. Learners can manipulate these representations within computer microworlds to work out differences between their incomplete, inaccurate mental models and the formal principles represented in the system.

White's research (1984, 1989) shows that novice learners within these environments benefit from structured experiences of progressive complexity which help them build and elaborate their mental models. Research by Brasell (1987) and others suggests that such symbolic-operational environments would be particularly powerful if directly connected to real time phenomena. These could help learners connect their more elaborated models to the real world experiences which they can explain.

LEARNING WITH MULTIMEDIA

This final section is the most speculative. Little research (particularly process research) has been done on learning with multimedia environments, in part because most efforts in the field are focused on development, and in part because the field is still evolving. However, multimedia present the prospect that the various advantages of the individual media described above can be brought together in a single instructional environment and strategically used to facilitate learning.

The term multimedia has been around for several decades (Brown, Lewis, & Harclerod, 1973). Until recently, the term has meant the use of several media devices, sometimes in a coordinated fashion, such as synchronized slides and audiotape, perhaps supplemented by video. However, advances in technology have combined these media so that information previously delivered by several devices are now seemlessly integrated into one. The computer plays a central role in this environment. It coordinates the use of various symbols systems—presenting text, then in another window presenting visuals. It also processes information it receives, collaborating with the learner to make subsequent selections and decisions.

The following sections review work on two, somewhat different but soon to be integrated approaches to multimedia environments: interactive videodisc environments and hypermedia environments. The literature reviewed reports on developments within these fields, speculates on the cognitive impact of these environments, and raises issues that must be addressed in future research.

Connecting Mental Models to the Real World with Interactive Video

Interactive video integrates computer and video technologies in a way that allows both video and computer-generated information to be displayed together. In some implementations this information is displayed on the same screen and can be overlayed. So for example, the video could present a view of a boulder rolling down a hill in one window on the screen. The computer could generate force vectors and overlay them on the moving object. In another window, a graph could be generated that plotted velocity or acceleration over time. Alternatively, the student may be given a workspace within which she or he could compute acceleration or velocity.

The Cognition and Technology Group at Vanderbilt University (1990; Sherwood, Kinzer, Bransford, & Franks, 1987; Sherwood, Kinzer, Hasselbring, & Bransford, 1987) has developed a series of interactive video-based, complex problem spaces (or "macrocontexts") that are anchored in realistic goals, activities, and situations. These macrocontexts provide semantically rich environments in which students and teachers can collaboratively explore concepts and principles in science, history, mathematics, and literature, and use these multiple perspectives to solve realistic problems. The Group contends that videodisc provides a more veridical representation of events than text, and that its dynamic, visual and spatial characteristics allow students to more easily form rich mental models of the problem situation.

Nationally, a number of interactive videodisc environments are now in the stages of development and formative evaluation. One such environment is *Palenque* (Wilson & Tally, 1989). *Palenque* is intended to be an entertainment and educational exploratory environment for children aged 8–14. With *Palenque*, the viewer becomes a member of an archaeological team of scientists and children exploring ancient Maya ruins in search of the tomb of Pacal, the 12-year-old ruler of Palenque during its heyday.

In an "explore mode" the viewer can use a joystick to engage in "virtual travel"; that is, the video uses a subjective camera perspective to allow the viewer to "see" what he or she would be seeing if actually there, walking and climbing among the ruins. This is accompanied by a dynamic you-are-here map. The child can use simulated research tools such as a camera, compass, and tape recorder. In the "museum mode" the viewer can browse through a database of relevant information including text, still photographs, motion video, graphics, and so on. These are organized into theme "rooms" such as "Maya glyphs" and the "tropical rain forest." In the "game mode," the viewer engages in such activities as putting back together fragmented glyphs and constructing a jungle symphony. Formative evaluation is examining the system's user friendliness, the appeal of the various components, and its comprehensibility.

These systems may be particularly powerful in representing social situations and tasks, such as interpersonal problem solving, foreign language learning, or moral decision making. Situational information needed to understand and solve these semantically rich problems is sometimes difficult to represent by computer alone and can be better represented with video. On the other hand, as mentioned earlier (Salomon, 1983), video information alone can easily be processed in a "mindless" and "shallow" way, thus reducing the inferences that viewers draw from it. With interactive video, the computer can be used to help the learner analyze the rich information present in a video scene and carefully think through all of the factors that impinge on the problem.

For example, Covey (1990) has created a particularly compelling moral case study, entitled *A Right to Die? The Case of Dax Cowart.* In this environment, students are faced with the real-life dilemma of a young man who, having just returned from the war in Vietnam, is involved in a flaming accident in which he is burned over 60 percent of his body and loses his sight. In addition, as part of this burn therapy he must be subjected to daily, painful antiseptic washings. He demands to have the treatments discontinued and be allowed to die. On the other hand, if the treatments are continued he can be rehabilitated to a functional but disabled life. The student is confronted with an important moral decision: should the treatments be discontinued? The goal of the program is not to "teach" or argue the student toward a specific position, but provide the viewer with a "moral sensorium" within which to explore these issues. Covey contends that to understand the moral position of another one must do more than "walk in his shoes," one must "live in his skin." With this program, which is based on a true case and filmed with the actual people involved, the student can see the patient's treatments and in effect "talk" to the patient, the patient's mother, and the doctors, a nurse, and a lawyer. The student is guided through a consideration of the issues of pain and suffering, competence and autonomy, quality of life, and the role of health professionals. Whichever decision the student makes, she or he is presented with contrary information intended to push them toward a deeper understanding of their position.

Cross-media research on the Dax case study is currently underway to examine the impact of video alone, text alone, and interactive video on the representation and processing of this information, and on the moral reasoning of learners. Also being examined is the interaction between these media and students' prior knowledge, experience, and opinions. Of particular interest will be the social and interpersonal cues embedded in the video information and how these are moderated by computer-generated text and guidance to affect the learners' construction of a model of the situation.

Stevens (1989) shows how these cues can be built into a system and used in problem solving. In this system, a subjective camera view is used to put the learner at the head of a conference table in the role of team leader. The task before the team of programmers is to review and critique program code generated by various members of the team. Critiques can, of course, be done in ways that generate defensiveness and otherwise reduce team productivity, and such incidents are built into the episode as it is played out. The task of the learner/team leader is to manage the meeting and interject comments at appropriate times to facilitate group process. The precise timing and nature of these interjections is left open and up to the learner. Successful behavior within the system must be responsive to social information embedded in the presentation. The learner can interrupt the session at a particular point, use various menus to construct a verbal statement and give it an affective/emotional loading. The feedback is also contextual; an expert system knowledge-base is used to present reactions of the team members as they might be in a real meeting.

Holland et al. (1986) indicate that mental models of social worlds are also filled with misconceptions and stereotypes. Typically, people believe social behavior to be more predictable at the level of the individual than it is actually. People tend to explain social behavior in terms of dispositions of actors rather than the character of the situation confronting the actor. Interactive video environments, such as the ones above, may help learners build models of social situations and use them to understand social behavior and solve social problems.

Navigating Through Symbolic Expressions with Hypermedia

To this point, the paper has spent a considerable amount of time discussing the relationship between media and the construction of situation models. Kintsch (1989), however, points out that some texts, such as literary texts, are studied in their own right. In these cases, a major component of the task is to understand a text in the context of other texts and cultural artifacts to which it refers, and within which it was constructed. This section describes an implementation of multimedia called "hypermedia" and speculates on its cognitive effects.

Although hypertext and hypermedia have become common terms only recently, they are ideas that have also been around for several decades. The terms were coined by Nelson (1974/1987) in the sixties but his thinking was strongly influenced by the even earlier work of Bush (1945). As defined by Nelson, hypertext is "nonlinear text." What it has come to mean in its many emerging implementations is a set of windows on the computer screen that are linked to information in a data base (Conklin, 1987). "Hypermedia" is an extension to include a variety of symbolic expressions beyond texts.

These terse definitions can benefit from an illustration. Picture a text document displayed in a window on the computer screen. This document can be searched by various means, including a Boolean key word search using logical functions such as AND and OR. Imagine that the document is an English translation of Plato's *Republic*, and that if desired the user could display the document in Greek, as well, in another window on the screen. In the English version, one could select a word and the computer could identify its corresponding word in the Greek text; this operation would be reciprocal. There may be other information connected to a word or passage in the text. For example, a passage could be connected to a contemporary scholarly article that comments on it; this article could be retrieved from the data base and be displayed on the screen. A reference to Homer would allow the user to retrieve and display the *Iliad*. Or, a word could be associated with a dictionary definition, or a diagram, or a sound, or a bit-mapped, high resolution photograph of an ancient artifact or sculpture or building. The name of a city or country could be linked to a map of it. The title of a play could be linked to a video enactment of its dramatization which could be displayed in yet another window.

Much of the educational development of hypermedia is occurring in a few universities, such as Project Perseus at Harvard (Crane, 1990), Intermedia at Brown University (Landow, 1989), and Hyperties at the University of Maryland (Marchionini & Schneiderman, 1988). The domains include the Greek classics, works of English literature, and technical material.

The potential cognitive effects of such systems become apparent when one compares their capabilities to the reading behavior of experts, as described in the previously mentioned Bazerman (1985) study. These experts would read very selectively, making strategic decisions based on a particular purpose and on highly developed schemata of their field. They scan tables of contents and read parts of articles selectively and in a person-ally constructed order. Sometimes they progress through the text rapidly, other times they slow down, moving back and forth within a text and across texts. This nonlinear reading would certainly appear to be facilitated by the richness of information and the nonlinear structure of hypertext.

The process may also be facilitated by an implementation of hypertext that is not yet widely used. Most current implementations of hypertext sys-tems are search-and-browse systems; that is, the learner is presented with an established database, which has been structured by an author, and the user is free to navigate through it in whatever way he or she may want. On the other hand, other systems (e.g., Kozma, 1989; Kozma & Van Roekel, 1986) allow learners to add their own information and construct their own relationships, perhaps symbolically representing them by graphic, node-and-link structures. Such systems can be made to correspond to the pro-cesses learners use when constructing interrelationships among concepts. As Salomon (1988) points out, this may prompt learners not only to think about ideas but to think about how they are interrelated and structured. More importantly, they provide an explicit model of information represen-tation that, under certain conditions, learners may come to use as mental models of their thinking.

Beyond the considerable literature that lauds the potential for such sys-tems and describes individual projects there is little research on hypertext to date. Those studies that have been done (e.g., Egan et al., 1989; Gay, Trumbull, & Mazur, in press; Marchionini, 1989) focus on the more rudi-mentary functions of hypertext (such as search functions) and relatively simple tasks (e.g., identifying specific information in text), rather than learning or problem solving. While there are some encouraging prelimi-nary findings in these studies to indicate that hypertext both calls on and develops cognitive skills in addition to those used with standard text, much more research is needed. The Bazerman (1985) study suggests that much of the reading behavior exhibited by expert physicists is due to their con-siderable domain knowledge and skill with the medium. Similar research is needed on the impact of domain knowledge and skills in hypertext.

Indeed, in a note of caution, Charney (1987) suggests that some of the very features that make hypertext so appealing, may make it more difficult to use for certain students. For example, the nonlinear nature of hypertext requires readers to decide what information to read and in what order; building such sequences is likely to be particularly difficult for readers new to a domain. By comparison, the author-determined sequence of informa-tion in text and the use of certain cues to signal structural relationships may be particularly facilitative of comprehension for novices. "Getting lost" in hypertext is another potential problem, particularly for novices who lack the extensive schemata that would allow them to easily locate new information within that previously encountered. Finally, lacking domain-based selection criteria, novices may end up reading a great deal of material that is not relevant to their purpose. While hypertext seems to hold some promise it also poses some challenges, challenges that warrant research in this area.

Summary and implications

Integrated multimedia environments bring together the symbolic and processing capabilities of various media described above to help learners connect their knowledge to other domains. Interactive videodisc environments hold the potential for helping learners build and analyze mental models of problem situations, particularly social situations. Hypermedia environments are designed to help the reader build links among texts and other symbolic expressions and construct meaning based on these relationships. While plausible rationales have been given for the expected effectiveness of such environments, these must be tested and in some cases serious questions have been raised. Nonetheless, instructional designers will find these to be powerful development environments and they have important implications for practice.

For example, these environments may dramatically change the nature of the media decisions made by instructional designers. Until now, the selection of media has been a macro-level decision. That is, the decision—should video be used or is audiotape sufficient?—has been based on various instructional considerations *in balance* and it applies to the entire instructional presentation and to all learners. The desirability of presenting visual information for one component of the task would have to be balanced against the increased cost for the entire presentation.

The structure of these traditional, macro-level decisions has effected the conduct of media research. The important question for media researchers has been: What is the overall impact of one medium versus another across learners, and is this impact going to be sufficient enough to justify the additional production and delivery costs that might be involved? This is the meta-question that has driven research on media for the past thirty years and has resulted in little understanding of learning with media.

On the other hand, media decisions for integrated multimedia environments will be micro-level decisions. With these environments it is possible to reconfigure a presentation on the fly in response to the needs of a particular learner. The moment to moment selection of appropriate media can respond to specific learner needs and task demands. While audio-linguistic or even text information may be sufficient for most of the presentation or for most learners, visual information can easily be presented to a particular learner, for a particular segment, at a particular moment, and for a particular purpose.

The macro-level decision still exists; the cost of such multimedia delivery environments is high, relative to other devices. However equipment costs are likely to continue to come down and they are, for the most part, one time costs. Production costs can actually be lower for such systems. Only selected segments need be videotaped; a single segment can be produced based on pedagogical grounds without having to incur the costs of video-taping the entire presentation. Design costs need not go up if the system is used to make these decisions on the fly so as to avoid the need for pro-gramming all possible branches in advance (Stevens, 1990).

A shift from macro to micro-level design decisions requires an under-standing of the moment-by-moment collaboration between a particular learner and the medium. They raise a different set of questions for the media researcher: What is the prior knowledge of a particular learner? How is this represented and structured and how does the learner operate on it to solve problems? What is the range among learners of such representations and operations? What symbol systems can best represent various compo-nents of the task domain? How do these correspond to the way learners rep-resent the task? What skills do the learners have in processing various symbol systems? How do they process various symbol systems together? How can the medium process these in a way that supports the learner?

Many of these questions were addressed in the research reviewed above and this research can inform micro-level media decisions. However, that these questions are now asked from within an integrated, multimedia envi-ronment will raise other, more novel questions, ones not yet addressed in research.

CONCLUSIONS

Do media influence learning? While Clark (1983) contends that media do not influence learning under any condition, the research reviewed in this article suggests that this position must be modified. While some students will learn a particular task regardless of delivery device, others will be able to take advantage of a particular medium's characteristics to help construct knowledge.

Various aspects of the learning process are influenced by the cognitively relevant characteristics of media: their technologies, symbol systems, and processing capabilities. For example, the serial processing of linguistic and pictorial information in books is very much influenced by the stability of this technology. Some learners rely on pictures to help construct a textbase and map it onto a model of the situation; others can provide this model from information in memory and pictures are not needed or audio presentations are sufficient. The processing of linguistic and visual information in television is very much influenced by the simultaneous presentation of these symbol systems and the information in their codes. Some learners use these to build rich representations of situations, particularly their dynamic aspects; others can supply this information from memory, and text or audio presentations will suffice. The process of learning with computers is influenced by the ability of the medium to dynamically represent formal constructs and instantiate procedural relationships under the learner's control. These are used by some learners to construct, structure, and modify mental models; other students can rely on prior knowledge and processes and the use of computers is unnecessary.

However, Clark (1983) contends that even if there are differences in learning outcomes, they are due to the method used, not the medium. With this distinction, Clark creates an unnecessary schism between medium and method. Medium and method have a more integral relationship; both are part of the design. Within a particular design, the medium enables and constrains the method; the method draws on and instantiates the capabilities of the medium. While some attributions of effect can be made to medium or method, there is much shared variance between them and a good design will integrate them. While in the various studies cited above learning was influenced by the methods used, it was in part because they took advantage of the medium's cognitively relevant capabilities to complement the learner's prior knowledge and cognitive skills. Many of these methods would have been difficult or impossible to implement in other media.

Finally, while Clark (1983) calls for a moratorium on media research, this article provides a rationale for additional research on media. There is a growing understanding of the mechanisms of learning with media, but a number of questions remain and the cognitive effects of the more recently developed environments are speculative. Research is needed to extend this understanding.

This research can itself be facilitated by the use of media. Computers provide a unique opportunity to examine learning processes and how these interact with the capabilities of a medium. Particularly useful is the computer's ability to collect moment-by-moment, time stamped log files of key presses, typed responses, menu selections, etc. These data, supplemented by videotapes of students working individually and thinking aloud can be used to examine the effects of media on learners' mental representations and cognitive processes (Ericsson & Simon, 1984). Videotapes of several students working together and talking can provide insights into how cognition is shared among students and between students and media (Roschelle & Pea, 1990). The integration of computer and video records will allow for powerful analyses of qualitative data and the sharing of these among researchers. The examination of the same "raw" qualitative data by psychologists, anthropologists, and sociologists can bring multiple disciplinary perspectives to bear on media research, as well as facilitate the linkage of these knowledge domains that too often go unconnected.

Ultimately, our ability to take advantage of the power of emerging technologies will depend on the creativity of designers, their ability to exploit the capabilities of the media, and our understanding of the relationship between these capabilities and learning. A moratorium on media research would only hurt these prospects.

NOTES

1.   Greeno also points out that at least in some cases information in the situation may be used directly without the need to construct and operate on mental models. Pictures can be considered either as symbolic expressions or as concrete objects in the environment. Pictures as situated objects may be a more efficient source for processing certain kinds of information, quite apart from how that information is represented in memory. For example, Larkin and Simon (1987) created formal computer models to analyze the number of processing steps required (i.e., computational efficiency) to extract information needed to solve problems in mechanics. Two types of data structures were created as they correspond to the same information presented linguistically or diagrammatically. They found considerable computational efficiency in the processing of the diagrammatic structure, such that it was easier for information to be searched and recognized in a diagram, and thus inferences based on this information were more easily made by the computer program. Similarly, Larkin (1989) contends that real objects (such as a coffee maker), as well as manipulatable diagrams of these (as they might be created in computer environments), facilitate cognitive tasks (such as making coffee) because they display the current state (e.g., the filter is currently empty) and thus reduce the need to retain this information in memory or make it easier to recover from memory failures. Such objects let important parts of the problem solving be done by perceptual rather than logical inference.

2.   The graphic objects used by di Sessa may not be symbolic. That is, the objects may not be viewed as having a referent in another domain, such as physics. Rather, the students may learn to operate on them directly in their own right without taking them to represent concrete objects or physical concepts. The objects used by White (1989) are specifically designed to symbolically represent these physical objects and concepts. However, the symbolic nature of objects remains subjective with reference to the learner, and this factor should be explicitly addressed in research with symbolic environments.

REFERENCES

Anderson, D.R., & Collins, P.A. (1988). *The impact on children's education: Television's influence on cognitive development.* Washington, DC: Office of Educational Research and Improvement.

Anderson, D.R., & Field, D. (1983). Children's attention to television: Implications for production. In M. Meyer (Ed.), *Children and the formal features of television.* Munich: Saur.

Anderson, D.R., & Lorch, E.P. (1983). Looking at television: Action or reaction? In J. Bryant & D.R. Anderson (Eds.), *Children's understanding of television.* New York: Academic Press.

Anderson, D.R., Alwitt, L.F., Lorch, E.P., & Levin, S.R. (1979). Watching children watch television. In G.A. Hale & M. Lewis (Eds.), *Attention and cognitive development.* New York: Plenum.

Anderson, D.R., Lorch, E.P., Field, D.E., & Sanders, J. (1981). The effects of TV program comprehensibility on preschool children's visual attention. *Child Development, 52,* 151–157.

Anderson, D.R., Lorch, E., Field, D., Collins, P., & Nathan, J. (1986). Television viewing at home: Age trends in visual attention and time with television. *Child Development, 57,* 1024–1033.

Anderson, J.R. (1985). *Cognitive psychology and its implications* (2nd ed.) New York: Freeman.

Anderson, R.C., Spiro, R.J., & Anderson, M.C. (1978). Schemata as scaffolding for the representation of information in discourse. *American Educational Research Journal, 15,* 433–440.

Baddeley, A. (1981). The concept of working memory: A view of its current state and probable future development. *Cognition, 10,* 17–23.

Baggett, P. (1979). Structurally equivalent stories in movie and text and the effect of the medium on recall. *Journal of Verbal Learning and Verbal Behavior, 18,* 333–356.

Baggett, P. (1984). Role of temporal overlap of visual and auditory material in forming dual media associations. *Journal of Educational Psychology, 76,* 408–417.

Baggett, P. (1989). Understanding visual and verbal messages. In H. Mandl & J. Levin (Eds.), *Knowledge acquisition from text and pictures.* Amsterdam: North-Holland.

Baggett, P., & Ehrenfeucht, A. (1982). Information in content equivalent movie and text stories. *Discourse Processes, 5,* 73–99.

Baggett, P., & Ehrenfeucht, A. (1983). Encoding and retaining information in the visuals and verbals of an educational movie. *Educational Communications and Technology Journal, 31*(1), 23–32.

Bayle, E. (1942). The nature and causes of regressive movements in reading. *Journal of Experimental Education, 11,* 16–36.

Bazerman, C. (1985). Physicists reading physics. *Written Communication, 2*(1), 3–23.

Beagles-Roos, J., & Gat, I. (1983). Specific impact of radio and television on children's story comprehension. *Journal of Educational Psychology, 75*(1), 128–137.

Brandsford, J.D., & Johnson, M.K. (1973). Contextual prerequisites for under-standing: Some investigations of comprehension and recall. *Journal of Verbal Learning and Verbal Behavior, 11,* 717–726.

Brasell, H. (1987). The effect of real-time laboratory graphing on learning graphic representations of distance and velocity. *Journal of Research in Science Teaching, 24*(4), 385–395.

Brown, A.L. (1980). Metacognitive development and reading. In R. Spiro, B. Bruce, & W. Brewer (Eds.) *Theoretical issues in reading comprehension.* Hillsdale, NJ: Erlbaum.

Brown, J.S., Collins, A., & Duguid, P. (1989). Situated cognition and the culture of learning. *Educational Researcher, 18*(1), 32–42.

Brown, J., Lewis, R., & Harclerod, F. (1973). *AV instruction: Technology, media, and method* (4th ed.) New York: McGraw-Hill.

Bush, V. (1945, July). As we may think. *Atlantic Monthly,* pp. 101–108.

Buswell, (1937). *How adults read.* Chicago: University of Chicago Press.

Clark, R. (1983). Reconsidering research on learning from media. *Review of Educational Research, 53*(4), 445–459.

Clement, J. (1983). A conceptual model discussed by Galileo and used intuitively by physics students. In D. Genter & A. Stevens (Eds.) *Mental models.* Hillsdale, NJ: Erlbaum.

Charney, D. (1987). Comprehending non-linear text: The role of discourse cues and reading strategies. In *Hypertext '87 Proceedings,* pp. 109–120.

Chi, M.T., Feltovich, P.J., & Glaser, R. (1981). Categorization and representation of physics problems by experts and novices. *Cognitive Science, 5,* 121–152.

Conklin, J. (1987). Hypertext: An introduction and survey. *IEEE Computer, 20*(9), 17–41.

Cognition and Technology Group at Vanderbilt, The (1990). Anchored instruction and its relationship to situated cognition. *Educational Researcher, 19*(6), 2–10.

Covey, P. (1990). *A right to die?: The case of Dax Cowart.* Presentation made at the Annual Conference of the American Educational Research Association, Boston, MA.

Crane, G. (1990). Challenging the individual: The tradition of hypermedia databases. *Academic Computing, 6*(11), 36–41.

di Sessa, A. (1982). Unlearning Aristotelian physics: A study of knowledge-based learning. *Cognitive Science, 6,* 37–75.

di Sessa, A. (1988). Knowledge in pieces. In G. Forman & P. Pufall (Eds.), *Constructivisim in the computer age.* Hillsdale, NJ: Erlbaum.

Dickson, W.P. (1985). Thought-provoking software: Juxtaposing symbol systems. *Educational Researcher, 14*(5), 30–38.

Egan, D.E., Remde, J.R., Landauer, T.K., Lochbaum, C.C., & Gomez, L.M. (1989). *Acquiring information in books and SuperBooks.* Paper presented at the Annual Meeting of the American Educational Research Association, San Francisco.

Ericsson, K., & Simon, H. (1984). *Protocol analysis: Verbal reports as data.* Cambridge, MA: MIT Press.

Gay, G., Trumbull, D., & Mazur, J. (in press). Designing and testing navigational strategies and guidance tools for a hypermedia program. *Journal of Educational Computing Research.*

Gibbons, J., Anderson, D.R., Smith, R., Field, D.E., & Rischer, C. (1986). Young children's recall and reconstruction of audio and audiovisual narratives. *Child Development*, *57*, 1014–1023.

Goodman, N. (1976). *Languages of art*. Indianapolis, IN: Bobbs-Merrill.

Greeno, J. (1989). Situations, mental models, and generative knowledge. In D. Khahr & K. Kotovsky (Eds.) *Complex information processing*. Hillsdale, NJ: Erlbaum.

Haas, C. (1989). "Seeing it on the screen isn't really seeing it": Computer writers' reading problems. In G. Hawisher & C. Selfe (Eds.), *Critical perspectives on computers and composition instruction*. New York: Teachers College Press.

Halliday, M.A., & Hasan, R. (1976). *Cohesion in English*. London: Longman.

Hayes, D.S., & Kelly, S.B. (1984). Young children's processing of television: Modality differences in the retention of temporal relations. *Journal of Experimental Child Psychology*, *38*, 505–514.

Hayes, D.S., Kelly, S.B., & Mandel M. (1986). Media differences in children's story synopses: Radio and television contrasted. *Journal of Educational Psychology*, *78*(5), 341–346.

Hegarty, M., & Just, M.A. (1989). Understanding machines from text and diagrams. In H. Mandl & J. Levin (Eds.), *Knowledge acquisition from text and pictures*. Amsterdam: North-Holland.

Hegarty, M., Just, M.A., & Morrison, I.R. (1988). Mental models of mechanical systems: Individual differences in qualitative and quantitative reasoning. *Cognitive Psychology*, *20*, 191–236.

Holland, J., Holyoak, K., Nisbett, R., & Thagard, P. (1986). *Induction: Processes of inference, learning, and discovery*. Cambridge, MA: MIT Press.

Huston, A., & Wright, J. (1983). Children's processing of television: The informative functions of formal features. In J. Bryant & D.R. Anderson (Eds.) *Children's understanding of television*. New York: Academic Press.

Just, M.A., & Carpenter, P.A. (1987). *The psychology of reading and language comprehension*. Newton, MA: Allyn & Bacon.

Kintsch, W. (1988). The role of knowledge in discourse comprehension: A construction-integration model. *Psychological Review*, *95*(2), 163–82.

Kintsch, W. (1989). Learning from text. In L.B. Resnick (Ed.), *Knowing and learning: Essays in honor of Robert Glaser*. Hillsdale, NJ: Erlbaum.

Kintsch, W., & van Dijk, T. (1978). Toward a model of text comprehension and production. *Psychological Review*, *85*(5), 363–394.

Kozma, R.B. (1989). *Principles underlying learning tool*. Paper presented at the Annual Meeting of the American Educational Research Association, San Francisco.

Kozma, R.B., & Van Roekel, J. (1986). *Learning tool*. Ann Arbor, MI: Arborworks.

Krendl, K.A., & Watkins, B. (1983). Understanding television: An exploratory inquiry into the reconstruction of narrative content. *Educational Communications and Technology Journal*, *31*(4), 201–212.

Kuntz, G.C., Drewniak, U., & Schott, F. (1989). *On-line and off-line assessment of self-regulation in learning from instructional text and picture*. Paper presented at the Annual Meeting of the American Educational Research Association, San Francisco.

LaBerge, D., & Samuels, S.J. (1974). Toward a theory of automatic information processing in reading. *Cognitive Psychology, 6,* 293–323.

Landow, G.P. (1989). Course assignments using hypertext: The example of Intermedia. *Journal of Research on Computing in Education, 21*(3), 349–365.

Larkin, J.H. (1983). The role of problem representation in physics. In D. Genter & A. Stevens (Eds.), *Mental models.* Hillsdale, NJ: Erlbaum.

Larkin, J.H. (1989). Display-based problem solving. In D. Khahr & K. Kotovsky (Eds.), *Complex information processing.* Hillsdale, NJ: Erlbaum.

Larkin, J.H., McDermott, J., Simon, D., & Simon, H. (1980). Expert and novice performance in solving physics problems. *Science, 80*(4450), 1335–1342.

Larkin, J.H., & Simon, H. (1987). Why a diagram is (sometimes) worth ten thousand words. *Cognitive Science, 11,* 65–100.

Levie, W., & Lentz, R. (1982). Effects of text illustrations: A review of research. *Educational Communications and Technology Journal, 30* (4), 195–232.

Marchionini, G. (1989). *Information seeking in electronic encyclopedias.* Paper presented at the Annual Meeting of the American Educational Research Association, San Francisco.

Marchionini, G., & Schneiderman, B. (1988). Finding facts vs. browsing knowledge in hypertext systems. *IEEE Computer, 21*(1), 70–80.

Mayer, R. (1984). Aids to prose comprehension. *Educational Psychologist, 19,* 30–42.

McCloskey, M. (1983). Naive theories of motion. In D. Genter & A. Stevens (Eds.), *Mental models.* Hillsdale, NJ: Erlbaum.

Meringoff, L. (1982). *What pictures can and can't do for children's story understanding.* Paper presented at the Annual Meeting of the American Educational Research Association, New York.

Meyer, B.J.F. (1975). *The organization of prose and its effects on memory.* Amsterdam: North-Holland.

Meyer, B.J.F. (1985). Signaling the structure of text. In D. Jonassen (Ed.), *The technology of text.* Englewood Cliffs, NJ: Educational Technology Publications.

Miller, G.A. (1956). The magical number seven plus or minus two: Some limits of our capacity for processing information. *Psychological Review, 63,* 81–97.

Minsky, M.A. (1975). A framework for representing knowledge. In P.H. Winston (Ed.), *The psychology of computer vision.* New York: McGraw-Hill.

Mokros, J., & Tinker, R. (1987). The impact of microcomputer-based labs on children's ability to interpret graphs. *Journal of Research in Science Teaching, 24*(4), 369–383.

Nelson, T. (1987/1974). *Computer lib.* Redmond, WA: Tempus Books.

Nugent, G.C. (1982). Pictures, audio, and print: Symbolic representation and effect on learning. *Educational Communications and Technology Journal, 30*(3), 163–174.

Perkins, D.N. (1985). The fingertip effect: How information-processing technology shapes thinking. *Educational Researcher, 14*(7), 11–17.

Pezdek, K., & Hartman, E.F. (1983). Children's television viewing: Attention and comprehension of auditory versus visual information. *Child Development, 54,* 1015–1023.

Pezdek, K., Lehrer, A., & Simon, S. (1984). The relationship between reading and cognitive processing of television and radio. *Child Development, 55,* 2072–2082.

Pezdek, K., & Stevens, E. (1984). Children's memory for auditory and visual information on television. *Developmental Psychology, 20,* 212–218.

Pressley, M. (1977). Imagery and children's learning: Putting the pictures in developmental perspective. *Review of Educational Research, 47*(4), 585–622.

Resnick, L. (1988). Learning in school and out. *Educational Researcher, 16*(9), 13–20.

Roschelle, J., & Pea, R. (1990). *Situated learning: Computer-based multimedia analysis of learning activities.* Paper presented at the Annual Conference of the American Educational Research Association, Boston.

Rusted, R., & Coltheart, V. (1979). The effect of pictures on the retention of novel words and prose passages. *Journal of Experimental Child Psychology, 28,* 516–524.

Salomon, G. (1974). What is learned and how it is taught: The interaction between media, message, task, and learner. In D. Olson (Ed.), *Media and symbols: The forms of expression, communication, and education.* Chicago: University of Chicago Press.

Salomon, G. (1979). *Interaction of media, cognition, and learning.* San Francisco: Jossey-Bass.

Salomon, G. (1983). The differential investment of mental effort in learning from different sources. *Educational Psychologist, 18*(1), 42–50.

Salomon, G. (1984). Television is "easy" and print is "tough"; The differential investment of mental effort in learning as a function of perceptions and attributions. *Journal of Educational Psychology, 76*(4), 647–658.

Salomon, G. (1988). AI in reverse: Computer tools that turn cognitive. *Journal of Educational Computing Research, 4*(2), 123–134.

Salomon, G., & Clark, R. (1977). Reexamining the methdology of research on media and technology in education. *Review of Educational Research, 47*(1), 99–120.

Schallert, D.L. (1980). The role of illustrations in reading. In R. Spiro, B. Bruce, & W. Brewer (Eds.), *Theoretical issues in reading comprehension.* Hillsdale, NJ: Erlbaum.

Schank, R.C., & Abelson, R.P. (1977). *Scripts, plans, goals, and understanding.* Hillsdale, NJ: Erlbaum.

Shebilske, W.L., & Fisher, D.F. (1983). Eye movements and context effects during reading of extended discourse. In K. Rayner (Ed.), *Eye movements in reading.* New York: Academic Press.

Shebilske, W.L., & Reid, L.S. (1979). Reading eye movements, macro-structure and comprehension. In P.A. Kolers, M.E. Wrolstad, & H. Bouma (Eds.), *Processing of visible language* (Vol. 1). New York: Plenum.

Sherwood, R., Kinzer, C., Bransford, J., & Franks, J. (1987). Some benefits of creating macro-contexts for science instruction: Initial findings. *Journal of Research in Science Teaching, 24*(5), 417–435.

Sherwood, R., Kinzer, C., Hasselbring, T., & Bransford, J. (1987). Macro-contexts for learning: Initial findings and issues. *Applied Cognitive Psychology, 1,* 93–108.

Simon, H.A. (1974). How big is a chunk? *Science, 183,* 482–88.

Snow, R. (1989). Aptitude-treatment interaction as a framework for reseearch on individual differences in learning. In P. Ackerman, R. Sternberg, & R. Glaser (Eds.), *Learning and individual differences.* New York: Freeman.

Stevens, S. (1989). Intelligent interactive video simulation of a code inspection. *Communications of the ACM, 32*(7), 832–43.

Stone, D., & Glock, M. (1981). How do young adults read directions with and without pictures? *Journal of Educational Psychology, 73*(3), 419–426.

Vygotsky, L.S. (1978). *Mind in society.* Cambridge, MA: Harvard University Press.

White, B. (1984). Designing computer games to help physics students understand Newton's laws of motion. *Cognition and Instruction, 1*(1), 69–108.

White, B. (1989). *A microworld-based approach to science education* (Technical Report). Newton, MA: Bolt Beranek & Newman.

White, B., & Frederiksen, J. (1987). *Causal model progressions as a foundation for intelligent learning environments.* (Technical Report). Newton, MA: Bolt Beranek & Newman.

Williams, M.D., Hollan, J.D., & Stevens, A.L. (1983). Human reasoning about a simple physical system. In D. Genter & A. Stevens (Eds.), *Mental models.* Hillsdale, NJ: Erlbaum.

Wilson, K. (1990). The "Palenque" Project: Formative evaluation in the design and development of an optical disc prototype. In B. Flagg (Ed.), *Formative evaluation for educational technologies.* Hillsdale, NJ: Erlbaum.

Winn, W. (1989). The design and use of instructional graphics In H. Mandl & J. Levin (Eds.), *Knowledge acquisition from text and pictures.* Amsterdam: North-Holland.

Wixson, K. (1984). Level of importance of postquestions and children's learning from text. *American Educational Research Jounral, 21*(2), 419–433.

Wright, J.C., Huston, A.C., Ross, R.P., Calvert, S.L., Tolandelli, D., Weeks, L.A., Raeissi, P., & Potts, R. (1984). Pace and continuity of television programs: Effects on children's attention and comprehension. *Developmental Psychology, 20*(4), 653–666.

CHAPTER 9

KOZMA REFRAMES AND EXTENDS HIS COUNTER ARGUMENT

Robert B. Kozma

Originally published as: Kozma, R.B. (1994). Will media influence learning? Reframing the debate. *Educational Technology Research and Development, 42*(2), 7–19. Reprinted by permission of the Publisher, the Association for Educational Communications and Technology and the author.

Do media influence learning? Ten years ago, Richard Clark (1983) reviewed the results of comparative research on educational media and claimed that they provide consistent evidence "…for the generalization that there are no learning benefits to be gained from employing any specific medium to deliver instruction" (p. 445). According to Clark, the results of those studies that appear to favor one medium over another are due not to the medium but to the method or content that are introduced along with the medium. Clark concludes that "…media do not influence learning under any conditions" (p. 445). Rather, "…media are mere vehicles that deliver instruction but do not influence student achievement any more than the truck that delivers our groceries causes changes in our nutrition" (p. 445).

It is time to revisit this question. Or perhaps, it is time to reframe it. Perhaps the appropriate question is not *do* but *will* media influence learning. Educational technology is a design science (Glaser, 1976; Simon, 1981), not a natural science. The phenomena that we study are the products of our own conceptions and devices. If there is no relationship between media and learning it may be because we have not yet *made* one. If we do not understand the potential relationship between media and learning, quite likely one will not be made. And finally, if we preclude consideration of a relationship in our theory and research by conceptualizing media as "mere vehicles," we are likely to never understand the potential for such a relationship.

There is a certain urgency about this question and a reason to revisit it now. In the not-too-distant future, we will be faced with a situation where telephone, cable television, and digital computer technologies will merge (Information Infrastructure Task Force, 1993; Stix, 1993). This capability presents the prospect of interactive video integrated with access to large multimedia data bases distributed among people in offices, classrooms, and living rooms all over the world. If by then we have not come to understand the relationship between media and learning—if we have not *forged* a relationship between media and learning—this capability may be used primarily for interactive soap operas and on-line purchasing of merchandise with automatic funds transfer. Its educational uses may be driven primarily by benevolent movie moguls who design "edutainment" virtual reality adventure games and the contribution of educational technologists will be minimal. Once again, we may find ourselves on the sidelines of our own game (Reigeluth, 1989).

In order to establish a relationship between media and learning we must first understand why we have failed to establish one so far. In large part, the source of this failure is due to the fact that our theories, research, and designs have been constrained by vestiges of the behavioral roots from which our discipline sprang (Richey, 1992; Winn, 1989, 1990). Embedded in the instructional presentations and criterion-referenced tests of our instructional designs (Dick & Carey, 1990) and embedded in the comparative media studies included in Clark's (1983) review are the primal stimuli and responses of the behavioral paradigm. Media "stimuli" are classified and differentiated based on surface features of their technologies and their effect on learning is compared using "responses" on a test. Missing in these studies are any mentalist notions or descriptions of the cognitive, affective, or social processes by which learning occurs. Also missing are descriptions of the underlying structure and functions of media which might serve as the causal mechanisms—or "first principles," to use Winn's (1989) term—that influence these processes. The theoretical frame of reference implicit in these studies—that of presentation and response—is aptly characterized by Clark's delivery truck metaphor: The medium is an inert conveyer of an active stimulus to which the learner makes a behavioral response.

However, as we have come to understand, learning is not the receptive response to instruction's "delivery." Rather, learning is an active, constructive, cognitive and social process by which the learner strategically manages available cognitive, physical, and social resources to create new knowledge by interacting with information in the environment and integrating it with information already stored in memory (Shuell, 1988). From this perspective, knowledge and learning are neither solely a property of the individual or of the environment. Rather, they are the reciprocal interaction between the learner's cognitive resources and aspects of the external environment (Greeno, 1988; Pea, 1993; Perkins, 1993; Salomon, 1993) and this interaction is strongly influenced by the extent to which internal and external resources fit together (Snow, 1992).

Consequently, we will understand the potential for a relationship between media and learning when we consider it as an interaction between cognitive processes and characteristics of the environment, so mediated (Salomon, 1993; Salomon, Perkins, & Globerson, 1991). Specifically, to understand the role of media in learning we must ground a theory of media in the cognitive and social processes by which knowledge is constructed, we must define media in ways that are compatible and complementary with these processes, we must conduct research on the mechanisms by which characteristics of media might interact with and influence these processes, and we must design our interventions in ways that embed media in these processes.

In this paper, I use the interaction between information and processes in the mind and those in the environment as a framework to examine the potential relationship between learning and media. I analyze the results of two significant and effective instructional environments to identify causal mechanisms by which media may have influenced learning. And I discuss the implications of this approach for a theory of, research on, and practice with educational media.

SUCCESSFUL INTERACTIONS IN TWO ENVIRONMENTS

ThinkerTools

Students' understanding of Newtonian mechanics is very different from that of experts. Expert physicists examine problem situations and see patterns based on underlying structure (Chi, Feltovich, & Glaser, 1981; Larkin, 1983). The mental models that they build of these situations include entities that correspond to the physical objects encountered in the problem situation, as well as entities that correspond to the formal constructs of physics that have no direct, concrete referent in the real world (e.g., force vectors). The relationships among these entities correspond to the laws of physics. Experts reason qualitatively with these models to construct and test problem solutions.

On the other hand, the mental models built by novices are composed primarily of entities that correspond to the familiar, visible objects mentioned in the problem statement (e.g., blocks, pulleys, inclined planes, etc.). They do not contain entities that represent formal physical constructs or relationships. Thus, the models that novices form are insufficient to determine a solution to the problem.

White (1984, 1993) developed a computer-based learning environment, called *ThinkerTools*, to address learning difficulties that students have in Newtonian mechanics. The curriculum for this microworld consists of four modules that present progressively sophisticated models of force and motion. Each module incorporates four phases: a motivation phase, a model evolution phase, a formalization phase, and a transfer phase.

In the motivation phase, the teacher describes real world situations involving forces acting upon objects, and students are asked to predict the outcome. The various outcomes are listed on the board without evaluative comment. Motivation is drawn from the conflict among the statements and from the learners' need to master their environment.

In the model evolution phase, students work in pairs to solve problems of the sort presented during the motivation phase and perform experiments using the microworld. On the screen of the computer students see two coordinated representational forms. In one, students are given a dot and a target and asked to "impart a force" on the dot so that it will hit the target at a specified speed. They do this with their joy stick by moving the stick right, left, up, or down to indicate the direction of the force. The second representation is a "data cross" that shows the amount of force imparted as decomposed force vectors, such that an arm of the cross (right, left, up, down) darkens one "unit" for each movement of the joy stick in the corresponding direction (i.e., one movement right and two movements up would darken the right arm of the cross one unit and the up arm two units). Correspondingly, an arrow appears next to the dot pointing in the vectoral direction of the forces; a "flame" emanates from the back of the arrow and a "swooshing" sound is made. The dot moves accordingly and behind it a series of small dots, called a "wake," appear at regular time intervals, spaced so that the faster the object moves the farther apart the dots appear. While conducting these exercises, students are asked to write down what happens.

These model evolution exercises are structured across modules so that the problems and activities become increasingly sophisticated. For example, in the first module students work only with motion in the horizontal (i.e., right and left) directions. In the second module, one student controls the horizontal force and the other student controls the vertical. Together they explore the combined vectoral forces in all four directions to maneuver the dot around a more complicated route to the target. The final model of force and motion includes motion in all directions, continuous motion, and representations of friction and gravity.

During the formalization phase, students must come up with a "law" that describes the behavior of the microworld. With early modules, students are given alternative laws and they must select the ones that best describe their experience. Students work together in small groups (three to five students) with the computer to test the different "laws" and decide which ones are supported by their results. The groups present their decisions to the class and these are debated. In subsequent modules, students must work together to invent their own laws and experiments. Thus, while the models become increasingly difficult, the students also receive less guidance.

During the transfer phase, students apply the laws that they have formulated to answer the predictive questions raised during the motivation phase. This is done by conducting experiments on the computer and with real world objects in the classroom to test the limits and qualifications of their laws.

This environment was used with 42 sixth-grade students for their 45 minute science class every day for two months (White, 1993). They were compared to 37 sixth graders in the same school who received the standard science curriculum (a unit on inventions) taught by the same teacher. They were also compared to two groups of 11th and 12th grade high school students in the same school system. One group had just completed 2-1/2 months studying Newtonian mechanics using a commercial textbook and traditional teaching methods; the second group of high school students was at the very beginning of their physics course. All of these students were given tests that required them to predict the outcomes of real world force situations. Both the students who used *ThinkerTools* and the high school students that studied mechanics performed significantly better on the tests than their respective control groups. However, the students using *ThinkerTools* both demonstrated significantly greater improvement and scored significantly higher than the high school students who were on the average six years older, had selected themselves into physics, and had been taught about force and motion using traditional methods.

The Jasper Woodbury Series

In schools, students frequently have difficulty drawing on the knowledge that they have of situations in the real world (Resnick, 1987). Conversely, the knowledge of solution strategies that they acquire in school is frequently stored in ways that are not evoked by problem situations that they encounter outside of school. This severely limits the transferability and utility of school-learned knowledge, what is sometimes called the "inert knowledge problem" (Whitehead, 1929).

The Cognition and Technology Group at Vanderbilt University has developed a set of videodisk-based problem situations in mathematics, called the *Jasper Woodbury Series* (Van Haneghan, Barron, Young, Williams, Vye, & Bransford, 1992; Cognition and Technology Group at Vanderbilt, 1992), that addresses this problem. The set provides teachers and middle school students with real-world contexts for learning complex mathematics problem solving. The videodisk is used to provide rich stories which embed both problems to be solved and data which can be used in the solutions. For example, in one story, the principal character, Jasper Woodbury, takes a river trip to examine a used boat, which he decides to buy. The problem, very briefly stated, is that because the running lights do not work, Jasper must determine if he can return to his home dock before sunset. The students are left to solve this problem. There are several major questions that are embedded in Jasper's decision: Does he have enough time to return home before sunset, and is there enough fuel in the boat's gas tank for the return trip? If there is not enough fuel, does Jasper have enough money to buy the necessary gas?

In the classroom, students work in groups with the teacher's guidance to determine the solution. The teacher encourages students to generate subordinate questions and identify relevant information needed to solve these problems. Students review segments of the video to search for information and separate relevant from irrelevant facts. They use the facts to solve the subordinate problems and then relate these solutions to the overall problem.

Students viewing the episode and receiving this instruction were compared to a control group (Van Hanenghan et al., 1992). This second group of students also viewed the boat episode. However, instead of receiving guidance in solving problems as they related to the problem context, they received instruction and practice in solving problems of the sort that Jasper would have to solve (distance, elapsed time, fuel consumption rate, etc.) but structured as word problems without specific reference to the Jasper story that they saw. In addition, they studied Polya's (1957) general model of strategies used to analyze and solve problems. Students were encouraged to use it to solve their word problems.

So, the difference between the two treatments was this: while both groups viewed problem contexts (i.e., the video story) and studied problem solving skills only the first group explicitly integrated problem solving and context. Students in this group scored significantly higher from pre- to posttest on questions related to the boat episode; the control group did not. In addition, the experimental group scored as well as the control group on a set of word problems like those that the control group received during practice sessions. Finally, the experimental group scored significantly higher than the control on a different, video-based story problem. The experimental group scored a mean of 58 percent on this transfer task, with several of these students scoring between 75–100 percent. The maximum control group score was 51 percent; their mean was 29 percent. Of particular significance was the sort of errors that students in the control group made. Some of these students mixed units (e.g., added hours and miles) or confused rates (e.g., minutes per mile and miles per minute) that indicated a lack of meaningfulness in the solution procedures they were attempting. Of those students who gave the correct answers to mathematical problems, few went on to show how these answers solved the overall problem. That is, while some students in the control group were able to acquire certain solution procedures they were unable to apply these to solve real world-like problems.

THE ROLE OF MEDIA

What contribution did media make to the learning documented above? To understand this, we must think about media not in terms of their surface features but in terms of their underlying structure and the causal mechanisms by which they might interact with cognitive and social processes. Media can be analyzed in terms of their cognitively relevant capabilities or attributes (Salomon, 1978). These include a medium's technology, symbol systems, and processing capabilities (Kozma, 1991). "Technology" is the physical, mechanical, or electronic capabilities of a medium that determine its function and, to some extent, its shape and other features.[1] These are the surface characteristics of media that we typically use to classify something as a "television," a "radio," and so on, in everyday language. From a theoretical perspective, however, the primary effect of a medium's technology is to enable and constrain the other two capabilities and these are the aspects of media that have more direct implications for cognitive processes. "Symbol systems" are sets of symbolic expressions by which information is communicated about a field of reference (Goodman, 1976). Examples of symbol systems include spoken language, printed text, pictures, numerals and formulae, musical scores, performed music, maps, graphs, and so on. "Processing capabilities" are the ability of a medium to operate on available symbol systems in specified ways. In general, information can be displayed, received, stored, retrieved, organized, translated, transformed, and evaluated among other processes.

Each medium can be defined and distinguished from others by a profile of these capabilities. Using this profile, a particular medium can be described in terms of its capability to present certain representations and perform certain operations in interaction with learners who are similarly engaged in internally constructing representations and operating on these. From an interactionist perspective, learning with media can be thought of as a complementary process within which representations are constructed and procedures performed, sometimes by the learner and sometimes by the medium (Kozma, 1991).

How did the capabilities of computers facilitate the learning that occurred in the *ThinkerTools* project (White, 1993)? First, the capability that computers have to present dynamic symbolic elements was used to create the representations of "objects in motion." This capability is very salient to a task domain for which motion is obviously important. It is also salient to novice students whose prior knowledge is either insufficient to create mental models of Newtonian motion or inaccurate such that the trajectories that they supply are contrary to scientific principles. Second, the capability of the computer to take input from the students and proceduralize these data was used to move the symbolic objects according to the laws of mechanics. That is, students could use the joy stick to "act" on these graphic objects in ways that corresponded to "force." Allowing students to manipulate "force" externally and examine the Newtonian effect on motion, as experts do internally with their mental models, quite likely made a significant contribution to the learning achieved in the White study.

What contribution did videodisk make to learning in the *Jasper* project (Van Hanenghan et al., 1992; Cognition and Technology Group at Vanderbilt, 1992)? Firstly, the capability of video to present complex, dynamic social contexts and events helped students construct rich, dynamic mental models of these situations. The detailed, dynamic nature of these mental models allows students to draw more inferences than they can from mental models constructed from text or even still pictures (Bransford, Sharp, Vye, Goldman, Hasselbring, Goin, O'Banion, Livernois, Saul, and the Cognition and Technology Group at Vanderbilt University, 1992). These structures are also more memorable than those constructed with text (Baggett, 1989). Had text been used instead of video, the construction of these mental models would rely less on information in the text and more on information in students' heads (Beagles-Roos & Gat, 1983; Meringoff, 1982), information that is likely to be incomplete or inaccurate for those with little prior knowledge.[2] Text also places more demands on reading ability for those who have not yet automated these skills. With these demands pre-empted by the video, the students can use their cognitive resources to learn the target problem solving strategies.

Secondly, the video contains a great deal of detail and information, information crucial to the solution of the problem. During the story, information about distances, available money, and other relevant conditions are embedded in objects and maps, and in what people say, do, and think, as this is acted out in the story. The random access capabilities of videodisk allow students to use a remote control device to pause, review, and search for information that they may have otherwise missed or forgotten. Identifying needed information and disembedding it from a context is an important component of learning to solve problems and this ability contributes to successful transfer and performance in subsequent real world situations.

Finally and most importantly, the visual and social nature of the story, as presented with video, is more likely to activate relevant situation-based prior knowledge so that students can use this to solve the problem. They are also more likely to connect their new learning to representations of situations as it is stored in memory. This will increase the likelihood that subsequently encountered similar problem situations will evoke the appropriate solution procedure. By repeating the same kinds of analyses and solutions in multiple contexts or situations with very different surface characteristics but common underlying task demands, these learned solution strategies are connected to a variety of situation schemas in memory and this promotes transfer across a variety of subsequently encountered problem situations (Spiro & Jehng, 1990). Application of the *Jasper Series* in the regular classroom involves several different video-based stories beyond the single one used in the study above. This should increase the likelihood that the strategies are recalled and applied in a wide variety of problem situations in the real world.

In summary, the learners in the *ThinkerTools* project benefited from the use of computers because the capabilities of this medium were employed to provide representations and perform or model operations that were salient to the task and that the learners had difficulty providing for themselves. Learners in the *Jasper* project benefited from the use of television because the capability of the medium was used to present problems embedded in complex social contexts that allowed students to connect their knowledge of solution procedures to real world-like problem situations. It is certainly the case that on occasion some learners, perhaps most, can and do supply useful representations and operations for themselves from the information that is available in the environment, regardless of the medium used. However, when learners have difficulty providing representations and operations that are sufficient for learning, either because of limited prior knowledge, limitations in working memory, or other reasons, they will likely benefit from the use of the capability of a particular medium to provide or model these representations and operations. Over time, these representations and operations become internalized such that students can generate for themselves what was generated for them by the medium (Salomon, 1993).

IMPLICATIONS FOR THEORY

How does the analysis above contribute to a theory of learning with media? Clark would say it does not. Attributing media effects to their capabilities or attributes invokes Clark's (1983) criticism of the media attribute approach. Clark does not consider attributes to be variables in media theory because they are neither necessary or unique to a particular medium. Attributes, according to Clark (1983), "...[are] not exclusive to any specific medium..." (p. 451) and "...many different media could present a given attribute so there [is] no necessary correspondence between attributes and media" (p. 452). To illustrate Clark's point, you could use dynamic pictures with either television, film, or a computer-generated animation and, therefore, this symbolic attribute is not exclusive or unique to television. Conversely, you can have a medium, such as television, without its associated attributes, such as dynamic pictures (e.g., one could show a still picture or static text on the screen), and therefore the attribute is not necessary for the medium.

However, a distinction must be made between attribute as a capability of a medium and the variability of its use. In the development of theory, Dubin (1969) defines an "attribute" as the property of a thing distinguished by the quality of being present, while a "variable" is the property of a thing that may be present in degree (p. 35). The *attributes* of a medium are its *capabilities*; the capabilities of a medium are always present. It is a necessary, defining attribute of television that it is capable of employing dynamic pictorial symbol systems, even if this capability is unused, and it is not at all a capability of radio. A medium is distinctive to the extent that its defining cluster of attributes is unique, that is, different from the defining clusters of other media. This has two implications for the focus of our theories: We must specify the causal mechanisms by which cognitive and social processes are influenced as students interact with a medium's defining capabilities (i.e., attributes). And we must specify the appropriate uses of these capabilities (i.e., variables), that is, the ways in which these capabilities may be used to influence the learning for particular students, tasks, and situations.

The use of dynamic visual symbol systems is a capability of video that distinguishes it from text and radio. Understanding how learners interact with video-based presentations and how this differs from the processing of text-based or audio-linguistic information is an important component of media theory and is crucial to understanding how media can influence learning. Both video and computers share the capability of displaying dynamic pictures but they are distinguished by the fact that the processing capability of computers can be used to move these pictures based on rules evoked by the decisions and actions of the users. Understanding the ways in which students use the unique processing capabilities of the computer is essential to understanding the influence the computer may have on learning and to building media theory. The other half of media theory is understanding when and how to employ these symbolic and processing capabilities so that cognitive and social processes, so influenced, result in learning for certain students, tasks, and situations.

However, Clark contends that even if such attributes are considered to be *media* attributes and even if research shows these attributes are associated with learning, they do not play a role in instructional theory unless the relationship between them is a *necessary* one. Clark contends that "...theories seek necessary conditions" (1983, p. 452) and such necessary conditions are "...the foundation of all instructional theories" (p. 453). On the other hand, Clark states that attributes are "...occasionally sufficient but not necessary contributors to learning" (p. 452) and therefore they "...may contribute to instructional design but not to theory development" (p. 451).

While Clark insists that instructional theory depends on necessary rather than sufficient conditions, Cohen and Nagel (1934) point out that the scientists concerned with necessary conditions are those interested in eliminating something undesirable, such as disease (p. 323). On the other hand, scientists interested in the production of something desirable, such as learning, are concerned with establishing conditions that are *sufficient* to bring it about (p. 323). Necessary conditions are those in whose absence an event cannot occur, while sufficient conditions are those in whose presence an event must occur (p. 322). It is of use to know those conditions without which learning will not occur. But for a design science, it is more important that instructional theories be based on those conditions under which learning *will* occur.

Given that learning fails to occur so frequently in our schools and work places, we must look for sufficient conditions in our theories, research, and designs. However, in constructing theories the sufficiency of conditions must be considered probabilisticly, rather than deterministicly as implied by Cohen and Nagel (1934). In the real world, as contrasted with the experimental laboratory, events are the outcomes of complex causal configurations which act conjointly. Causes which may be sufficient for learning in one situation may result in different net effects or may be canceled out as they are joined by other causes in different situations, even though the same causal mechanisms are at work in each (House, 1991). Consequently, our media theories and research must reflect both the capabilities of media and the complexities of the social situations within which they are used.

IMPLICATIONS FOR RESEARCH

The foundational assumptions and goals that guide educational research are shifting from a view of the world as a set of law-like relationships between observable causes and effects that act uniformly across similar situations to a world of interacting causes that join together to produce events (House, 1991). Within this paradigm, the goals of research are to isolate, as much as possible, the causal entities and structures that produce events and to describe, as much as possible, the complex interactions of these events in particular social situations. Rather than causes and effects, then, we are looking for causal mechanisms, which are the underlying processes that produce events. And rather than general laws we are looking for sufficient tendencies, which are the net effects of these mechanisms as they operate in complex social situations. Consequently, the goal of research for applied or design scientists is to identify the particular causal elements that "tip the balance" (to use House's term) and produce desired events within specific situations.

The goals of specifying mechanisms and describing interactions roughly correspond to the analytic and systemic approaches to educational research described by Salomon (1991) and issues of internal and external validity raised by Ross and Morrison (1989). The goal of the analytic approach is to manipulate and control situations so as to increase internal validity and isolate specific causal mechanisms and processes. In the past, this has typically been done by conducting experimental studies (of the sort reviewed by Clark) in which an independent variable is isolated by the experimental design and its effect on a dependent variable is measured. This approach has resulted in limited understanding of the phenomena, primarily because the "cause" and the "effect" were examined but rarely the "causal mechanism." This is similar to examining the effect of a tornado descending on a town by taking photographs before and after the event. These photographs allow us to observe the extent of the damage but not the process by which the damage was wrought. To understand this process we would need to make fine-grained, moment-by-moment observations.

The goals of the analytic approach would be furthered, then, by observations of the phenomenon throughout the period of change and by a high density of observations relative to the rate of change (Siegler & Crowley, 1991). These goals can also benefit from including "process" as well as "outcome" data in our observations. The use of think aloud protocols (Ericsson & Simon, 1993), eye fixations, and log files of events increases the amount of information that we have on the processes by which change occurs as learners interact with our interventions in certain ways. Methodologies that provide more direct access to causal mechanisms reduce the need for comparative experimental designs which are structured so that conclusions about mechanisms are drawn indirectly by inference.

The second approach discussed by Salomon (1991) is the systemic approach. This approach is based on the assumption that each event, component, or action in the classroom has the potential of affecting the classroom as a whole. These variables act on each other in interdependent ways. Changing one variable may have dramatic and perhaps unanticipated effects as it propagates through the complex web of relationships among variables in the system. The goal of this approach is to describe the patterns of relationships among a system of components and events as they interact and mutually define each other in real situations. Observing the interaction of these variables as it occurs in natural settings increases the external validity of research findings.

Salomon (1991) suggests the use of quantitative methods, such as Guttman's Smallest Space Analysis (Guttman, 1969), to statistically establish the interrelationship among variables such as use of the computer, teacher talk, social interaction among students, perceived self-efficacy, ability, effort, excitement, and achievement. The use of this statistical analysis over time can show the shifting interrelationships as an intervention is introduced into the classroom. Alternatively, ethnographic or naturalistic methods can be used to identify and analyze the "whys," "hows," and interrelationships of various instructional dimensions as they emerge in classroom activity (Neuman, 1989). Prolonged observation, interviews, and artifact analysis provide a richness of detail about the social processes within which cognition is embedded. Such details are often missing from quantitative data.

Salomon (1991) points out the complementarity between analytic and systemic approaches. They can be used together to identify causal mechanisms and then to observe how they interact in complex social situations. Related more specifically to media research, the analytic approach and process methodologies can be used to isolate particular media attributes and observe how learners' interactions with these influence learning processes. The systemic approach and quantitative or ethnographic methodologies can be used in classroom situations to examine how these media-related causal mechanisms interact with other mechanisms to influence learning conjointly. Brown (1992) describes how she uses a coordinated mix-and-match approach where large scale studies are complemented by in-depth analyses of a few individuals or groups of the children. This coordinated approach is used to specify the roles of teacher, students, curricula, and computer support within the classroom context.

White (1993) used a variety of research approaches in her *ThinkerTools* project. In addition to collecting achievement and transfer data, she made observations of group discussions in the classroom, examined students' notebooks, and interviewed students and asked them to think out loud while they solved problems.

But for the most part, these approaches are not yet commonly used. The extended research methods recommended here would generate additional information on the relationship between media and learning over the use of traditional methods alone. For example, future research on the *Jasper* project would benefit from the collection of data on how it is that groups of students decompose and solve problems and how it is that they use video to do this. How often do students generate questions and what kinds are they? Do they use the video to answer these questions? If they do not search the video, is the information that they generate recalled from a previous viewing or is it based on general, world knowledge? If they use information in the video what information is used and how do they search for it? How does this information, in turn, influence subsequent questions or the discourse among students? Research on this project would also benefit from controlled studies in which groups of students receive similar information embedded in text-based or video-based stories. How do students process these stories differently? How do they search them differently? What information do they remember from each and is it structured differently?

Answers to questions such as these provide both a list of elemental, media-related causal mechanisms and descriptions of how they interact differently with other mechanisms in a range of educational situations. This information informs both theory and practice much more than information from comparative studies that neither examine mechanisms or contextualize their findings.

IMPLICATIONS FOR PRACTICE

Clark (1983, 1985) would contend that the findings in the studies cited above confound medium with content or method and the learning achieved was due to these latter factors, not the medium used. Consequently, it is the selection of the method not the medium that is of practical importance for learning. Selection of media, Clark would say, deals only with the efficiency or expense of delivering these methods. He contends that "...when we begin to separate method from medium we may begin to explain more significant amounts of learning variance" (Clark, 1983, p. 449).

Quite certainly the posting of motivational questions, the progression of models, the formulation of "laws," the guidance of teachers, and the use of student groups all contributed to learning in the *ThinkerTools* project. And the use of socially rich contexts, the decomposition of problems, the particular strategies used to solve problems, the guidance of teachers, and the use of student groups all contributed to learning in the *Jasper* project. But the fact that other factors contribute to learning does not preempt a role for media.

Indeed, Clark's separation of media from method creates an unnecessary and undesirable schism between the two. Medium and method should have a more integral relationship (Kozma, 1991; Ross & Morrison, 1989; Winn, 1989). Both are part of the instructional design. In good designs, a medium's capabilities enable methods and the methods that are used take advantage of these capabilities. If media are going to influence learning, method *must* be confounded with medium. Media must be designed to give us powerful new methods, and our methods must take appropriate advantage of a medium's capabilities.

Learning resulted in the *ThinkerTools* project precisely because White (1984, 1993) used the computer's capabilities to create symbolic representations similar to the mental representations that experts create for themselves and she made these representations respond to students' manipulations much like mental representations behave when experts reason with them. In the *Jasper* project, video's capability to display dynamic pictures was used to present complex social situations that help students associate solution strategies with problem contexts.

The integration of media and method, in turn, with the educational context is also important (De Corte, 1993). The image of students working one-on-one with a computer in isolation from other students, or even a teacher, evokes memories of the teaching machine and the Skinner Box, a paradigm that has been rejected for good reason. Media will only make a significant contribution to learning in our schools if their application is designed into complex social and cultural environments of learning (Newman, Griffin, & Cole, 1989; Pea, 1992) and made widely accessible, especially to those students most at risk of school failure (Kozma & Croninger, 1992). And media will contribute to school reform only to the extent that these systems are designed around the constraints and tasks that confront teachers and classrooms (Cuban, 1986; Kerr, 1989).

Traditional models of instructional design do not address the complex interrelationships among media, method, and situation. In general, they are not compatible with constructivist, social models of learning, being as they are derived from behavioral models (Winn, 1989). Perhaps it is also time to reframe our notions of design along with our notions of media. Perhaps a more productive approach would be to view the design process is a dynamic, creative interaction—or conversation, to use Schön's term (1987)—between the designer, the situation, and the medium in which the design both shapes and is shaped by each of these factors. The capabilities of a medium constrain what it is designers can do, as do features of a situation. But these capabilities and features also enable designers; they provide the designer with resources and suggest things that might be done with them. Media capabilities have changed considerably since the time of the studies reviewed by Clark (1983); they will change even more in the near future. These developing capabilities may, in turn, change the ways in which designers interact with media and enable more powerful designs which emerge from this interaction. But this change will depend as much on the mind set of designers as on the capabilities of media. This requires a shift in perspective.

From an interactionist perspective, the "conversation" between designer, medium, and situation does not stop when the design is "finished." The result of the design process is not an inert, objective object. Rather, this object can be viewed as a rhetorical statement that the designer makes about desirable actions, beliefs, and values (Buchanan, 1989). In this way, the designed object is the first turn in a conversation between the designer and the intended users. The design itself does not emerge until the users interact with it—take their turn in the conversation. The emergent design will be influenced by the goals, beliefs, and knowledge of the users, as well as the intentions of the designer, as embedded in the designed object. The conversation will be different for different users and perhaps for subsequent uses by the same user. From this perspective, the task of the designer is to use the capabilities of the medium to create objects that generate interesting and effective "conversations"—ones that influence learning.

The emerging National Information Infrastructure (NII) will be an excellent test bed for our evolving theories, research methodologies, and instructional designs. The NII will combine telephone, video, and computer technologies into one seamless, interactive digital medium (Information Infrastructure Task Force, 1993; Stix, 1993). This network will connect homes, business, and schools. An understanding of the way that media capabilities, instructional methods, and cognitive processes interact in complex social situations will allow us to take advantage of these capabilities. The combined capabilities of these media, and the access to a range of social situations and processes that they bring, provide designers with powerful new tools that they can use to construct their designs.

With these capabilities, students in science classes can combine data on local water quality with self-generated video stories about the personal importance of their lake or stream and post these in a national or regional resource-base of text, video, and data. Data points can be aggregated across regions and analyzed to determine trends and the stories can be examined to build meaning and personal relevance out of these findings. In their social studies classes these students can study environmental legislation by observing congressional debates and sending email to their representatives. Or students from different locations can engage in voice-video debates to discuss the relative impact of water quality legislation, water diversion, or environment-related plant closings on the quality of water and on their quality of life.

How this new technology will be used is not yet clear. But enabled by its capabilities, liberated by new models of design, and informed by media theory and research, designers may find new ways to engage students in interactions within these technological environments, interactions that may tip the balance in favor of learning.

CONCLUSION

The field of educational technology is reexamining its foundational assumptions and questions (Duffy & Jonassen, 1992; Hlynka & Belland, 1991). This article is meant to contribute to that effort. I believe that if we move from "Do media influence learning?" to "In what ways can we use the capabilities of media to influence learning for particular students, tasks, and situations?" we will both advance the development of our field and contribute to the restructuring of schools and the improvement of education and training.

NOTES

1.   It is important to note that because technology changes over time, so too does the definition of a particular medium. For example, the advancing speed and capacity of CPUs have made it possible to employ pictures and other dynamic symbol systems with computers in a way that was not possible before the 1970s. Thus, the definition of computers has changed to include these symbol systems. Early studies of computer-based instruction (such as those reviewed by Clark, 1985) were actually studying a different, less capable medium than we are examining here.

2.   Quite likely, this is the reason why learning concepts that are dissonant with prior knowledge is so difficult with text (Dole, Niederhauser, & Hayes, 1991). With text, the information that students remember is their prior knowledge; often, they do not even perceive a dissonance between prior knowledge and information in the text, even when they are prompted to do so.

REFERENCES

Baggett, P. (1989). Understanding visual and verbal messages. In H. Mandl & J. Levin (Eds.), *Knowledge acquisition from text and pictures* (pp. 101–124). Amsterdam: Elsevier.

Beagles-Roos, J., & Gat, I. (1983). Specific impact of radio and television on children's story comprehension. *Journal of Educational Psychology, 75*(1), 128–137.

Bransford, J., Sharp, D., Vye, N., Goldman, S., Hasselbring, T., Goin, L, O'Banion, K., Livernois, J., Saul, E., and the Cognition and Technology Group at Vanderbilt (1992). *MOST environments for accelerating literacy development.* Presentation at the NATO Advanced Study Institute on Psychological and Educational Foundations of Technology-Based Learning Environments, Kolymbari, Crete.

Brown, A. (1992). Design experiments: Theoretical and methodological challenges in creating complex interventions in classroom settings. *Journal of the Learning Sciences, 2*(2), 141–178.

Buchanan, R. (1989). Declaration by design: Rhetoric, argument, and demonstration in design practice. In V. Margolin (Eds.), *Design discourse* (pp. 91–109).

Chi, M., Feltovich, P., & Glaser, R. (1981). Categorization and representation of physics problems by experts and novices. *Cognitive Science, 5,* 121–152.

Clark, R. (1985). Confounding in educational computing research. *Journal of Educational Computing Research, 1*(2), 137–148.

Clark, R.E. (1983). Reconsidering research on learning from media. *Review of Educational Research, 53*(4), 445–459.

Cognition and Technology Group at Vanderbilt (1992). An anchored instruction approach to cognitive skills acquisition and intelligent tutoring. In J.W. Regian & V. Shute (Eds.), *Cognitive approaches to automated instruction* (pp. 135–170). Hillsdale, NJ: Erlbaum.

Cohen, M., & Nagel, E. (1934). *An introduction to logic and scientific method.* New York: Harcourt Brace.

Cuban, L. (1986). *Teachers and machines.* New York: Teachers College Press.

Dick, W., & Carey, L. (1990). *The systematic design of instruction* (3rd ed.). Glenview, IL: Scott, Foresman and Co.

De Corte, E. (1993). *Psychological aspects of changes in learning supported by informatics.* Paper presented at the meeting on Informatics and Changes in Learning, Gmunden, Austria.

Dole, J., Niederhauser, D., & Hayes, M. (1991). *The role of reading in conceptual change in science.* Paper presented at the Annual Meeting of the American Educational Research Association, Chicago.

Dubin, R. (1969). *Theory building.* New York: Free Press.

Duffy, T., & Jonassen, D. (1992). *Constructivism and the technology of instruction: A conversation.* Hillsdale, NJ: Erlbaum.

Ericsson, K.A., & Simon, H. (1993). *Protocol analysis: Verbal reports as data* (2nd ed.). Cambridge, MA: MIT Press.

Glaser, R. (1976). Components of a psychology of instruction: Toward a science of design. *Review of Educational Research, 46*(1), 29–39.

Goodman, N. (1976). *Languages of art.* Indianapolis, IN: Hackett.

Greeno, J. (1988). Situations, mental models, and generative knowledge. In D. Klahr & K. Kotovsky (Eds.), *Complex information processing* (pp. 285–318). Hillsdale, NJ: Erlbaum.

Guttman, L. (1969). A general nonmetric technique for finding the smallest coordinate space for a configuration of points. *Psychometrics, 33,* 465–506.

Hlynka, D., & Belland, J. (1991). *Paradigms regained: The uses of illuminative, semiotic, and post-modern criticism as modes of inquiry in educational technology.* Englewood Cliffs, NJ: Educational Technology Publications.

House, E. (1991). Realism in research. *Educational Researcher, 20*(6), 2–9.

Information Infrastructure Task Force (1993). *The National Information Infrastructure: Agenda for action.* Washington, DC: U.S. Department of Commerce.

Kerr, S. (1989). Technology, teachers, and the search for school reform. *Educational Technology Research and Development, 37*(4), 5–18.

Kozma, R. (1991). Learning with media. *Review of Educational Research, 61*(2), 179–212.

Kozma, R., &. Croninger, R. (1992). Technology and the fate of at-risk students. *Education and Urban Society, 24*(4), 440–453.

Larkin, J. (1983). The role of problem representation in physics. In D. Gentner & A. Stevens (Eds.), *Mental models* (pp. 75–98). Hillsdale, NJ: Erlbaum.

Meringoff, L. (1982). *What pictures can and can't do for children's story understanding.* Paper presented at the Annual Meeting of the American Educational Research Association, New York.

Neuman, D. (1989). Naturalistic inquiry and computer-based instruction: Rationale, procedures, and potential. *Educational Technology Research and Development, 37*(3), 39–52.

Newman, D., Griffin, P., & Cole, M. (1989). *The construction zone: Working for cognitive change in school.* New York: Cambridge University Press.

Pea, R. (1992). Augmenting the discourse of learning with computer-based learning environments. In M.L.E. De Corte & L. Verschaffel (Eds.), *Computer-based learning environments and problem solving* (pp. 313–344). New York: Springer-Verlag.

Pea, R. (1993). Practices of distributed intelligence and designs for education. In G. Salomon (Ed.) *Distributed cognitions.* New York: Cambridge University Press.

Perkins, D. (1993). Person plus: A distributed view of thinking and learning. In G. Salomon (Ed.), *Distributed cognitions* (pp. 88–110). New York: Cambridge University Press.

Polya, G. (1957). *How to solve it.* Princeton, NJ: Princeton University Press.

Reigeluth, C. (1989). Educational technology at the crossroads: New mindsets and new directions. *Educational Technology Research and Development, 37*(1), 67–80.

Resnick, L. (1987). Learning in school and out. *Educational Researcher, 16*(9), 13–20.

Richey, R. (1992). *Designing instruction for the adult learner.* London: Kogan.

Ross, S., & Morrison, G. (1989), In search of a happy medium in instructional technology research: Issues concerning external validity, media replications, and learner control. *Educational Technology Research and Development, 37*(1), 19–34.

Salomon, G. (1978). *Interaction of media, cognition, and learning.* San Francisco: Jossey-Bass.

Salomon, G. (1991). Transcending the qualitative-quantitative debate: The analytic and systemic approaches to educational research. *Educational Researcher, 20*(6), 10–18.

Salomon, G. (1993). No distribution without individuals' cognition. In G. Salomon (Ed.), *Distributed cognition* (pp. 111–138). New York: Cambridge University Press.

Salomon, G., Perkins, D., & Globerson, T. (1991). Partners in cognition: Extending human intelligence with intelligent technologies. *Educational Researcher, 20*(3), 2–9.

Schön, D. (1987). *Educating the reflective practitioner.* San Francisco: Jossey-Bass.

Shuell, T. (1988). The role of the student in learning from instruction. *Contemporary Educational Psychology, 13*, 276–295.

Siegler, R., & Crowley, K. (1991). The microgenetic method. *American Psychologist, 46*(6), 606–620.

Simon, H. (1981). *The sciences of the artificial* (2nd ed.). Cambridge, MA: MIT Press.

Snow, R. (1992). Aptitutde theory: Yesterday, today, and tomorrow. *Educational Psychologist, 27*(1), 5–32.

Spiro, R., &. Jehng, J. (1990). Cognitive flexibility and hypertext: Theory and technology for the nonlinear and multidimensional traversal of complex subject matter. In D.N. & R. Spiro (Eds.), *Cognition, education, and multimedia* (pp. 163–206). Hillsdale, NJ: Erlbaum.

Stix, G. (1993). Domesticating cyberspace. *Scientific American, 269*(2), 100–110.

Van Haneghan, J., Barron, L., Young, M., Williams, S., Vye, N., & Bransford, J. (1992). The Jasper Series: An experiment with new ways to enhance mathematical thinking. In D. Halpern (Eds.), *Enhancing thinking skills in the sciences and mathematics* (pp. 15–38). Hillsdale, NJ: Erlbaum.

White, B. (1984). Designing computer activities to help physics students understand Newton's laws of motion. *Cognition and Instruction, 1*(1), 69–108.

White, B. (1993). ThinkerTools: Causal models, conceptual change, and science education. *Cognition and Instruction, 10*(1), 1–100.

Whitehead, A.N. (1929). *The aims of education.* New York: Macmillan.

Winn, W. (1989). Toward a rationale and theoretical basis for educational technology. *Educational Technology Research and Development, 37*(1), 35–46.

Winn, W. (1990). Some implications of cognitive theory for instructional design. *Instructional Science, 19*(1), 53–69.

CHAPTER 10

AN ANALYSIS OF KOZMA AND CLARK'S ARGUMENTS

Gary R. Morrison

Originally published as: Morrison, G. R. (1994). The media effects question: "Unresolvable" or asking the right question? *Educational Technology Research and Development, 42*(2), 41–44. Reprinted by permission of the Publisher, the Association for Educational Communications and Technology and the author.

When I reviewed the Kozma article for publication, I wondered if a rejection recommendation would be similar to some high commission in the dark ages suggesting that we have already discovered all knowledge and there was no need to pursue additional avenues. Instead, the reviewers felt Kozma had a valid view that should be openly debated to further the knowledge and theory of the field.

Kozma has suggested that Clark's "Do media influence learning?" question should be reframed to ask if "...*will* media influence learning." After reading Kozma's article several times, Clark's reply, Clark's original article (Clark, 1983), and Knowlton's (1964) original article I have concluded that Kozma is asking a different question than Clark to the extent that the two are only tangentially related.

KOZMA'S EXAMPLES

To support his reframing of Clark's question, Kozma describes two environments to illustrate his point. The first is *ThinkerTools* (White, 1984, 1993) and the *Jasper Woodbury Series* (Cognition and Technology Group at Vanderbilt, 1992). These two studies, however, suggest that the issue is not reframing Clark's question, but asking a different question.

According to Kozma, *ThinkerTools* allow students to manipulate objects on a computer which behave according to rules derived from Newtonian mechanics. The study Kozma cites (White, 1993) compared sixth-grade students who used *ThinkerTools* to a similar group of sixth graders studying a standard curriculum unit on inventions. The experimental group was also compared to a high school physics class who had studied Newtonian mechanics using traditional methods and a high school class who had not studied the topic. The results support the effectiveness of *ThinkerTools* to teach Newtonian mechanics as measured by a posttest. The study, however, is inappropriately designed for interpretation as a basic research study to provide evidence for the contribution of the media to learning. Kozma suggests that it was the ability of the computer to present motion and react to the learners' input. One must ask, however, what would have been the result if the instructor had taken the control sixth-grade class to a billiard parlor and allowed them to conduct similar experiments? Might the more concrete hands on experience in the billiards parlor also produce the same effect? If similar results are obtained, are the results due to the medium or the strategy?

In the *Jasper Woodbury Series* the students viewed a math problem which required several calculations to determine if the story character could return to the place of origin. Both the experimental and control groups viewed the presentation of the problem, however, the experimental group received additional interactive video instruction on problem solving using the problem context. The control group received only structured word problems without the context of the Jasper story. The experimental group scored significantly higher than the control group on problems related to the boat episode and the same as the control group on problems similar to the control group's practice items. Kozma attributed this superior performance to the additional video instruction which provided a rich context for the instruction. This conclusion that the video was the key factor in the superior performance of the experimental group is highly suspect considering that other research has shown that story problems rich in contextual information improve performance (e.g., Dorsey-Davis, Ross, & Morrison, 1991; Ross & Anand, 1987).

In both of the above studies, the control group received a different instructional strategy (e.g., manipulation of objects vs. traditional instructional, and contextual examples versus abstract examples). As a result, neither study is appropriate to answer the question proposed by Kozma, nor does either support his contention that media affects learning. The studies simply show that the instructional materials are effective for achieving the objectives. In addition, the studies do not allow the researchers or one interpreting the results to determine how much of the variability is due to the strategy and how much is due to the medium.

THE INTERDEPENDENCE OF STRATEGY AND MEDIA

Kozma identifies five capabilities of the medium in the studies that he interprets as facilitating learning. First was the ability to represent moving objects on the screen. Second was allowing students to manipulate objects (e.g., a microworld). Third was the ability to present complex contexts which generated dynamic mental images. Fourth was the ability to search and display information. Fifth was the ability to present a visual and social context for the story. Not one of these attributes is unique to the investigated media. For example, moving objects were represented in film and video in both concrete (actual objects) and abstract (artistic representations) forms long before the invention of the computer. The "Newtonian" objects could be manipulated on a billiard table in a highly enactive mode. Data searching is by no means limited to the computer, although the computer is often faster and more efficient. And, rich context for instruction could also be created in many different media formats.

I would suggest that it is not the capabilities of the media that facilitated the learning, but the creative development of the instructional strategy which actively engaged the learners. One could argue that it was the design of the strategy that created an environment for the student to test the Newtonian laws and it was the scripting that created the rich context. In the final instructional unit, the strategy and the media are so interdependent that it is almost impossible to separate them. In two recent studies (Morrison, Ross, & Baldwin, 1992; Ross, Morrison, & O'Dell, J. K., 1989) we found no difference in achievement scores when students were taught math problems using familiar contexts (e.g., sports, animals, business, education, etc.). Unlike the *Jasper* program, our materials were text based. If we were to repeat our study and use the abilities identified by Kozma as facilitating the *Jasper* program (e.g., pictures and increased amount of information) we would need to completely redesign our instructional strategy as mere implementation of the medium's attributes would not be feasible in the existing design.

IS REFRAMING THE QUESTION THE ISSUE?

Rather than reframing Clark's question, it seems more productive to consider the effectiveness of the whole unit of instruction rather than the individual components. Richey (1992) describes this type of research as developmental research which focuses on the "production of knowledge based on situation-specific problem solving." Richey makes a distinction between those studies that investigate the product and those that investigate the process used to develop the product. Of interest are the Type 1 studies which are both context and product specific and the Type 2 studies which are context specific. Both address the issue of the effectiveness of the instructional product. The two studies described by Kozma are context and product specific and serve to produce knowledge about problem solving skills in a specific situation. The evaluation methodology used by the studies is also similar to the evaluation Briggs (1977) proposed as a step of the instructional systems development model. That is, the final version of the instruction should be compared with an alternate form if available to determine its effectiveness. Similarly, *ThinkerTools* was compared to a group who studied scientific invention and to a group who learned Newtonian physics by a traditional teaching method.

This developmental research perspective then, is used to study the impact of the product on student learning. Issues of determining variability as related to strategy and medium are unimportant because the emphasis is on the synergism created through the interaction of the components and the instructional environment. Although context specific, the results would be of value to other designers when designing strategies for similar content structures.

A related issue is the use of a media replication design proposed by Ross and Morrison (1989). Each of these studies could be repeated using a media replication design that would use different media to deliver equivalent content with an instructional strategy designed to exploit the capabilities of the medium. For example, the White (1993) *ThinkerTools* study could be replicated using billiard parlor strategy for the control group. Similarly, the Jasper study could be replicated using a design similar to Ross and Anand (1987), Morrison, Ross, and O'Dell (1988) and Ross, Morrison, and O'Dell (1988) by presenting the same materials in two different formats such as interactive video and television or interactive video and print. A difference between groups would then suggest further research to determine *why* a particular strategy was more effective in a particular medium.

Answers to developmental research questions and those questions derived from media replication studies should produce more fruitful information for the instructional designer. Practitioners, it would seem, would be more interested in which strategies work and with what media such strategies are (a) most easily implemented, (b) most efficient, and (c) most cost effective. Knowing the effectiveness of a manipulative strategy such as used in *ThinkerTools,* or the use of context rich environment, as in *Jasper,* would probably provide more of a creative stimulus for a designer than the knowledge that a computer allows for learner input, can animate objects, and that a video disc can be paused and reviewed.

The research suggested by Kozma provides additional support to the argument against media comparison studies. As the interdependence of instructional strategy and utilization of a medium's capabilities (e.g., immediate feedback, user input, animation, controllable objects) increases in strength with interactive technologies like computer-based instruction, such research has less and less relevance. When controls are added to separate the effects of the strategy and medium, the resulting instructional strategy may be compromised to the point of being meaningless and/or artificial. I would suggest that instructional technology researchers continue with both basic, applied, and developmental research to determine the most effective strategies for accomplishing a given task.

REFERENCES

Briggs, L.J. (1977). Introduction. In L.J. Briggs (Ed.), *Instructional design* (pp. 5–18). Englewood Cliffs, NJ: Educational Technology Publications.

Clark, R.E. (1983). Reconsidering the research on learning from media. *Review of Educational Research, 53*, 445–459.

Cognition and Technology Group at Vanderbilt. (1992). An anchored instruction approach to cognitive skills acquisition and intelligence tutoring. In J.W. Regian & V. Schute (Eds.), *Cognitive approaches to automated instruction* (pp. 135–170). Hillsdale, NJ: Erlbaum.

Dorsey-Davis, J.D., Ross, S.M., & Morrison, G.R. (1991). The role of rewording and context personalization in the solving of mathematical word problems. *Journal of Educational Psychology, 83*, 61–68.

Knowlton, J. (1964). A conceptual scheme for the audiovisual field. *Bulletin of the School of Education: Indiana University, 40*,1–44.

Kozma, R.B. (1994). Will media influence learning? Reframing the debate. *Educational Technology, Research, and Development* (this issue).

Morrison, G.R., Ross, S.M., & Baldwin, W. (1992). Learner control of context and instructional support in learning elementary school mathematics. *Educational Technology, Research, & Development, 40*, 5–13.

Morrison, G.R., Ross, S.M., & O'Dell, J. (1988). Text density as a design variable in instructional displays. *Educational Communications and Technology Journal, 36*(2), 103–115.

Richey, R.C. (1992). Designing Instruction for the Adult Learner: Systemic Training Theory and Practice. Bristol, PA: Kogan Page.

Ross, S.M., & Anand, P.G. (1987). A computer-based strategy for personalizing verbal problems in teaching mathematics. *Educational Communications and Technology Journal, 35*, 151–162.

Ross, S.M., & Morrison, G.R. (1989). In search of a happy medium in instructional technology research: Issue concerning external validity, media replications, and learner control. *Educational Technology Research, and Development, 37,* 19–34.

Ross, S.M., Morrison, G.R., & O'Dell, J.K. (1989). Uses and effects of learner control of context and instructional support in computer-based instruction. *Educational Technology Research, and Development, 37,* 29–39.

Ross, S.M., Morrison, G.R., & O'Dell, J. (1988). Obtaining more out of less text in CBI: Effects of varied text density levels as a function of learner characteristics and control strategy. *Educational Communications and Technology Journal, 36,* 131–142.

White, B. (1984). Designing computer activities to help physics students understand Newton's laws of motion. *Cognition and Instruction, 1,* 69–108.

White, B. (1993). ThinkerTools: Causal models, conceptual change, and science education. *Cognition and Instruction, 10,* 1–100.

CHAPTER 11

THE MEDIA VERSUS
METHODS ISSUE

Richard E. Clark

Originally published as: Clark, R.E. (1994) Media will never influence learning. *Educational Technology Research and Development, 42*(2), 21–29. Reprinted with permission of the publisher, the Association for Educational Communications and Technology.

INTRODUCTION

The purpose of this discussion is to explain and sharpen different points of view about the impact of media and attributes of media on learning, motivation and efficiency gains from instruction. This paper is an attempt to summarize my arguments about the research and theory in this area and to respond to Robert Kozma's criticism of my earlier discussion of these issues. I will first briefly summarize my arguments about media effects; next I will attempt to characterize the many reactions to the controversial claim that media do not influence learning or motivation (Clark, 1983, 1985a). Finally, I will respond to the specific criticisms advanced by Robert Kozma (1993, this issue).

A Brief History of Media Research

The claim of "no learning benefits" from media has been made and substantiated many times in the past. Many researchers have argued that media have differential economic benefits but not learning benefits. For example, in the first Handbook of Research on Teaching, Lumsdaine (1963) concluded that the benefits of media were primarily economic and that their use was "to develop the technology of instructional method" (p. 669). Mielke (1968) was eloquent on the topic in an article he wrote for the now-defunct *Educational Broadcasting Review* (Mielke, 1968) titled "Questioning the Questions of ETV Research." He predicted that adequately designed research on the learning benefits of various media would yield no significant differences between treatments. Another example of the argument came from this century's most prolific media research reviewer, Wilbur Schramm, who claimed (Schramm, 1977) that learning is influenced more by the content and instructional strategy in a medium than by the type of medium. Levie and Dickey (1977) made the same point as Schramm in his chapter on media and technology research in the second *Handbook of Research on Teaching*. Finally, this was the conclusion I reached with Gavriel Salomon in our review in the third, and most recent, *Handbook of Research on Teaching* (Clark & Salomon, 1986). It is therefore a bit of a mystery why my restatement of the claim of "no differences expected" a decade ago (Clark, 1983) received so much attention. A colleague has suggested that previous discussions of this argument have put the claim in very tentative terms (as befits our training as researchers) and left the door open to media effects on learning. I made the explicit and clear claim that there were no learning benefits possible and urged that we not continue to waste effort on the question until a "new theory" was developed. I intended to stimulate discussion and I was not disappointed. Before I describe the reactions however, the discussion turns next to a brief review of the argument.

The Important Aspects of the Learning From Media Argument

My early articles (Clark, 1983, 1985a) claimed, in part, that media are "mere vehicles that deliver instruction but do not influence student achievement any more than the truck that delivers our groceries causes changes in our nutrition" (1983, p. 445). The articles presented evidence in support of the hypothesis that instructional methods had been confounded with media and that it is methods which influence learning. Further, I claimed, that any necessary teaching method could be designed into a variety of media presentations. I also questioned the unique contributions of media attributes. Gavriel Salomon and others (Salomon, 1979) had argued that it was not the medium which influenced learning but instead certain attributes of media that can be modeled by learners and can shape the development of unique "cognitive processes." Examples of media attributes are the capacity of television and movies to "zoom" into detail or to "unwrap" three-dimensional objects into two dimensions. The problem with the media attribute argument is that there is strong evidence that many very different media attributes accomplish the same learning goal (e.g., there are a variety of equally effective ways to highlight details other than "zooming"). In every attempt to replicate the published media attribute studies (see studies cited by Clark, 1985c; Clark & Sugrue, 1989), a number of very different media attributes served the same or similar cognitive functions. This point is critical to my argument. If there is no single media attribute that serves a unique cognitive effect for some learning task, then the attributes must be proxies for some other variables that are instrumental in learning gains.

A "Replaceability" Challenge

It may be useful to apply the following "armchair experimental criteria" to any situation where it appears that media or attributes of media have been instrumental in fostering learning gains: *We need to ask whether there are other media or another set of media attributes that would yield similar learning gains.* The question is critical because if different media or attributes yield similar learning gains and facilitate achievement of necessary performance criteria, then in a design science or an instructional technology, we must always choose the *less expensive* way to achieve a learning goal. We must also form our theories around the underlying structural features of the "shared properties" of the interchangeable variables and not base theory on the irrelevant surface features. I challenge Robert Kozma and other colleagues in this area to find evidence, in a well-designed study, of any instance of media, multimedia, or media attributes that are *not* replaceable by a different set of media and attributes to achieve similar learning results for any given student and learning task. This "replaceability" test is the key to my argument since if a treatment can be replaced by another treatment with similar results, the "cause" of the results is in some shared (and uncontrolled) properties of both treatments. Of course it is important for instructional designers to know that there are a variety of treatments that will produce a desired learning goal. However, the utility of this knowledge is largely economic. The designer can and must choose the less expensive and most cognitively efficient way to represent and deliver instruction. It cannot be argued that any given medium or attribute must be present in order for learning to occur, only that certain media and attributes are more efficient for certain learners, learning goals and tasks. This allows the discussion, and our mental set as theorists, to shift from media attributes as causal in learning to media attributes as causal in the cost-effectiveness of learning. While this may seem a small shift in the representation of the problem, it would have major consequences for instructional research, theory and for design. Cognitive instructional theory can shift to a concern with instructional methods that support the "structural" elements of cognitive processing during learning and transfer.

What is an Instructional Method, and How is it Different From a Medium?

An instructional method is any way to shape information that activates, supplants or compensates for the cognitive processes necessary for achievement or motivation (Salomon, 1979). For example, students often need an example to connect new information in a learning task with information in their prior experience. If students cannot (or will not) give themselves an adequate example, an instructional presentation must provide it for them. It is likely that many different types of examples, with many different attributes presented by many different media would serve similar cognitive functions for any given student. Instructional technology attempts to specify the need for and type of instructional methods required for the essential psychological support of students as they learn. Delivery technology formats and packages essential instructional methods based on available resources and the cost-effectiveness qualities of media attributes for specific learners and learning contexts.

A Confusion of Technologies

In a presentation for the Association for Educational Communications and Technology at their 1987 Atlanta convention I attributed our media research and practice problem to a "confusion of technologies" (Clark, 1987). Instructional or training design technologies draw on psychological and social-psychological research to select necessary information and objectives (as a result of task analysis) and design instructional methods and environments that enhance achievement. A very different technology—delivery technology—is necessary to provide efficient and timely *access* to those methods and environments. Both technologies make vital but very different contributions to education. Delivery technologies influence the cost and access of instruction and information. Design technologies make it possible to influence student achievement. In my view, there is a long history of a basic confusion between these two technologies that strangles our study of the contributions of media.

Motivation With Media

I also claimed that media not only fail to influence learning, they are also not directly responsible for motivating learning. Here I agreed whole-heartedly with the views of Salomon (1984) and others who draw on the new cognitive theories which attribute motivation to learners' beliefs and expectations about their reactions to external events—not to external events alone. There is compelling research evidence that students' beliefs about their chances to learn from any given media are different for different students and for the same students at different times.

WHAT ARE THE COUNTER-ARGUMENTS?

While there have been a great variety of counter-arguments, I categorize them into four types of rebuttals to the basic argument; (1) reasoning based on the usual uses of a medium: (2) the meta-analysis evidence; (3) problems with empiricism and logical positivism; and (4) a lingering hope for media attributes.

Usual Uses

The majority of informal letters which I received took Marshall McLuhan's view that media and method were identical and inseparable. I think of it as the usual uses argument. It seems to develop because media specialists generate beliefs about the "best" contents and methods for each medium. So, for example, television is usually thought to convey "realistic," visual, real time, documentary information. Computers most often give semantically dense simulations of complex phenomena as well as drill and practice. Textbooks have tended to focus on the development of encyclopedic knowledge with illustrated examples and heavy verbal content. Many writers seemed to suggest that these "methods" were somehow intrinsic to a given medium. My argument is that the usual uses of a medium do not limit the methods or content it is capable of presenting. Computers can present "realistic" visual, real time documentary information and television can present semantically dense simulations. The method is the simulation or the real time depiction. A good example of this point was uncovered in one of the earliest and largest (and best designed) studies of computers by Suppes (in Clark, 1983) during the 1960s. In a study of computers versus teachers using drill and practice in mathematics, Suppes' colleagues found that one of his control school districts had messed up the data collection by delivering more drill and practice in mathematics than was permitted by the study—using teachers and not computers. The result was that in that school district, mathematics achievement increased at exactly the same rate as it did in districts where computers were giving drill and practice. Suppes concluded then that it was not the medium but the drill and practice method which influenced achievement but noted that the cost of the intervention might have been less with computers.

Meta-analytic Evidence

Meta-analytic reviews of media research have produced evidence for the positive learning benefits of research with various media, particularly computers (see reviews in Clark, 1983, 1985a,b). These analyses report an approximate 20 percent increase in final exam scores following computer-based instruction (CBI) when it is compared to "traditional" forms of instruction (generally "live instruction"). After a number of discussions, Kulik (1985), one of the primary authors of many of the meta-analytic surveys, agreed that it is not the computer but the teaching method built into CBI that accounts for the learning gains in those studies. More important, Kulik agreed that the methods used in CBI can be and are used by teachers in live instruction (Kulik, 1985). In fact, I reanalyzed a 30 percent sample of the studies he used and found that when the same instructional design group produces CBT and presents the live instruction with which it is compared in many studies, there is no achievement difference between the CBT and live conditions (Clark, 1985c). To characterize the fact that these powerful methods can and are used in a variety of media, Kulik coined the catchy phrase "…diffusion of the innovative treatment to the control condition" (Kulik, 1985, p. 386). This statement more or less acknowledges that most of the studies which are grist for the meta-analytic mill, are confounded because the teaching method is not controlled (if it were controlled it could not "diffuse" anywhere).

Empiricism Envy

Cunningham (1986) did not dispute my argument that media made no difference to learning or motivation but argued against my empirically-based claims that instructional methods were responsible for achievement gains. Cunningham is well trained as a quantitative researcher but is increasingly attracted to qualitative research and not to empirical method or logical positivism. I think his argument was with the unreconstructed empiricism of my argument rather than with the theoretical claims. I agreed with him that my claim that it is instructional methods which account for learning gains is a hypothesis, not a conclusion (Clark, 1986).

Necessary Media Attributes

A number of researchers have argued with my claim about the unique contribution of what Gavriel Salomon calls "media attributes." Remember that the capacity of movies to "zoom" into detail or to "unwrap" three-dimensional objects has led some to claim that new media have attributes that make unique cognitive representations available (Salomon, 1979). A few go so far as to claim that new "intelligence" might be possible as a result of exposure to these attributes (e.g., Salomon, Perkins & Globerson, 1991). I presented evidence (Clark, 1985a,b) that many very different media attributes could accomplish the same learning goal (i.e., there were a variety of equally effective ways to highlight details other than "zooming") and so no one media attribute has a unique cognitive effect.

Petkovitch and Tennyson (1984) took me to task with an argument which I still do not completely understand but which seems to be related to the attributes argument. They seemed to agree that media comparison studies are useless but claimed that certain media attributes make necessary contributions to learning. The evidence they offered was a study where a computer simulation was used to teach students some skills required to fly a plane. I responded that people learned to fly planes before computers were developed and therefore the media attributes required to learn were obviously neither exclusive to computers nor necessary for learning to fly. A similar and more extensive argument has been made by Kozma (1991). The next section of this paper addresses Kozma's points in this debate and in his earlier work.

Kozma's Reframed Argument about the Influence of Media on Learning

First, it is important to notice that Kozma agrees with me that there is *no* compelling evidence in the past 70 years of published and unpublished research that media cause learning increases under any conditions. Like all other researchers who have made a careful study of the arguments and research studies, he reaches a conclusion that is compatible with my claims

(Clark, 1983). Kozma then asks that we reframe the argument about the future possibilities of media as causal agents in learning. In his discussion (this issue) Kozma interprets my claim that media attributes are not "necessary" variables in learning studies by quoting scholars from the philosophy of science who suggest that "sufficient conditions" are important to a design science. Kozma states that "...scientists concerned with necessary conditions are those interested in eliminating something undesirable, such as disease ... On the other hand, scientists interested in the production of something desirable, such as learning, are concerned with establishing conditions that are sufficient to bring it about ... Necessary conditions are those in whose absence an event cannot occur, while sufficient conditions are those in whose presence an event must occur" (p. 19). Kozma offers those studies where media attribute treatments are sufficient for learning as evidence for the value of attribute research.

This argument contains some of the most important elements of our disagreement. My reply is relatively simple. When a study demonstrates that media attributes are sufficient to cause learning, the study has failed to control for instructional method and is therefore confounded. It is true that in some cases instructional treatments containing media attributes are sufficient to cause learning. When this happens, the necessary condition to cause learning is embedded in the "sufficient" treatment. We know that the active ingredient in successful media treatments is not the media attributes because in all known attempts to replicate these studies, different attributes produce similar learning results—provided that the required instructional method is present in the compared versions of the media attributes. That necessary condition or "active ingredient" of the treatment which was sufficient to cause learning from instruction is best characterized as an instructional method which activates, compensates or supplants the cognitive processes necessary for learning to occur (Salomon, 1979). In other words, any treatment that is sufficient for learning must embody whatever is necessary to cause learning.

Structural and Surface Features of Research Constructs

The concepts of "necessary" and "sufficient" are similar to the concepts of "structural" and "surface" features in research on the role of analogies in transfer during problem solving (e.g., Gick & Holyoak, 1987). Surface features of analogies are those whose characteristics are of only limited and domain specific importance. For example, in science and mathematics instruction, irrelevant features of analogies often cause misconceptions in learning. When told that an atom is like the solar system, students often believe that electrons must attract each other and be attracted to the nucleus of the atom because planets are attracted to each other and to the sun by gravity. Gravity is a surface feature that is important to understanding the solar system but not the atom. The structural (necessary) features that underlie both systems are central bodies (nucleus, sun) that are encircled by rotating spheres (electrons, planets). The point that I had hoped to make in my earlier reviews is that media attributes are surface features of learning systems. Those surface features may affect the economics but not the learning effectiveness of instruction. Instructional methods are structural (necessary) features of media attribute studies. On the other hand, instructional methods may be surface features of treatments concerned with the economics of learning.

I accept the point that whenever learning occurs, some medium or mix of media must be present to deliver instruction. However, if learning occurs as a result of exposure to any media, the learning is caused by the instructional method embedded in the media presentation. Method is the inclusion of one of a number of possible representations of a cognitive process or strategy which is necessary for learning but which the students cannot or will not provide for themselves. Kozma accuses me of creating an "unnecessary and undesirable schism" (p. 19) between method and medium. My claim is that Kozma has confounded the two constructs. He is asking you to consider media as an integral aspect of "method." I am suggesting that if we take his advice, we will continue to misinterpret the research on instructional media and learning and continue to fail in our efforts to construct powerful learning environments for all students.

All methods required for learning can be delivered by a variety of media and media attributes. It is method which is the "active ingredient" or active independent variable that may or may not be delivered by the medium to influence learning. The derivation and delivery of a method to support learning is always necessary. A great variety of media "translations" of any given method are sufficient to cause learning. Therefore, aside from the identification of necessary methods for learners and tasks, it is important to derive media that are capable of delivering the method at the least expensive rate and in the speediest fashion. Media influence cost or speed (efficiency) of learning but methods are causal in learning.

Let me try to illustrate my point one more time with a medical analogy. People often have preferences for one or another way to use a chemical medicine prescribed by a physician to improve health. Some people will argue for tablets and others for liquid or injected forms of treatment. Is it "sufficient" that one take a tablet medicine? Only if the tablet contains the active ingredient required to help us. Different forms of a medicine might help us provided that they all contain the same "method" or active ingredient. The different forms of medicine are similar to different media. The "media" include a variety of tablets, liquid suspensions, suppositories or injections. All of these different media are often capable of delivering a "necessary" active chemical ingredient with different levels of efficiency, but with more or less equal effects on our physical symptoms. The active chemical ingredient of these medical media is analogous to the necessary "method" in instruction. We could not construct an adequate medical "design science" using different (sufficient) forms of delivery media alone and it would be irrelevant to measure whether these delivery forms reduce our symptoms (unless we were concerned with the effects of belief on health). Scientific arguments about the necessary or sufficient nature of oral ingestion of tablets versus an injection of the liquid form of a medicine would be largely irrelevant. Yet the discussion of delivery forms for medicine is very important. Each of these delivery forms have different *efficiency* characteristics. Some forms of delivery get the active ingredient to the patient much faster (or slower) in quantities which are more "pure" or more "diluted" at greater or less cost to the patient. For this reason I disagree with Kozma's suggestion that we not separate medium and method in instructional research. Instead I claim that our failure to separate medium from method has caused enormous confounding and waste in a very important and expensive research area. We continue to invest heavily in expensive media in the hope that they will produce gains in learning. When learning gains are found, we attribute them to the delivery medium not to the active ingredient in instruction. When learning gains are absent, we assume we have chosen the wrong mix of media. In any event, many educators and business trainers are convinced that they must invest scarce resources in newer media in order to insure learning, performance or motivational gains.

Evidence for Kozma's View

Finally, Kozma's evidence for his view is to describe the latest round of studies that utilize the currently fashionable media—*ThinkerTools* to teach force and motion problem solutions and the *Jasper Woodbury Series* intended to help students solve mathematics problems (see Kozma, this issue). These studies were not designed so that their results would provide evidence about the claims being made in this dispute. The research conducted to validate these very creative instructional programs did not control for the sources of confounding that lie at the root of the argument. The computer-based *ThinkerTools* program was compared with a "standard" curriculum for teaching force and motion. It is not clear whether the standard curriculum used similar instructional methods but it is very doubtful. The videodisc-based *Jasper* program group was compared with a control group that did not receive instruction in "decomposition and solution strategies." One must question whether this missing instruction could have been delivered with a very different medium or set of media attributes? One must assume that these comparisons confound method and content in the same way that many previous studies in this area fail to control for important alternative hypotheses. One way to begin to answer questions about the structural necessity of media attributes is to ask whether other learners have achieved similar learning results with different instructional treatments? Have learners acquired problem-solving techniques similar to those presented in *ThinkerTools* or *Jasper* in the past? If so, the media attributes available from expensive computers and video disks are not structurally important in learning problem-solving skills. Yet in making this point, I do not want to appear to be critical of the developers of these two excellent programs. The substantive point of both design activities was to explore the utility of different combinations of instructional method.

CONCLUSION

Kozma agrees with me that evidence does not yet support the claim that media or media attributes influence learning. However, he hopes that future media and research will be more positive. He accepts the claim that in thousands of media research studies conducted over a period of 70 years we have failed to find compelling causal evidence that media or media attributes influence learning in any essential and structural way. However, Kozma remains optimistic that with careful consideration of cognitive processes, we will find a critical connection between media attributes and learning. He suggests that my insistence that educational researchers separate these two classes of variables will retard a very promising area of research.

In brief, my claim is that media research is a triumph of enthusiasm over substantive examination of structural processes in learning and instruction. Media and their attributes have important influences on the cost or speed of learning but only the use of adequate instructional methods will influence learning. I define methods as the provision of cognitive processes or strategies that are necessary for learning but which students can not or will not provide for themselves. I claim that absolutely any necessary teaching method can be delivered to students by many media or a variety of mixtures of media attributes—with similar learning results.

The media research question is only one of a number of similarly confounded questions in educational research. It is difficult for alternative questions to gain acceptance, even though adequate research exists to refute invalid but intuitively appealing beliefs. The development of an instructional design science is necessary but very complex. Part of the difficulty, in my view, is that we tend to encourage students (and faculty) to begin with educational and instructional *solutions* and search for problems that can be solved by those solutions. Thus we begin with an enthusiasm for some medium, or individualized instruction, or deschooling—and search for a "sufficient" and visible context in which to establish evidence for our solution. Negative evidence is suspect and we are predisposed to believe that it is flawed. In the case of media research, 70 years of largely negative evidence has been and continues to be ignored by many researchers. Positive evidence is accepted easily because it confirms our expectations and helps to attract research support. We need a greater appreciation for negative evidence and to begin with a focus on the problem (e.g., the need to increase achievement, or access to instruction, or to address the labor intensiveness of instruction) and then search relevant research literatures for robust, research-based theories that can support the development of a variety of solutions to those problems. If we begin by implicitly and explicitly attempting to validate a belief about the solutions to largely unexamined problems, we are less open to evidence that our intuitions might be very far off the mark.

If the arguments advanced here have failed to convince you, I ask you to consider one or two questions as you reason about media research. Whenever you have found a medium or set of media attributes which you believe will cause learning for some learners on a given task, ask yourself if another (similar) set of attributes would lead to the same learning result. If you suspect that there may be an alternative set or mix of media that would give similar results, ask yourself what is causing these similar results. It is likely that when different media treatments of the same informational content to the same students yield similar learning results, the cause of the results can be found in a "method" which the two treatments share in common. Design science (and a world with limited resources and many competing problems) requires that you choose the least expensive solution and give up your enthusiasm for the belief that media attributes cause learning.

REFERENCES

Clark, R.E. (1983). Reconsidering research on learning from media. *Review of Educational Research, 53*(4), 445–459.

Clark, R.E. (1985a). Confounding in educational computing research. *Journal of Educational Computing Research, 1*(2), 445–460.

Clark, R.E. (1985b). The importance of treatment explication in computer-based instruction research. *Journal of Educational Computing Research, 1*(3), 389–394.

Clark, R.E. (1985c). Evidence for confounding in computer-based instruction studies: Analyzing the meta analyses. *Educational Communication and Technology Journal, 33*(4).

Clark, R.E. (1986). Absolutes and angst in educational technology research: A reply to Don Cunningham. *Educational Communication and Technology Journal, 34*(1), 8–10.

Clark, R.E. (1987). *Which technology for what purpose.* Paper presented at an invited symposium for the annual meeting of the Association for Educational Communications and Technology, Atlanta, GA.

Clark, R.E., & Salomon, G. (1986). Media in teaching. In M. Wittrock (Ed.), *Handbook of research on teaching* (3rd ed.). New York: Macmillan.

Clark, R.E., & Sugrue, B.M. (1989). Research on instructional media, 1978–1988. In D. Ely (Ed.), *Educational media yearbook 1987–88.* Littletown, CO: Libraries Unlimited.

Cunningham, D.J. (1986). Good guys and bad guys. *Educational Communications and Technology Journal, 34*(1), 3–7.

Gick, M., & Holyoak, K. (1987). Cognitive basis of knowledge transfer. In S.M. Cormier & S.D. Hagman (Eds.), *Transfer of learning.* New York: Academic Press.

Kozma, R.B. (1991). Learning with media. *Review of Educational Research, 61*(2), 179–212.

Kozma, R.B. (1993, September). *Will media influence learning? Reframing the debate.* Paper presented at the International Meeting of the EARLI, Aix en Provence.

Kulik, J.A. (1985). The importance of outcome studies: A reply to Clark. *Educational Communications and Technology Journal, 34*(1), 381–386.

Levie, W.H., & Dickie, K. (1973) The analysis and application of media. In R. Travers (Ed.), *The Second Handbook of research on Teaching.* Chicago: Rand McNalley.

Lumsdaine, A.A. (1963). Instruments and media of instruction. In N. Gage (Ed.), *Handbook of research on teaching.* Chicago: Rand McNally.

Mielke, K.W. (1968). Questioning the questions of ETV research. *Educational Broadcasting, 2,* 6–15.

Petkovich, M.D., & Tennyson, .R.D. (1984). Clark's "Learning from media": A critique. *Educational Communications and Technology Journal, 32*(4), 233–241.

Salomon, G. (1979). *Interaction of media, cognition and learning.* San Francisco: Jossey Bass.

Salomon, G. (1984). Television is easy and print is "tough": The differential investment of mental effort in learning as a function of perceptions and attributions. *Journal of Educational Psychology, 76*(4), 647–658.

Salomon, G., Perkins, D.N., & Globerson, T. (1991). Partners in cognition: Extending human intelligence with intelligent technologies. *Educational Researcher, 20*(2), 2–9.

Schramm, W. (1977). *Big media, little media.* Beverly Hills, CA: Sage.

Winn, W. (1990). Media and instructional methods. In D.R. Garrison & D. Shale (Eds.), *Education at a distance: From issues to practice.* Malabar, FL: Krieger.

CHAPTER 12

ARE METHODS "REPLACEABLE"?

A Reply to Critics in the ETR & D Special Issue on the Debate

Richard E. Clark

Originally published as: Clark, R.E. (1994). Media and method. *Educational Technology Research and Development, 42*(3), 7–10. Reprinted with permission of the publisher, the Association for Educational Communications and Technology.

One way for me to view the several perspectives offered by the authors of the articles in the special "debate" issue of ETRD (Vol. 42 #2) is to look at their "degree of fit" to the arguments I have advanced and take issue where the differences are great. Using this approach I would discuss my agreement on nearly all of the points raised by Shrock and Morrison, and I would express my empathy for many of the issues raised by Reiser. On the other hand I would take Jonassen, Campbell and Davidson to task for attributing to me, and to Kozma, points of view, values and assumptions that neither of us entertained, let alone expressed in what we wrote. However, the Editor has wisely imposed severe space limitations on our replies, ruling out a blow-by-blow reply. So, while I'm comforted by finding like-minded colleagues on this topic, I'm searching for a key issue that would help me focus my response to the concerns of my colleagues. With this in mind, I selected only one of the many interesting questions raised by the contributors for discussion: Are instructional methods replaceable or interchangeable?

I have claimed that whenever one finds one medium or media attribute that seems to produce desired learning outcomes, there is ample evidence from both quantitative and qualitative inquiry that the substitution of another medium and/or attribute of a medium will produce the same or similar learning outcomes. I suggested that this fact must be interpreted as evidence that "instructional methods" are the underlying element of all "substitutable" media and attributes of media. Reiser agreed that media were replaceable but suggested that we try to "...find evidence of an instructional method that is not replaceable by a different method to achieve similar learning results" (p. 48). Shrock noted that "...perhaps there is no one method required to attain a given learning outcome" (p. 50). While this is a complex issue that requires more space for full discussion, let me try a brief review of some of the issues this challenge raises.

Three key points form the heart of my argument about media and method: First, that *when learning is influenced by external events, those events must support cognitive processes or structures that are required for learning goals by students who are unable or unwilling to provide them for themselves.* The specification for these external events is what I am calling an "instructional method." At this initial level of analysis, "other things being equal," instructional methods are not "replaceable" unless learning theories about relevant cognitive processes and structures change, requiring a parallel change in methods. Theory at this basic level specifies the characteristics of human cognitive structures and processes, general knowledge types and motivational mechanisms that are common to all human beings. Media variables have not proved useful at this basic level of analysis when learning is the measured outcome. In fact, there is no cognitive learning theory that I have encountered where media, media attributes or any symbol system are included as variables that are related to learning. In all cases where the effects of these variables on learning has been examined, compelling rival hypotheses about measured effects have been found (Clark, 1983). In fact, there is no reason to believe or expect, based on nearly a century of media research and the past eighty years of cognitive learning research, that any media variable will ever be an instructional method as the term is defined above.

The second key issue is that *instructional designers, developers and researchers often fail to adequately link their work to the basic and applied research on learning from instruction.* As a consequence, we are too often unaware of the evidence about important cognitive processes necessary to achieve desired performance on learning tasks. Our enthusiasm for media and our focus on context (often expressed as a concern with "ecological validity") lead us to ignore or misinterpret basic research. Compounding this problem, is a tendency to ignore the "construct validity" of variables used in the design of field studies and successful instructional programs based on new media platforms. At the design stage, this leads us to avoid a careful analysis of the definition and measurement issues associated with instructional methods and corresponding cognitive processes. The result is *many different "operational definitions" of familiar instructional methods that are used interchangeably in design with very different results.* Methods get confounded with the medium being used for delivery or the symbolic mode being used to express or communicate information. For example, the instructional method of "feedback" is part of most instructional programs presented in a variety of media. Yet the term "feedback" covers a multitude of very different instructional activities and functions that result in very different cognitive consequences, regardless of the medium used to provide feedback (see, for example, the discussion by Cronbach & Snow, 1977). So different methods are called by similar names and are developed and implemented in idiosyncratic ways that produce unanticipated, and sometimes negative and conflicting cognitive consequences that, in turn, may lead to different performance outcomes. Reigeluth (1992) gives a number of engaging examples of this phenomenon in the emerging literature on intelligent tutoring systems.

Part of the solution to this dilemma would be to acknowledge that among the requirements for good design are: (a) a plausible model of the general cognitive processes required to learn and perform for specific tasks (e.g., the monitoring and correction of errors during practice is a critical cognitive process "method" some learners have difficulty engaging); (b) an "operational definition" of the required cognitive processes derived from an analysis of solid research studies (e.g., recognizing that external monitoring support is provided by a measurable but still "generic" method called "feedback"); and, (c) a plan for developing an "externalized" cognitive process support in an instructional program designed to be effective and efficient for specific people in a specific context employing a known delivery medium (e.g., a specification for how feedback needs to be shaped, phrased, and delivered in a specific mediated instructional program where real people are learning to perform real tasks under specific resource constraints). In the final stages of this approach to design, methods such as feedback can be placed in a great variety of modes and symbol systems, depending on (among other things) whether the monitoring must be: immediate or delayed; information about learning activities and/ or motivation; correcting or confirming of learner strategies; and in verbal or pictorial form. The selection of media and symbol systems are critical at this final stage in design and development because of such factors as learner preferences, available media, and the available time and funds; the preferred mode and medium used to express and deliver a method like feedback is likely to be specific to one set of learners and learning goals.

A third factor that contributes to the confounding of media and methods is that, when we are conducting design and development for delivery by new media, *we tend to ignore basic and applied research if that research was conducted with older media. We too often act as if we believe that each new delivery technology requires a new theory of learning and performance. Thus, we "reinvent the wheel" constantly but inadequately.* The problem here is that designers and media producers look to previous programs developed for specific contexts and media for methods to use in new programs. If the medium in question is new, the chances of previous research specific to that medium are slim and they conclude that "there is no research" and so draw on their own personal history to design programs and so "reinvent the wheel." If they find research based on the "medium of choice," designers are prone to assume that attractive features of media attributes or symbolic modes from a previous program may be necessary to influence learning. They often treat the evaluation of a specific program as if it produced generalizable theory about learning and all components of these programs as "independent variables."

These issues are not new. They are often discussed in our literature and a number of remedies have been suggested by thoughtful critics of design and development including for example, Heinich (1984), Hooper and Hannifin (1991), Landa, (1983), Ohlsson, (1993), Reigeluth (1983, 1992), Ross and Morrison (1988), and Winn (1990), among others. The problem is that the solutions are not disseminated widely enough, nor are they generally accepted by more than a small number of people in our field.

One of the results of the confusion caused by our confounded research, design and development is a fragmentation of research and practice in our field. A number of us simply "give up" on quantitative research and embrace phenominology and related qualitative methods as their sole inquiry tool. This frees us to reinvent theory and practice while designing instruction with exciting new technologies. Others generate radical constructivist and contextual theories, partly due to their frustration with narrow-minded researchers who try to make direct application of descriptive theories without regard for the complexity of intervening processes and local conditions. Our instructional technology graduate programs tend to split away from parent disciplines where learning theory and methodology are taught (Clark, 1978). This split tends to give technology faculty more control over curriculum, and reduce the effort they must spend to keep abreast of new developments in research. It serves students because those who are primarily interested in finding applications for new media can focus their efforts on new media and not be bothered with difficult course work in advanced learning theory and the technology of research. The result is a theoretical and methodological "tower of Babel" where we can no longer communicate, learn from each other or build systematic theories that inform practice.

AN EXAMPLE OF ADEQUATE INSTRUCTIONAL DESIGN
AND MEDIA DEVELOPMENT

Space prevents a full description of the rationale for and examples of instructional design that draws on the results of basic research and design research (also called "prescriptive research"). One good example of a design system firmly grounded in basic and applied research can be found in Anderson (1983, 1990) who makes full use of cognitive descriptive theories of learning and expertise in his development of his ACT* design theory. Gagne, Yekovich, and Yekovich (1993) have extended Anderson's design theory and described how it might be applied to school tasks such as learning to read and write, and to important content areas such as mathematics and science. Anderson has applied his own theory to many local applications including the development of a computer-based program called "LISP Tutor" for training people to use the LISP programming language (e.g., Anderson, Farrell & Sauers, 1984).

Anderson (1983) makes the point that design theories should be "generic" in that they should accommodate any learning task and any set of learners. Development and delivery theories must be "local" in that they must apply design theories to a specific context where real people live and work. At this local level we find constraints in values, beliefs, misconceptions, knowledge and resources that must influence the way we implement our design. At this level, we will find specific media attributes and delivery vehicles that are the most efficient way to "instantiate" or translate instructional methods that have themselves survived the transition from descriptive and design theories to serve the specific needs of a specific group of learners. At the "local level," we only have the option to choose a medium that will deliver the method that will influence the necessary cognitive process for the desired learning task performance. We must translate the "generic" and irreplaceable method to suit the individuals who reside in the specific context we are serving. We would have reasonable disagreements about whether it is possible to present some methods via certain media in the chosen symbol system or within the time or budget available to achieve a desired performance. For example, it is impossible to present pictures via audio and very inefficient to present immediate feedback that is sensitive to a broad variety of learner performance problems with broadcast television or radio.

ARE METHODS REPLACEABLE?

The final answer to the question "Are methods replaceable or interchangeable?" depends on the level or stage in the design process. At the first level or generic stage, methods are defined in terms of the cognitive process they support. At this stage they are not replaceable. However, at the local level, when generic methods are translated into symbol systems for conveyance by media to particular learners in specific contexts, then multiple instances of a required generic method may be possible. Each instance could have a different efficiency characteristic for any given learner.

REFERENCES

Anderson, J.R. (1983). *The architecture of cognition.* Beverly Hills, CA: Sage.

Anderson, J.R. (1990). *Cognitive psychology and its implications* (3rd ed.). New York: W.H. Freeman.

Anderson, J.R., Farrell, R., & Sauers, R. (1984). Learning to program in LISP. *Cognitive Science, 8,* 87–129.

Clark, R.E. (1978). Doctoral research in educational technology. *Educational Communications and Technology Journal, 53,* 445–459.

Clark, R.E. (1983). Reconsidering research on learning from media. *Review of Educational Research, 53,* 445–459.

Clark, R.E. (1989). The future of technology in educational psychology. In M. Wittrock & F. Farley (Eds.), *The future of educational psychology.* Hillsdale, NJ: LEA.

Clark, R.E. (In Press). Media and learning. In T. Husen & T.N. Postlethwaite (Eds.), *The international encyclopedia of education.* London: Pergamon Press.

Cronbach, L.J., & Snow, R.E. (1977). *Aptitudes and instructional methods.* New York: Irvington Press.

Gagne, E.D., Yekovich, C.W., & Yekovich, F.R. (1983). *The cognitive psychology of school learning* (2nd ed.). New York: Harper Collins College Publishers.

Heinich, R. (1984). The proper study of educational technology. *Educational Communications and Technology Journal, 32*(2), 67–87.

Hooper, S., & Hannifin, M.J. (1991). Psychological perspectives on emerging instructional technologies: A critical analysis. *Educational Psychologist, 26*(1): 69–95.

Landa, L.N. (1983). The algo-heuristic theory of instruction. In C.M. Reigeluth (Ed.), *Instructional design theories and models.* Hillsdale NJ: LEA.

Ohlsson, S. (1993). Impact of cognitive theory on the practice of courseware authoring. *Journal of Computer Assisted Learning, 9,* 194–221.

Reigeluth, C.M. (1983). Instructional design: What is it and why is it? In C.M. Reigeluth (Ed.), *Instructional design theories and models.* Hillsdale NJ: LEA.

Reigeluth, C.M. (1992). New directions for educational technology. In E. Scanlon & T. O'Shea (Eds.), *New directions in educational technology.* New York: Springer-Verlag.

Ross, S.M., & Morrison, G.R. (1988). In search of a happy medium in instructional technology research: Issues concerning external validity, media replications, and learner control. *Educational Technology Research and Development, 37*(1), 19–33.

Winn, W. (1990). Media and instructional methods. In D.R. Garrison & D. Shale (Eds.), *Education at a distance: From issues to practice.* Malabar, FL: Krieger.

CHAPTER 13

NEW DIRECTIONS

An Argument for Research-based Performance Technology

Richard E. Clark and Fred Estes

Originally published as: Clark R.E. & Estes, F. (1998). Technology or craft: What are we doing? *Educational Technology, 38*(5), 5–11. Reprinted by permission of Educational Technology Magazine.

Tech - nol - o - gy (tek-'nä-le-jē) *n. pl.* -gies

The application of science, especially to industrial or commercial objectives. The entire body of methods and materials used to achieve such objectives.

Craft (kraft, kräft) n. pl. crafts.

Skill or ability in something ... Proficiency; expertness ... Indicates work, art or practice of, for example, woodcraft, stagecraft.[1]

The origin of this essay was a request from the Editor, Larry Lipsitz, for a reflective article on where we currently stand and where we are going in Educational Technology. His concern is based, in part, on the perception of a number of people who have monitored educational technology scholarship over the years (e.g., Clark, 1983, 1988a,b, 1994a; Cuban, 1986; Ellul, 1990; Heinich, 1984; Kaufman, 1998; Kearsley, 1998) that well-designed research and evaluation does not provide evidence for expected educational technology results. In addition, many scholars since the turn of the century, have suggested that our field is founded on a shared misunderstanding of technology and thus cannot hope to find the best solutions to many of the problems it is addressing.

Our involvement in this issue is both personal and professional. For a number of years, both of us have balanced teaching, research and practice in educational technology. We both experience more people today who are enthusiastic about educational technology solutions that have face validity and seem intuitively correct but lack supporting evidence. We also notice, along with Greg Kearsley (1998) and others, that most people in our field continue to define technology as "machines and media." Even more distressing is our impression that good evidence more often suggests a lack of effectiveness for many uses of educational technology as it is currently defined and practiced, despite the enthusiasm we experience from students, colleagues, the general public and industry professionals. Recent examples of such enthusiasms are directed at distance education, virtual reality and multi media. We realize that pressures from employers limit the amount of time professionals have available to master a complex and sometimes conflicting research literature even more today than even a decade ago. We are very aware of the enthusiastic testimonials for these "new technologies" from people who are effective in communicating and persuading others to use them. And we are very alarmed by the increasing number of our students and colleagues who ignore the lack of research evidence to support technology enthusiasm. Too many people simply do not trust research. We get the impression that much of this distrust comes from a lack of support one finds in the research for people's intuition about the benefits of educational technology. Their reasoning seems to suggest that if research does not find evidence for something that seems so powerful, then research as an inquiry strategy must be flawed. Since researchers often seem to disagree, too many of our colleagues get the impression that the social and educational sciences are "opinion" and that all opinions are equally valid. This phenomenon is not limited to educational technology but can be found in all social and organizational issues. One consequence we notice is that more people advocate a greater proportion of failed or limited educational and organizational strategies which do not measure up when subjected to robust evaluation (see for example the discussion of organizational change and empowerment motivation strategies by Golembiewski & Sun; 1990; Newman, Edwards, & Raju, 1989; and reviews of comparative media studies by Clark, 1983, 1994a). As part of this trend, we have also noticed the tendency of university educational technology programs to become increasingly insular, reduce the emphasis on the technology of research and avoid the responsibility to correct students' intuitive beliefs about technological solutions (Clark, 1978, 1988a). The result is a gradual eroding and splintering of our field.

THE PURPOSE OF THIS ARTICLE

In this article, and those that follow in this series, we will make the argument that the reason this field is languishing at a time when there is great international interest in educational technology, is that we have confused craft and technology and we have too narrowly focused educational technology on media and distance education as we attempt to solve educational problems.

We will contend that what too many educational technologists have been describing in the pages of this journal and others is not technology but craft. While craft is valuable and, in the absence of technology, the only alternative solution to problems, confusing the two approaches is deadly. Even worse, our craft has too often been targeted on the wrong problems and solutions. We will also suggest that the medieval origin of craft encourages too many of us to advocate solutions and then go in search of educational problems the solution may help. We will suggest that in order to connect with root sciences, technology development must begin with a clear understanding and validation of problems to be solved and consider solutions only after a careful consideration of the problem. In this essay, we will describe the positive and negative qualities of both craft and technology and give examples of the consequences of emphasizing one over the other. We will urge a greater blending of the two approaches. In forthcoming essays we will describe, in some detail, how a technology of education develops; how we can foster its development in environments where people have many demands on their time, and how we might change this field so that it is oriented towards the appropriate blending of technology and craft to solve educational problems.

EDUCATIONAL TECHNOLOGY AND EDUCATIONAL CRAFT

As most dictionary definitions indicate, technology is the application of scientific knowledge to solving practical problems (Heinich, 1984; Galbraith, 1967). The chain of events that lead from science to technology to educational practice is what John Dewey (1900) called a "linking science... between theory and practical work" (p. 110). Our technology of education has produced diverse offspring such as improved tests for selection, aptitude and achievement measurement; effective organizational strategies such as change tactics; new cognitive theories of motivation applied to instruction; modular scheduling and approaches to school consolidation; job and task analysis; modular building designs; instructional design models and teaching methods. All of these issues and problems are also addressed by craft. In craft we see emphases in areas such as learning styles such as the Meyers-Briggs instrument, empowerment motivation strategies, and competency models. So we cannot distinguish between the two approaches on the basis of the problem they attempt to solve. Two of the key defining elements of a technology are the connection between the root science and the practical problem being solved by the technology and the generalizability of the solution once it is developed. One of our concerns is that the problems we have been attempting to solve are not always those their root science was addressing and usually are not problems that can be solved by media. The best example of this problem is our obsession with media in all of its current and electronic forms (e.g., Clark, 1983; 1994a; 1994b). The development of the connection between science and effective technology is accomplished with the use of "linking sciences and technologies" for applying scientific theory and models to the solving of practical problems (Bruner, 1964; Clark, 1988a; Dewey, 1900; Glaser, 1987; Simon, 1981). Further, we suggest that too many of us have unintentionally been engaged in educational craft which is experience based, marginally effective where it was developed and not reliably transferrable to a new situation. We will also argue that craft approaches allow us to easily confuse the connection between problem and solution.

What Is Educational Craft and What Are its Benefits?

Much of human knowledge is based on craft. The person developing a craft solution to a problem draws on fortunate accidents, personal experience, insight and the expertise of others to fashion a solution and revise it through trial and error. Craft is then passed on through a system of expert-based instruction and practice-based apprenticeships. In many instances, evaluation studies indicate that craft solutions are successful in the setting where they are designed. Craft is also quite easy to learn and its use seldom requires much training or prior experience. Craft approaches produce a body of knowledge and expertise that is sometimes personal but more often passed on through guilds, unions, professional associations or other collections of experts and student novices. Teaching and training are largely craft-based activities despite the role of colleges and universities in the training of school teachers and business trainers. Many instructional design and development strategies are largely craft based. Medicine was a craft when it was developed and has been making a gradual transition to technology over the past century. Building trades such as carpentry, stone masonry and construction planning began as craft and gradually evolved into engineering. Presently, engineering is largely a technology although it draws on its craft origins when the root science of a problem is absent or inadequate. The reasons for the evolution from craft to technology in medicine and engineering are pragmatic. Technology works better when success is evaluated (Dewey, 1900). Thus, the development of fields of knowledge tend to follow a pattern where early insights are gained through craft and then, as the field matures, the limitations of craft motivate an emphasis on science and its related technologies. What has apparently happened in educational technology is that we continue to develop craft solutions when science and technology are available, but we are calling what we do "technology."

What Is Wrong with Craft Solutions?

If craft solutions often work, even if their success is limited to a very specific setting, why discourage their use? There are at least three serious faults in a craft solution—they are indeterminate, non transferrable and unconnected to a systematic knowledge base.

One of the most important flaws of a craft is that its solutions have indeterminate causes. We do not know why they work. Craft solutions are seldom linked to a larger body of knowledge where established scientific principle and causes are explained. While people who develop the craft have explanations for why they work, closer scrutiny indicates that these explanations are seldom correct (Clark, 1988b; Gage, 1985; Heinich, 1984; Shulman, 1986). This means that we are in doubt about which part of the craft solution is the "active ingredient" that leads to measured outcomes. Thus, most craft solutions contain elements that are either inefficient and/ or counter productive (in that they may cause unintended side effects). However, by itself, this fault is not always destructive—only inefficient. So we do not know why they work, in fact some of them do work and do solve important problems. Do we need to know why they work? Must we be able to identify their active ingredients and relate them to a larger body of research and theory? The answer to these questions is "No, we do not need to know why they work, unless we want to transfer the solution beyond its initial context." The key utility of any insight is in its generalizability. If knowledge was context specific, we would have to invent a new solution each time we encountered the same problem in a new context, or with different people or tasks. Clark (1988a) has argued that we do not often learn about the lack of generalizability of craft solutions because they often carry the strong endorsement of their original developers or from people in the original application context. Since these endorsements are based on the actual experiences of real people in real settings, they are trusted more than the cautions and concerns of research and evaluation specialists who are perceived as less experienced in the real world.

According to historian Barbara Ward (1962) the difference between craft and technology is as profound as the difference between primitive and advanced societies. In her essay's on the development of modern civilizations, Ward gives technology the credit for the efficiencies that permit the development of advanced societies. She provides historical evidence to support her view that "...there is virtually no science in tribal society. There is a good deal of practical experience, skilled work and early technique. It seems possible, for instance, that primitive farming developed as a result of close observation of nature's cycle ... but the idea of controlling things by grasping the inner law of their construction is absent" (p. 47). Understanding the "inner law" is the essence of science and technology. Yet, she argues, members of modern technological societies do not necessarily understand science and technology nor recognize their impact on our social and economic achievement. Many historians have described the tendency in modern civilizations to "scientize" craft using scientific language and measurement technologies (Ellul, 1990).

Thus, the second problem with craft solutions is that they are situated. Because they are unconnected to a body of systematically gathered scientific knowledge, they are seldom transferrable to new settings and/or people. Craft developments are one of the primary reasons why the literature on the transfer of training and the "external validity" of solutions is so dismal (e.g., Stolovitch, 1997). Since we seldom repeat transfer or impact evaluation on interventions that have been found to be effective in previous evaluations, we are not often aware of transfer failures. So, solutions which have been effective once, are touted to others who try them and are unaware that they do not work in a new setting. Concern about craft and technology has led to a series of reports from the National Academy of Sciences in the United States (Druckman & Bjork, 1991, 1994) on educational and psychological technologies and evaluations of craft solutions.

Finally, the third negative impact of craft is that the lack of a body of connected scientific theory about the problems being addressed, leads us to believe that science is irrelevant (or at best only a body of "opinion") and problems can best be solved in an ad hoc, intuitive fashion. Craft encourages fads, gurus and magical thinking about problems and solutions. The philosopher Dewey's attraction to science as a way to solve practical problems stemmed from his concern about our failure to provide teachers with effective strategies at the turn of the century. His concerns are still valid today. As a result of our failure to use science, he wrote, educators must "...fall back upon mere routine traditions of ... teaching, or fly to the latest fad [or] panacea peddled out in ... journals ... just as the old physician relied upon his magic formula" (Dewey, 1900, p. 113). Craft is based on the development of arbitrary, mechanistic procedures that are perceived to solve problems in a specific setting. Those procedures develop over time through trial and error adjustments in the problem-solving developed and implemented by experts in a specific context. Craft can be a very effective way to solve a problem. It allowed early human cultures to fashion fire on demand and build extraordinary monuments such as Stonehenge and the Inca cities of South America without the root sciences and mathematics that now serve engineers. It also permits organizational specialists to fashion policies and procedures that foster change and growth in specific situations and allows teachers to foster more-or-less random but sometimes extraordinary learning benefits for individual students or classroom based groups. Yet, the limitations of craft knowledge are not fully appreciated.

Clark (1988a), calling on the theories of Anderson (1993) and others (e.g., Rummelhart & Norman, 1981) has suggested that the lack of generalizability problem with craft mirrors the transfer problems we find in studies of human cognition. Craft mirrors a type of knowledge used by the cognitive system to overcome the limitations on working memory and thinking. When conscious knowledge is used to solve a problem, it gradually becomes automated and unconscious. This automated knowledge is used to make decisions, solve problems and perform all routine human activities. With procedural knowledge we have an efficient mental procedure that is highly effective only in very limited situations which "...fail in general but work in specific cases" (Rummelhart & Norman, 1981, p. 338). This is the reason that craft is dangerous. It has a limited utility but people usually attempt to over generalize it without checking results. The fact that it is limited, context bound, generally inadequate yet effective in one setting, distracts us from real solutions to problems and leaves us overconfident about what we have accomplished. Yet, many educators are unaware of the transfer limits of knowledge and persist in believing that most expertise is widely generalizable. This leads to attempts to teach "learning to learn" and "analogical thinking" skills in schools when most research suggests that general reasoning and learning skills cannot be acquired by most students. When evaluation of these programs are negative, educators tend to blame technology. Thus, our unhealthy reliance on craft, and our tendency in the past two decades to call craft "technology," has eroded the support for educational technology.

One example of the problems created by craft is in the media selection area. Even the most recent model in this area (e.g., Cantor, 1988) is intelligently presented but like all past models, does not link advice to research on current cognitive theories of learning or instruction. Similarly, the most recent book on training and instructional design (e.g., Gagne & Medsker, 1996) suggests craft-based media selection procedures. Most professionals seem to support the intuitive correctness of instructional design and development models that propose connections between various media and different types of learning and information content. We do not doubt the occasional effectiveness of these selection schemes but are concerned about the reliability, internal validity and generalizability of the results. Media selection schemes are usually built on the intuitive assumption that any given media will support some but not other learning outcomes and information content. This assumption has been demonstrated to be incorrect since research has failed to establish any causal links between media and learning (Clark, 1983, 1994a). The indirect result of this situation is that schools, government and industry often invest in newer media on the craft-based promise that "new technology" will improve learning gains.

What Is Educational Technology?

Technology is a process whereby practical problems are identified and solved using interventions based firmly on sound scientific theory, principles and measurement. Scientific principles and the situations they attempt to explain are linked to a larger body of theoretical models that have been validated through systematic experimentation. Because educational scientists are concerned with both internal and external (ecological) validity, the results of an educational technology has the potential for generalizability and reproducibility. Landa (1983), in a very interesting discussion of the relationship between basic science and practical application, refers to the distinction between descriptive and prescriptive research. Another focus of a science-based technology is the value placed on the specification of the problem being solved. Since science must be clear about the problem being solved, a great deal of emphasis is placed on problem specification and measurement. This insures that causes and effects will be clearly defined and measured in a way that can be replicated. Finally, there is an engineering component to all social and educational technologies. Engineering strategies are the bridge between the problem, the science representing our knowledge about the causes and operation of the problem, and the intervention that is expected to solve the problem.

Examples of social and educational technologies are innovations such as the bail-bond process in our legal system (Reichen & Boruch, 1974); change strategies for self-destructive health and addition behaviors (Prochaska, Norcross, & Diclemente, 1994), cognitive task analysis strategies for training and education (Clark & Estes, 1996) and John Anderson's (1993) ACT-R training design system and Anderson's (1993) tutor for the LISP programming language. In each case, these technologies started with a practical problem whose solution was socially and economically valued.

In the case of Prochaska et al. (1994), addictive behaviors and self-destructive health habits are extraordinarily expensive components of our health care system.

The researchers associated with these technologies all started with the same barriers to overcome. First, they faced a profession where there were many dissimilar solutions available for the problem but none of the solutions seemed generalizable. In many instances, the available solutions seemed to work in one setting or with one type of person and cause greater problems for another (Prochaska et al., 1994). This seems to be the situation in instructional design where a variety of craft-based approaches to instruction can lead to measured learning gains for some students and learning content in one setting but lead to "learning loss" for other students, content and settings (Clark, 1988b).

What Is Wrong with Technology Solutions?

So, if educational technology solutions are more robust and generalizable than craft solutions, why don't we all embrace technology? As the dates on the citations for this article will demonstrate, the suggestion that we adopt technology has been around for nearly a century yet it has not been eagerly accepted. This implies that we have failed to solve some of its most important problems. In our view, there are at least three main barriers that inhibit the support for authentic educational technology—non scientists cannot see themselves contributing to technology development; technology requires much more "front end" analysis of problems and impulsive problem solvers are not inclined to wait; and, we do not yet have an adequate process for translating scientific theory and principles into reliably effective technological solutions.

In the first place, people easily get the impression that only people who are trained and functioning as scientists can participate in technology development. Since the various social sciences are difficult to master and require experience monitoring developing bodies of research and theory, most people opt for craft. Craft solutions seem only to require strong analytical skills, creativity, focused motivation and expertise in the setting where the problem is being solved. In fact, as Kearsley (1998) has implied, the aptitudes required for the successful development of a craft are also the basis for most successful technologies. Even in engineering and medicine, various types of knowledge are required to realize the full development of a new technology. These skills include diverse areas such as communication and media production; graphic arts and drawing; computer systems and programming design and development; measurement and evaluation; and project management—to mention only a few specialities. Our beliefs about the levels and types of skills necessary to develop technology are inaccurate as a number of writers in this field have tried to point out over the years. Robert Heinich was not a scientist and yet he was one of the early people in our field who urged us toward a technology focus (Heinich, 1984). He was fond of pointing out that technology is, by its nature and complexity, a group process where everyone has a role in problem identification, intervention design, development, implementation and evaluation. What must bind us together is a commitment to science-based problems and a belief that we can effectively coordinate our separate contributions to the end result.

The second issue that inhibits our support for educational technology is that it takes considerably longer to develop a technology than to devise a craft solution. The extra time is often required at the beginning of the process in order to insure that the real problem has been identified and that the science used for the solution is connected to the problem in prior research and theory. It also requires that impatient educational managers resist their inclination to suggest and implement solutions before problems are thoroughly validated and metrics are available to measure impact. Our experience suggests that most educational problem descriptions are brief and inadequate and most solutions are selected and implemented before there is an adequate understanding of the problem context. Since careful evaluation of results is a rare event, we find that having a solution underway or implemented is considered a successful achievement by most educational managers. If structural engineers and architects worked the same way, most of our buildings would sink into soft ground, be destroyed by earthquakes or other natural disasters and/or fail to serve the needs of those who work in them. Part of the reason for this impulsiveness is a public or a business environment that wants "results" quickly. Since we seldom compare the costs and benefits of craft and technology, we do not have rational data to offer in defense of the careful front-end analysis required by technology. Clark (1994) has provided such data in a rare study comparing a craft and a technology approach to the solution of a knowledge problem in a European organization. He found that while a technology-based training approach required 30 times more front-end effort than its craft predecessor, the technology was so efficient that its delivery and impact cut the time required to implement the solution by half and therefore the financial cost was about half as much as the craft approach. In addition, the technology solution was available for transfer to other parts of the organization and was successfully transferred to different organizations.

The third barrier to the continuing development of educational technology is that we have not yet found an adequate system for connecting basic research, practical problems and the constraints that face interventions in modern educational organizations. We know that we cannot simply "apply" research findings to practical problems and solve them. We need to develop a process that is similar to the "scoping" strategies in engineering or the "diagnosis and triage" approaches used in medicine. There are many first hand accounts of such strategies (see for example, Prochaska et al., 1994) but no systematic study of the issue. We will have much more to say about this issue in a later article in this series. Before this problem is addressed, we need to briefly examine the reason technology is resisted by educators.

Why Do Educators Generally Resist Technology?

Fred Kerlinger, whose books on research methodology have trained generations of students, suggested that educators have actively resisted research-based principles in the past because "Educators have little patience with what they conceive to be 'impractical, ivory tower' research... the net effect of their impatience is a pervading anti-intellectualism that has a devastating effect on research in education" (Kerlinger, 1977, p. 6). Robert Heinich went even farther when he provided evidence that teachers will resist instructional technologies (one of the many categories of educational technology). He wrote that "organized teacher activity parallels the craft union movement in industry. The ways in which the labor movement tried to protect its members from the encroachment of technology are very similar to how teacher groups seek to maintain the labor-intensive character of instruction (Heinich, 1984, pp. 77–78). Katz (1966) describes the historical development of the craft versus science split in Schools of Education. He argues that early in this century, due to their craft focus, "...educationists rejected the option of adherence to any one of the established scientific disciplines, proclaimed themselves to be outspokenly eclectic, and failed to develop a distinctive mode of inquiry or a set of criteria for organizing data for their self-proclaimed science. In the process, they lost all criteria for limiting the nature of their inquiry and instead, tried to construct a discipline through an indiscriminate survey of all factors loosely associated with schools [and] ... became marked by the survey outlook" (p. 332). In the process, Katz argues, education preserved some of the surface trappings of quantitative measurement and science, but cut itself off from advances in scientific methodology; ignored technology development in related professions; severed theoretical connection to related disciplines; and maintained its primary emphasis on craft. The recent emphasis on "post-modernist" philosophy in education is simply the most recent manifestation of a long tradition.

SUMMARY AND CONCLUSION

We believe that our field is producing craft and calling it "technology." The result of this confusion can be found in a number of distressing research and evaluation reports on the lack of effectiveness of many of our popular interventions. Reviews and methodological studies of our work suggest that too many programs are based on ad hoc, non transferrable and isolated solutions to problems that often do not represent the ones we were trying to solve. Yet we are presenting the solutions as if they were effective, derived from scientific theories and models and generalizable to different people, tasks and contexts. When adequate measurement and evaluation establishes that solutions we believe to be science based do not generalize, our reaction has often been to reject science and research as "mere opinion" and foster qualitative evaluation strategies that give us the results we expected. It is too often the case that these rejected solutions were ether "scientized" craft or poor technology. These negative results are very dramatic at a time when educational technology (when defined as media and distance education) is experiencing very enthusiastic international support. Complicating this picture is a distressing tendency for educational technology graduate programs in universities to drift farther and farther away from science over the past two decades. This trend is in the opposite direction from developments in fields such as medicine and engineering where, along with the National Academy of Sciences, we agree that technology is more secure in recent decades. We suggest that part of the reason for our problem is that craft solutions can be developed with little or no training or commitment to science. Since robust evaluation is seldom implemented in educational settings, we tend to be unaware of the transfer failures resulting from attempts to generalize craft solutions. In addition, the technology of education has not yet been fully developed and the necessary participation of non scientists has not been planned or encouraged. Yet we must find ways to encourage increased attention on a wider definition of educational technology. Only with a science-based technology will we be able to produce reliable, generalizable and effective solutions to educational problems. In our next article, we will review accounts of technology development strategies. Our goal is to foster the systematic development of a true educational technology by people from a variety of non-scientific backgrounds and expertise.

NOTE

1.   Morris, W. (Ed.). (1973). *The American Heritage dictionary of the English language.* Boston: Houghton Mifflin Company.

REFERENCES

Anderson, J.R. (1993). *Rules of the mind.* Hillsdale, NJ: Lawrence Erlbaum Publishers.

Bruner, J.S. (1964), The course of cognitive growth. *American Psychologist, 19,* 1–15.

Cantor, J.A. (1988). Research and development into a comprehensive media selection model. *Journal of Instructional Psychology, 15*(3), 118–131.

Clark, R.E. (1978). Doctoral research training in Educational Technology. *Educational Communication and Technology Journal, 26*(2), 165–173.

Clark, R.E. (1983). Reconsidering the research on learning from media. *Review of Educational Research, 53*(4), 445–459.

Clark, R.E. (1988a). The future of technology in educational psychology, In M.C. Wittrock & F. Farley (Eds.), *The future of educational psychology.* Hillsdale, NJ: Lawrence Erlbaum Publishers.

Clark, R.E. (1988b). When teaching kills learning: Research on mathemathantics. In H. Mandl, E. DeCorte, N. Bennett, & H.F. Friedrich (Eds.), *Learning and instruction: European research in an international context* (Vol. 2.2, pp. 1–22). Oxford: Pergamon.

Clark, R.E. (1994a). Media will never influence learning. *Educational Technology Research and Development, 42*(3), 21–29.

Clark, R.E. (1994b). How the cognitive sciences are changing our profession. In H. Stolovitch & E. Keeps (Eds.), *Handbook of Human Performance Technology.* New York: Macmillan.

Clark, R.E. (1995). A history of instructional psychology. *International Encyclopedia of Education* (2nd ed.). Oxford: Pergamon Press Ltd.

Clark, R.E., & Estes, F. (1996). Cognitive task analysis. *International Journal of Educational Research, 25*(5), 403–417.

Cuban, L. (1986). *Teachers and machines: The classroom use of technology since 1920.* New York: Teachers College Press.

Dewey, J. (1900). Psychology and social practice. *The Psychological Review, 7,* 105–124.

Druckman, D., & Bjork, R.A. (1991). *In the mind's eye: Enhancing human performance.* Washington, DC: National Academy Press.

Druckman, D., & Bjork, R.A. (1994). *Learning, remembering and believing.* Washington, DC: National Academy Press.

Ellul, J. (1990). *The technology bluff.* Grand Rapids, MI: Eerdmans Publishing Co.

Galbraith, J.K. (1967). *The new industrial state.* Boston: Houghton Mifflin.

Gage, N. (1985). *Hard gains in the soft sciences: The case of pedagogy.* Phi Delta Kappa, Center on Evaluation, Development and Research, Bloomington, IN.

Gagne, R., & Medsker (1996). *The conditions of learning: Training applications.* Fort Worth, TX: Harcourt Brace College Publishers.

Glaser, R. (1987). Further notes toward a psychology of instruction, In R. Glaser (Ed.), *Advances in instructional psychology* (Vol. III). Hillsdale, NJ: Lawrence Erlbaum Associates.

Golembiewski, R.T., & Sun, B.C. (1990). Positive-finding bias in QWL studies: Rigor and outcomes in a large sample. *Journal of Management, 16,* 665–674.

Heinich, R. (1984). The proper study of instructional technology. *Educational Communications and Technology Journal, 32*(2), 67–87.

Katz, M.B. (1966). From theory to survey in graduate schools of education. *Journal of Higher Education, 23*, 225–334.

Kaufman, R. (1998, January-February), The internet as the ultimate technology and panacea. *Educational Technology*, pp. 63–64.

Kearsley, G. (1998, March-April) Educational technology: A critique. *Educational Technology*, pp. 47–51.

Kerlinger, F. (1977, September) The influence of research on education practice. *Educational Researcher*, p. 50–62.

Landa, L.N. (1983). Descriptive and prescriptive theories of learning and instruction: An analysis of their relationships and interactions. In C. Reigeluth (Ed.), *Instructional design theory and models*. Hillsdale NJ: Lawrence Erlbaum Associates.

Newman, G.A., Edwards, J.E., & Raju, N.S. (1989). Organizational development interventions: A meta-analysis of their effects on satisfaction and other attitudes. *Personnel Psychology, 42*, 461–489.

Prochaska, J.O., Norcross, J., & Diclemente, C.C. (1994). *Changing for good*. New York: Avon Books.

Reichen, H.W., & Boruch , R.F. (1974). *Social experimentation: A method for planning and evaluating social intervention*. New York: Academic Press.

Rummelhart, D.E., & Norman, D.A. (1981). Analogical processes in thinking. In J.R. Anderson (Ed.), *Cognitive skills and their acquisition*. Hillsdale, NJ: Lawrence Erlbaum Publishers.

Shulman, L.S. (1986). Paradigms and research programs in the study of teaching: A contemporary prospective. In M. Wittrock (Ed.), *Handbook of research on teaching* (3rd ed.). New York: Macmillan.

Simon, H. (1981). *The sciences of the artificial* (2nd ed.). Cambridge, MA: MIT Press.

Stolovitch, H.D. (1997). Introduction to the special issue on transfer of training-transfer of learning. *Performance Improvement Quarterly, 10*(2).

Ward, B. (1962). *The rich nations and the poor nations*. New York: Norton.

CHAPTER 14

NEW DIRECTIONS

How to Develop "Authentic Technologies"

Richard E. Clark and Fred Estes

Originally published as: Clark, R.E. & Estes, F. (1999). The development of authentic educational technologies. *Educational Technology, 39*(2), 5–16. Reprinted by permission of Educational Technology Magazine.

The goal of this article is to briefly describe how an authentic technology develops and to give two examples of current social and educational technologies. Our deeper purpose is to encourage a dialogue between educational technologists about the conceptual structure of our research and practice. We agree with Greg Kearsley (1998) that our field needs a new conceptual basis and that our new understanding "must be one that does not assume a logical/rational world..." (p. 51). We believe that our problems are opportunities for a developmental step forward. In other places we have described our concerns about a number of distressing features of this field's current dilemma in previous articles (Clark 1983, 1988a,b; 1994a,b; Clark & Estes, 1998) and only summarize them briefly here.

The main source of concern for most observers of our field is a persistent irrelevance in our inquiry and practice. In the past we have attributed the cause of the problem, in part, to a history of mindless and demonstrably wrong advocacy of popular electronic media to foster motivation and learning. It is also very troubling that most university-based educational technology programs have continued to abdicate their responsibility to confront these problems (Clark, 1978, 1989). The recent glut of students, rushing to Internet-based, multimedia, distance education has not served to discipline our academic programs.

In this series of articles, we discuss the conceptual difficulties that we believe have led to what we now view as a crisis in our field. In our previous article (Clark & Estes, 1998) we described the consequences of our almost exclusive conceptual patronage of indefensible, craft-based points of view. In that article, we suggested that we do not have, and never have had, an educational "technology." While there are notable exceptions, our analysis of the field suggests that when we succeed, it is often because we generate limited, contextualized, non-transferable craft solutions to educational problems. We share the concerns voiced by other critics of our field who suggest that we are not committed to understanding or using the science that illuminates the problems we confront. Instead, educational technologists tend to "scientize" craft by citing research studies that are often poorly designed and largely irrelevant (Clark, 1989) to support interventions that seldom generalize beyond their initial application. We asked for a dialogue concerning the benefits of committing ourselves to authentic science-based educational technology.

John Dewey was making a similar complaint about the craft basis of all of education nearly a century ago (Dewey, 1900). The situation has improved somewhat since then but nearly the same set of concerns has been recently voiced by the National Academy of Sciences and by the National Research Council in this decade (Druckman & Bjork, 1991, 1994). The ninety-year span between these two discussions underscores the duration, difficulty and extent of the challenge. Yet in this article we want to turn away from emphasizing the negative. We agree with colleagues such as Stellan Ohlsson (1996) who notice that pointing out errors and assigning blame may be necessary for error correction in learning about anything. We hope that a dialogue based on rational discourse, replicable evidence, error correction by accepting responsibility for mistakes and providing positive examples and a willingness to serve as our own, most severe critic, will move us forward.

WHAT IS AN "AUTHENTIC TECHNOLOGY?

Our technology scorecard is not entirely negative. It is possible to be thrilled by some of the recent, very effective developments in social and educational research and practice based on authentic technologies. We define an "authentic educational technology" as educational solutions resulting from a systematic analysis that identifies the problem being solved, selects and translates appropriate, well-designed research and applies it to design culturally appropriate educational solutions.

We expect that craft solutions will always be necessary and will always make a significant contribution to solving educational problems. We urge collaboration between research-trained technologists and educational craftspeople of the kind that made *Sesame Street* an extraordinary success in the 1970s. The development of Sesame Street required the close collaboration of child development and instructional psychology researchers on the one hand, and a variety of art and television craft specialties, on the other. Its worldwide success in raising reading and math scores for children, and its adoption in over 80 nations of the world, indicate the potential power of authentic technology. Our problem now is not to encourage craft; it is to develop research-trained technologists who can collaborate productively with creative educational craftspeople. We believe that this kind of collaboration has resulted in effective authentic technology traditions in medicine and engineering.

While positive examples of authentic performance and educational technologies are rare, and often developed outside of educational technology, they can serve as both evidence of, and as models for, future developments. In this article, we want to draw on two examples of authentic educational technology and use them to illustrate an approach and a direction for the future. We will choose one example from recent developments in drug abuse prevention and treatment and another from instructional design. Our discussion will attempt to answer four questions: (1) What problem is being solved by an authentic technology? (2) What body of research and theory addresses the problem most effectively? (3) How do we translate research into effective technologies? (What is the science to technology "spiral"?), and (4) How do we determine that a technology has "solved" an educational problem? (What is the generalizability of technology and how is it demonstrated to be better than a craft solution?).

WHAT PROBLEM IS BEING SOLVED BY AUTHENTIC TECHNOLOGY?

We must begin our search for the development of authentic and effective educational technologies by being clear about the problem we are solving with a new technology. One of the most damaging traditions in educational technology is our temptation to advocate educational solutions apart from a clear analysis of the specific problem needing to be solved. For example, Rossett and Czech (1996) find that many professionals with graduate level training in instructional design and performance technology admit to doing little or no problem analysis. Solutions must be specifically targeted to a type of problem or we run the risk of providing an elegant and expensive solution for the wrong problem. It appears that educational technologists often advocate media to solve learning problems when the strongest evidence supports the conclusion that media do not influence learning (Clark, 1983, 1994a). Electronic media are more likely to solve problems in instructional delivery such as those associated with access, cost and learning time. Educational and performance technologists tend to skip this essential and initial step in technology development. When we advocate a solution without a clearly limited description of its application boundaries and limitations, we do ourselves and our clients a disservice. When we are not clear about the problem being solved it is impossible to connect with the research that will help us find a solution.

Many critics of educational technology have made these points. Roger Kaufman (1998), for example, has been eloquent in pointing out that "...we are getting things backward. Again, instead of focusing on the results and payoffs for whatever we deliver, we are slipping back into old responses that have made many earlier good ideas fail for the wrong reasons ... the ultimate panacea ... is now the Internet ... *(Many educational technologists)* ... seem committed to the view that this is 'the answer to end all answers' ... Constructivists ... and others who have a 'solution' in search of a problem ... find ... satisfactions unrestricted by objectives or purposes" (italics added, p. 63). The "what is the problem being solved" issue is especially vexing since it was educational technology that successfully championed the specification of learning and instructional objectives in the 1960s and 1970s as a way to introduce alternative instructional design and delivery media to schools.

So, what problems should be solved? How do we analyze problems prior to solving them? While we are not aware of any comprehensive "problem domain" analyses, it seems reasonable to assume that problem definitions must be drawn from the existing body of experimental research and theory. For example, problems that involve the *motivation* of students to learn seem to us to connect with a very different body of experiments and theory than problems concerning student *access* to instruction and information. Motivational and access problems tend to be addressed by research and theory that is quite different than *learning* or *performance* problems. Within each of these more-or-less separate research areas, one finds many sub-varieties of specific problems.

For example, research on motivation seems to focus on two different types of motivational problems, commitment and mental effort. Commitment is defined as persistence at a task over time in the face of distractions. Mental effort is defined as the number of non-automatic elaborations used to learn or solve novel tasks and problems. See, for example, the discussion of motivational "indexes" in chapter 1 of Pintrich and Schunk (1996). The reader can imagine other research and theory driven taxonomies of problems. For example, a powerful way to understand learning problems is to draw on cognitive learning theories and break problems into "declarative" and "procedural or propositional" issues (e.g., Anderson, 1993; van Merrënboer, 1998). The learning of declarative knowledge can then be broken down further into different types of declarative knowledge such as processes, concepts and principles, and so on. A similar analysis could be performed on educational "access" issues. This is the area that may eventually prove most fruitful for multimedia, Internet, Intranet and distance educational technology specialists concerned with "delivery" efficiencies.

We turn next to two current examples of authentic technologies, one focused on drug abuse prevention and treatment and another focused on learning and performance. Each of these authentic technologies began with a very clear analysis and understanding of the problem being solved. In fact, both of these examples are successful, in part, because their developers refused to consider specific solutions until the problem being solved was more clearly understood. In the first example, Prochaska et al.'s (1994) technology for substance abuse treatment, a reanalysis of the problem being solved was a key element in finding a new solution to a very old problem.

EXAMPLES OF PROBLEM-FOCUSED AUTHENTIC TECHNOLOGIES: PROCHASKA'S SIX-STAGE CHANGE PROGRAM

Many readers may not be aware that the health care systems of many of the largest nations in the world have recently changed their approach to the treatment of substance abuse. Most nations have now adopted the exciting new "six-stage change technology" developed by James Prochaska, a professor of psychology who specializes in drug abuse prevention, and his colleagues. Prochaska's father died from the complications of alcohol abuse when he was a teenager. Thus, perhaps more than his colleagues, Prochaska was distressed that the evaluations of our most powerful substance abuse treatment approaches indicated that they were only effective in about 2 to 3 percent of cases. After many years of research on the topic, he came reluctantly to the point where he felt the need to "start again."

He vividly describes (Prochaska et al., 1994) the exact moment, during a summer vacation in Cape Cod, when his insight about the problem being solved by the over 400 therapies attempting to prevent drug abuse, led him to a new technology. As he searched for a better way, he was impressed with recent work in psychology that attempted to categorize the many different psychotherapeutic approaches by the problems that each solved best.

Essentially, Prochaska realized that most of the therapies used in drug abuse treatment were not focused directly on modifying substance abuse. Most of these therapies were solving many different types of problems. Existential therapy, for example, was focused on identifying life goals and solving "meaning of life" problems, not on changing habitual and destructive drug addiction behaviors. Psychoanalytic therapies emphasize the analysis of resistance and emotional arousal. Nether of these therapies directly addressed the problem of getting addicted people to change their self-destructive behavior or to maintain a change. His insight, simple to describe but very complex in origin, was to reanalyze the problems being solved. He reasoned that there must be "clusters" of theories and approaches that focus on different "stages" in the complex series of events that precede the decision to actively avoid harmfully addictive substances.

Prochaska identified six stages or problems to be solved by treatment technologies (and developed a six-stage technology for change). Those stages are: (1) Pre-contemplation (Do I have a problem?); (2) Contemplation (Do I want to do anything about my problem?); (3) Preparation (I want to do something, so what options are open to me?); (4) Action (I'm now changing my habits. Will this treatment plan help me withdraw from addictive substances effectively?); (5) Maintenance (What will help me stay away from addictive substances and the contexts which lead me to abuse?), and (6) Termination (I did it!). Thus, in our view, Prochaska's contribution to a new worldwide technology for treating one of the most destructive problems confronting society was to reconceptualize the problem being solved.

Compare Prochaska's approach to the myriad of self-help programs available in bookstores and on the Internet. While some of them are worthless nonsense, many of these programs are developed by practitioners who have been successful in helping others quit smoking, lose weight, assert themselves, manage their time or any of a number of positive changes to improve their lives. These successful programs are most often based on their personal experience in working with clients and on insight, serendipity, and trial and error. This is characteristic of craft knowledge (Clark & Estes, 1998) and often craft-based knowledge is the best and most useful knowledge we have in a particular area, at any given point in time. The problem that concerns us is our failure to move beyond craft-based knowledge and build a science-based technology where we do have the necessary scientific knowledge.

The problem with craft-based solutions is that (1) we don't know why they work or when they will work, (2) it is difficult to transfer these programs to other people, other problems, or other social settings, and (3) they are unconnected to our knowledge of the way the world works, our science, because we have not determined the cause and effect principles involved. The infomercial features a new program every month because these successful programs usually turn out to be highly situated in a partic-ular context and only applicable to certain types of people, under certain conditions. To make it more confusing, the conditions of applicability are unknown.

Does this mean that we should spurn craft-based knowledge and demean the practitioners who create and use these programs? Not at all. To para-phrase Teddy Roosevelt, we should do all we can, with what best we know now, wherever we are now, with whatever tools we have now. To do less would be to fail in our responsibility to do the best we can to solve real prob-lems in real time and to forgo the opportunity to improve the lives of oth-ers. However, to remain content with craft approaches is to fail to in our responsibility to create better solutions. To go beyond craft requires the col-laboration of practitioners, technologists, scientists, craftspeople and artists.

EXAMPLES OF PROBLEM-FOCUSED AUTHENTIC TECHNOLOGIES: E. GAGNE AND J. VAN MERRIËNBOER

In the past, most of our instructional design systems were varieties of the Instructional Systems Design (ISD). While space prevents a discussion of the problems in this model, suffice it to say that it was very strong on pro-cess and very weak on instructional method. Many ISD models exist and most attempt to provide process sequences and procedures for producing instructional materials. The effectiveness of instruction produced using the ISD model varied greatly depending on who was implementing the model. This is a finding that tends to indicate a craft product. In general, the prob-lem being solved by the ISD model was not learning, but instead ISD mod-els solved process problems for the identification, design and development of training. Most ISD models ignored current research on learning or instruction.

Recently, two individuals have succeeded in translating the cognitive research on learning into highly effective instructional design technolo-gies. Ellen Gagne, Robert Gagne's daughter and a professor at Catholic University, has described a very effective approach to designing instruction for K-12 classrooms based on the huge body of cognitive learning research generated by John R. Anderson (1993) and others. Jeroen van Merrën-boer, a Dutch educational technologist and professor at the University of Twente, has translated a similar body of research into a design model to facilitate the learning of complex technical knowledge for adults.

Both of these authors divide their time between research and technol-ogy development. Both have invested the effort required to master the large body of research that supports the design systems they developed. Both have clearly begun with an analysis of the learning problems their systems are designed to solve. Both systems would now profit from collaborations with craft experts. The books and articles that describe both design systems begin with a clear description and analysis of the declarative and procedural knowledge supported by the design models. Both systems draw on the construct and operational definitions used in cognitive learning research when defining the types of knowledge and instructional methods in their design systems. Each can serve as a model for the development of future, problem-focused instructional and training design systems as cognitive learning theory evolves. Both show great promise as solutions to complex learning problems. Both technologies selected the best body of research on the learning of complex knowledge as the basis for the solutions that are suggested.

WHAT BODY OF RESEARCH AND THEORY SHOULD BE USED TO DEVELOP AUTHENTIC TECHNOLOGIES?

We suggest three criteria for choosing research to be translated and applied in an authentic technology. First, we need to choose the most comprehensive, experimentally verified theory that predicts the outcomes (problems to be solved) of interest to the new technology. Second, the independent variables and interventions described in the theory must be morally, ethically and practically acceptable in the target application environments. Third, the theory and related experimental studies that provide evidence for the theory, must permit a description of the "active ingredient" that causes or alleviates the problems being solved in a way that permits "no plausible alternative explanation."

Selecting Appropriate Research

In the first place, technologists must look for comprehensive theories. In choosing theory, we must go beyond the limited and narrowly focused theories that are often available. For example, if our problem involves adults, research with children may often be relevant. If the problem exists in a school setting, research conducted in the military or business may be relevant. Thus, we must conduct the widest search possible for the most inclusive and robust theories. We must also avoid the temptation to choose a theory because it fits our bias or reflects our current experiences or beliefs. We must be willing to change our minds if well-designed experiments fail to confirm our prejudices or our experience.

For example, Ford (1992) counts over thirty-two, research-based theories of motivation to learn. He notes that many of these theories overlap.

Pintrich and Schunk (1996) describe four different theories of motivational learning goal orientation developed by researchers who have given different construct names to almost exactly the same constructs. Because of this duplication and lack of communication among researchers, we need to be very cautious in picking among a large body of theories. In fact, since only one or two motivation theories attempt to incorporate the others (e.g., Ford, 1992) the choice in the motivational area is made easier.

The problem is made more difficult as the number and diversity of comprehensive theories increases. This is certainly the case when one considers research on learning and instruction. The field is ripe with many small and large theoretical efforts (see for example a discussion by Clark, 1988a). Yet most researchers who have recently attempted to produce design technologies have settled on the comprehensive body of research produced by John R. Anderson (1993). Other bodies of research-based theory might eventually produce authentic technologies that have different strengths because they focus on different learning problems.

This complexity suggests that the many types of expertise required to produce authentic educational technologies development will require team efforts. Highly collaborative teams composed of researchers, designers, and representatives of the target audience will most likely be more successful than individuals who try to represent very different and diverse experience. Prochaska and van Merriënboer discuss their own collaborations with colleagues possessing different but complementary knowledge. Prochaska made the decision to accept all major theories but focus the technology based on those theories on the type of problem that reflected one of the six stages in the cycle of change in addictive behavior. This way he and his colleagues did not have to discard many powerful theories, they merely used them appropriately. The design technology of van Merrënboer is focused on the most effective theories on the learning of complex knowledge.

Moral, Ethical and Cultural Issues

On the second issue, our search for practical, moral, cultural and ethical acceptability requires a personal knowledge of the application context for a technology. One of us had a personal epiphany on this issue in India when we made a remark to an Indian colleague about India's "population problem." We were politely but firmly told that "India does not have a population problem, it has a food supply problem." At that point, we learned at the deepest level that the way a problem is defined in the application setting for a technology determines, in large part, the receptiveness of people in the setting for the solution being developed.

In our initial analysis, we must ask whether the problems and solutions addressed by a specific technology will be acceptable to our clients. Robert Heinich (1984) has addressed similar acceptability problems in the educational technology literature. Prochaska wisely did not discard theories that were philosophically acceptable to their advocates and prospective clients. He selected the set of theories that could be used practically to solve at least one of the problems addressed at one or more of the six stages in the cycle of change for addictive behaviors. He tried to find many small theories that were aimed at each change stage. He and his colleagues reasoned that at least one or more of the cluster of theories at each stage would be acceptable to clients who were going to use the resulting technology.

While Prochaska solved his acceptability problem by choosing many theories but assigning them to an appropriate stage in the change process, van Merrënboer is not allowed a similar luxury. He has selected a specific set of theories to translate and now runs the risk of alienating educational technologists who support different theories. We need a constant dialogue about the adequacy and limitations of alternative theories of learning and instruction.

Yet, one of our biggest concerns in this area is that many educational technologists have philosophical and belief barriers to accepting any technology based on experimental science and quantitative research. Many of these barriers get expressed as "post modernist" views of science. We suggest that those concerned about the potential of science to inform educational technology practice read the eloquent defense of this point of view by Nathan Myhrovold (1998) in a recent issue of *Science*. Myhrovold serves as the chief technology officer for Microsoft Corporation. It is our impression that much (but not all) of the resistance to using science to develop new educational technologies is based on stereotypes and a lack of understanding about research and scientific method.

Identifying Active Ingredients for Authentic Technologies

Finally, authentic technology design requires an operational definition of the generic "active ingredient" in the independent variables and interventions that have been used in successful experiments that verified the theory being adopted. A quick example can be found among shopper strategies for purchasing the least expensive in the "over the counter" remedies available in drug stores. The active ingredient in aspirin is 5 mg of an acid compound. This ingredient is available in equal amounts, and with equal impact no matter what medium carries it (e.g., gum, tablet, or liquid suspension) or what "brand" it sells under. Thus all aspirin products that contain the required 5mg. of active ingredient have a more or less equal biological impact, but not the same price.

Clark (1983,1994a) argued that the two active ingredients influencing learning from electronic media delivered instruction are the "instructional methods" and the "task knowledge" embedded in instructional frames. A method was defined as any external representation of a cognitive process necessary for the learning and application of task knowledge of students who could not, or would not, provide the cognitive process for themselves. Task knowledge is defined as the various types of declarative and procedural knowledge necessary to perform the task but unavailable to learners before instruction. The ID technology of van Merrënboer (1998) presents many other important active ingredients.

Identifying active ingredients in research and theory is one of the most creative acts required for technology development. It is a skill that is not well understood or taught and it is seldom modeled adequately. We have been impressed with the discussions about this issue by Reigeluth (1983), Gage (1985) and Landa (1983). Clark (1983, 1988a) described an approach to this problem for delivery and instructional technologies. Clark (In press) describes examples of the approach for motivation technologies. Essentially we must be able to identify the generic causal agents that influence the problems we are solving at the deepest, most structural level in order to develop the most effective technology.

For example, a popular craft-based solution to motivational problems in work settings is to provide "employee empowerment." This involves allowing employees to form work teams that make decisions about how they will perform a job. In some settings these empowered teams have been very successful, in other settings they have failed miserably and expensively. An "active ingredient" analysis of the empowerment intervention suggests that when it succeeds, it does so because those applying it feel that they will gain significant control and become more successful. In some cultures and work settings, being permitted to make decisions about one's job is considered to be a speedy way to fail at the job and therefore is rejected. So the active ingredient in these studies could be called "control beliefs" and defined as any job condition that the individual or team perceives as resulting in increased control or success.

This active ingredient analysis is most obvious to researchers who understand the modern "expectancy-control" theories of motivation (Clark, In press). Without active ingredient analysis, empowerment interventions run the risk of expensive failure at work, in navigation rules for Internet and computer-based distance education and in the classroom. Thus, ingredient analysis is also the basis for the generalizability advantage of an authentic technology over a craft. The more we are aware of the active and necessary ingredients that form the basis of the interventions suggested by technologies, the greater the chance that the technology will transfer to new settings, people and varieties of tasks. Identifying active ingredients in instructional treatments is the extraordinary strength of both the Ellen Gagne and van Merrënboer design technologies. Both of these technologists are very clear about the key elements of their interventions.

HOW DO WE TRANSLATE RESEARCH INTO EFFECTIVE TECHNOLOGIES?

Those who have attempted to apply research findings have learned quickly, and sometimes painfully, that such transfers are not direct or easy. Learning about positive correlations between age and height, on the one hand, and learning and time on the other hand, should not lead us to expect that we will necessarily grow taller and smarter if we only wait for time to pass. Yet this kind of twisted logic can be found in many existing instructional media technologies. Because we find learning correlated with the use of new electronic technologies, we wrongly assume that providing more technology will produce learning advantages. We need a way to conceptualize the process by which theories are developed, and active ingredients are identified and translated into technology. Our suggestion is to focus on the four stages in a "science to technology spiral."

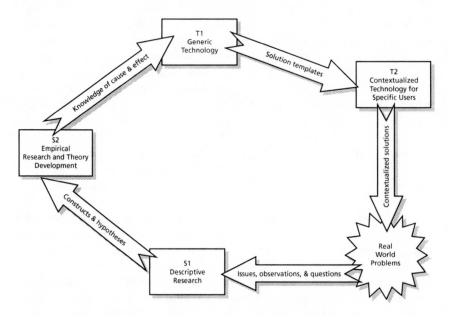

Figure 1.   Development Cycle of a Science-based Technology

We suggest a four-stage model for describing the process by which science develops and is, in turn, translated into social or behavioral technology. We briefly describe the model and then apply it to understanding the translations that occur in the two authentic technologies we are using as examples. The four stages that characterize the movement from science to technology we will call: (1) Descriptive research; (2) Experimental verification of theory; (3) Generic Technology (T1); and (4) Contextualized Technology (T2). The first two stages are commonly associated with science. The final two stages define technology development.

Stage 1: Descriptive Scientific Research Stage (S1)

In stage 1, descriptive research attempts to produce reliable measurement and description of variables and processes of interest. At this stage, very creative new ideas are explored. Nothing is rejected if it can be measured. Construct definition, measurement and hypothesis generation are the key descriptive goals. Both qualitative and quantitative methods attempt to tease out new variables and processes of interest to scientific research. In fact, it is possible that many descriptive research problems result from analyses of craft solutions. Since all craft solutions that are successful in any setting contain elements that might have been sufficient to solve the problem once, many successful technologies have resulted from descriptive reasoning about why the craft solution worked.

Yet no technology results directly and immediately from stage one inquiry. Hypotheses developed here need to be tested at the next stage before they are useful. The survey methods, naturalistic observations, thinking experiments, literature searches for construct validation, path analysis and LISREL or structured equation models used at this stage all serve to define key variables and provide evidence for relationships between variables. This leads to important hypotheses that need to be tested and linked into theories at the next stage. Conclusions about the factors that cause a problem cannot be drawn and no interventions or authentic technologies can be developed based on descriptive data.

Most educational technologists do not conduct descriptive research. Most do not even review the research that has been conducted at this stage unless there is a question about the definition or psychometric properties of constructs that are being considered for inclusion in a technology. The research conducted at this state is often very creative and naturalistic. For example, in the 1850s, the Viennese physician Semmelweis noticed that four times as many women died of symptoms called "childbirth fever" in a birth clinic staffed by physicians than in a similar clinic staffed by midwives. He could not describe the cause of the deaths until a physician friend cut himself with a knife he had used for dissecting cadavers and died of symptoms identical to childbirth fever. Semmelweis connected these two events and reasoned that since physicians who delivered babies in their clinic had often been dissecting cadavers just before the delivery, he suggests that "cadaverous matter" may have been causing the deaths through transmission by the physicians. He planned an experiment to validate his descriptive observation. He asked physicians to wash their hands before attending childbirth. Subsequent deaths in the physician's clinic fell to the level of the midwife's clinic. His experiment was an example of science at stage 2.

Stage 2: Scientific Experiments and Theory Development (S2)

In stage 2, theory development and the experimental verification of theories is carried out through the testing of hypotheses suggested at the descriptive level. Theories are built, checked in experiments and revised. Theoretical paradigms compete for attention. Quantitative and qualitative methodologies cooperate to test the key hypotheses in theories. Those theories that encompass the greatest range of phenomenon and survive experimental tests, continue. Confounding and artifact are eliminated from the typical experimental designs that test competing theories. The unconfirmed or narrow theories should fail but sometimes survive out of the ignorance or ego problems of researchers and journal editors. Rival hypotheses and alternative explanations for the effects measured in controlled studies are explored and, if possible, eliminated. Active ingredients that produce measured results are identified. Paradigms shift and change with shifts in evidence and fashion. Advanced theories that survive this stage are ripe for the development of authentic technologies.

Semmelweis's hand washing experiment is a good example of the long history of connections between science and technology. While there was no effective knowledge of micro organisms in the 1850s, Semmelweis's instructions that doctors wash their hands before attending women in childbirth decreased deaths. He assumed that the active ingredient causing death was "cadaverous matter" and that hand washing would eliminate the problem.

Stage 3: Generic Technology Development (T1)

In stage 3, generic technologies are developed based on the strongest and most successful theoretical paradigms that have survived scrutiny at stage 2. This is the state where a generic active ingredient analysis is critical. Technologies must first be developed in a generic or decontextualized state so as not to confuse the issues surrounding the many unique limiting features of the setting or context in which they are being applied. For example, we need first to know that a need to feel in control is the active ingredient that drives motivational commitment to learning goals. Only then can we introduce the many conflicting types of control issues one finds in different application settings. (The issue of setting-specific translations of the active ingredients is introduced in the next stage). The goal at this stage is to generate a model that explains how to solve the problems that served as dependent variables in prior research.

Reigeluth (1983) notices that the reasoning at this stage is "backwards." Whereas research starts by trying to find a treatment that will "predict" changes in a dependent variable. Technology at the generic stage starts with the dependent or "problem" variable and attempts to incorporate the active ingredient into a generic treatment or intervention that will solve the undesired problem.

Prochaska's change strategy exists only at the generic T1 stage. He and his colleagues wisely decided to design a generic technology that could be "translated" by psychologists in many treatment or prevention settings. This permitted the addition of local features that increased the cultural acceptability of the treatments without diluting the active ingredient. This is one of the strengths (and some have complained, one of the weaknesses) of his system. Its strength is that the generic, "active ingredient" description of the key elements of the successful interventions at every stage allows all users to translate the T1 ingredients in a way that will make them acceptable to their clients. Yet the clarity of the description of the T1 solutions permits users to make reliable and accurate applications in a great variety of culturally different settings.

Van Merrënboer used a similar strategy for his instructional design technology. He has a generic T1 system that cannot succeed without being procedurally translated for application in any specific application. He notes that his system "does not … focus on ready made procedures to support the process of instructional design" (van Merrënboer, 1998, p. 1). He explains that it is to be "applied in conjunction with an ISD-model in order to receive support for the activities not treated in the model such as needs assessment, needs analysis, production of instructional materials, implementation, delivery and summative evaluation" (p. 3). Presumably, other T1 authentic technologies could be developed to accommodate the additional "activities."

Stage 4: Specific Technology Development (T2)

In stage 4, generic (T2) technologies are translated for specific settings, people and tasks. An educational technology that is acceptable and effective in a North American K-12 classroom may not be acceptable in a Chilean K-12 classroom. An educational technology developed for San Jose, California may not be acceptable in San Pedro, California. The children's television series "Sesame Street" was eventually adopted for use in over 80 nations. In many of those settings, there were controversies about the almost total focus of the program on "cognitive skills" and an absence of "social skills" training. In other countries, the scripts had to be edited and new versions of the program were produced to change elements such as gender roles, situations, relationships and songs to make them culturally acceptable.

At this final stage, the generic T1 technology is shaped and translated for the unique cultural beliefs, expectations, knowledge and value patterns found in a specific application setting. The specificity of T2 technologies vary, depending on the novelty of the cultural expectations and values held by users who will experience the technology. It is also critical to note that only T1 technologies should be transferred between different settings. Since T2 technologies are specific to a context, one would not expect the intact transfer of T2 interventions to a different context to succeed.

Translating generic T1 technologies into specific T2 applications requires a great deal of experience with the culture and expectations found in the target setting. We are not aware of any science that informs this process and so we need to rely on existing craft, systems approaches and on a "trial and revise" correction cycle. Imagine a need to transfer a T1 technology for teaching concepts to a specific setting. It is easy to see how the knowledge and learning strategies people need to learn and perform can be described in a generic way. A concept is defined the same regardless of the context in which it is taught or learned.

Yet critical elements of instructional presentations such as our specific choice of the examples, simulations, and analogies used to illustrate concepts can and should change depending on local constraints. Important among those constraints are teacher's and learner's beliefs. For example, the usefulness of certain types or formats for examples; the value placed on humor or a rejection of humor as "frivolous"; whether instructional decisions are typically made by learners or system managers; and the efficacy beliefs of learners and system managers, name only a few of many constraining beliefs. Much more work remains to be done at the T2 level to insure adequate translation of generic technologies.

Roles and Responsibilities.

A few words about the various roles in this spiraling cycle of science to technology may clarify the dimensions of the type of collaboration we are calling for. First, while no one can juggle all the roles simultaneously, many people play more than one role. For example, practitioners who are responsible for implementing and delivering solutions to clients may function as technologists at the T2 level while adapting a T1 technology for use in their specific organizations and clients, then shift to a craft role in improvising a part of the solution set where our scientific knowledge is missing or incomplete. So people may move among various roles as their needs, interests, and opportunities allow.

Second, it is clear that all the roles are necessary for optimal solutions of real world problems. Scientists add to our knowledge of the world, but it is not their job to apply that knowledge. Technologists use knowledge as the raw material to forge solutions at both the T1 and T2 levels. Practitioners deliver these solutions in the real world and employ craft to fill in the gaps of our knowledge. Craftspeople are those ingenious people who devise ways to make things work, even if they do not know why it works. For example, before there was a technology of anesthesia, a craft approach to pain relief was to give a patient as much whiskey as they could consume. At that time, whiskey was a responsible and compassionate (if dangerous) intervention. Today, however, when we have a technology of anesthesia based on scientific knowledge, the use of whiskey is not an acceptable practice. We deplore the persistence of craft approaches when the state of our knowledge permits the development of authentic technology.

HOW DO WE DETERMINE THAT A TECHNOLOGY HAS "SOLVED" AN EDUCATIONAL PROBLEM?

Since substantive, multidimensional evaluation is seldom performed on educational interventions, the case for authentic technologies is more difficult. If we require adequate evaluation of interventions, the clear superiority of authentic technology over craft will be evident. Too many practitioners experience research as a complex, error-filled process where competing claims are voiced constantly. Whereas information about craft solutions are most often based on "personal or organizational experience testimony" where the positive is emphasized and failures are not mentioned. To paraphrase an old saying in the media area, "The invisible virtues of craft are compared with the very visible mistakes made as we develop research-based authentic technologies."

We are attracted to a combination of formative evaluation (in progress checks accompanied by a revise cycle) and the adoption of a more elaborate version of the Kirkpatrick (1994) four level evaluation model used in business settings for summative evaluation. Kirkpatrick's model permits us to distinguish among (1) motivation (like it?), (2) learning (learn it?), (3) application (use it?), and (4) results (payoff?). This is a check on the needs analysis and problem analysis that began the design cycle in the first place).

Formative evaluation can be performed at all of the four stages in the development of a technology. Outcome evaluation can most persuasively be performed only on T2 technologies but because of the indeterminate nature of the T1 to T2 translations, considerable uncertainty always remains about what has caused any measured gain (or lack of gain) at any of the four Kirkpatrick evaluation levels. It is discouraging that so little evaluation is performed on any educational innovation. This pattern makes it difficult to compare the effectiveness of authentic technologies with craft solutions. When evaluation is performed, it is often badly designed and focused mainly on reactions (which can be inversely related to learning, behavior and results) and secondarily on learning (and most learning evaluation is focused on memory for facts). We seldom evaluate transfer or results, and yet our goals are almost always to achieve transfer and to solve the problem that began the development process in the first place.

THE PARTNERSHIP NEEDED TO DEVELOP AUTHENTIC TECHNOLOGIES

One of the important implications of the Spiral Model of Science and Technology is the need for the collaboration of practitioners, technologists, and scientists. We feel that much of the controversy in this area results from two mistaken beliefs. One is that a good professional should do it all from basic, descriptive research to implementing the polished T2 solution set. The second is that some roles in this cycle are inherently more worthy of respect than others.

The first belief is a common, yet impossible problem. No one person can perform all the roles in the cycle simultaneously. First, the demands and opportunities of the organizations we work in put us all in different situations. Universities afford time for research and reflection; school classrooms and business settings demand swift, effective action, and consultancies provide an overview of the same problem in many settings and the bridge between theory and practice. Second, we all have different strengths and skills as a result of our aptitudes, interests, and focused experiences. The special skills and instincts we develop that make us so good in one role may be counterproductive in another role. A dispassionate, deeply analytical, and reflective approach will serve the researcher very well, but will be fatal to the classroom teacher and business trainer who need to respond fluidly and immediately.

The second misconception is related and deeply troubling. Unless we understand the roles of our collaborators in different phases of the cycle and can develop true respect for their contributions and the constraints they work under, we will not be able to collaborate effectively. Practitioners are not less worthy or less valuable than researchers; they are not simply people who could not make it in research. Researchers are not impractical nerds doomed by their timid souls to spend their cloistered lives proving the obvious at great expense to the taxpayers. Each role has a unique contribution to make and a need to partner with all the other roles to add to our knowledge and to solve real problems.

SUMMARY AND CONCLUSIONS

We are proposing collaboration between educational researchers and craftspeople on the development of authentic technologies. We believe that only with a commitment to authentic technologies can we hope to solve persistent problems with the utility and relevance of our educational technology interventions. We argue in this article, and an earlier discussion (Clark & Estes, 1998) that most of our current work can be described as limited and non-generalizable craft. We define an "authentic educational technology" as educational solutions resulting from a systematic analysis that identifies the problem being solved, selects and translates appropriate, well-designed research and applies it to design culturally appropriate educational solutions. We presume that educational technologists will want to take advantage of the extraordinary advances over the past two decades in the social and behavioral sciences in order to solve pressing educational problems.

In order to do so, we provide some preliminary answers to four troubling questions: (1) What problem is being solved by an authentic technology? (2) What body of research and theory addresses the problem most effectively? (3) How do we translate research into effective technologies? and, (4) How do we determine that a technology has "solved" an educational problem? As we attempt to answer those questions, we suggest that authentic technology design requires first a clear analysis and validation of the problem being solved and a determination to avoid our present error of "advocating solutions and looking for problems they will solve." A preliminary taxonomy of educational problem types was proposed centering on access to educational resources; the economics of educational treatments and outcomes; learning and performance issues; and motivation to learn and perform.

Next we recommended a strategy for identifying robust research that, when analyzed, will yield a generic model of the solution to an educational problem. We asked for three assurances when selecting research. First, that we choose the most comprehensive, experimentally verified theory that predicts the outcomes (problems to be solved) of interest to the new technology. Second, the independent variables and interventions described in the theory must be morally, ethically and practically acceptable in the target application environments. Third, the theory and related experimental studies that provide evidence for the theory, must permit a description of the "active ingredient" that causes or alleviates the problems being solved in a way that permits "no plausible alternative explanation." We clearly understand that each of these issues permits alternative views and respectful dialogue about alternatives between colleagues who may choose to disagree.

We then described a "science to technology" cycle. This cycle helps our understanding of the events that occur as basic science becomes applied science, and applied science is transformed into effective technologies. We proposed a four-stage cycle: (1) descriptive science where hypotheses are identified; (2) experimental research where theories are validated; (3) a generic technology (T1) stage where the analysis of research and theory permits us to identify the "active ingredient" in the research interventions or treatments that influenced the types of problems we want to solve; and (4) a contextualized (T2) stage where the active ingredient of the solution is translated for specific settings, cultures, and people. Our focus was on the two technology stages.

In T1, for example, we advised technologists to seek a generic "active ingredient." An example of an active ingredient is the active compound in aspirin. No matter how many brands or types of aspirin one encounters, we can be certain that the key component is the active ingredient. We gave many examples of the active ingredients in T1 educational technologies.

The second or T2 stage of technology development, knowing the chemical makeup of this acid compound is equivalent to describing a T1 generic technology. Yet in order to "take" or "administer" aspirin, we must combine the active compound into a variety of buffer and delivery media. Aspirin can be combined with a number of inert compounds and fluid suspensions and delivered orally or through injection, suppositories or skin patch. Oral delivery can take the form of swallowed tablets or liquid suspensions, sublingual tablets or liquid or a chewed gum. We acknowledge that both T1 and T2 technologies require collaborative work between people and teams with differing expertise. Our models for collaborations between craftspeople, artists and scientists include successful authentic technologies such as "Sesame Street," the Prochaska Six-Stage Model for Change for the treatment of drug abuse (Prochaska et al., 1994), the instructional system designed by E. Gagne (Gagne et al., 1993), and van Merriënboer's Complex Cognitive Skills Training model (van Merriënboer, 1998). Finally, we propose adopting a version of the Kirkpatrick (1994) four level evaluation design for use in both formative and summative evaluation so that we can check the results of all authentic technologies and compare then with craft solutions.

We are deeply aware that space considerations required us to give only cursory descriptions of ideas and approaches that are very complex and, in a few cases, controversial. Our purpose in this article is to shift the direction of our dialogue a bit. We invite questions, suggestions and alternative views. We only hope that we can be constantly clear about the criteria we will use to determine which ideas will prevail. Our criteria emphasize measured gains that reflect a solution to the problem targeted by our technology. We know that this discussion is not finished. In our next installment, we will describe some of the replies and ideas that have been proposed about these ideas.

REFERENCES

Anderson, J.R. (1993). *Rules of the mind.* Hillsdale NJ: Lawrence Erlbaum Publishers.

Clark, R.E. (1978). Doctoral research training in educational technology. *Educational Communication and Technology Journal, 26*(2), 165–173

Clark, R.E. (1983). Reconsidering the research on learning from media. *Review of Educational Research, 53*(4), 445–459.

Clark, R.E. (1988a). The future of technology in educational psychology. In M.C. Wittrock & F. Farley (Eds.), *The future of educational psychology.* Hillsdale, NJ: Lawrence Erlbaum Publishers.

Clark, R.E. (1988b). When teaching kills learning: Research on mathemathantics. In H. Mandl, E. DeCorte, N. Bennett, & H.F. Friedrich (Eds.), *Learning and instruction: European research in an international context* (Vol. 2.2, pp. 1–22). Oxford: Pergamon.

Clark, R.E. (1989). The future of technology in educational psychology. In M. Wittrock & F. Farley (Eds.), *The future of educational psychology.* Hillsdale NJ: Lawrence Erlbaum Publishers.

Clark, R.E. (1994a). Media will never influence learning. *Educational Technology Research and Development, 42*(3), 21–29.

Clark, R.E. (1994b). How the cognitive sciences are changing our profession. In H. Stolovitch & E. Keeps (Eds.), *Handbook of human performance technology.* New York: Macmillan.

Clark, R.E. (1998, October). Motivating performance. *Performance Improvement, 37*(8), 39–47.

Clark, R.E. (In press). The CANE model of motivation to learn and to work: A two-stage theory process of goal commitment and effort. In J. Lowyck (Ed.), *Trends in corporate training.* Leuven: University of Leuven Press.

Clark, R.E., & Estes, F. (1998). Technology or craft: What are we doing? *Educational Technology*, pp. 5–11.

Dewey, J. (1900). Psychology and educational practice. *The Psychological Review, 7*, 105–124.

Druckman, D., & Bjork, R.A. (1991). *In the mind's eye: Enhancing human performance.* Washington, DC: National Academy Press.

Druckman, D., & Bjork, R.A. (1994). *Learning, remembering and believing.* Washington, DC: National Academy Press.

Ford, M. (1992). *Motivating humans.* Newberry Park, CA: Sage.

Gage, N. (1985). *Hard gains in the soft sciences: The case of pedagogy.* Phi Delta Kappa, Center on Evaluation, Development and Research, Bloomington, IN.

Gagne, E., Yekovich, C., & Yekovich, F. (1993). *The cognitive psychology of school learning* (2nd ed.). New York: Harper Collins College Publishers.

Heinich, R. (1984). The proper study of instructional technology. *Educational Communications and Technology Journal, 32*(2), 67–87.

Kaufman, R. (1998, January-February). The Internet as the ultimate technology and panacea. *Educational Technology, 38*(1), 63–64.

Kearsley, G. (1998, March-April). Educational technology: A critique. *Educational Technology, 38*(2), 57–61.

Kirkpatrick, D.L. (1994). *Evaluating training programs: The four levels.* San Francisco: Berrett-Kohler Publishers.

Landa, L.N. (1983). The algo-heuristic theory of instruction. In C. Reigeluth (Ed.), *Instructional design theories and models.* Hillsdale, NJ: Lawrence Erlbaum Publishers.

Myhrovold, N. (1998, October 23). Supporting science. *Science* (282), 621–622.

Ohlsson, S. (1996). Learning from error and the design of task environments. *International Journal of Educational Research, 25*(5), 419–448.

Pintrich, P.R., & Schunk, D.H. (1996). *Motivation in education: Theory, research and application.* Englewood Cliffs, NJ: Prentice-Hall.

Prochaska, J.O., Norcross, J.C., & Diclemente, C.C. (1994). *Changing for good.* New York: Avon Books.

Reigeluth, C.M. (1983). Instructional design, what is it and why is it? In C. Reigeluth (Ed.), *Instructional design theories and models.* Hillsdale, NJ: Lawrence Erlbaum Publishers.

Rossett, A., & Czech, C. (1996). They really wanna but ... The aftermath of professional preparation in performance technology. *Performance Improvement Quarterly, 8*(4), 114–132.

van Merriënboer, J.J.G. (1998). *Training complex cognitive skills,* Englewood Cliffs, NJ: Educational Technology Publications.

CHAPTER 15

NEW DIRECTIONS

Cognitive and Motivational Research Issues for Multimedia Instruction

Richard E. Clark

Originally published as: Clark, R.E. (1999), Yin and Yang cognitive motivational processes operating in multimedia learning environments. In J. van Merrienböer (Ed.), *Cognition and multimedia design.* Herleen, Netherlands: Open University Press. Reprinted by permission of the Open University Press.

ABSTRACT

The purpose of this discussion is to make the point that the complexity and flexibility of multimedia instructional environments can be beneficial but may also bring a large and almost unrecognized danger. Instructional conditions associated with multimedia environments that both help and hinder student learning motivation are described. The first part of the presentation attempts to link research on complex learning and cognitive load on the one hand, and motivational variables that are necessary to support learning, on the other hand. Following Pajares (1996) the discussion engages in "intertheoretical cross talk" (p. 569) and so draws freely on the many small theories and research hypotheses suggested by research in a variety of learning and motivation traditions, keeping in mind the cautions of Gery D'Ydewalle

(1987) concerning the many problems with motivational constructs. Five hypotheses are suggested that attempt to explain why motivation for complex learning may sometimes be damaged by multimedia instructional conditions that, for example, overload working memory and/or provide new learning strategies.

Hypothesis 1.   As cognitive load increases, mental effort increases linearly and positively.

Hypothesis 2.   Mental effort has an inverted U relationship with task self efficacy so that self efficacy decreases as task novelty increases and vice versa.

Hypothesis 3.   At the "efficacy threshold" effort stops and an automated cognitive "default" directs attention to different or novel goals.

Hypothesis 4.   As knowledge automates, mental effort decreases and learner overconfidence is a danger.

Hypothesis 5.   Persistence at a learning task is a positive, linear, multiplicative function of domain self efficacy, mood and task value. Below a "control threshold," persistence stops and an automated default focuses attention on novel goals.

An explanation for multimedia instruction (MMI) features that may damage or aid learning is drawn from cognitive motivation research, specifically from expectancy-control theory and from cognitive learning theory. The purpose of the five hypotheses is to generate additional research to help explain the many kinds of mistakes and learning failures that are caused by links between motivational and learning processes. A "yin and yang" model is proposed to explain the learning failures associated with instruction in novel, declarative knowledge on the one hand and the use of more familiar, automated, procedural knowledge, on the other hand. It will be suggested that when motivational problems are encountered when learning declarative knowledge, they are caused by "yin processes" that substitute different, novel and unintended learning goals and strategies for the ones intended by MMI systems. When motivation problems are encountered during procedural learning, they are caused by "yang processes" that elicit familiar, automated but unsuccessful learning goals and strategies for over confident students. Where research-based solutions are available for motivational problems, they are described.

INTRODUCTION

Instructional research is rich with studies of important learning and motivational processes that operate during complex learning (e.g., Anderson, 1993; Bandura, 1977, 1997; Bower, 1983; Gagne, et al., 1993; Gagne & Medsker, 1996; Pintrich & Schunk, 1996). Cognitive research on the executive processes that are thought to control learning activities has provided us with the potential to improve the impact of instruction. One source of this improvement is to use the flexibility and resources of multimedia, computer-based technologies for designing and delivering instruction that compensates for student information processing and study skill deficits. Newer media provide potentially cost-effective access to a great variety of instructional simulations, formats, symbol systems, monitoring and feedback capabilities on the one hand, and information scaffolding methods that might aid cognitive processing during learning, on the other hand. Multi media instructional systems, from the viewpoint of the learner, are characterized by: (a) Information rich displays where almost all visual and auditory formats and symbolic modes can be presented at once, if desired; (b) the potential for high levels of real time interactivity (transactions) between the system and individual learners; and (c) maximum learner control of instructional access, pacing, scheduling, feedback, and structure. Dillon and Gabbard (1998) have provided a recent review of research on the effects of various design and formatting features in "hypermedia" on learning. They define hypermedia as "...a generic term covering hypertext, multimedia and related applications involving the chunking of information into nodes that could be selected dynamically" (Dillon & Gabbard, 1998, p. 323). After reviewing studies conducted in the past decade, they came to a conclusion similar to earlier reviews by Clark (1983, 1994a,b). Essentially, the evidence in multimedia and hypertext research suggests that all learning benefits from the newer media also cause learning problems for some learners. They summarize their review by suggesting that only rapid searching, learner control and accommodating learner styles occasionally help increase learning in multimedia instructional environments. They also indicate that each of these benefits can harm learning for some students.

MOTIVATIONAL PROCESSES THAT SUPPORT OR INHIBIT COMPLEX LEARNING

Most reviews of instructional design for MMI environments focus on types of knowledge and strategies for knowledge acquisition and more or less ignore motivational issues. Yet, knowledge cannot be acquired and used without appropriate motivational levels (Pintrich & Schunk, 1996). Whereas knowledge provides substance and organization to behavior, motivation provides "...the process whereby goal-directed activity is instigated and sustained" (Pintrich & Schunk, 1996, p. 4). Motivation is also concerned with the amount and quality of the "mental effort" people invest in achieving goals. Mental effort is defined as "the number of non-automatic elaborations necessary to solve a problem" (Salomon, 1984, p. 231). Elaborations are enhanced by instructional methods such as examples and analogies, the cognitive mechanisms that connect new declarative knowledge to previously learned information (Gagne et al., 1993). These two elements of motivation, active and sustained goal pursuit (committed persistence) on the one hand, and mental effort, on the other hand, are the primary outcomes investigated in motivation research and the primary focus of this discussion. Mental effort is the engine that provides the energy necessary to support complex learning. Complex learning is the essential ingredient of "knowledge work" that is the primary source of the products and services that support large and small business and government organizations (Cascio, 1995). Motivational studies have found that cognitive motivation accounts for between 12 percent (Helmke, 1987) and 38 percent (Fyans & Maehr, 1987) of the variance on academic learning tasks. The model presented here derives, in part, from an analysis of motivation research by Pintrich and Schunk (1996); from the Motivational Systems Theory (MST) proposed by Martin Ford (1992); and from recent work on cognitive effort by Bandura (1997), Salomon (1984) and Clark (in press) among others. It is intended to serve as an update on an older motivational design model presented by Keller (1987).

Expectancy-Control Model of Motivation to Learn and to Solve Problems

The following discussion of motivational problems that occur in complex learning environments is drawn from cognitive motivation theory, often called "expectancy-control theory." Many motivation researchers (e.g., Friedman & Lackey, 1991; Heckhausen & Schulz, 1995; Shapiro, Schwartz, & Austin, 1996) share the implicit and explicit belief that the ability to gain and maintain a sense of personal and group control or effectiveness is the essential goal of all motivated behavior. Expectancy-control researchers assume that committed behavior is rational (although not always logical or effective). Persistence at a learning or problem solving goal over time is presumed to result from an explicit or implicit analysis of the "control potential" value of achievement or learning goals.

The general hypothesis that seems to underlie expectancy control theories is that the more we perceive the achievement of learning goals to bring increased control or effectiveness, the more we are motivated to persist at those goals when faced with distractions. When convinced that a learning goal will decrease our effectiveness or control, learners are less willing to continue pursuing the goal and the more inclined they are to select an alternative goal. While different individuals and cultures might adopt radically different preferred methods for achieving control, the value for control is thought to be one of the most dominant and crucial human "universals" (Brown, 1991). Evidence for the benefits of achieving and maintaining stable "control beliefs" through adequate "self regulation" (Carver & Scheier, 1998) across developmental stages (Heckhausen & Schulz, 1995) is provided in studies of academic learning and problem solving (e.g., Bandura, 1997), psychotherapy (Wegner, 1997), and medicine (Shapiro, Schwartz, & Austin, 1996; Enserink, 1999). Evidence for the destructive effects of beliefs that control has been lost or compromised have also been provided by many researchers (e.g., Peters et al., 1998; Shoham & Rohrbaugh, 1998; Wegner, 1997).

What Aspects of Learning Does Motivation Support?

Pintrich and Schunk (1996) have suggested that our diverse body of current motivation research tends to focus on a number of "indexes" or outcomes. These indexes are the problems that motivation researchers are attempting to understand and solve. Examples of these outcomes are goal choice (the passive and active selection of learning or performance goals), commitment (persistence at a learning goal over time, in the face of distractions), mental effort (employing conscious, non-automatic cognitive strategies to facilitate goal achievement) and performance (measures of learning goal success). All of these indexes have, at one time or another, been used to characterize motivation to learn and to define the variables examined in motivation research. Since goal commitment and mental effort seem to be the key motivational issues in most adult learning and work settings, the theoretical model chosen for this discussion is drawn from the CANE (Commitment and Necessary Effort) model described by Clark (in press).

The goal in this discussion is to provide a motivational explanation for the cognitive overload issues raised by Sweller (1999) and the destructive effects of instructional methods described by Clark (1982, 1989) and Lohman (1986). The discussion of motivational processes that operate in MMI learning environments has been divided into seven, interrelated hypotheses. Evidence for each hypothesis will be discussed in turn. Then suggestions are made for how designers in MMI environments might unintentionally cause learning problems and how design rules might avoid problems and enhance motivation to persist and invest maximum mental effort for learning goals.

COGNITIVE LOAD AND MENTAL EFFORT

The discussion begins with a suggested connection between students' perception of the cognitive load they expect and experience during learning and the amount of mental effort they invest to learn from instruction. A primary assumption supporting this discussion is that intrinsic learner perceptions of cognitive load are often more powerful than extrinsic, "objective" measures of cognitive load.

Hypothesis 1. As cognitive load increases, mental effort increases linearly and positively.

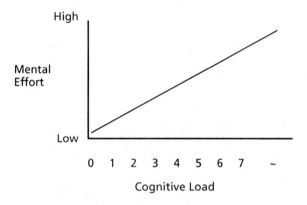

Many studies have found evidence for a direct connection between cognitive load and mental effort (Miller, 1956; Paas, 1992; Sweller, 1999). Presumably, all students continually monitor the extent of the novelty and difficulty posed by a learning goal (Pintrich & Schunk, 1996). Judgements of task difficulty appear to directly influence the amount of mental effort invested in a learning task (Clark, in press; Salomon, 1984). Since perceived difficulty is primarily (but not entirely) a function of cognitive load, "other things being equal" we could expect a positive and linear relationship between these two variables.

The more instructional elements that must be consciously manipulated by elaboration or reorganization, and the more "non automatic" cognitive strategies that must be developed to manage these cognitive manipulations, the more mental effort that must be invested to achieve learning goals. As the number of items that must be processed in working memory increase, mental effort must necessarily increase if learning is to be successful. We also know that maximum learning gains are achieved with the maximum levels of challenge a student can tolerate successfully (Locke, 1990; Locke & Latham, 1990). In order to insure that cognitive load is high enough to insure maximum learning gains but not so high as to overwhelm students, some way to measure mental effort needs to be included in instructional systems.

The Measurement of Intrinsic Cognitive Load and Mental Effort

The purpose of focusing on the relationship between load and effort is that it is difficult to accurately measure "intrinsic" cognitive load because of the large variation between learners in prior knowledge that can be used to elaborate information resident in working memory (Sweller, 1999). Instead, it seems better to attempt to measure mental effort since each student's effort will be directly related to their individual perceptions of their own cognitive load (Bandura, 1997; Pintrich & Schunk, 1996; Salomon, 1983). The measurement of effort is not yet well developed.

Salmon (1983) has defined mental effort as our perception of the mental energy required to use "non automatic" knowledge to solve problems, learn or transfer knowledge to new tasks. The measurement of the use of non-automatic knowledge is not well developed (but see a review by Cennamo, 1989). Instruments currently available include a variety of post-task, self-report measures (Bandura, 1997; Schwarzer, 1992); indirect estimates of latencies and time to complete tasks (e.g., Corno & Kanfer, 1993; Dweck, 1989) and dual-task measures (e.g., rhythmic finger tapping while engaged in complex learning and practice; additional examples described by Cennamo, 1989). The most efficient measures are those that only require post-task, Likert-style, self report estimates of how "difficult" or how much "thinking" the task required. The reliability of these self-report measures is often quite high (e.g., Dweck, 1989).

The most robust measures seem to those associated with "dual tasks" that interrupt learners at different stages during instruction and ask them to perform an unrelated and interfering task or operation (e.g., finger tapping or solving mental mathematics problems) while they are under time pressure to complete the learning task (e.g., Peters et al., 1998). The more that the dual task performance is delayed or interrupted, the more mental effort a person is presumed to be experiencing.

MENTAL EFFORT AND SELF EFFICACY

Mental effort is difficult to observe directly so it is necessary to search for indirect measures. Bandura (1997) and Salomon (1981, 1983, 1984) have argued that task-specific self efficacy is greatly influenced by mental effort expenditures. Presumably, the experience of mental effort influences our personal efficacy expectations about a learning task. Thus, task-specific self efficacy can be described as an important indicator of past mental effort investments and past intrinsic cognitive load experienced during the learning. The second hypothesis describes the expected shape of the relationship between mental effort and specific self efficacy.

Hypothesis 2.   Mental effort has an inverted U relationship with task self efficacy so that self efficacy decreases as task novelty increases and vice versa.

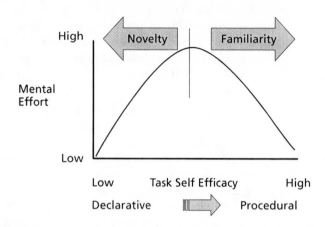

Bandura (1997) has defined self efficacy as "...beliefs in one's capabilities to organize and execute courses of action required to produce given attainments" (p. 3). Self report measures of self efficacy have been found to be highly reliable and accurate predictors of academic achievement regardless of student ability level, prior knowledge or age (Bandura, 1997; Pajares, 1996; Pintrich & Schunk, 1996). For example, Pajares and Miller (1994) found that mathematics self efficacy was a better predictor of math achievement than was prior mathematics knowledge or the value students placed on mathematics knowledge. Bandura (1997) suggests that efficacy beliefs mediate the effects of skills on performance by influencing effort and persistence. Thus, one powerful reason for perceived self efficacy's success in predicting academic achievement may lie in its association with mental effort. Self report measures of efficacy simply ask students to report their own assessment of the learning or problem solving "difficulty" they experienced. Since difficulty judgements are largely due to students' experience of their cognitive load they experienced in past learning and problem solving tasks in a particular subject matter area, perceived self efficacy is highly predictive of current and future mental effort (Bandura, 1997; Salomon, 1981, 1984).

Evidence also exists to support claims that the more specific the set of tasks being addressed by a self efficacy questionnaire, the more robust the prediction of mental effort and learning (Bong & Clark, in press; Pajares & Miller, 1994). For example, Algebra self efficacy is a better predictor of mental effort invested in algebra than is mathematics self efficacy or academic self efficacy (Pajares & Miller, 1994). Bong (1997) has provided evidence that this finding is due, in large part, to the more accurate judgements of cognitive load coming from assessments of more specific tasks. She has found that students can accurately judge their self efficacy for tasks they have never performed because they assess the similarity of familiar tasks or observations of the performance of other students who they judge to be similar in experience and ability and generalize their expectations to unfamiliar but similar tasks. The larger the scope of the tasks being assessed with a self-efficacy measure, the more variation in cognitive load one would expect. Variations in load would tend to be handled by "averaging" and produce summary self-efficacy assessments that were less predictive of the amount of effort invested in any specific learning task.

Inverted U Relationship Between Self Efficacy and Mental Effort

While many studies have reported a linear and positive relationship between self efficacy and mental effort (e.g., Covington, 1992), a number of motivation researchers suggest that the shape of this relationship is an "inverted U" (Clark, in press; Salomon, 1983). The reason for this suggestion requires a bit of explanation. When confronting a challenging and novel learning task, self efficacy tends to be low because of the amount of conscious, declarative knowledge that must be manipulated. As learning progresses satisfactorily, declarative knowledge gradually automates and efficacy increases. As knowledge becomes more and more automated, effort decreases even though self efficacy continues to increase. The more familiar the goal and the more knowledge and skill we believe we have gained in the pursuit of similar goals, the less effort we are inclined to invest. The rationale for this relationship can be understood by reference to cognitive theories of knowledge types (e.g., Anderson, 1983, 1993; Gagne et al., 1993). Automated expertise, developed over many hundreds of hours of practice, requires no cognitive effort to express. The more that learning requires the acquisition and use of conscious, non-automatic, declarative knowledge, the more cognitive effort is required (Anderson, 1983, 1993; Salomon, 1981, 1983, 1984). The more perceived mental effort required, the lower the specific self-efficacy judgements learners assign to themselves. The more novel and difficult we perceive the goal to be, the more challenge we expect in the task and the lower our perceived self efficacy. Bandura (1997) has commented on this phenomenon and advises that the most effective learners and performers possess extremely high domain-general self efficacy but much lower short-term and specific self efficacy. The utility of this mix of self-efficacy levels seems to be to encourage the use of the greatest amount of mental effort for new learning and for the solving of novel problems.

COGNITIVE OVERLOAD AND THE EFFICACY DEFAULT

From the preceding discussion, it seems reasonable to assume that the maximum amount and quality of complex learning takes place in a narrow range between too little and too much cognitive load, mental effort and self efficacy (Snow, 1977). What happens when cognitive load exceeds working memory capacity? Evidence from a number of areas in psychology suggests that learners may establish an "efficacy threshold" where increasing amounts of perceived or "intrinsic" cognitive load results in a number of automated default behaviors.

Hypothesis 3. At the "Efficacy Threshold" effort stops and an automated cognitive "Default" directs attention to different or novel goals.

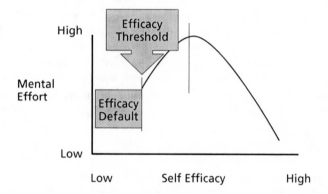

It is likely that when tasks are perceived as impossible, self efficacy issues lead us to avoid the goal at hand (Clark, in press; Salomon, 1981, 1983, 1984). This hypothesis assumes that mental effort slows then stops at either exceptionally low or high self efficacy levels. The phenomenon is implicit in the hypothesized inverted U relationship between efficacy and effort. The more novel and difficult the learning goal is perceived to be, the more effort we expend until the novelty grows beyond an efficacy threshold.

Salomon (1984) for example, presented evidence that our perceptions of the difficulty of learning from various media greatly influenced perceptions about the amount of conscious, non-automatic mental elaborations required to learn or solve problems. He found that people who believed that a medium (e.g., print) was very difficult, worked significantly harder to learn a task from that medium than they invested in the same learning task presented on another medium (video) they had judged to be much easier. He also found that people who believed that a learning task was impossible expended no effort. Instead, they reported looking for "other things to do."

There is recent evidence that when the efficacy threshold is experienced during cognitive overload, an automated "default" occurs that forces learners away from the immediate learning goal and towards novel or different performance goals (e.g., mistakes that they had been trying to avoid or yielding to distractions through mental fantasy or "day dreaming" or activities available in their immediate environment such as computer games or social interaction). Snow (1977) has termed this default the "Zone of Intolerable Problemicity" (ZIP) in a parody of Vygotsky's "Zone of proximal development." Evidence for the ZIP reaction to increasing cognitive load can be found in a variety of research areas including studies of psychotherapy processes and cognitive load theory.

Wegner's Ironic Monitoring System Model

Wegner (1997) has provided evidence for a process he calls "Ironic" mechanisms in mental control. He presents evidence that when working memory is overloaded by anxiety or fears, the result is that an "ironic monitoring system" causes an automated cognitive efficacy threshold default. The monitoring system is characterized as unconscious, uninterruptible, "...searches for mental content signaling a failure to create the intended state of mind" and introduces "...different, unwelcome and unintended behavior" (p. 148). Unintended behavior can range from "slips of the tongue" (embarrassing expressions people try to avoid or thoughts that one wishes not to experience or to express publically) and extend to more complex mistakes that one may be attempting to avoid. He and his colleagues provide evidence for the impact of the ironic process on people with high levels of anxiety, depression, anger and eating disorders (Wegner, 1997).

Shoham and Rohrbaugh (1997) draw on cognitive expectancy-control theory and attribute the ironic process to a perceived loss of control. They describe the downward spiral of control loss that afflicts many people who seek psychotherapy because they cannot learn to control intrusive fears, thoughts or mistakes. Initial control problems with, for example, intrusive and obsessive thoughts about mistakes or failures, encourage helpful friends and family to urge the person to "stop thinking about it." The more a person tries not to think or worry about something negative, the more that cognitive overload occurs and unwelcome, intrusive thoughts occur in working memory. The more that these thoughts are experienced, the greater the perceived loss of control which lowers our self efficacy for control of our own thinking. The result is that the efficacy threshold widens and intrusive thoughts increase. This "cycle of despair" (Shoham & Rohrbaugh, 1997, p. 152) is described as a pattern where helpful suggestions are offered, failure to control mistakes and intrusive thoughts when trying to implement the helpful suggestions produces an increased perception of loss of control (lowered specific self efficacy). The resulting higher failure level produces an even greater increase in the strength of "helpful suggestions" and even more dramatic failures ensue.

The ironic monitoring system is contrasted with an opposing, "intentional monitoring system" that is "...conscious, effortful and interruptible... (and) searches for mental content consistent with the intended state of mind." (Wegner, 1997, p. 148). This system is the one that we hope is operating when learning is taking place. It focuses attention on assigned learning goals and activities and encourages the retrieval and reorganization of appropriate prior knowledge schemas. In order to maintain the intentional system, students must, at all times, believe that they are experiencing a personally manageable level of novelty and difficulty in instructional displays.

Sarbin's Strategic Action Model

A process similar to the ironic and intentional systems has been proposed by Sarbin (1997) who describes cognitive reactions to events that conflict with our self efficacy. Sarbin suggests that monitoring processes are sensitive to efficacy conflicts in the form of hostility, extreme difficulty, novelty and unexpected events. When learning goals focus attention on more novel, declarative and complex information, efficacy conflicts are more likely. Metacognitive processes map internal and external events containing efficacy conflicts that violate expectations, beliefs and values in order to determine how much and what kind of mental and physical effort is required to handle the conflict. Conflict results in strategic actions of various types that are designed to reduce the conflict and achieve a social confirmation of the result. Sarbin's system provides a much richer array of reactions to efficacy problems than the Wegner ironic default theory.

Five Types of Strategic Actions

Sarbin (1997) describes five types of strategic action that are deployed by most people to handle threats to efficacy: (1) Instrumental acts that seek to change the external environment through "fight or flight," ritual acts (such as prayer) or "letters to the editor of newspapers," (2) Tranquilizing and Releasing Acts that attempt to change internal states through acts such as their use of narcotic drugs, physical exercise, compulsive gambling and sex; (3) Attention development that focuses attention on consistent input (to balance the conflict) through neurotic behaviors such as conversion reactions, imaginary worlds; hypochondriasis, or projection; (4) Changing beliefs and values that attempt to modify perceptions of the event so that the new perception disconfirms the threat or conflict such as "reframing" or "reinterpreting" the event; and (5) Escape behaviors such as depression, helplessness and quitting or dropping out.

Each of these reaction strategies have alternatives that are helpful (reframing the event) and those that are potentially harmful (narcotic drug use) and destructive. The alternatives that are more helpful seem to be learned over time whereas many of the more destructive alternatives may be in the form of automated procedural knowledge. It is also interesting that some of Sarbin's 5 strategies involve changing the environment (Instrumental Acts), others involve changing the self (Changing Beliefs) and some involve avoiding the problem (Tranquilizing and Releasing, Attention development, and Escape). Sarbin's (1997) suggestion of internal and external strategies connect nicely with the developmental theory of motivation suggested by Heckhausen and Schultz (1995). They offer evidence that younger people tend to choose "primary" or external strategies when faced with negative feedback about their performance under conditions of excessive challenge or conflict, whereas adults tend to select more "secondary" and internal strategies in the same context. It is also likely that with both internal and external strategies, the more destructive reactions to conflict or efficacy challenges come from people with overloaded working memory. When working memory is exceeded, the more recently learned (and presumably more effective and less destructive) strategies will be inhibited in favor of the older (childish?) and more automatic and destructive alternatives. This is the essence of the Ironic default.

Learning Failures Due to Consistency Checking, Feedback, Split Attention and Redundancy

In addition to the ironic and agency models, Vosniadou et al. (1988) describe studies in prose learning where cognitive overload during consistency checking of propositions in prose stories produces a default that increases errors. Students who were overloaded failed to note that new propositions in prose stores were similar to those already encountered and so incorrectly classified them as new and different. This knowledge-based default seems to cause a cognitive reversion to previously learned and more automated but more general and less effective propositions.

Kluger and DiNisi (1998) describe feedback interventions that reduce or prevent learning. Presumably, learning progress feedback influences learning because it focuses students' attention on the gap between current knowledge and learning goals (Kluger & DiNisi, 1998). Feedback that focuses attention on a learner's mistakes or that encourages a comparative ranking of learners appears to often result in efficacy defaults. Corrective feedback (emphasizing mistakes and the avoidance of mistakes) may often unintentionally result in an efficacy default and the operation of the ironic process. In this scenario, corrective feedback would actually "suggest" or "enable" mistakes and a sense of helplessness in students who were trying to avoid those mistakes. This scenario seems to reflect Wegner's (1997) ironic default and Sarbin's (1997) Attention Development where learners attempt to do what is consistent with the immediate content of cognition. If fear of mistakes is current in working memory, then committing mistakes brings the cognitive system back into balance and eliminates conflict. Kluger and DiNisi (1998) argue that feedback emphasizing the gap between current learning progress and intended learning goals is much more successful in directing mental effort to relevant learning problems and preventing efficacy defaults. Students experiencing efficacy defaults could be called "under confident." It appears that under confident may benefit from reassurance that the learning task can be made more manageable, by reducing cognitive load. One way to reduce load is to divide a larger task into a series of smaller, more specific and tractable tasks (Clark, in press).

Split Attention and Redundancy Effects

Sweller (1999) describes two types of instructional conditions that often cause students to exceed the limitations on their working memory. The split-attention effect "occurs when learners are faced with multiple sources of information that must be integrated before they can be understood" (p. 22). This effect often occurs when graphic displays and their verbal "explanation" are separated from each other and when neither source of information can "stand alone" and so both sources must be considered together in order for effective learning to occur. The mental effort required to integrate graphic and text components of a display can overload working memory and contribute to an efficacy threshold default. A related phenomenon called the "redundancy effect" occurs when both textual and graphic material on some topic are redundant. Sweller (1999) presents evidence that when students attempt to master the redundant graphic and text information the effort results in an unnecessary and sometimes negative effect on the cognitive load in working memory. Presumably, students invest unnecessary mental effort to integrate redundant messages. It may also be the case that when integration of the redundant messages fails (as it must because no integration is possible) students' perception of failure enhances the violation of the efficacy threshold. The split-attention effect can be eliminated if graphic and verbal information on a topic are fully integrated. The redundancy effect can be eliminated if instructional displays provide only one form of information about a topic (or two fully integrated forms). It would be interesting to investigate the nature of the working memory failures caused by overloading working memory with the split-attention or redundancy effect. Cognitive motivation theory would suggest that overloaded learners in these two conditions would default to focusing on different or novel learning goals (or non learning goals).

Yin and Yang Processes

Attempts to explain learning failures caused by perceptions of working memory overload suggest that dual metacognitive monitoring processes operate during learning. Each of these processes searches for different, opposing conditions. They are, in the terms of Chinese philosophy, a balanced "Yin and Yang" duality. This second century feature of Taoist thought, hypothesized a duality in nature where all important forces manifest themselves through opposition. The opposing Yin "difference" processes come into play when working memory is overloaded or is perceived to be overloaded. Yin processes express themselves most often during the learning of novel, different, declarative knowledge. Yin processes are characterized in part by the "ironic" monitoring system described by Wegner (1997). This aspect of metacognition is more automated and it searches for evidence of failure and other "different" and feared results in working memory when learning complex declarative knowledge. Wegner (1997) suggests that the ironic monitoring system "tests whether the operating process is needed by searching for mental contents inconsistent with the intended state" (p. 34). When working memory is overloaded and self efficacy falls below a threshold, the monitoring process is not able to call up previously learned coping behaviors and a default forces the expression of unintended behaviors including self-defeating activities (such as mistakes one is trying to avoid or thoughts of escape from the failure situation) that are the subject of anxious concerns faced by many students. The effect of Yin processes is to focus attention and elaborative activity on different, inconsistent and unintended goals and connections in working memory and long term declarative memory.

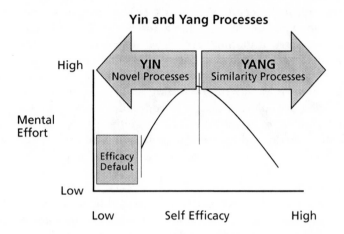

Yin and Yang Processes

Yang effects are associated with "similarity" processes and events during the reorganization, modification and extension of procedural knowledge. Learning is facilitated by drawing on previously learned procedural knowledge in the form of discrete "similarity" associations supported by "spreading activation" (Anderson, 1993) and other "flow of control" based learning and performance processes (Anderson, 1983, 1990; E. Gagne et al., 1993) tend to be used more when learning or problem solving requires the use or practice of procedural knowledge. Yang activities are evaluated by the "intentional monitoring system" described by Wegner (1997) and they facilitate conscious, effortful attention to goal-compatible knowledge in long term memory that are similar to intended learning goals.

Sarbin's (1997) strategic action model begins with the same events as Wegner's. As cognition moves more toward the declarative "Yin" side, barriers to goals tend to become more novel, unexpected, and difficult to overcome. This kind of experience produces more internal conflict and threat so people select (or default to) strategies that attempt to reduce the resulting conflict and difficulty. As efficacy is threatened, a number of learned and automated strategies might be employed by learners. Each of Sarbin's strategic action types seem to have variations that are more productive, while others seem more destructive. Some of those strategies seem to emphasize habit and automated reactions to difficulty and danger (e.g., fight or flight, narcotic drugs, neurotic projection) and some emphasize more helpful learned strategies (e.g., reframing, letters to the editor of newspapers, exercise, seeking out other views of events).

Ordinarily, the Yin and Yang processes collaborate effectively to both foster intended learning behaviors and to avoid unintended activities. When students perceive that the learning goal they are pursuing is impossible (because of cognitive overload or a misunderstanding of events), the efficacy default can take many forms. The most destructive forms of the efficacy default seem to occur when working memory is overloaded and more helpful coping strategies are unavailable because their expression requires working memory space.

Efficacy Threshold Summary

When a learning or problem solving task is perceived as excessively novel and difficult, and/or maximum cognitive load is exceeded, a learner's efficacy threshold is violated. The result is an automated "efficacy default" where either lowered task self efficacy or, in extreme cases, helplessness is experienced. Under default conditions, learning and problem solving goals are abandoned in favor of either new goals or the operation of an automated monitoring system that searches out and expresses anything that learners have been trying to avoid including feared mistakes, distracting thoughts or goals and inadequate learning strategies. It is important to note that the "efficacy threshold" default is both automated and that it focuses attention on new or different goals, thoughts and strategies that distract learners from intended learning goals. The positive but opposite system is learned, conscious and focuses attention on information that is similar or compatible with resident learning goals. These "Yin and Yang" opposing cognitive systems are hypothesized to moderate the interaction between the conscious, learned, positive and helpful similarity or compatibility functions that function in the learning of declarative knowledge on the one hand, and the unconscious, automated, negative and hurtful novelty processes that support the learning of procedural knowledge, on the other hand.

Mental Effort Problems Not Caused by Motivational Processes

While many learning problems seem to be caused by the efficacy consequences of very difficult and novel learning tasks, motivation problems are not the only cause of depressed learning outcomes. Efficacy defaults seem most often to happen to anxious, inexperienced learners. The less experienced and more anxious students seem to be the most vulnerable to learning problems. Yet, Clark (1982, 1989) and Lohman (1986) have presented evidence from aptitude-treatment interaction studies that certain attempts to help anxious and lower prior knowledge students can cause learning and motivation deficits for the highest ability students. It appears that when instructional designers include instruction in learning strategies along with instructional information for all learners, more experienced and able learners often suffer as a result. More experienced learners apparently attempt to make use of new learning strategies and in doing so, interfere with the use of their own previously automated, effective learning strategies that serve similar purpose. This was the case in a study by Salomon (1974) where high verbal ability subjects had their performance depressed significantly below untreated controls by a treatment that helped them actively manipulate the unfolding of three-dimensional objects into two dimensions. Evidence was presented that high verbal subjects had automated the verbal translation and manipulation of spatial information. Attempts to get these high verbal subjects to use muscular-spatial manipulation strategies depressed performance on delayed post tests significantly lower than untreated control groups because of the interference of their already automated verbal strategies. In these studies, task demands that are perceived as similar to previously experienced conditions elicit automated cognitive strategies that inhibit the learning of novel procedures for cognitive processing. It is notable that in the Salomon study, the higher the verbal ability, the more that spatial rotation performance was depressed by this novel method of depicting the unfolding task. Lohman (1986) argued that: "...with extensive practice, learners become increasingly dissimilar in the cognitive structures they assemble, thus rendering a common instructional treatment less useful for an increasingly larger proportion of subjects ... According to this hypothesis, then, direct instruction of cognitive skills is more likely to be successful for those who have not already developed and tuned a substantial body of procedural knowledge in the domain of interest" (p. 198).

OVERCONFIDENT MISTAKES WHEN USING AUTOMATED KNOWLEDGE

The discussion turns next to problems caused not by a lack of efficacy but instead by too much efficacy in the face of mistakes during learning and problem solving. In this instance, learners continue to work at learning but make mistakes and do not take responsibility for their mistakes because they are overconfident.

Hypothesis 4. As knowledge automates, mental effort decreases and learner overconfidence is a danger.

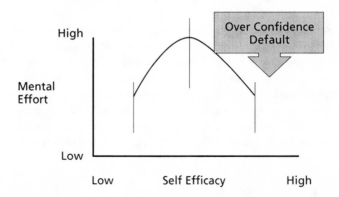

One indicator of learning problems caused by too much efficacy occurs when people with adequate prior knowledge are making mistakes on a task they are actively pursuing (if people are avoiding a task, they have a commitment or persistence problem). Once actively involved in a task, excessive efficacy (over confidence) problems show up as mistakes due to inappropriate approaches to a learning or problem solving goal. Bandura (1997) notes that these errors "arise from misjudgements of personal efficacy rather than from performance ambiguities or constraints" (p. 70). He suggests that when people select plans and strategies to handle learning (and other) goals, they based their decisions, in part, on their past performance in goals situations that they judge to be similar. Since similarity judgements can be misleading, experienced learners may apply previously automated learning strategies that they believe to be appropriate when, in fact, the strategy is causing them to make mistakes. Bandura (1997) suggests that the optimum self efficacy for specific learning tasks should be on the moderate to low side (to promote the maximum use of mindful mental effort) and moderate to high for the larger domain of knowledge represented by the task (to promote persistence and commitment to learning goals).

Yates et al. (1998) describe a series of studies designed to assess the effects of overconfidence in self assessment of knowledge and strategies. In general, they conclude that "...people's probability judgements about their general knowledge are higher than the proportion of questions they actually answer correctly" (p. 91). This overconfidence finding seems to hold true for a great variety of cultures and nations (except for Japan and Singapore). Yates et al. (1998) also noted that in most experiments where a "cost" is assigned to wrong judgements about one's knowledge, overconfidence tends to disappear. Presumably, when wrong judgements are perceived to damage efficacy, overconfidence decreases. There is recent and compelling evidence that when general (domain) self efficacy is slightly higher than is warranted, emotional well being is enhanced (see for example the discussion in Bandura, 1997). However, the proportion of students who use familiar and automated learning strategies when new or modified strategies need to be developed may be severely underestimated as a source of errors during instruction. If these students have the capability to generate the new learning strategies that are required, and if overconfidence leads them to reject responsibility for the errors they make, the problem can be very damaging. This may have been the case in the analysis of displacement errors by Ohlsson (1996).

Automated Displacement Models

Instead of mistakes caused by efficacy defaults and novelty seeking, displacement models suggest that earlier, more automated but incorrect knowledge and strategies interfere with the learning of new and often more specific knowledge. Ohlsson (1996) has described a displacement model that describes the origin and correction of common mistakes made during concept learning. He suggests that "similarity checking" is a critical element in most new learning. When learning a concept, students must develop schemas containing a set of attributes that define the concept. Mammals, for example, are defined as hairy, warm-blooded animals who give birth to live young who are suckled. When practicing the learning of new concept definitions, students are asked to classify a set of examples and non examples. Learners must try to select examples that contain the defining attributes of the target concepts. For example, when presented with examples of animals such as "dog, cat, bird, horse, whale, shark," students are expected to identify birds and sharks as "non mammals" because they do not have all of the defining features. When self efficacy is extremely high it is more likely that learners will displace the new classification knowledge in favor of older, more familiar, more automated and often more general knowledge. The result, in terms of the example above, is that knowledge acquired previous to the current lesson will suggest that "whales" are examples of fish. Many children learn early that everything that swims is a "fish" and so incorrectly use this earlier knowledge in an overconfident way (Farrington, 1997). Dougherty et al. (1999) describe processes in memory that support "likelihood" judgements necessary to support concept learning. Their MINERVA-DM model accounts for many of the errors that students seem to make when judging the similarity of current task demands and familiar, task-specific knowledge and strategies already resident in memory. They make the point that these judgements can be made without the benefit of higher cognitive processes and therefore may be prone to many different kinds of error that contribute to overconfidence.

Perkin's "Disrationalia" Defaults

Perkins and Grotzer (1997) described a number of behaviors that seem to stem from "...the pattern driven character of cognition as well as ego defense and other mechanisms" (p. 1125). They describe four default tendencies including learning strategies that are "Hasty (impulsive, insufficient investment in deep processing and examining alternatives); Narrow (failure to challenge assumptions, examine other points of view), Fuzzy (careless, imprecise ...); and Sprawling (generally disorganized, failure to advance or conclude)" (Perkins & Grotzer, 1997, p. 1125). They advise instructional designers and teachers to emphasize domain and task specific strategies that help students toward more reflective, strategic, and self monitoring in their approach to learning tasks.

Seductive Details

The destructive effects of overconfidence may be one of the factors that cause the seductive detail effect described by researchers such as Harp and Mayer (1998). In a series of studies, Harp and Mayer (1998) inserted irrelevant information into lessons about natural processes such as lightning. Learning goals required students to recall details and solve problems using their knowledge of factors and processes that cause lightning. Instructional displays provided the information necessary to learn but some treatments also included engaging but irrelevant information such as pictures of buildings, trees and people who had been struck by lightning and pictures of people in situations where they were exposed to danger from lightning. When seductive details were available, learning was depressed. All learners finished the lessons within the same time limits despite the presence of irrelevant and seductive details in experimental groups. One interesting feature of the Harp and Mayer (1997) study was their attempt to determine the exact cause of the depressed learning based on previous hypotheses. For example, they found that placing the seductive details earlier in a lesson caused significantly more learning problems than when the same details occurred later in lessons. They concluded that seductive details cause students to generate inaccurate learning goals. As a result of the inaccurate goals, the students searched long term memory for irrelevant knowledge and constructed knowledge schemas that were not helpful. The effort spent to form schemas based on irrelevant information "diverts" attention away from intended goals and thus learning is depressed. While Harp and Mayer (1997) did not measure learner confidence or efficacy, we could assume that those who received seductive details were confident that the new (and irrelevant) learning goals they generated were useful.

To this point, the discussion has focused on the motivational processes that lead to changes in mental effort. However, there are other motivational outcomes that are influenced by motivation. Pintrich and Schunk (1996, see ch. 2) describe these outcome variables or "indexes." In addition to mental effort, commitment or persistence is a very important outcome variable. The discussion turns next to persistence problems in complex MMI learning environments.

Motivational Variables Supporting Persistence at Learning Tasks

While many researchers have examined the variables that influence task choice and commitment (e.g., Bandura, 1997; Dweck & Leggett, 1988; Erez & Earley, 1993; Keller, 1987; Locke, 1990; Locke & Latham, 1990; Schwarzer, 1992), Martin Ford's (1992) Motivational Systems Theory provides the most comprehensive and coherent view of the factors that influence task persistence for adults during complex learning tasks. Commitment is defined in many studies as persistence at a task over time in the face of distractions. As a result of his analysis of 32 motivational theories and related research Ford (1992) indicates that there are three variables which, if taken together, appear to offer the best prediction of the strength of our persistence during learning, problem solving and other performance goals. The three variables influencing goal persistence are: (1) goal value (as we strengthen our belief that achievement of a learning goal will increase our personal control or effectiveness, our persistence at the goal is hypothesized to increase); (2) mood or emotions (positive emotions facilitate persistence and negative emotions discourage persistence); and (3) personal agency (beliefs concerning the extent to which our ability and contextual factors will facilitate goal achievement—as our expected chances for success increase, goal persistence is also hypothesized to increase).

Hypothesis 5.   Persistence at a learning task is a positive, linear, multiplicative function of domain self efficacy, mood and task value. Below a control threshold, persistence stops and an automated default focuses attention on divergent goals with more control potential.

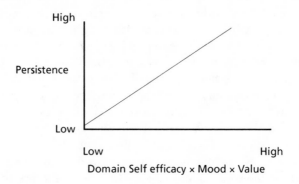

The hypothesized relationship between the three variables is multiplicative. This implies that if the value of any one of the variables reaches a threshold level, goal persistence stops. When persistence stops, an automated "control default" is hypothesized to direct attention to novel goals that hold more control potential. In this discussion, each variable will be described in turn by focusing first on evidence for its negative influence on persistence, its measurement and then on interventions that have been found to increase its positive effects on persistence. It will be argued that as values for the task, positive mood and agency increase, persistence at a task will also increase. However, when either control value, mood or agency fall below a threshold level, persistence stops and another destructive cognitive default takes over and redirects attention to novel goals.

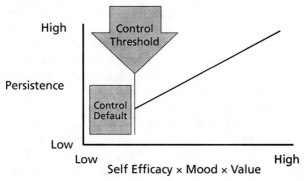

Below a control threshold, persistence stops and an automated control default focuses attention on goals with more control potential

Control Values and Persistence

Some of the best and most recent research on learning goal value has been conducted by Eccles and Wigfield (1995) who have found compelling evidence for the impact of three different types of control values on persistence in educational settings. The three types are: utility, interest, and importance values for learning or problem solving tasks. The first type of value, utility, is defined as the "usefulness of the task for individuals in terms of their future goals, including career goals ... [and] is related more to the ends in the means-ends analysis of a task" (Pintrich & Schunk, 1996, p. 295). This implies that utility value is placed on goal outcomes or ends, but not on the means or process used to achieve the outcome. Utility value is the one used to justify a less desirable experience that is endured in order to achieve a more desirable end or result. The second type of value, interest, is defined as the enjoyment or intrinsic curiosity people experience when performing tasks that have subjective interest. The third type, importance, or attainment value, represents the significance to a person of doing well on a task because success confirms their own beliefs about themselves and their skills. Importance value might sustain persistence at a goal when a learner believed that the goal represented a challenge in an area of their own special skill or aptitude. All three of these types of values contribute to our estimate of the control potential of goal persistence. Eccles and Wigfield (1995) summarize tests of these value types by confirmatory factor analysis and their relationship to goal persistence in a number of studies.

Choosing or Assigning Learning Goals

An issue related to control values concerns recent "learner control" and "constructivist" strategies embedded in instructional systems (e.g., Jonasson, 1991; Merrill, 1991). Arguments about the utility of allowing learners to "explore" or "discover" learning goals and content have raged for a century. Recent versions of this argument by constructivist theories (Jonassen, 1991) suggest that only a high amount of learner control is effective in promoting individual learning benefits. Since most instructional systems cannot allow students to choose their own learning goals, will assigned or "forced" learning goals reduce persistence as suggested by Jonassen (1991)? Locke and Latham's (1990) studies have provided evidence that people do not have to participate in goal setting in order to make a strong commitment to assigned goals. In cases where participatory goal setting is not possible, they find that value for the goal is enhanced if people perceive the goal to be: (1) assigned by a legitimate, trusted authority with an "inspiring vision" that reflects a "convincing rationale" for the goal, and who; (2) provides expectation of outstanding performance and who gives; (3) "ownership" to individuals and teams for accomplishments; (4) expresses appropriate confidence in individual and team capabilities; while (5) providing task-focused feedback on progress that includes supportive but corrective suggestions for mistakes. There is some evidence that while discovery or learner control over some goals is valuable for experts or advanced learners, those with lower prior knowledge encounter major learning problems with this instructional strategy (Clark, 1982, 1989; Merrill, 1991). This problem comes in the form of a control value default where automated yin processes dominate cognition.

Emotion and Goal Persistence

In addition to values, the current emotional state of an individual or group is also hypothesized to influence task commitment. The general hypothesis resulting from research on emotion and commitment suggests that as mood becomes more positive, persistence becomes more likely, frequent and stronger in the face of distractions and vice versa (Boekaerts,

1993; Bower, 1995; Ford, 1992). Negative moods are characterized as sadness, fear, depression and anger (Ford, 1992). These negative mood states inhibit commitment (Bower, 1995). Positive moods are characterized by happiness, joy, contentment and optimism. Positive emotions have been found to foster commitment (Bower, 1995; Ford, 1992). In research, mood states are indicated by people's memory for information congruent with their self-reported mood state; ratings of the enjoyableness of mood congruent information or commitments; affiliation preferences for people with similar mood states; social comparisons with mood-congruent people at work; and a focus on the positive or negative aspects of goals as moods change (Bower, 1995). Expectancy-control theorists suggest that negative mood states lead to lowered expectations that success or control will be achieved by a work goal and negative moods focus people on past errors and failures (Boekaerts, 1993; Bower, 1995). In fact, there are suggestions (e.g., Shapiro et al., 1996; Weiner, 1986) that one of the origins of negative emotions is the perception that we are denied adequate control in specific situations. For example, Weiner (1986) suggests that depression sometimes results from the self perception that we are lacking in critical skills or ability to achieve a necessary goal, and that anger is the emotional product of the cognitive belief that some external agent has threatened our self control.

Izard (1993) has presented evidence of four separate mechanisms that generate the same emotion in any individual. Only one of those systems is cognitive and under the control of the individual. Other, non-cognitive emotion activation systems include habitual or automated emotional reactions to events (Anderson, 1990, 1993) plus neural, biochemical and hormonal processes (Izard, 1993). This research suggests that the origins of emotions are not always under our direct control. Yet Bower (1995) makes the point that emotions can be influenced by environmental and cognitive events even when their origins are biological or neurological. This claim seems to be supported by recent evidence concerning the extent of the placebo effect in mood disorders such as depression. For example, Enserink (1999) reviews the meta analyses of anti depressant drug trials and concludes that 75 percent of the effects of new drugs such as Prozac are due to expectancy beliefs and not to biological factors.

Mood Problems: Hot/Cool System Model

A different source of evidence for a mood-related "control threshold" default comes from a recent theory suggested by Metcalfe and Mischel (1999) to explain failures in volition, self control and the delay of gratification in children and adults. They hypothesize a "hot/cool system ... that enables—and undermines—self-control or 'willpower' ... essential to the execution of difficult to achieve intentions" (Metcalfe & Mischel, 1999, p. 3). The "...hot emotional system is specialized for quick emotional processing and responding on the basis of unconditional or conditional trigger features... (and) deals with the kinds of automatic responses to both appetitive and fear producing unconditioned stimuli and their learned associates ... that have been relatively neglected in studies of human cognition" (italics in original text, Metcalfe & Mischel, 1999, p. 6). When the hot system is activated by strong, negative emotions such as those accompanying cognitive overload, the result is "...a range of self-defeating and self-destructive behaviors such as Impulsivity and failures of self-control, irrational fears, and addictions of many sorts" (p. 16). The cognitive default that results directs learners' attention and persistence away from the goals and intentions at hand and toward different and often self-defeating goals or behaviors. Metcalfe and Mischel (1999) hypothesize that automated cognitive defaults result from environmentally enabled but inherited predispositions that are more or less present at birth. Recent studies reported in Science (Bower, 1999) following new "dynamic systems models" of skill development in children provide support for the argument that novelty seeking is an early (3 to 6 month) default when food or other reasons for exploration are not fulfilled. These defaults tend to moderate over time but when anxiety or negative emotions reach a peak, and/or working memory is overloaded, an automated Yin default, often involving a search for different or novel goals, is the result.

Emotion Measurement and Intervention

Bower (1995) describes a number of techniques for assessing emotional state and levels in research that could be adopted to MMI systems including: affiliation preferences (students report preferring to affiliate with people who share the same emotional state); recall of information related to our mood state (people tend to remember more information congruent with their current mood state); and the time spent looking, listening and reading information related to mood state (more time is spent attending to mood congruent information). The assessment of changing moods may be possible by noticing when people compare themselves with people whose mood is more positive (if they are moving toward a negative mood) or with people whose mood is negative (if they are shifting to more positive moods). This "reversed" social comparison process seems to accentuate the direction in which mood is moving by increasing the differences between ourselves and others whose mood is different. Boekaerts (1993) reminds us that self report measures of "stress" can also be used to evaluate negative emotion related performance problems.

Interventions that have been found to change negative mood states have included listening to music that is perceived to be positive; writing or telling about a positive mood-related experience; watching a movie or listening to stories that emphasize positive mood states (Bower, 1995); and emotion control training through "environmental control strategies" including the choice of learning context and "positive self talk" (Corno & Kanfer, 1993). There are also indications that trusted enthusiastic, positive, energetic teachers and learner "models" encourage positive emotions in others and support learning goal persistence (Bandura, 1997).

Personal Agency and Goal Persistence

In addition to values and mood, the final factor found to influence active persistence is our personal agency beliefs. Personal agency consists of two concerns: first, Ford (1992) provides evidence that we engage in a "domain" (general) self efficacy analysis of whether we have the knowledge required to achieve the goal ("Can I do it?), and second, we consider the barriers to our performance in the goal setting ("Will I be permitted to do it?"). The more that we believe we might be able and permitted to achieve a learning or problem solving goal, the more likely we are to choose and commit ourselves to the goal. The self efficacy "can I do it?" question engages our memory about our ability and prior experience with similar learning goals. This review seems often to be implemented at a general and shallow level during this stage in the motivational process (Ford, 1992). Bandura (1997) refers to a more general self efficacy that projects our perceived self confidence for a class of tasks based on our interpretations of our past experience. He contrasts this domain self efficacy with the very task-specific efficacy that is based on immediate experience and that influences persistence at a learning goal. He clearly recommends that domain efficacy should be high (to promote goal commitment and persistence) but that specific self efficacy should be lower (to maximize mental effort).

The mechanism for the analysis of the general, domain self efficacy component of agency may be similar to our "meta memory" or "feeling of knowing" experiences (Nelson, 1988) found in the familiar experience of "knowing that I know a fact (e.g., a person's name) without at the moment being able to remember the fact that I want to recall." Self efficacy analysis for persistence is similar to memory analysis in that we guess whether we have capability to achieve a goal without deeply analyzing our self efficacy or the exact knowledge and expertise demands of the goal we are considering. While it seems that many people may slightly overestimate their ability to achieve a goal (Nelson, 1988; Yates et al., 1998), the errors that are made in personal agency judgements tend to occur when learners confuse their familiarity with the goal statement with their ability to achieve the goal (Reder & Ritter, 1992).

Interventions Fostering Personal Agency and Persistence

Personal agency involves both our memory of past performance on task domains similar to those we are considering and beliefs about the support available in the environment where the goal is pursued. Most measures of personal agency are based on self report (Ford, 1992). Locke (1990) and Locke and Latham (1990) suggest that goal persistence increases, and temporary failure or negative feedback is handled much more successfully, when we believe that: (1) the goal is possible to achieve within the time and resources available; (2) we have the knowledge to achieve the goal; (3) more specific, explicit and difficult goals are chosen; (4) newly learned skills are directly relevant to goal achievement; and, (5) learning "help" and support are available. Bandura (1997) recommends three types of agency interventions: First, we should provide mastery-oriented training experiences where increasingly challenging tasks representing large goals are accomplished. This intervention requires that we have analyzed the prior knowledge necessary to achieve learning goals. In addition, Bandura recommends that learning support systems focus feedback on task success on ability and effort and feedback about failure on task goals and away from the learner. For example, when people succeed at learning goals, the best feedback suggests that the person invested "good effort" and that they "have an ability for this kind of task." When learning difficulties occur, mistakes and failures should be attributed to external, goal related causes.

Another way of fostering personal agency at work is to expose people who make many mistakes to "coping models" (Bandura, 1997) who are perceived to be from similar backgrounds and who have selected difficult goals and are succeeding only gradually and with difficulty. This approach is most important for people who may have different cultural origins than the majority of the learners served by an instructional system. Finally, Bandura stresses the need to discourage people from using self-defeating biases as they appraise their own capabilities. He recommends an approach described by Goldfried and Robbins (1982) where people learn to modify their standards of self evaluation and personal appraisals of their efficacy. Taylor et al. (1998) suggest a specific series of visualization strategies that help people cope with control or efficacy default problems. They suggest teaching learners to create a series of visual images and "self talk" explanations of events, including: (1) visualize themselves at the computer screen in a state of frustration, helplessness, fear and anxiety; (2) visualize and verbally describe the steps and stages in the process of achieving learning goals (a concrete procedure for learning should be taught); (3) visualize possible distractions, interruptions and problems experienced while studying and imagine how each can be overcome. Their studies demonstrate a 66 percent greater increase in successful goal completion for students who used their visualization and coping strategies (Taylor et al., 1998).

Context Barriers and Goal Persistence

Context beliefs are another key aspect of personal agency. Commitments are also based on beliefs about the contextual barriers in the environment where the goal is pursued or where knowledge will be transferred and used. People who believe that personal prejudice, policy or procedural barriers exist in the performance environment are reluctant to make a commitment to learning goals. Ford (1992) suggests that components of the instruction must reassure students that they will be encouraged to use the skills they have learned and that no unfair or unusual barriers to the use of the knowledge exist in the application environment.

SUMMARY AND CONCLUSIONS

Multimedia Instructional (MMI) technology provides a number of exciting benefits to the many challenges facing educators interested in fostering efficient and effective complex learning. This new technology makes it possible to present a dazzling variety of information rich displays where almost all visual and auditory formats and symbolic modes can be presented at once, if desired. In addition, they bring the potential for high levels of real time interactivity (transactions) between the system and individual learners and the possibility of maximum learner control of instructional access, pacing, scheduling, feedback, and structure. Yet these new information options can also present increased opportunities to damage learning and discourage learners. In order to maximize the positive potential of MMI and reduce its potential danger, it is suggested that MMI designers incorporate cognitive motivation research into the instructional design, delivery and evaluation process. Excellent design systems for complex learning are incomplete without key motivational components. The suggestion is made that designers should monitor two essential "indexes" of motivation (Pintrich & Schunk, 1996), mental effort and persistence. Mental effort is characterized as amount of energy invested in the conscious, deliberate and cognitive elaborative processing required to learn novel declarative knowledge. Persistence is described as the extent to which students "stick at" a learning task over time and in the face of external or internal distractions.

In previous research, mental effort has been found to be correlated with cognitive load and task-specific self efficacy. It is argued that the relationship between efficacy and mental effort takes the form of an inverted U. This relationship is complex because there is evidence that at the upper and lower limits of self efficacy, all effort stops and learning problems can occur. Evidence from a variety of research traditions is presented to describe the nature of efficacy defaults, including Wegner's (1997) "ironic monitoring system" and Sarbin's "strategic action system" and studies by Sweller (1999), suggesting that as learning tasks become more novel and declarative and cognitive load increases, an "efficacy default" can occur. In an efficacy default state, learners express more automated, unintended, feared and destructive behaviors and/or drop out of the MMI system. When efficacy defaults are experienced many times, a state of helplessness may occur for lower ability, less experienced, more anxious and more vulnerable learners.

On the other side of the efficacy continuum, as procedural knowledge is learned and automated, self efficacy often increases to its maximum and an "overconfident" default may occur. Evidence for the overconfidence default is presented from research by, for example, Ohlsson (1996) on displacement errors, Perkins and Grotzer's (1997) "disrationalia default," and Harp and Meyer's (1998) "seductive details" research. In an overconfident state, learners may misjudge learning goals, use wrong learning strategies, make mistakes and refuse to take responsibility for their mistakes and reject corrective feedback.

In addition to the toxic defaults that accompany very high or very low efficacy, a "control default" discourages learners from persisting at MMI learning goals over time and in the face of distractions. Mental effort can be adequate yet learning can be damaged if students fail to persist by withdrawing or procrastinating. Ford's (1992) motivational systems theory is used to describe the three variables that are thought to directly influence the amount of persistence students invest in learning tasks. Ford (1992) describes a multiplicative relationship between control values, mood and agency (domain self efficacy and expectancy beliefs about the application context for what is learned). Clark (in press) has described these three variables as a series of questions students ask themselves constantly as they learn: "Will the knowledge I gain help me become more effective?" (control value); "Do I feel like learning this information?" (mood); and "Can I do it? And if I can will I be encouraged/permitted to use what I learn later?" (agency). Since the relationship between all three variables is multiplicative (value × mood × agency), if the value of any one variable slips below a tolerance threshold, persistence and learning stop. Unlike the defaults at both low and high levels of self efficacy, there is no comparable default at very high levels of value, mood or agency.

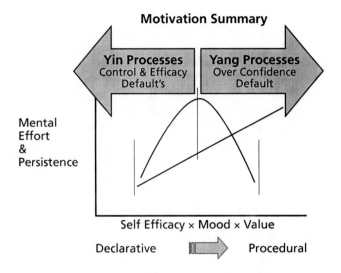

A balanced, cognitive "Yin and Yang" process model is suggested to help understand the types of mental processes that lead to default behavior. It is suggested that as learning tasks become more novel and declarative, cognitive load increases and students must find different and novel learning strategies to achieve learning goals. These "Yin" (different, novel) processes lead to both efficacy and control defaults where automated behaviors tend to force students into different and/or novel and destructive goals and mistakes. When learning goals emphasize the acquisition or use of automated procedural knowledge, "Yang" (similarity, familiar) processes search working declarative and procedural memory for familiar learning strategies and goals. Yang processes can lead to over confident defaults. Essentially, Yin processes result from more novel goals and at extreme levels, introduce novel mistakes. Yang processes result from the use of familiar, often automated knowledge, and introduce familiarity (over confident) mistakes and a rejection of responsibility.

Since learner self efficacy, value, mood and agency can be monitored through self report questions, it is suggested that MMI designers monitor subtle changes in these variables, and changes in the indicators of mental effort (increasing numbers of mistakes on practice exercises) and persistence (delay, poor scheduling of work, dropping out). As we develop more subtle and effective ways to handle motivational issues in complex learning environments, we may find methods for collecting efficacy, value, mood and agency profiles of each learner in order to intervene before default precursors reach potentially harmful levels. Large individual and cultural differences exist to influence student efficacy and control beliefs. We need to collect learner-specific information about instructionally controllable events perceived as reducing or increasing task and domain self efficacy, control values, mood and context beliefs (agency). Until the time when such information is available, MMI designers and developers are advised to: (1) Avoid the urge to use the full display capacity of MMI systems to format, color, animate, exemplify, link and provide endless alternatives to learners. Emphasize only the critical instructional information necessary to compile, encode, elaborate and practice knowledge; (2) be alert to the possibility that any instructional format or method that helps one student may be perceived as threatening or discouraging to another student; (3) Focus feedback on the gap between specific learning goals and immediate learning, not on the learner's "wrong behavior" or intentions; (4) Attempt to maintain each learner at low to moderate levels of immediate task self efficacy by always providing instruction at a cognitive load that reflects the maximum challenge possible without risking efficacy, overconfident or control defaults and yet encourage positive domain self efficacy to maintain persistence; and (5) avoid the temptation to provide learning strategy instruction for more experienced or higher ability students if that instruction might interfere with previously automated learning strategies.

REFERENCES

Anderson, J.R. (1983). *The architecture of cognition.* Cambridge, MA: Harvard University Press.

Anderson, J.R. (1990). *The adaptive character of thought.* Hillsdale, NJ: Lawrence Erlbaum Publishers.

Anderson, J.R. (1993). *Rules of the mind.* Hillsdale, NJ: Lawrence Erlbaum Publishers.

Bandura, A. (1977). *Social learning theory.* Englewood Cliffs, NJ: Prentice-Hall.

Bandura, A. (1997). *Self efficacy: The exercise of control.* New York: W. H. Freeman.

Baumeister, R.F., Boden, J.M., & Smart, L. (1996). Relation of threatened egotism to violence and aggression: The dark side of high self esteem. *Psychological Review, 103*(1), 5-33.

Boekaerts, M. (1991). Subjective competence, appraisals, and self-assessment. *Learning and Instruction 1,* 1–17.

Boekaerts, M. (1993). Being concerned with well-being and with learning. *Educational Psychologist, 28*(2), 149–167.

Bong, M. (1997). Generality of academic self-efficacy judgements: Evidence of hierarchical relations. *Journal of Educational Psychology, 89*(4), 696–709.

Bong, M., & Clark, R.E. (In press). Comparison between self-concept and self-efficacy in academic motivation research. *Journal of Educational Psychology.*

Bower, G.H. (1983). Affect and cognition. In D. Broadbent (Ed.), *Functional aspects of human memory* (pp. 149–163). London: The Royal Society.

Bower, G.H. (1995, September). *Emotion and social judgements.* Monograph published by the Federation of Behavioral, Psychological and Cognitive Sciences as part of the Science and Public Policy Seminars, Washington, DC.

Brown, D.E. (1991). *Human universals.* Philadelphia, PA: Temple University Press.

Carver, C.S., & Scheier, M.F. (1998). *On the self-regulation of behavior.* New York: Cambridge University Press.

Cascio, W.F. (1995). Whither industrial and organizational psychology in a changing world of work? *American Psychologist, 50*(11), 928–939.

Cennamo, K.S. (1989). *Factors influencing mental effort: A theoretical overview and review of literature.* Paper presented at the annual meeting of the Association for Educational Communications and Technology, Dallas TX. [ERIC Ed 379-313]

Clark, R.E. (1982). Antagonism between achievement and enjoyment in ATI studies. *Educational Psychologist, 17*(2), 92–101.

Clark, R.E. (1983). Reconsidering research on learning from media. *Review of Educational Research, 53*(4), 445–459.

Clark, R.E. (1989). When teaching kills learning: Research on mathemathantics. In H. Mandl, E. DeCorte, N. Bennett, & H.F. Friedrich (Eds.), *Learning and Instruction in an international context,* Vol: 22: *Analysis of complex skills and complex knowledge domains.* New York: Pergamon Press.

Clark, R.E. (1992). Human performance interventions for Irish organisations. *Irish Journal of Psychology, 13*(1), 1–16.

Clark, R.E. (1994a). Media and method. *Educational Technology Research and Development, 42*(3), 7–10.

Clark, R.E. (1994b). Media will never influence learning. *Educational Technology Research and Development, 42*(3), 21–29.

Clark, R.E. (1998). Motivating performance: Part 1—Diagnosing and solving motivation problems. *Performance Improvement, 37*(8), 39–47.

Clark, R.E. (in press). The CANE model of motivation to learn and to work: A two-stage process of goal commitment and effort. In J. Lowyck (Ed.), *Trends in corporate training.* Leuven: University of Leuven.

Clark. R.E., & Estes, F. (1996). Cognitive task analysis. *International Journal of Educational Research, 25*(5), 403–416.

Corno, L., & Kanfer, R. (1993). The role of volition in learning and performance. In L. Darling-Hammond (Ed.), *Review of research in education* (Vol. 19). Washington, DC: American Educational Research Association.

Covington, M.V. (1962). *Making the grade: A self-worth perspective on motivation and school reform.* Cambridge: Cambridge University Press.

Dillon, A., & Gabbard, R. (1998). Hypermedia as an educational technology: A review of the quantitative research literature on learning comprehension, control and style. *Review of Educational Research, 68*(3), 322–349.

Dougherty, M.R.P., Gettys, C.F., & Ogden, E.E. (1999). MINERVA-DM: A memory process model for judgements of likelihood. *Psychological Review, 106*(1), 180–209.

Dweck, C.S. (1989). Motivation. In A. Lesgold & R. Glaser (Eds.), *Foundations for a psychology of education.* Hillsdale, NJ: Lawrence Erlbaum Associates.

Dweck, C.S. & Leggett, E. (1988). A social cognitive approach to motivation and personality. *Psychological Review, 95*, 256–273.

D'Ydewalle, G. (1987). Is it still worthwhile to investigate the impact of motivation on learning? In E. De Corte, H. Lodewijks, R. Parmentier, & P. Spoan (Eds.), *Learning and instruction* (Vol. I, pp. 191–200). Elmsford, NY: Pergamon Press.

Eccles, J., & Wigfield, A. (1995). In the mind of the actor: The structure of adolescents' achievement task values and expectancy-related beliefs. *Personality and Social Psychology Bulletin, 21,* 215–225.

Enserink, M. (1999, April). Can the placebo be the cure? *Science, 284,* 238–240.

Erez, M., & Earley, P.C. (1993). *Culture, self-identity and work.* Oxford: Oxford University Press.

Farrington, J. (1997, May). *The impact of structural features and context on improving transfer in concept acquisition.* Unpublished doctoral dissertation, School of Education, University of Southern California.

Feather, N. (1982). Human values and the prediction of action: An expectancy-valence analysis. In N. Feather (Ed.), *Expectations and actions: Expectancy-value models in psychology.* Hillsdale, NJ: Erlbaum.

Ford, M.E. (1992). *Motivating humans: Goals, emotions and personal agency beliefs.* Newberry Park, CA: Sage.

Friedman, M.I., & Lackey, G.H. Jr. (1991). *The psychology of human control: A general theory of purposeful behavior.* New York: Praeger Publishers.

Gagne, R.M., & Medsker, K.L. (1996). *The conditions of learning: Training applications.* New York: Harcourt Brace College Publishers.

Gagne, E.D., Yekovich, C., & Yekovich, F. (1993). *The cognitive psychology of school learning.* New York: Harper Collins.

Goldfried, M.R., & Robbins, C., (1982). On the facilitation of self-efficacy. *Cognitive Therapy and Research, 6,* 361–379.

Harp, S.F., & Mayer, R. (1997). The role of interest in learning from scientific text and illustrations: On the distinction between emotional interest and cognitive interest. *Journal of Educational Psychology, 89*(1), 92–102.

Harp, S.F., & Mayer, R. (1998). How seductive details do their damage: A theory of cognitive interest in science learning. *Journal of Educational Psychology, 89*(1), 92–102.

Heckhausen, J., & Schultz, R. (1995). A life-span theory of control. *Psychological Review, 102*(2), 284–304.

Helmke, A. (1987). Affective student characteristics and cognitive development: Problems, pitfalls, perspectives. *International Journal of Educational Research, 13*(8), 915–932.

Highley, D. (1994, May). *Effects of a "Learning to Learn" course on at risk students' motivation, self-regulated learning processes and academic achievement.* Unpublished doctoral dissertation, University of Southern California, Division of Educational Psychology, Los Angeles, CA.

Izard, C.E. (1993). Four systems for emotion activation: Cognitive and non cognitive processes. *Psychological Review, 100*(1), 68–90.

Jonassen, D.J. (1991). Objectivism versus constructivsm: Do we need a new philosophical paradigm? *Educational Technology Research and Development, 39*(3), 5–14.

Keller, J.M. (1987). Development and use of the ARCS model of instructional design. *Journal of Instructional Development, 10*(3), 2–10.

Kluger, A.N., & DiNisi, A. (1996). Feedback Interventions: Toward the understanding of a two-edged sword. *Current Directions in Psychological Science, 7*(3), 67–72.

Locke, E.A. (1990). Motivation through conscious goal setting. *Applied and Preventive Psychology,* (5), 117–124.

Locke, E.A., & Latham, G.P. (1990). *A theory of goal setting and task performance.* Englewood Cliffs, NJ: Prentice-Hall.

Lohman, D. (1986). Predicting mathemathantic effects in the teaching of higher order thinking skills. *Educational Psychologist, 21*(3), 191–208.

Merrill, M.D. (1991). Constructivism and instructional design. *Educational Technology, 31*(5), 45–53.

Metcalfe, J., & Mischel, W. (1999). A hot/cool-system analysis of delay of gratification: Dynamics of willpower. *Psychological Review, 106*(1), 3–19.

Miller, G.A. (1956). The magical number seven plus or minus two: Some limits on our capacity for processing information. *Psychological Review, 63,* 81–97.

Nelson, T.O. (1988). Predictive accuracy of the feeling of knowing across different criterion tasks and across different subject populations and individuals. In M.M. Greenberg, P. Morris, & R.N. Sykes (Eds.), *Practical aspects of memory* (Vol. 2). New York: Wiley.

Offerman, L.R., & Gowing, M.K. (1990). Organizations of the future. *American Psychologist, 45,* 95–108.

Ohlsson, S. (1996). Learning from performance errors. *Psychological Review, 103*(2), 241–262.

Paas, F. (1992). Training strategies for attaining problems solving skills in statistics: A cognitive load approach. *Journal of Educational Psychology, 84,* 429–434.

Pajares, F. (1996). Self-efficacy beliefs in academic settings. *Review of Educational Research, 66*(4), 543–578.

Pajares, F., & Miller, M.D. (1994). The role of self-efficacy and self-concept beliefs in mathematical problem solving: A path analysis. *Journal of Educational Psychology, 86,* 193–203.

Perkins, D.N., & Grotzer, T.A. (1997, October). Teaching intelligence. *American Psychologist, 52*(10), 1125–1133.

Peters, M., Godaert, G.L.R., Ballieux, R., van Vliet, M., Willemsen, J., Sweep, F.C.G.J., & Heijnen, C. (1998). Cardiovascular and endocrine responses to experimental stress: Effects of mental effort and controllability. *Psychoneuroendocrinology, 23*(1), 1–17.

Pintrich, P.R., & Schunk, D.H. (1996). *Motivation in education: Theory, research and applications.* Englewood Cliffs, NJ: Prentice-Hall.

Reder, L.M., & Ritter, F.E. (1992). What determines initial feeling of knowing? Familiarity with question terms, not with the answer. *Journal of Experimental Psychology: Learning, Memory and Cognition, 18,* 435–451.

Salomon, G. (1974). Internalization of filmic operations in relation to individual differences. *Journal of Educational Psychology, 66,* 499–511.

Salomon, G. (1981). *Communication and education: Social and psychological interactions.* Beverly Hills CA: Sage.

Salomon, G. (1983). The differential investment of effort in learning from different sources. *Educational Psychologist, 18*(1), 42–50.

Salomon, G. (1984). Television is "easy" and print is "tough": The differential investment of mental effort in learning as a function of perceptions and attributions. *Journal of Educational Psychology, 76,* 774–786.

Sarbin, T.R. (1997). On the futility of psychiatric diagnostic manuals (DSM's) and the return of personal agency. *Applied and Preventive Psychology, 6,* 233–243.

Schunk, D.H. (1989). Self efficacy and achievement behaviors. *Educational Psychology Review, 1,* 173–208.

Schwarzer, R. (1992). *Self efficacy: Thought control of action.* Washington, DC: Hemisphere.

Shoham, V., & Rohrbaugh, M. (1998). Interrupting ironic processes. *Psychological Science, 8*(3), 151–153.

Shapiro Jr., D.H., Schwartz, C.E., & Austin, J.A. (1996). Controlling ourselves, controlling our world: Psychology's role in understanding positive and negative consequences of seeking and gaining control. *American Psychologist, 51*(12), 1213–1230.

Snow, R.E. (1977). Research on aptitudes: A progress report. In L.J. Shulman (Ed.), *Review of research in education* (Vol. 4, pp. 50–105). Itasca, IL: Peacock.

Sweller, J. (1999, July 1). *From cognitive architecture to instructional design.* Invited paper read at van Merrienboer's inaugural seminar "Cognition and Multimedia Design." Open University of the Netherlands. Heerlen, Netherlands.

Taylor, S.E. , Pham, Ll., Rivkin, I., & Armor, D. (1998). Harnessing the imagination: Mental simulation, self regulation and coping. *American Psychologist, 53*(4) 429–439.

Van Merriënboer, J.J.G. (1998). *Training complex cognitive skills.* Englewood Cliffs, NJ: Educational Technology Publications.

Vosniadou, S., Pearson, P.D., & Rogers, T. (1988). What causes children's failures to detect inconsistencies in text? Representation versus comparison difficulties. *Journal of Educational Psychology, 80*(1), 27–39.

Wegner, D.M. (1994). Ironic processes of mental control. *Psychological Review, 101*(1), 34–52.

Wegner, D.M. (1997). When the antidote is the poison: Ironic mental control processes. *Psychological Science, 8*(3), 148–150.

Weiner, B. (1986). *An attributional theory of motivation and emotion.* New York: Springer-Verlag.

Weiner, B. (1990). History of motivational research in education. *Journal of Educational Psychology, 80,* 616–622.

Wigfield, A. (1997). Reading motivation: A domain-specific approach to motivation. *Educational Psychologist, 32*(2) 59–68.

Yates, J., Lee, J., Shinotsuka, H., Patalano, A., & Sieck, W.R. (1998). Cross cultural variations in probability judgement accuracy: Beyond general knowledge—overconfidence? *Organizational Behavior and Human Decision Processes, 74*(2), 89–107.

CHAPTER 16

NEW DIRECTIONS

Evaluating Distance Education Technologies

Richard E. Clark

Originally published as: Clark, R.E. (2000). Evaluating distance education: Strategies and cautions. *The Quarterly Review of Distance Education*, *1*(1), 5–18. Used by permission. Some parts of this article were also published in: Clark, R.E. (1994). Assessment of distance learning technology. In E.L. Baker & H.F. O'Neil, Jr. (Eds.), *Technology assessment*. Hillsdale, NJ: Lawrence Erlbaum.

ABSTRACT

The four goals of this discussion are to: (a) Discourage distance education evaluation questions and tactics which have not proved useful in the past; (b) Persuade distance education evaluation designers to distinguish between the effects of two distinctly different technologies; delivery technology and instructional technology; (c) Offer brief descriptions of evaluation plans, questions and examples associated with delivery technologies on the one hand, and instructional technology on the other, and (d) discuss issues related to the cost effectiveness evaluation of distance education. The emphasis in the article is to discuss evaluation strategies that give an accurate picture of the substantive contributions made by distance education programs—and to help the reader avoid historical pitfalls in technology evaluation.

FORMING AND ASKING EVALUATION QUESTIONS

For at least the past fifty years, various types of distance education programs have attracted different groups of enthusiastic supporters. Every
major mass communication technology, including film, radio, television,
and (currently) the Internet, have been used to transmit instruction and
support education at a distance. Each of these "new" media have experienced similar problems providing credible evidence of solid educational
success (Clark, 1995). Since the time lag between each technology tends to
be approximately the span of a generation, there is a temptation for current advocates to ignore the past and assume that their "new technology" is
unique (Clark & Salomon, 1986). One damaging result of a failure to learn
from the past is that damaging mistakes tend to be repeated. For example,
a recent comprehensive review of research and evaluation studies on
"hypermedia" in distance education (Dillon & Gabbard, 1999) pointed out
serious problems with available evidence of impact. The goal of this article
is to suggest evaluation strategies designed to avoid past mistakes and provide defensible evidence for distance education successes.

What is Evaluation?

Evaluation is the process by which we judge the worthwhileness of something in order to make decisions (Baker, 1991). Technology assessment
encompasses a number of analytic and measurement strategies that help us
make "worthwhileness" judgements about distance education programs.
Judgements made during the development of a program are termed "formative." Evaluation that seeks to describe the impact of an operating program is often referred to as "summative." Since our values govern both
formative and summative evaluation activities, we need to be clear about
the kinds of distance education evaluation questions that will meet the
needs of the clients for distance education—students and their communities. The questions we decide to ask about distance education and the evaluation instruments we employ will necessarily keep us ignorant about some
matters while informing us about others. Evaluation questions carry
implicit assumptions and beliefs about the significance of different elements of distance education and their impact on desired outcomes. For
example, if we ask whether a new teaching medium produces more student
achievement than traditional media, we have assumed that media are able
to influence student learning. Yet this assumption has been seriously questioned (Clark 1994a,b, 1992a; Clark & Estes, 1998, 1999; Clark & Salomon,
1986; Gardner & Salomon, 1986).

One of the most important recommendations underlying this discussion is that all evaluations should explicitly investigate the relative benefit of two different but compatible types of distance education technologies found in every distance education program. One technology influences the delivery of instruction and another technology influences learning from instruction.

Delivery Technology

Delivery technology is characterized by the equipment, machines and media that provide access to instruction. Familiar examples of delivery technology are books, computers and teachers. Instructional technology seeks to influence the learning of students. Examples of instructional technology are ways to sequence and structure lessons, the use of examples, provisions for practice, and tests. Instructional technology is transported to the student by delivery technology. Any instructional technology can be provided to students by a variety of delivery technologies. For example, information, examples, practice and tests can all be delivered to students by either books, computers and/or teachers.

Delivery and instructional technologies are typically confused in distance education evaluation. Student achievement gains or losses influenced by instructional technology are most often attributed to delivery technologies. Reductions in the cost or time it takes to access special student populations (e.g., rural or disadvantaged students) are incorrectly attributed to instructional technology. Confusion about technological benefits can lead to inappropriate and expensive policy mistakes. At the root of the confusion one finds many different definitions of technology (Clark, 1992b).

Which Technology for What Purpose?

It its most general sense, the term "technology" suggests the application of science and experience to solving problems (Clark & Estes, 1998, 1999; Heinich, 1984). The major obstacle in our past struggle to understand the contribution of new technology in distance education is that we have confused the contributions of these two different technologies. One distinct class of technologies results from the application of various scientific and engineering principles to the development and use of equipment, materials and procedures that record and transmit instruction. These educational media technologies are associated with the physical sciences that have produced the new electronic multimedia (e.g., fiber optics, interactive video disc and computers). Delivery technologies increase student access to learning resources which is one of the most important goals of distance education.

Instructional or Learning Technology

A second type of technology applies various social science principles and past experience to develop instructional methods and curriculum choices (Reigeluth, 1983, 1987). This instructional technology draws primarily on research in teaching, learning and motivation to enhance student achievement. The "products" of an instructional technology are new instructional design theories (Gagne, Briggs, & Wager, 1992; Merrill, Jones, & Li, 1992; Reigeluth, 1983, 1987), teaching methods and motivational strategies (Clark, 1998; Clark & Salomon, 1986; Weiner, 1992) which can be embedded in "courseware" (instructional materials) for distance education. A primary goal of this discussion is to recommend that all evaluations of distance education programs attempt to provide reliable and valid determinations of the separate influences of delivery and instructional technologies.

Separating Delivery and Instructional Evaluation Questions

Support for a separate consideration of delivery and instructional technologies in evaluation is well established in the research literature but rare in evaluations or program planning. Wilbur Schramm, historically the most established reviewer of media studies in education, concluded (Schramm, 1977) that "...learning seems to be affected more by what is delivered than by the delivery medium" (p. 273). More recently, analyses of media and technology research that compared the learning benefits of different media (Allen, 1971; Clark, 1983, 1985; Clark & Salomon, 1986; Gardner & Salomon, 1986; Jamison, Suppes, & Wells, 1974; Kearsley, Hunter, & Sidel, 1983; Levie & Dickie, 1973; Lumsdaine, 1963; Mielke, 1968; Salomon, 1981; Schramm, 1977; Winn, 1982) could be summarized with the analogy that media "...do not influence learning any more than the truck that delivers groceries influences the nutrition of a community" (Clark, 1983, p. 445). Distance education media are vehicles that transport instruction to students. The choice of vehicle influences the important outcomes of student access, and the speed or cost of the delivery but *not* the learning impact of the instruction that is delivered to the "consumer." Delivery vehicles indiscriminately carry helpful, hurtful and neutral instruction.

CHOOSING CRITICAL INDICATORS FOR EVALUATION

Among the specific issues that must be addressed in future evaluations of local applications of distance education technology are: What aspects of evaluation planning enhance the usefulness of information for decision makers? and How might we collect information that will aid in our judgement about the different influences of the delivery and instructional features of the program? (Baker, 1989; Clark, 1985; Congress of the United States, 1989a; 1989b). While a number of evaluation concerns apply to some but not all programs, three generalizations seem useful to all; (a) Adopt an early concern for evaluation, (b) Use a multi-level evaluation plan, and (c) Conduct formal cost-effectiveness analyses.

Adopt an Early Concern for Evaluation

Both evaluation specialists and administrative decision makers need to be involved early and actively in distance education system design. Past experience suggests that waiting until a system is designed before thinking about evaluation has been a familiar but very wasteful pattern (Baker, 1989). It is critical to have early "base line" information about, for example, exactly what set of conditions are being replaced by new distance education programs. One way to accomplish this would be to spend an ample amount of time during the program planning stages carefully describing the specific problems we wish the new approach to solve. We should describe how we will measure the current conditions (e.g., a base line measure of the existing situation including the views and impressions of the stakeholders) and thoroughly discuss what we believe to be the *alternative* solutions to the problem(s).

If an evaluation plan is developed as the program is planned and implemented, a number of advantages are realized. In the area of computer assisted learning, Henry Levin (1983, 1988; Levin & Meister, 1985) describes eight exemplary cost-effectiveness evaluation programs. Each of these good examples collected baseline measures of the problems they were trying to solve. Each of the eight programs began their concern with evaluation at the start of their planning.

Early evaluation makes it possible to determine which aspects of a distance education program were positive and which were negative. Negative aspects can then be modified and the positive accentuated to achieve maximum benefit. For example, most distance education programs attempt to bring a much richer set of curriculum choices and quality teaching to K-12 school programs. Program planners might begin with an analysis of options (the variety of media available to deliver new curricula) and their audience (e.g., measure the number of students who would enroll in new courses). Early concern with evaluation results in the collection of information on both the need and the audience for distance education as well as the existing alternatives.

Another advantage of early evaluation involvement is that an ongoing evaluation plan can be developed. Too often programs are developed and implemented, then at some later stage the program planners remember that "we have to do some evaluation." As a result, very little is learned about the program being studied which is useful either for the immediate program or for other distance education ventures. It is early evaluation planning that most often yields useful information and yet it is a rare phenomenon. Levin noted that his search for adequate cost effectiveness evaluations was difficult. He found that only one in six published reports was adequately designed. Since most reports are not published, one suspects that early evaluation is not our typical procedure at the moment. The second general direction that is useful for all distance education programs is to adopt a multi-level evaluation plan.

Use a Multi-Level Evaluation Plan

The two levels of evaluation that most often seem to give useful development information are measures of: (a) participant reactions, and (b) the achievement of program objectives. Participant reactions to distance education program effectiveness is the most common (and unfortunately, often the only) level of evaluation attempted by distance educators. Typically, this level of evaluation employs printed forms containing a combination of questions designed to inquire about the "feelings" and "impressions" of different groups who are involved in the program. A common question is "How would you rate the quality of the teaching in this program?" (typically rated on a five-point scale that ranges from Exceptional through Average to Poor). Items such as "List what you think are the STRONG [or WEAK] points of the program?" permit the respondent to write in personal views and comments. Questionnaire forms are most often used for reactions because they protect the anonymity of respondents and therefore, we presume, increase the candor of the responses. Forms are often sent to all of the program participants but are filled out and returned by only a small percentage of those who receive them.

Participant reactions are useful provided that they do not serve as the *only* level of evaluation data. There is clear evidence that when reaction data is used to measure learning or other achievement goals, the information can often indicate the exact opposite of what actually happened. Clark (1982) has provided evidence of strong inverse relationships between reactions and learning where students who indicate that they have learned a great deal are found, on closer inspection, to have learned very little or even had their learning damaged by instruction.

Reaction evaluation should be used primarily to uncover both informal participant impressions and *unanticipated* benefits and problems. They can also give indications of how much motivation participants experienced as a result of the program. Reaction items should be divided between those that deal with the medium (e.g., ease of access, reliability or technical quality of transmission or machines, space allocation issues) and those associated with the instruction (e.g., the quality of teaching, how things learned in the program were used outside of class).

The advantage of collecting participant reactions is that program mangers get informal impressions of the programs and often uncover unanticipated results. For example, the Northeastern Utah Tele-learning project, which uses microcomputer-based instruction transmitted between remote schools over telephone lines, found an unexpected problem because they used open-ended reaction forms (Congress of the United States, 1989). Students complained that in the early stages of the program it was very difficult to contact a teacher to get help when it was needed.

On the other hand, the Interact Instructional Television Network in Houston, Texas (Congress of the United States, 1989) used a similar instrument and discovered an unexpected positive outcome of their project. It was observed that students in small television reception rooms tended to help each other a great deal during the instructional program. They could help while the program was continuing without disrupting the teacher or other students. This "peer tutoring" seemed to be having a positive impact on student learning and motivation. Upon closer inspection, the tutoring activity seemed to be due to the fact that the microphone which the students used to communicate with the teacher at another location had to be turned on to function. When the microphone was turned off, the students could consult among themselves before they turned it on to answer a question or discuss a point with the teacher. When following up on the peer tutoring finding, the Houston project uncovered the fact that some of the tutors hired to supervise the student television reception rooms were demanding that the students "keep quiet" which discouraged the peer tutoring. The tutors had assumed that talking indicated a "discipline problem" that had to be corrected. Once discovered, the peer tutoring might be encouraged and its barriers eliminated (e.g., though adjusting the training of tutors as in the Houston example).

The problem with participant reaction data is that it is most often collected in such a way that it not a reliable or a valid indicator of program effects. Yet, unreliable information might occasionally provide useful information as it did in the Houston project. Questionnaire data can be representative if evaluators select a random sample of participants large enough to engage a meaningful number of each group involved in the project. To increase participation evaluators have found it useful to send each randomly chosen participant a card telling them that they have been selected, that their response is vital and to expect the questionnaire soon. Follow-up notes to all those chosen can encourage laggards to send in their forms without violating anonymity. Depending on the numbers involved in the entire program, a small (5 to 10 percent) random sample of participants can give a very accurate impression of the reactions of the entire group (see Fowler, 1984 for a discussion of sample size in evaluation studies).

Questionnaires should be used at various stages in the program development, including very early on. Unanticipated problems and benefits uncovered by questionnaires usually require much more careful study. For example, when students in most distance education programs are asked, a majority will typically state that they would *not* continue to elect a distance education option if they could choose a "traditional class" as they did in the Northeastern Utah Tele-learning Project (Congress of the United States, 1989). The fact that students would elect a traditional program if one was offered does not indicate that the Utah project failed. Upon closer inspection it is often found, as is suspected in the Utah case, that students sometimes feel isolated in distance education settings and would therefore select more traditional options for social and "non academic" reasons. This is particularity true of middle school and high school students. They typically have strong social needs which are not always met in distance education programs.

Other problems which can be spotted using the "early warning system" of reaction questionnaires are communication problems between participants, the extent and impact of technical difficulties, inappropriate implementation of plans, and opportunities to extend the program into new areas. Yet in even the best of circumstances, reaction forms will not give solid information about the achievement of most delivery and instructional goals. For this purpose, programs need to adopt a second level of evaluation.

Achievement of Program Objectives

The second and most substantive evaluation goal is to focus on program objectives. Formal measurement of objectives is usually considered by evaluation specialists to be the most crucial information to be gathered. Objectives should be divided into at least two categories, those associated with delivery and those associated with instruction. One category of outcome that is common to both types of technology is cost-benefit and cost-effectiveness. In cost-benefit and cost-effectiveness evaluation, we attempt to measure "bang for the buck," that is, the cost of the impact obtained from various features of the program. The discussion turns next to outcomes specific to instructional technology, then to delivery technology outcomes and finally to cost-benefit and cost-effectiveness measurement.

Instructional technology objectives include changes in student learning, values, motivation, and the transfer of and application of knowledge outside of the classroom. These important goals are influenced by the "courseware" or instructional programs that are developed and/or chosen and transmitted to distant learners. In some cases, instruction is designed by teachers. In other cases, already-developed courseware is purchased and transmitted to remote sites. The instructional decisions that are embedded in each lesson influence student learning and motivation. Different teaching method and curriculum options have very different effects on student learning, which might be explored in evaluation. So, distance education evaluation might include at least the following seven types of questions related to instructional technology:

1. Which of the curriculum and teaching method choices in a given distance education program impacted student achievement and subsequent ability to use (transfer) the knowledge acquired outside of the instructional setting?

Achievement can be tested with teacher-made or standardized achievement tests. Increasingly schools are interested in the extent to which students transfer what they learn outside of school. Transfer might be estimated by open-ended questions on reaction forms. If the school district has other schools receiving similar curricula from different delivery forms, an obvious opportunity exists to check on any achievement or motivation differences between the options. When possible, alternative teaching methods and curriculum choices should be explored in order to maximize the learning of different kinds of students. For example, highly structured and supportive instruction might be contrasted with a more "learner directed" and discovery approach to curriculum (Clark, 1983, 1985). Many programs have found that students who are anxious or have learning problems profit a great deal from added structure and support, whereas students who are more independent and able tend to benefit more from a discovery approach (Clark, 1983).

2. What influenced student and teacher *motivation* to learn and invest effort in making this program a success?

Current theories of motivation (Clark, 1998; Weiner, 1992) have introduced a very counterintuitive element in distance education programs and evaluation. Formerly, it was thought that media choices greatly influenced both student and teacher motivation. The recent cognitive approach to motivation suggests that it is influenced by beliefs and expectations and is therefore due to individual differences in beliefs about media and *not* to the media per se (Clark, 1994, 1983; Salomon, 1984). Yet, a number of recent studies of media preferences (Dillon & Gabbard, 1998) agree with older landmark studies by, for example, O'Neil, Anderson, and Freeman, that "In general, students' attitudes are positive while instructors' attitudes are negative" (1986, p. 977).

There is recent but solid evidence that when students expect that a new medium will make learning easier and more "entertaining," they like it. However, there is also good evidence that their liking does not lead them to work harder (Clark, 1994a; Saettler, 1968). Quite to the contrary, the more they think a medium makes learning "easy," the less effort they will invest to learn (Kozma, 1991; Mielke, 1968; Salomon, 1984). This effect has been explained as a student misjudgment about the kind of effort that is required to learn based on our previous experience and expectations. For example, American students typically assume that television is an "easier" medium than books or teachers, probably because of their use of the medium for entertainment. This reaction on the part of our students is quite different than that of Israeli students who, on the average, have been found to invest more effort in television because their early experiences with television have been less entertaining and more demanding intellectually (Salomon, 1984).

There is additional evidence that students will not invest effort if they believe a medium to be very difficult. With American children, this is sometimes the reason for their lack of willingness to read (Kozma, 1991; Salomon, 1984). So the greatest motivation is invested in media and instructional programs that are perceived as being moderately difficult. This evidence would suggest that one way to influence student motivation would be to select "moderately difficult" media. However the evidence also suggests that student and teacher beliefs about media difficulty change over time, sometimes radically (Clark, 1994). The more stable predictor of motivation seems to be student beliefs about their own ability and the demands placed on them by different instructional tasks (Salomon, 1984). This would suggest that we should evaluate the students' perceptions and beliefs about the *learning tasks* contained within the media employed by distance education programs and their own *self efficacy* as learners. This form of evaluation could be embedded in reaction questionnaires.

3.   Which of the curriculum and teaching method choices in a given distance education program impacted: (a) student and teacher values for what was learned and, (b) subsequent motivation to teach

and learn and to use what was learned outside of the instructional setting?

Reaction questionnaires which are carefully constructed and administered will give a good indication of student and teacher values related to the program, teaching and the curriculum. Negative value statements do not always reflect negatively on the program (recall the students in the Utah project who liked traditional classrooms better than distance education because of social opportunities). Generally one hopes to foster a positive value for learning and new curriculum options with distance education. Shifts in attitude that result from *changes* in the program can be monitored *if* reaction forms are sent periodically (every few months) throughout the development stages.

4.   Which of the curriculum and teaching method choices in a given distance education program impacted the cultivation of different kinds of knowledge including procedural skills *and* higher order thinking, learning-to-learn and metacognitive skills?

While higher order skill learning is more difficult to assess than ordinary "achievement," few programs have been successful in this area. One good example of a technology-based thinking skills program is the Higher Order Thinking Skills (HOTS) program that focuses on Chapter 1 (disadvantaged) students (Congress of the United States, 1989a; 1989b). The program originates at the University of Arizona and is distributed to member schools in many states. Teachers in the program use computer lessons, class exercises and discussion to increase the thinking and study skills of students. HOTS evaluation involves the ongoing use of standardized tests, noting changes in the quality of questions students ask and analyses of their class assignments. While a few formal measures of thinking and study skills exist (and more are being developed), program managers might consult with evaluation specialists about selecting and developing tests to measure problem solving and study skill development (Congress of the United States, 1989; Levin & Meister, 1985). While learning, values and study skills are important instructional outcomes for distance education, the delivery technology will influence yet another type of outcome.

Delivery Technology

Delivery technology transmits various forms of instruction to students. The dramatic increase of computers and Internet access in schools and at home has resulted in more attention to technology delivery benefits (Dillon & Gabbard, 1998). Evaluation questions associated with delivery technologies include attempts to assess the effect of medium on (a) student *access* to a greater variety of curriculum choices, (b) school or program *utilization of resources*, and (c) the *reliability* of delivery choices. Questions one typically finds in the evaluation of media include:

5.   Did the distance education media maximize student access to new, and/or high quality courses and teaching when compared with other delivery choices?

Access to new or beneficial courses and instructional techniques or teachers is one of the primary objectives of most distance education programs. Collecting access data often involves comparisons between different ways to deliver courses or the size of enrollments in classes both before and during the implementation of the program. For example, the Share-Ed program in Beaver County, Oklahoma (Congress of the United States, 1989a; 1989b) used a new fiber optic network to provide new curriculum to rural schools. They collected participant reactions on the advantages of the increased curriculum choices offered to students who are allowed to take college credit courses in high school as a result of the new system. These reactions, when combined with baseline and process data on actual enrollments, provide good evidence of the extent of access provided by the innovation. Evaluators should carefully consider increased or enhanced access of minority, older or widely dispersed student groups.

While "access" usually suggests the availability of new curriculum options, it can also imply teacher access to students on a more personal level. Teachers in the Houston, Texas InterAct Instructional Television systems (Congress of the United States, 1989a; 1989b) report problems with their personal and immediate access to students during instruction in order to "check their reactions or mood" and adjust their teaching accordingly. On the other hand, teachers using computer delivered courses often report increased "individualized" access to students and enjoy the opportunity to "watch them learn."

6.   Did the media influence the utilization of school and community educational resources (e.g., space, equipment, skilled teachers, new courseware developed at one site but not readily available at others)?

It is often the case that because distance education programs are recorded and distributed to many different sites, the best teachers are made available to many more students. Evaluators might track statistics about how the background and/or training of teachers in distance programs compare with district averages. An instance of a different kind of utilization is to be found in the Beaver County, Oklahoma Share-Ed program (Congress of the United States, 1989a; 1989b). The local telephone company was installing fiber optic communication lines to improve local service. The system was capable of handling far greater transmission volume than the existing usage anticipated in the communities served. The school system's use of fiber optic lines for television and voice transmission for distance education utilized unused space on the system. Since distance education courses are often provided to fewer students per school than the average course, they often make use of underutilized rooms (e.g., storage spaces) and equipment.

7.   Are distance education media more reliable than other alternatives?

One of the primary concerns expressed by the critics of distance media is their technical reliability. In the Beaver County, Oklahoma television system for example, the reaction forms used in evaluation only picked up technical problems when the students were asked to describe "weak points" of the system. None of the administrators noticed technical problems, 11 percent of the teachers mentioned reliability, but 36 percent of the students responded to the reaction form by going into detail about microphone feedback, distracting equipment, out-of-focus pictures, equipment noises and color problems. This difference in reporting reliability problems probably stems from the amount of experience each group had with the actual television transmission.

However, program evaluation should establish regular checks by technical staff on these problems in order to judge the severity of participant reactions and make repairs when necessary. When technical transmission problems are not solved, they can decrease achievement scores and reduce participant commitment to the system.

In successful distance education programs, delivery (media) technology and instructional technology must work together. The delivery features of new media must be employed so that they will eventually save precious educational resources. Curriculum and instructional design must be utilized so that they support the effective learning and transfer of important concepts. Instruction must be developed to reflect the special delivery characteristics of different media. In addition however, communities and funding agencies are increasingly concerned not only with the effectiveness but also the cost of distance education programs. Cost is a "goal" or "outcome" of both delivery and instructional technologies.

Cost-Effectiveness Evaluation

During an evaluation of the separate delivery and instructional value of distance education program effectiveness, *cost* data should also be collected. This parallel activity allows us to combine "effectiveness" (i.e., delivery and instructional outcomes) with "cost" data to provide cost-effectiveness information to decision makers. Cost-effectiveness evaluation requires that the cost of two or more different alternative technology options are compared for the same outcome measures (Levin, 1983).

In many ways, cost-effectiveness ratios are the most interesting information we can supply to school officials, taxpayers and their elected representatives. Limited educational resources will eventually require a much greater emphasis on both the monetary and time cost of new programs.

Delivery Technology Cost

Evaluations that precede the introduction of new media should explore the costs of various alternatives. In many cases, older technologies (e.g., tutors, books, cassette television programs, the mail system) are cheaper in monetary cost. Evaluations of costs should always consider trade-offs with cheaper and more traditional delivery options. There are evaluation data that indicate, for example, that tutors who are trained and paid minimum wage are much cheaper than computers for many instructional tasks (Levin, 1983). An excellent discussion of cost-effectiveness analysis is provided by Fletcher (1990) who reviews previous studies and presents cost data for interactive video disc programs used in military training. He notes that some programs divide costs into categories such as: (a) initial investment; (b) technology support (maintenance and replacement) and, (c) operating costs—other programs lump all costs together. He advises that separation gives a better picture of the source of costs and helps cost containment. He notes that cost-effectiveness ratios vary widely in past reports. Some studies find huge cost benefits for technology-based distance education. Other studies report large cost disadvantages.

Clearly this question involves a number of factors, many of which have not yet been identified. Fletcher implies that cost-effectiveness analyses can be (and are) manipulated when he suggests that "basically, these cost ratios can be as low as we want, depending on the actual equipment being simulated" (Fletcher, 1990, p. 19). Evaluations that are conducted during the introduction and maintenance of a distance education program are advised to adopt the "ingredients" costing approach described below.

Instructional Technology Cost

There are a great variety of different school and community goals that influence evaluation criteria under the general heading of instructional effectiveness costs. The cost required to increase student motivation, learning and transfer is being questioned with greater frequency (Jamison, Suppes, & Wells, 1974; Congress of the United States, 1989a; 1989b). School districts may wish to consider collecting cost data as a way to support the development of policy. The development of an instructional technology yields a variety of teaching, motivation and transfer outcomes at very different monetary costs (Congress of the United States, 1989a; Levin & Meister, 1985).

Besides monetary cost, schools are increasingly interested in the time costs associated with the mastery of different learning or performance goals. Some types of learning tasks consume much more "teaching time" and/or "learning time" (Clark & Sugrue, 1989). For example, it takes much longer to teach a student study skills than to teach memorization of facts. It also takes longer for a student to learn procedural knowledge to the point where it becomes automatic—about 100 hours of practice for even simple procedures is the current estimate (Clark, 1989; Gagne, Briggs, & Wager, 1992). Fletcher (1990) reviews a number of military applications of computer-based instruction and finds time savings to average about 30 percent across many different sites. It is therefore likely that there will be more and more emphasis on the time costs of different instructional technology options.

In some applications, the cheapest and/or quickest options are not necessarily the best. Students who learn cheaper or faster do not necessarily learn better. The new "cognitive" learning theories provide the insight that it may be more important to know *how* students reach learning goals than to know that they get correct answers on examinations. It often takes longer for students to learn in such a way that their correct answer on a test reflects "deep cognitive processing" and the exercise of higher order cognitive learning skills, than to take a surface level shortcut (Clark & Voogel, 1985; Merrill, Jones, & Li, 1992). Educators need to be wary of focusing evaluations on time savings at the expense of the quality of learning.

Generally, once a distance education team has worked out the list of goals associated with both monetary and time costs, an evaluation design can be chosen. One of the first issues to be confronted is the choice of how the data reflecting costs will be gathered. While there are a number of methods, one seems particularly applicable to both delivery and instructional technologies—Levin's (Levin, 1983, 1988; Levin & Meister, 1985) *ingredients* method.

The Ingredients Methods of Determining Costs

While there are a number of emerging ways to determine local costs and efficiencies, one of the soundest and most comprehensive is the "ingredients method" developed by Henry Levin at Stanford University (Levin, 1983, 1988). It "requires identification of all of the ingredients required for the ... [distance education] intervention, a valuation or costing of those ingredients and a summation of the costs to determine the cost of the intervention" (Levin, 1988, p. 3). In the K-12 setting, cost is defined as the value of what is given up by using resources in one way rather than for its next best alternative use. For example, if teacher time is given up then it may not be used for other purposes. Therefore, the cost of teacher time is assessed by assigning a value to what is lost when teachers are assigned to distance education technology programs.

The ingredients method is implemented in two stages. In the first stage, all necessary program ingredients are listed. The identification of ingredients requires that we list distance education program necessities associated with five categories: (a) personnel, (b) facilities, (c) equipment, (d) materials and supplies and (e) all other. In the second stage, each of the ingredients listed in each of the five categories is valued.

Space limitations preclude a complete description of the ingredients method but a review of Levin (1988; Levin & Meister, 1985) will provide most of the information needed to determine ingredient costs. Levin gives specific technology examples which are very relevant to the kinds of programs now evolving in many schools, and he urges complete listings of ingredients. For example, he requires that all "donated" time of volunteers and outside organizations be included as a personnel ingredient if it is necessary for the conduct of the program. He reasons that failure to cost donated time will give an unrealistic picture of the "replication" expense. He also claims (Levin & Meister, 1985) that, in the rare instance where one finds a complete costing of technology-based programs, one often finds evidence that the organizational climate greatly influences cost-benefit ratios. He presents evidence that when the same distance education program is presented in many different sites, the cost of implementation can vary by 400 percent (Levin & Meister, 1985). Some organizational designs seem much more efficient than others for technology-based, distance education program delivery.

CONCLUSION

In the past, distance education evaluations have typically been conducted as "afterthoughts" and have relied heavily on reaction questionnaires which may be unreliable and nonrepresentative of the participants involved. Even when evaluations attempted to collect information about changes in student achievement, questions were asked which confused the separate contributions of delivery media and instructional technology.

In order to identify the strong features of distance education programs and eliminate weak features, more robust evaluation plans must be adopted in the future. These plans should be firmly based on the experience of those who have struggled with technology evaluations in the past (Levin, 1988). Three features are recommended: First, evaluation should begin at the start of distance education program planning. An early commitment to evaluation will provide much more useful information about the strengths of a program as it develops. Changes can be made during the formative stage in time to strengthen the plan. The second recommendation is that all programs should adopt a multi-level evaluation plan. The different roles of qualitative (e.g., questionnaires, diaries and open-ended participant reactions) and quantitative (e.g., student achievement scores, monetary costs) data should be decided. Delivery and instructional evaluation should be separated and a variety of goals assessed. Finally, new techniques are available for cost-effectiveness evaluation of distance education programs. Levin's "ingredients" method is suggested.

REFERENCES

Allen, W.H. (1971). Instructional media research: Past, present and future. *Audio Visual Communication Review 19*, 5–18.

Baker, E.L. (1989). *Technology assessment: Policy and methodological issues. Air Force Systems Command.* Proceedings of the 2nd Intelligent Tutoring Systems Research Forum, pp. 151–158.

Baker, E.L. (1991). Technology assessment: Policy and methodological issues for training. In H. Burns, J.W., Parlett, & C.L. Redfield (Eds.), *Intelligent tutoring systems* (pp. 243–263). Hillsdale, NJ: Lawrence Erlbaum Associates.

Benjamin, L.T. (1988). A history of teaching machines. *American Psychologist, 43*(9), 703–712.

Clark, R.E. (1998). Motivating performance: Part 1—Diagnosing and solving motivation problems. *Performance Improvement, 37*(8), 39–46.

Clark, R.E. (1995). Media and learning, In T. Husen & T. N. Postlethwaite (Eds.), *The International Encyclopedia of Education* (2nd ed.). Oxford: Pergammon.

Clark, R.E. (1994a). Media and method. *Educational Technology Research and Development, 42*(3), 7–10.

Clark, R.E. (1994b). Media will never influence learning. *Educational Technology Research and Development, 42*(3), 21–29.

Clark, R.E. (1994c). Assessment of distance learning technology. In E.L. Baker & H.F. O'Neil, Jr. (Eds.), *Technology assessment*. Hillsdale, NJ: Lawrence Erlbaum.

Clark, R.E. (1992a). Dangers in the evaluation of instructional media. *Academic Medicine,* 67(12), 819–820.

Clark, R.E. (1992b). Six definitions of media in search of a theory. In D.P. Ely & B.B. Minor (Eds.), *Educational media and technology yearbook, 1992* (Vol. 18, pp. 65–76). Littletown Co: Libraries Unlimited Inc.

Clark, R.E. (1992c). Media use in education. In M. Alkin (Ed.), *Encyclopedia of Educational Research* (6th ed., pp. 805–814. New York: Macmillian.

Clark, R.E. (1989). Current progress and future directions in research on instructional technology. *Educational Technology Research and Development,* 37(1), 57–66.

Clark, R.E. (1985). Evidence for confounding in computer-based instruction studies: Analyzing the meta-analyses. *Educational Communication and Technology Journal, 33*(4), 249–262.

Clark, R.E. (1983). Reconsidering research on learning from media. *Review of Educational Research, 53*(4), 445–459.

Clark, R.E. (1982). Antagonism between achievement and enjoyment in ATI studies. *Educational Psychologist, 17*(2).

Clark R.E., & Craig, T.G. (1992). Research and theory on multimedia learning effects. In M. Giardina (Ed.), *Interactive multimedia learning environments.* New York: Springer Verlag.

Clark, R.E., & Estes, F. (1999). The development of authentic educational technologies. *Educational Technology,* 39(2), 5–16.

Clark, R.E., & Estes, F. (1998). Technology or craft: What are we doing? *Educational Technology,* 38(5), 5–11.

Clark, R.E., & Salomon, G. (1986). Media in teaching. In M.C. Wittrock (Ed.), *Third handbook of research on teaching* (pp. 464–478). New York: Macmillan.

Clark, R.E., & Voogel, A. (1985). Transfer of training for instructional design. *Educational Communication and Technology Journal, 33*(2), 113–123.

Congress of the United States, Office of Technology Assessment. (1989a, September). *Power on: New tools for teaching and learning.* Washington, DC: U.S. Government Printing Office.

Congress of the United States, Office of Technology Assessment. (1989b, December). *Linking for learning: A new course for education* [OTA-SET-430]. Washington, DC: U.S. Government Printing Office.

Cuban, L. (1986). *Teachers and machines: The classroom use of technology since 1920.* New York: Teachers College Press.

Dillon, A., & Gabbard, R. (1999). Hypermedia as an educational technology: A review of the quantitative research literature on learner comprehension, control and style. *Review of Educational Research, 68*(3), 322–349.

Fletcher, D. (1990). *Effectiveness and cost of interactive videodisc instruction in defense training and education* [Institute for Defense Analysis Paper P-2372]. Alexadria, Virginia: Institute for Defense Analysis.

Fowler, F.J. (1984). *Survey research methods.* Beverly Hills, CA: Sage.

Gagne, R.M., Briggs, L.J., & Wager, W.W. (1992). *Principles of instructional design.* New York: Harcourt Brace Jovanovich.

Gardner, H., & Salomon, G. (1986, January). The computer as educator: Lessons from television research. *Educational Researcher,* pp. 13–19.

Heinich, R. (1984). The proper study of instructional technology. *Educational Communication and Technology Journal, 32*(2), 67–87.

Jamison, D., Suppes, P., & Wells, S. (1974). The effectiveness of alternative instructional media: A survey. *Review of Educational Research, 44,* 1–68.

Kearsley, G., Hunter, B., & Sidel, R.J. (1983). Two decades of computer based instruction: What have we learned? *T.H.E. Journal, 10,* 88–96.

Kozma, R.B. (1991). Learning with media. *Review of Educational Research, 61*(2), 179–211.

Levie, W.H., & Dickie, K. (1973) The analysis and application of media. In R.M.W. Travers (Ed.), *Second handbook of research on teaching.* Chicago: Rand McNally.

Levin, H.H. (1983). *Cost effectiveness: A primer.* Beverly Hills, CA: Sage.

Levin, H.H. (1988, May). The economics of computer-assisted instruction. In press for a special issue of the *Peabody Journal of Education* to be edited by J.J. Bosco, Tate Center, Western Michigan University.

Levin, H.M., & Meister, G.R. (1985). *Educational technology and computers: Promises, promises, always promises* [Report No. 85-A13]. Stanford, CA: Center for Educational Research at Stanford, School of Education, Stanford University.

Lumsdaine, A. (1963). Instruments and media of instruction. In N.L. Gage (Ed.), *Handbook of research on teaching.* Chicago: Rand McNally.

Merrill, D.M., Jones, M.K., & Li, Z. (1992, June). Instructional theory: Classes of transactions. *Educational Technology 36*(3), pp. 30–37.

Mielke, K. (1968). Questioning the questions of ETV research. *Educational Broadcasting Review, 2,* 6–15.

O'Neil, Jr., H., Anderson, C.L., & Freeman, J. (1986). Research on teaching in the armed forces. In M.C. Wittrock (Ed.), *Handbook of research on teaching* (3rd ed.). New York: MacMillian.

Reigeluth, C. (1983). *Instructional design: Theories and models.* Hillsdale NJ: Lawrence Erlbaum Associates.

Reigeluth, C.M. (1987). *Instructional theories in action.* Hillsdale, NJ: Lawrence Erlbaum Associates.

Saettler, P.A. (1968). *A history of instructional technology.* New York: McGraw Hill.

Salomon, G. (1981). *Communication and education.* Beverly Hills, CA: Sage.

Salomon, G. (1984). Television is "easy" and print is "tough": The differential investment of mental effort in learning as a function of perceptions and attributions. *Journal of Educational Psychology, 76*(4), 647–658.

Schramm, W. (1977). *Big media, little media.* Beverly Hills, CA: Sage.

Weiner, B. (1992). *Human motivation: Metaphors, theories and research.* Newbury Park, CA: Sage.

Winn, W. (1982). Visualization in learning and instruction. *Educational Communication and Technology Journal, 30*(1), 3–25.

CHAPTER 17

THE EQUIVALENT EVALUATION OF INSTRUCTIONAL MEDIA

The Next Round of Media Comparison Studies

Gary R. Morrison

For over 40 years, scholars in the field of instructional technology have suggested that asking which medium is better is an invalid research question (Clark, 1983, 1985, 1994; Clark & Salomon, 1986; Knowlton, 1964; Levie & Dickie, 1973; Morrison, Ross, & Kemp, 2001). Knowlton suggested that this lack of support for the superiority of any media over another was predicted 40 years prior to his 1964 article. The suggestion of Clark and Salomon (1986) that as new media emerge, researchers are apt to compare the new media to the old media to determine which is "better" is still true today. A primary focus of distance education research has been on media comparison studies. Many of these studies were designed to determine if courses offered at-a-distance are as effective as traditional classroom courses. This paper will examine the issues of distance education research and propose appropriate evaluation and research questions.

THE NEXT ROUND

The introduction and growth of the Internet, increasing bandwidth, and more powerful browsers have contributed to the increased interest and growth of distance education delivery systems in higher education, business, military, and K-12 settings. As predicted by Clark and Salomon (1986), researchers produced a number of studies designed to determine the "effectiveness" of distance education courses compared to traditional classroom courses. A number of papers have reviewed the research in distance education (Anglin & Morrison, 2000; McIssac & Gunawardena, 1996). The following section examines these studies and their rationale.

Media Comparison Studies in Distance Education

Media comparison studies are a common form of research in distance education. McIsaac and Gunawardena (1996) found that almost 25 percent of the distance education research focused on media comparisons that yielded no significant differences. In a more recent review, Moore and Thompson's (1997) analysis of the effectiveness of distance education found numerous media comparison studies conducted in the 1980s and 1990s. Similarly, Barry and Runyan (1995), concluded that distance learning in the military "appears to have a secure and even bright future" based on their review of nine media comparison studies conducted on military courses (p. 44). This research methodology is often used to evaluate distance education courses rather than more traditional project evaluation approaches (Lockee, Burton, & Cross, 1999).

A typical approach in distance education research is to compare student performance in a course taught at-a-distance to a traditional course taught on campus. For example, Souder (1993) compared the learning achievement in a course delivered via satellite to a traditional classroom setting. The study was described as a "natural experiment" that allowed for the direct comparison of the two methodologies. Students in the three different university settings were compared on a performance test and a research paper. Additional data were collected with two survey instruments. The study produced some significant differences in performance. The design, however, failed to control for differences in GPA and years of experience that could easily account for the significant differences. This research methodology is often used as an evaluation of distance education courses as opposed to a more traditional project evaluation.

The "Need" for Media Comparison Studies in Distance Education

Why is there an abundance of media comparison studies in the distance education literature? One reason for media comparison studies is the need to determine if the new technology is as effective as the existing technology (Clark, 1985). For example, Schacter (1999) suggests that politicians and policymakers are searching for information concerning the effectiveness of various instructional technologies to determine which will improve educational outcomes and are worth the investment. The need to demonstrate that students taking a course at-a-distance are receiving the same quality of instruction as the students taking the same course on campus is one compelling reason for conducting such studies (Lockee et al., 1999).

Equal or Equivalent?

Instructional technologists and educators would probably agree that student performance in a distance education course should be at least equal if not better than student performance in a traditional course. We would find a delivery system such as distance education unacceptable if students consistently performed lower than students in a traditional class. The instructional environments of the traditional and at-a-distance course can vary greatly in resources, seat time, student characteristics, methods of communication, and instructional strategies employed. They are not *equal* in the instructional environment each creates. For example, the traditional classroom heavily depends on synchronous communication between the instructor and students. In the at-a-distance course the instructor and students may rely more on asynchronous communications. As an instructional technologist, it would be impossible to create equal learning environments given the distributed nature of the distance learners and the expectations of regularly scheduled class meetings of the traditional course.

Rather than creating equal learning environments, Simonson, Schlosser, and Hanson (1999) propose that designers create *equivalent* learning experiences. Although the instructional environment of the two courses will differ, the *instructional methods* should produce equivalent learner outcomes. When important and effective instructional methods are developed for one type of instructional delivery, a functionally similar (but not identical) method should be provided in an alternative type of instructional delivery. This will insure that neither group of students are forced to suffer an inadequate instructional method because of the limitations of the medium being used to deliver instruction to them. For example, in an on campus course we might have students present their research paper and then answer questions from their peers. In an online course an equivalent method might require the student to post a paper on the course website and then facilitate a discussion of the paper using a discussion board or mailing list for several days. We would consider each of these strategies as effective if the students achieved the objectives for the assignment. If equivalent outcomes (i.e., the objectives were achieved) were found, then we could consider the two learning experiences as equivalent.

EVALUATION WITHOUT ONE-UPSMANSHIP

There are two general concerns of interest to individuals involved with the design and delivery of distance education courses. First, does the course provide quality instruction that produces student achievement equivalent to courses delivered by other means? Second, what instructional strategies are most effective in a distance education environment? This section will discuss these two questions to illustrate how to avoid an ill-fated media comparison study.

Evaluation

Evaluation is the process of judging the worth of something (Scriven, 1967). In instructional technology it is often judging the worth or effectiveness of an instructional intervention such as a distance education course. When evaluating an instructional intervention, it is typically not necessary to perform formal research using control and experimental groups with a detailed statistical analysis. Rather, one can gather data relative to pre and post-instruction performance. The value of the course is judged based on performance relative to course goals and/or objectives (Morrison et al., 2001).

Considering student performance data helps the researcher to determine if a program is instructionally effective. Such a narrowly focused approach, however, ignores other intangible outcomes that have direct implications for designing new courses or interventions (Morrison et al., 2001). Clark (2000) proposes a multi-level evaluation approach for distance education courses that incorporates not only student performance data, but emphasizes the identification of unintended outcomes of the course. In an early study involving the evaluation of broadcast television courses at the University of Mid-America, the focus was on evaluating the distance education course rather than comparing the course to similar on campus offerings. Course evaluations included a variety of data including performance measures, surveys, and interviews. Two key findings from these early distance education studies were the role television played in pacing the students' work and the need for contact with the instructor (Brown, 1975a,b).

In a more recent project, we evaluated a course offering using two-way audio and video that included a group of students on campus and one at a remote site 90 miles away (Morrison, Bland, & Ross, 1992). The instructor made only minor adaptations to the traditional course for this offering. If we had collected only data on student performance we would have found that both sections performed equally well. Through surveys and interviews, the students at the remote location expressed an anxiety about the delivery method. The compressed video system used for the course displayed their image of the remote site on one of the monitors at both locations while the instructor was shown on the other monitor. Seeing themselves on camera all the time caused an unnecessary anxiety throughout the course. As a result, modifications were made in the system to display graphics on the second monitor in both classrooms when students were not interacting. These two examples illustrate the need to collect data beyond student performance measures when evaluating a distance education course. The additional information provided insights into unintended outcomes that are useful to others when planning similar instructional interventions.

Media Replication Research

With an increasing interest in technology to deliver instruction at-a-distance it seems natural to question the effectiveness of both traditional and new teaching strategies in a different environment. However, it does not make sense to compare student performance in a traditional course to a distance education course. Using a media replication approach (Ross & Morrison, 1989), researchers can compare the effectiveness of an instructional method in two different technologies of instruction. This comparison across technologies will further our theoretical understanding of different facets of the delivery system such as the social context and time factors as well as how to effectively apply the method.

As an example of media replication consider the following in the context of a seminar course that emphasizes discussion. A seminar course often relies on discussion between the students and with the instructor. Classroom discussions are synchronous and are typically limited to class time. A course offered online is not bound by the same classroom-meeting time frame of the more traditional class. A graduate level seminar course might only meet one evening a week and have a different topic of discussion each week. In contrast, the same seminar offered online would require different discussion strategies. A research study might ask how student discussions differ between a classroom and an online course. By using a media replication strategy, the method used in the classroom course might follow a more traditional format of the instructor asking a question to start the discussion and then facilitating the student interactions. Although it is possible to hold a synchronous online chat for three or four hours, there is a fatigue factor to consider as well as interest due to constraints of the technology (although, it is harder to create a verbose reply!). The method used in the online course might be an asynchronous discussion using either a mailing list or discussion forum for posting responses. An analysis of the two discussions might reveal that the online discussion lasts a full seven days as opposed to a single evening, the online posts are given more thought, and the online students are more likely to seek additional references to support their arguments (Weiss & Morrison, 1998). If students in both treatments achieve the objectives, then the two strategies are considered equivalent. If the online discussion was found to be significantly or qualitatively better, then future research might investigate its use in both an online and classroom course. Research questions might ask if it is the asynchronous time frame, having access to additional reading materials while posting comments, or the lack of face-to-face contact of the online discussion that influences the discussion.

Schwier (2001) provides several analyses of traditional and virtual classrooms with suggestions for research. These comparisons provide ideas for media replication studies to further our understanding of which strategies to use for effective distance education teaching. For example, Schwier indicates that the intimacy in a traditional classroom is potentially high while the intimacy in a virtual classroom is variable and can even be anonymous. One aspect of intimacy is instructor immediacy, which is a predictor of instructor effectiveness (Anderson, 1979; Mehrabian, 1969). A media replication study might investigate how instructor intimacy is affected by different strategies in the traditional course and in an online course.

CONCLUSIONS

Distance educators and instructional technologists need to select valid research questions that will lead to a better understanding of the technologies and further the development of related distance education theories. Researchers need to clarify their intent when evaluating distance education courses and select an evaluation approach similar to those proposed by Clark (2000) rather than attempting to compare two delivery systems. When a comparison of strategies is needed between two technologies, the researcher should consider the use of a media replication (Ross & Morrison, 1989) or other appropriate research strategy as described by Ross and Morrison (1996). Better research will help us answer questions about the design of future courseware and delivery systems as well as support the development and refinement of distance education theories.

REFERENCES

Anderson, J.F. (1979). Teacher immediacy as a predictor of teaching effectiveness. *Communication Yearbook, 3*, 543–559.

Anglin, G.J., & Morrison, G.R. (2000). An analysis of distance education research: Implications for the instructional technologist. *Quarterly Review of Distance Education, 1*(3), 189–194.

Barry, M., & Runyan, G.B. (1995). A review of distance-learning studies in the U.S. military. *American Journal of Distance Education, 9*(3), 37–47.

Brown, L.A. (1975a). *Accounting I* (First offering. Course evaluation report (ED159970). Lincoln, NE: University of Mid-America.

Brown, L.A. (1975b). *Learner responses to the use of television in UMA courses* (ED159969). Lincoln, NE: University of Mid-America.

Clark, R.E. (1983). Reconsidering the research on media. *Review of Educational Research, 53*(4), 445–459.

Clark, R.E. (1985). *Choosing educational technologies: Lessons from the past and directions for the future.* Invited address to the United Nations Educational Scientific and Cultural Organization (UNESCO) Conference titled: "Children in an Information Age: Tomorrow's Problems Today." Varna, Bulgaria.

Clark, R.E. (1994). Media will never influence learning. *Educational Technology Research and Development, 42*(2), 21–29.

Clark, R.E. (2000). Evaluating distance education: Strategies and cautions. *Quarterly Review of Distance Education, 1*(1), 3–16.

Clark, R.E., & Salomon, G. (1986). Media in teaching. In M.C. Wittrock (Ed.), *Second handbook of research on teaching* (pp. 464–478). New York: Macmillan.

Knowlton, J.Q. (1964). A conceptual scheme for the audiovisual field. *Bulletin of the School of Education, Indiana University, 40*(3), 1–44.

Levie, W.H., & Dickie, K.E. (1973). The analysis and application of media. In R.M.W. Travers (Ed.), *Second handbook of research on teaching.* Chicago: Rand McNally.

Lockee, B.B., Burton, J.K., & Cross, L.H. (1999). No comparison: Distance education finds a new use for "no significant difference." *Educational Technology Research and Development, 47*(3), 33–42.

McIsaac, M., & Gunawardena, C. (Eds.). (1996). *Distance education.* New York: Simon & Schuster MacMillan.

Mehrabian, A. (1969). *Nonverbal communication.* Chicago: Aldine-Atherton.

Moore, M.G., & Thompson, M.M. (1997). *The effects of distance education* (Vol. 15, 2nd ed.). University Park, PA: American Center for the Study of Distance Education.

Morrison, G.R., Bland, K., & Ross, S.M. (1992). *Evaluation of the first learning link classes: Spring, 1992.* Memphis, TN: Memphis State University.

Morrison, G.R., Ross, S.M., & Kemp, J.E. (2001). *Designing effective instruction* (3rd ed.). New York: John Wiley & Sons, Inc.

Ross, S.M., & Morrison, G.R. (1989). In search of a happy medium in instructional technology research: Issues concerning external validity, media replications, and learner control. *Educational Technology Research and Development, 37*(1), 19–33.

Ross, S.M., & Morrison, G.R. (1996). Experimental research methods. In D.J. Jonassen (Ed.), *Handbook of research on educational communications and technology* (pp. 1148–1170). New York: Simon & Schuster Macmillan.

Schacter, J. (1999). *The impact of educational technology on student achievement: What the most current research has to say.* Milken Family Education. Available: http://www.mff.org/publications/publications.taf?page=161 [1999, 2/1/99].

Schwier, R.A. (2001). Catalysts, emphases, and elements of virtual learning communities: Implications for research and practice. *Quarterly Review of Distance Education, 2*(1), 5–18.

Scriven, M. (Ed.). (1967). *The methodology of evaluation* (Vol. 1). Chicago: Rand McNally.

Simonson, M., Schlosser, C.A., & Hanson, D. (1999). Theory and distance education: A new discussion. *American Journal of Distance Education, 13*(1), 60–75.

Souder, W.E. (1993). The effectiveness of traditional vs. satellite delivery in three management of technology master's degree programs. *American Journal of Distance Education, 7*(1), 37–53.

Weiss, R., & Morrison, G.R. (1998, February 18–20). *Evaluation of a graduate seminar conducted by listserv.* Presented at the 1998 annual meeting of the Association of Educational Communications and Technology, St. Louis, MO.

CHAPTER 18

WHAT IS NEXT IN THE MEDIA AND METHODS DEBATE?

Richard E. Clark

The debate about the learning benefits of media has extended over eighty years. While the arguments have evolved, the debate is still very much alive. An increasing number of universities with instructional technology degree programs are using the debate as a teaching tool. A number of faculty ask students to familiarize themselves with debate positions to better understand the process of using research to make design and development decisions (see examples in the web site addresses described in the Preface to this book). In some cases, the debate has become a question on "end of program" university examinations. In addition, the recently renewed enthusiasm for distance education has led yet another group of technology advocates to seek media comparison evidence. Thus, the goal of this final chapter is to bring the argument up to date as this book goes to press.

THREE NEW DEVELOPMENTS

After discussing contemporary views with many of the key contributors to the debate, it is my view that a number of key positions have evolved significantly in the last few years. This chapter identifies at least three important trends: First, Bob Kozma, the most active debater, now agrees that there is no past evidence for a causal connection between media (or media attributes) and learning. Yet he holds out hope that new and less restrictive research methods will find evidence for the benefit of more complex interactions between media and learners. The second change is a product of recent developments in cognitive instructional psychology. We now understand much more about the way that different modes of information are processed in "working memory." Some researchers believe that these new insights will help designers format a number of the display components of the visual and aural information in multimedia instruction. This chapter will briefly describe the research of John Sweller from Australia and Richard Mayer from U.C. Santa Barbara concerning these developments. Third, Tom Cobb at the Université du Québec à Montréal Canada has suggested an approach called "cognitive efficiencies" that might offer new insights about the benefits of instructional media and media attributes. Cobb's approach is very compatible with the new information about working memory and provides a new set of hypotheses for research.

KOZMA'S CURRENT POSITION

Kozma (1994b) in an article for the *School Library Media Quarterly*, suggests that "Perhaps it is time to go beyond our concern with 'proving' that media 'cause' learning so that we can begin to explore the question in more complex ways ... we should ask ... in what ways can we use the capabilities of media to influence learning for particular students, tasks and situations?". His view is that research designs drawn from behavioral psychology have forced the question into unnaturally simplified forms that strangle the complex, multifaceted processes that characterize instructional interactions with new electronic media. He argues that our current research designs do not permit any evidence for unique learning benefits from media. Yet he believes in the potential of new media to enhance learning if it is used correctly by instructional designers. Kozma (1994b) suggests four approaches to questions about media and learning: (1) ground all theories of learning in the cognitive and social processes that support knowledge construction; (2) Define media in ways that are "compatible" with knowledge construction processes; (3) conduct research on the ways that characteristics of media interact with and influence construction processes; and (4) design instruction in ways that embed the use of media in knowledge construction processes. He goes on to describe a number of "possible" or "suggestive" uses of various kinds of media. For example,

> ...the processing capabilities of computers can influence the mental representations and cognitive processes of learners. Their transformation capabilities can connect symbolic expressions (such as graphs) to the actual world. Their proceduralizing capabilities can allow students to manipulate dynamic, symbolic representations of abstract, formal constructs that are frequently

missing from their mental models in order to construct more accurate and complete mental representations of complex phenomena.

CLARK'S CURRENT POSITION

Kozma's recent recommendations for research on media and learning are nearly identical to the view that Gabi Salomon and I made at the end of our Third Handbook of Research on Teaching article (see the last part of Chapter 3 in this book) fifteen years ago. Salomon and I agreed with Kozma that there is no evidence for a causal connection between media and learning.

Where we continue to disagree is about the future benefit to be derived from asking about whether media or media attributes are "causal" in learning and about the future benefits of conducting what he terms "qualitative, cognitive and social case studies and other innovative methodologies ... (rather than) traditional experimental studies" (personal communication, June 2, 2001). I share Kozma's enthusiasm about qualitative data and case study methods. Yet the data that result from these approaches are primarily useful for hypothesis construction or evaluation and do not permit conclusions about, or generalizations to, future instructional events. One distressing feature of current thinking about research design is that when a traditional design does not provide evidence for a set of variables we "know" to be powerful, we throw out the design and offer the speculative hope of results with a different set of designs. When scientific methods applied to instructional media questions does not provide the evidence we expect for the benefits of media, some reject scientific method. In general, there is a disturbing recent trend in media research to "kill the messenger" when we do not like the message. Yet it is possible that Kozma's future hopes for limited but important effects of media attributes might find support in future research.

Kozma (1994b) recommends embedding the study of media attributes in research and theory about cognitive knowledge construction processes. I agree totally and suggested a similar approach in my work with Gavriel Salomon (Chapter 3). In fact, it was not until the cognitive, multifaceted research recommended by Kozma was designed and conducted in the 1970s and 1980s that I made the clear statement that media and attributes of media do not have unique effects on learning. Gavriel Salomon agreed with me. Salomon was responsible for many of those early cognitive studies. While the research designs Kozma suggests for the future have been conducted for many years in the past, compelling results are not yet forthcoming. Kozma (1994b) acknowledges that no clear evidence exists for the benefit of the methodology he recommends. Yet it is possible that we might find limited benefits in the future.

Kozma may be suggesting something very similar to the argument that Gary Morrison advances in Chapter 17. Morrison recommends media comparisons for the "equivalent" evaluation of different delivery platforms for instruction. I understand Morrison's suggestion to be something like the following: Different mixes of media provide different types or "affordances" for presenting similar instructional methods. Morrison discusses this strategy in reference to the evaluation of distance education courses and a comparison with the design and impact of "live" on-campus versions of the same course. He suggests the following example of how equivalent evaluation can identify beneficial instructional methods in different settings and media:

> Classroom discussions are synchronous and are typically limited to class time. A course offered online is not bound by the same classroom-meeting time frame of the more traditional class. A graduate level seminar course might only meet one evening a week and have a different topic of discussion each week. In contrast, the same seminar offered online would require different discussion strategies. A research study might ask how student discussions differ between a classroom and an online course. By using a media replication strategy, the method used in the classroom course might follow a more traditional format of the instructor asking a question to start the discussion and then facilitating the student interactions. Although it is possible to hold a synchronous online chat for three or four hours, there is a fatigue factor to consider as well as interest due to constraints of the technology (although, it is harder to create a verbose reply!). The method used in the online course might be an asynchronous discussion using either a mailing list or discussion forum for posting responses. An analysis of the two discussions might reveal that the online discussion lasts a full seven days as opposed to a single evening, the online posts are given more thought, and the online students are more likely to seek additional references to support their arguments (Weiss & Morrison, 1998). If students in both treatments achieve the objectives, then the two strategies are considered equivalent. If the online discussion was found to be significantly or qualitatively better, then future research might investigate its use in both an online and classroom course. Research questions might ask if it is the asynchronous time frame, having access to additional reading materials while posting comments, or the lack of face-to-face contact of the online discussion that influences the discussion. (Morrison, this volume, Chapter 17, pp. 323–324)

Yet Kozma's point seems to go beyond equivalency of results. I suspect that he believes evidence will be forthcoming that for some learners (perhaps only one or two people) a very specific and possibly complex set of media attributes, perhaps including features such as the immediacy of interaction, *will be* important for the achievement of learning objectives on some learning tasks at some point. He wants to find methodologies that will identify these suspected benefits for individuals under specific task and prior knowledge conditions.

One of the conditions where cognitive benefits might be available is suggested by new research on processes that underlie working memory function during learning from instruction.

RECENT EVIDENCE ABOUT VISUAL AND AUDITORY BUFFERS IN WORKING MEMORY

Recently, Mousavi, Lowe, and Sweller (1995) and Mayer (1997) have claimed that presenting novel and difficult science concepts to learners in both auditory and visual symbolic modes results in more learning than information presented in either mode alone—provided that the two modes of information are integrated with each other in time and space. This is the current incarnation of the dated "dual processing theory" (Paivio, 1986). Mousavi et al. (1995) and Mayer's (1997) explanation for their findings is that working memory is connected to both auditory and visual "buffers" that specialize in storing different symbolic representations of information to be learned in each of the two modes. Conscious consideration of information to be learned or used in problem solving is very brief (approximately 3–9 seconds) unless the learner is able to repeat or elaborate. Failure to hold information in short term memory requires that the learner use perceptual and motivational resources to again review information that has been forgotten. Presumably, working memory can independently access identical information content in two different modalities (visual and auditory) from each of the two buffers and therefore increase the duration and quality of information available to learners during cognitive processing (see a discussion of these sensory memory buffers in Bruning et al., 1999, Chapter 2). Thus, providing information to be learned in two integrated modes (pictorial depiction accompanied by auditory narrative) might extend the representational duration of key science concepts during learning for some learners for a vital few seconds.

It is critical to note that Mayer (1997) limits this "learning efficiency" impact of both visual and aural modes of instruction to a very small group of learners. The increased efficiency was primarily useful for students who had a very low prior knowledge and very high visual ability and it primarily influenced recall of information. One might wonder what percentage of students received a significantly enhanced efficiency from both visual and aural forms of instruction? Yet, this area deserves more attention from media researchers since it fits nicely with the current interest in "multimedia instruction." It may also be an example of a unique sensory mode effect on retention during learning described by Kozma (1998).

Split Attention and Redundancy Problems

A related line of research conducted by Sweller (1999) and his colleagues offers cautionary information on the misuse of the sensory mode evidence in multimedia format and design strategies (see Chapter 15). Sweller (1999) describes two types of instructional conditions that often cause students to exceed the limitations on their working memory and so cause learning problems. The split-attention effect "occurs when learners are faced with multiple sources of information (about the same topic) that must be integrated before they can be understood" (p. 22). This effect often occurs when graphic displays and their verbal or aural "explanation" are separated from each other in space and/or time and when neither source of information can "stand alone" and so both sources must be considered together in order for effective learning to occur. The mental effort required to integrate graphic and text components of a display often overload working memory and cause learning difficulties for many learners.

A related phenomenon called the "redundancy effect" occurs when both textual and graphic material on some topic are redundant. Sweller (1999) presents evidence that when students attempt to master the redundant graphic and text information the effort results in an unnecessary and sometimes negative effect on the cognitive load in working memory. Presumably, students invest unnecessary mental effort to integrate redundant messages. It may also be the case that when integration of the redundant messages fails (as it must because no integration is possible) students' perception of failure enhances the violation of the efficacy threshold. The split-attention effect can be eliminated if graphic and verbal information on a topic are fully integrated. The redundancy effect can be eliminated if instructional displays provide only one form of information about a topic (or two fully integrated forms). It would be interesting to investigate the nature of the working memory failures caused by overloading working memory with the split-attention or redundancy effect. Cognitive motivation theory would suggest that overloaded learners in these two conditions would default to focusing on different or novel learning goals (or non learning goals).

Another promising area to examine for evidence of media and media attribute effects on learning is to ask about their capacity to speed learning or make it less effortful or expensive. A recent development in this area which may have solid promise for future research is a recent suggestion to conduct studies on "cognitive efficiencies"

RESEARCH ON COGNITIVE EFFICIENCIES FROM MEDIA

Tom Cobb, a second language learning researcher in Canada has published a criticism of the "media does not cause learning" argument (Cobb, 1997). Cobb makes a very interesting proposal to study the "efficiencies" in learning due to different mixes of media, symbolic modes and media attributes. He suggests that some media and symbolic modes lead to quicker and/or less demanding learning and performance outcomes than other media or symbolic modes for some people and some learning tasks. This prediction sounds very much like Kozma's expectations.

One way to think about Cobb's idea is to generate a question with at least two, interactive independent variables: the media or representational mode used for presenting an instructional method (for instance, an example presented in pictorial or verbal modes or both), and the individual or group differences that would predispose learners to process the method easier and/or faster during learning (for instance, high visual but low verbal ability learners will likely learn faster from pictures than from narrative descriptions of examples). The cost of learning to the student and the instructional provider is, after all, one of the most important issues for those concerned with the delivery of instruction to large numbers of students.

Translating Cobb's suggestion leads to a possible generic hypothesis to guide new research questions in this new area: *Whenever any instructional method is necessary for learning to occur, different media or symbolic modes will have different learning efficiencies for different learners.* Let's consider some examples of this hypothesis and then explore ideas from various research traditions that might advance research on cognitive efficiencies.

The Value of Cognitive Efficiency Studies

To some extent, many of our past research on learning might have unexplored efficiency components. Very few researchers measure the time it takes their subjects to finish learning tasks. Most learning tasks are time limited so that individual differences in learning ability or motivation influence outcome variance. Very few studies report subjects' view of task difficulty and the amount of "mental effort" they perceived was necessary to succeed at various instructional treatments. The small subset of studies that collect information about "time to learn" or "instructional time" (e.g., Benjamin & Bjork, 2000; Reynolds & Walberg, 1991; Thiede & Dunlosky, 1999) and "perceived mental effort to learn" (e.g., Gimino, 2000; Paas, Van Merriënboer, & Adam, 1994; Salomon, 1984) could be plumbed for cognitive efficiency insights. Whenever treatments using similar instructional methods were presented in different symbolic modes or media produce significantly different time and/or effort consequences, we'll find an example of an important cognitive efficiency.

This limitation will give an advantage to learners who more easily process information in the mode and format in which it is presented. If we allowed much more time, is it possible that those who initially failed to learn would catch up? This is one of the key issues debated in the research on the role of intelligence in learning (e.g., Ohlsson, 1998).

Examples of Cognitive Efficiency Questions

Cobb (1997) illustrates research in cognitive efficiencies by inventing a situation where we want to teach someone to recognize the song of a specific species of bird. He describes different media/modes of presenting bird songs to learners including audio recordings and musical notation. He asks "How many hours are needed to learn a bird song with a recording vs. with sheet music?" (p. 26). This approach is entirely consistent with my argument. Some isomorphic representation (example or simulation) of a bird song is a necessary method for recognizing a novel bird song. This method can be translated into a variety of sensory and symbolic modes. Cobb suggests that we show learners the musical notation for the song or play an audio recording of the song. If enough time is allowed for learners and if their motivation is adequate to support their persistence in difficult treatments such as the musical notation of the bird song, then all treatments should eventually produce learning. Yet few media specialists would consider teaching bird songs with musical notation to a majority of learners with adequate hearing and auditory discrimination ability. Is it possible however, that the two modes have different efficiency characteristics for different learners? While the example requires a stretch of the imagination, consider learners who have musical training and auditory discrimination problems. It seems plausible to assume that this small subset of learners might be able to recognize bird songs more efficiently with musical notation than with audio recordings.

Anderson's Economic Theory of Cognition

John Anderson's (1990, 1991) rational theory of cognition is another fertile area for understanding the cognitive efficiencies available from various symbolic modes or media. Anderson has presented compelling evidence that cognitive learning follows Bayesian Statistical formulations of the relationship between the perceived "cost" of mental effort and expected learning "gain." Like most of John Anderson's research, this theory requires considerable effort to understand. His theory of expertise development (Anderson, 1993) was not well understood until it was explained by Ellen Gagne (Gagne et al., 1993). Yet the benefit of his theory for media researchers may be worth the cost of learning and extending it to media and symbolic modes. For example, Anderson presents compelling evidence that when learning concepts, our normative beliefs about the most efficient ways to identify the defining features of concepts control our scanning and selection of features in instructional displays. He suggests that these efficiency beliefs will control both the types of displays we will favor and the rules that we use to determine which of the many features of presented examples and non examples we will use to determine the central tendency of concept definitions. He also provides examples and explanatory economic formulas for the learning of principles and the solving of problems. These three types of knowledge content and tasks (concepts, principles and problem solving) are very similar to the knowledge types used in current instructional design and media production theories.

Five Conditions Needed to Investigate Cognitive Efficiencies

Research on cognitive efficiencies is a compelling opportunity. It seems possible that various features of old and new media may permit some people to learn quicker or with less mental effort. How might we go about investigating this possibility?

First, researchers need a way to conceptualize and measure the cognitive demand of instruction and learning task. The best approach has been described by John Sweller and his colleagues (Paas et al., 1994). Our measurement of mental effort must be consistent with the constructs found in the theories we are testing. We must challenge ourselves to go beyond the self-report of mental effort used in most motivation studies. Our operational definitions of effort must include direct and unobtrusive indicators as well as self report protocols. A recent study of the most promising methods of measuring mental effort during instruction was conducted by Gimino (2000).

Second, we need a commitment to the measurement of the amount of time it takes similar learners to achieve a specific learning criterion in instructional studies. These time measurements must be based on a careful analysis of the context where the learning is occurring and where it will be transferred when it is used (see, Benjamin & Bjork, 2000; Reynolds & Walberg, 1991; Thiede & Dunlosky, 1999 for examples).

Third, we must find temporary solutions to disputes about the measurement of "cognitive processes" during learning (Ohlsson, 1998). As in the case of mental effort, our measurement of cognitive processes is now largely determined by self report which has been found to be inaccurate for more complex learning tasks (Gimino, 2000). We need more creative and more objective ways to observe and measure cognitive processing.

Fourth, we need cost-benefit and cost-effectiveness protocols that are conservative and are connected to research in other areas of learning and performance. I've been impressed with the careful work and excellent insights of Henry Levin from Stanford on the cost effectiveness of computer-based instruction (Levin, Glass, & Meister, 1987). His "replacement method" of determining costs is a very conservative estimate of the economic gains from using technology in a school setting. A recent article by Lombard et al. (1998) is a good place to start for those interested in the larger social costs and benefits of technology. While Lombard et al.'s approach is focused on health psychology and the economic benefit of psychological treatment, it can be adapted to our concern with cognitive efficiency in instruction.

Finally, we need a theory to guide our questions. My recommendation is that we begin with Anderson's (1990, 1991, 1993) rational theory and build on it. We all should remain open to other economically-focused theories of learning and performance. However, we should not be open to shallow, repetitive, narrow and atheoretical research in this area. Since our past research on media and learning suffered from a lack of theoretical focus, our future work on integrated visual and aural information and on cognitive efficiencies should not make the same mistakes.

REFERENCES

Anderson, J.R (1990). *The adaptive character of thought.* Hillsdale, NJ: Lawrence Erlbaum Publishers.

Anderson, J.R. (1991). Is human cognition adaptive? *Behavioral and Brain Sciences, 14*(3), 471–517.

Anderson, J.R. (1993). *Rules of the mind.* Hillsdale, NJ: Lawrence Erlbaum Publishers.

Benjamin, A.S., & Bjork, R.A. (2000). On the relationship between recognition speed and accuracy for words rehearsed via rote versus elaborative rehearsal. *Journal of Experimental Psychology: Learning, Memory and Cognition, 26*(3), 638–648.

Bruning, R.H., Schraw, G., & Ronning, R. (1999). *Cognitive psychology and instruction* (3rd ed.). Upper Saddle River, NJ: Simon and Schuster.

Clark, R.E. (1983). Reconsidering research on learning from media. *Review of Educational Research, 53*(4), 445–459.

Clark, R.E. (1994a). Media will never influence learning. *Educational Technology Research and Development, 42*(2), 21–30.

Clark, R.E. (1994b). Media and method. *Educational Technology Research and Development, 42*(3), 7–10.

Cronbach, L.J., & Snow, R.E. (1977). *Aptitude and instructional method.* New York: Irvington Press.

Cobb, T. (1997). Cognitive efficiency: Toward a revised theory of media. *Educational Technology Research and Development, 45*(4), 21–35.

Gagne, E.D., Yekovich, C., & Yekovich, F. (1993). *The cognitive psychology of school learning* (2nd ed.). New York: Harper Collins.

Gimino, A. (2000). *Factors that influence student's investment of mental effort in academic tasks: A validation and exploratory study.* Unpublished dissertation, Rossier School of Education, University of Southern California.

Kozma, R. (1994a). Will media influence learning: Reframing the debate. *Educational Technology Research and Development, 42*(3), 1–19.

Kozma, R.B. (1994b, Summer). The influence of media on learning: The debate continues. *School Library Media Quarterly, 22*(4), 233–239. Accessed at: http://www.ala.org/aasl/SLMR/slmr_resources/select_kozma.html in July of 2001.

Levin, H., Glass, G., & Meister, G.R. (1987). Cost-effectiveness of computer assisted instruction. *Evaluation Review, 11*(1) 50–72.

Lombard, D., Haddock, C.K., Talcott, G.W., & Reynes, R. (1998). Cost-effectiveness analysis: A primer for psychologists. *Applied and Preventive Psychology, 7,* 101–108.

Mayer, R. (1997). Multimedia learning: Are we asking the right questions? *Educational Psychologist, 32*(1), 1–19.

Mousavi, S., Lowe, R., & Sweller, J (1995). Reducing cognitive load by mixing auditory and visual presentation modes. *Journal of Educational Psychology, 87,* 319–334.

Ohlsson, S. (1998). Spearman's g = Anderson's ACT?: Reflections on the locus of generality in human cognition. *The Journal of The Learning Sciences, 7*(1), 135–145.

Paas, F., Van Merriënboer, J.J., & Adam, J. (1994). Measurement of cognitive load in instructional research. *Perceptual and Motor Skills, 79,* 419–430.

Paivio, A. (1986). *Mental representations: A dual encoding approach.* Oxford: Oxford University Press.

Reynolds, A., & Walberg, H. (1991). A structural model of science achievement. *Journal of Educational Psychology, 83*(1), 97–107.

Salomon, G. (1984). Television is "easy" and print is "tough": The differential investment of mental effort in learning as a function of perceptions and attributions. *Journal of Educational Psychology, 76*(4), 647–658.

Thiede, K., & Dunlosky, J. (1999). Toward a general model of self-regulated study: An analysis of selection of items for study and self-paced study time. *Journal of Experimental Psychology: Learning, Memory and Cognition, 25*(4), 1024–1037.

Weiss, R., & Morrison, G.R. (1998, February 18–20). *Evaluation of a graduate seminar conducted by listserv.* Presented at the 1998 annual meeting of the Association of Educational Communications and Technology, St. Louis, MO.

A BIOGRAPHY OF RICHARD E. CLARK

Michael Molenda

To be published in Molenda, M. (in press, Spring 2002). Richard E. Clark. In A. Kovalchick & K. Dawson (Eds.), *Educational technology: An encyclopedia.* Santa Barbara, CA: ABC-CLIO Publishers. Used by permission.

Richard E. Clark, Ed.D., is Professor of Educational Psychology at University of Southern California, where he has been a member of the faculty and has held various administrative posts since 1978, including Division Head, Educational Psychology and Technology, and Director, Professional Studies and Community Programs. He has been elected a Fellow of the American Psychological Association (Division 15, Educational Psychology), the American Psychological Society, and the Association for Applied Psychology, exceptional recognition for someone who does not have a degree in psychology.

He is best known among educational technology professionals as a critic of the theory that media have direct causative influence on specific types of learning. His publication in 1983 of "Reconsidering Research on Learning From Media" (Clark, 1983) touched off a controversy sometimes summarized as the media-methods debate. Throughout the 1980s and early 1990s he continued to defend his position through point-counterpoint articles in professional journals and panel discussions at academic conferences.

Clark has devoted his efforts since then to exploring what *does* work, the positive side of his media critique. This quest has led him into study, in turn, of human cognition, instructional methods, instructional design processes, motivation theory, and performance interventions. In 2001 he was focusing on writing several books to synthesize these studies into a cognitively-based theory of designing learning environments incorporating motivational features to maximize the transfer of learning to real-world accomplishments.

Clark's professional quests have been shaped by his life experiences, like most other people. Born September 15, 1940 in Howell, Michigan, near Detroit, he was the eldest of nine children, so he took on parental type responsibilities early. From his mother he learned the indispensability of making lists and planning ahead in order to cope with the demands of taking care of others as well as oneself. He attended a small rural elementary school that featured multi grade organization, not as a progressive experiment, but as a necessity. The inquisitive child was able to move ahead without hindrance, reading "above his grade level" right from the start. As he says, "I didn't get bored with school until high school." High school was more conventional, leading to the more conventional sort of indifference to academics. However, during his teen years Clark suffered a back injury that led to a lifelong disability that altered the course of his life. A doctor warned him that he had better prepare to make his way in the world with his mind since his physical capabilities would be limited. From that point young Dick began to plan for post-secondary education, the first in his family history to do so.

After a false start at the University of Michigan he found a place and a mentor—Bob Dye—at Western Michigan University, majoring in History and Political Science, graduating in 1963. Looking for a practical career and needing financial aid, he took advantage of an offer of a full scholarship to enter the then-new Annenberg School for Communication at the University of Pennsylvania to study journalism. By the time he completed the master's degree he was married and had a son, so finding a job became a top priority. Coincidentally, the founder of the Annenberg School, Walter H. Annenberg, was also the owner of Philadelphia television station WFIL which was undergoing a strike at the time. Annenberg hired virtually all the School's graduates to fill vacant jobs at the station, including Clark, who became an associate producer. Such an entry level job did not provide enough income to support a family, so Clark took another position, working mornings at WFIL and evenings at WHYY, the public television station in Philadelphia.

After about a year, an opportunity arose out of connections made while producing a public television series, "The Compleat Gardener." It led to the agricultural extension program at Rutgers University, where Clark had responsibility for a radio network and other communication operations. Shortly, though, Bob Dye, his mentor at his alma mater, Western Michigan

University, beckoned. There he became director of broadcasting, including oversight of a campus-wide dial-access audiovisual delivery system. The position also included an appointment as assistant professor in General Studies. As he now seemed to be on a career path in higher education rather than commercial television, Clark realized that he would need to undertake doctoral studies at some point.

After exploring options for doctoral study, in 1967 Clark decided on the Mass Communications program at Indiana University, attracted by the chance to work with Keith Mielke, then a leading researcher on the effects of television on children, later senior researcher for Children's Television Workshop. After a year, Clark qualified for an NDEA fellowship and transferred to the Ed.D. program in the Educational Media (soon to be Instructional Systems Technology) department, entering what was to become his ultimate professional home, the School of Education.

In Instructional Systems Technology (IST) he was influenced by researchers such as Malcolm Fleming, who encouraged young researchers to have confidence and pursue their own interests, and Gavriel Salomon, who pursued hard—and important—questions. His classmates included a number of future leaders of the field, including Sivasailam Thiagarajan, Thomas Schwen, W. Howard Levie, Diane Dormant, and Harold Stolovitch.

On completing doctoral studies, Clark was recruited to Stanford University, in 1971 joining the staff in the Research and Development Center on Teaching, later becoming one of the founding leaders of the ERIC Clearinghouse on Educational Media and Technology (known as Information and Technology in 2001). Although he had an adjunct appointment in the School of Education, this was not a tenure-track position, so when Syracuse University asked him to become associate professor, later full professor, and chair of the instructional technology program in 1974 he left Stanford for Syracuse.

The Syracuse program, then known as Area of Instructional Technology, had recently gone through major curriculum revision, but Clark felt that inquiry was not sufficiently embedded in the graduate program. In a detailed memo to the faculty he argued,

> ...my personal concern is to communicate my strong desire that we grow away from the training of people who are primarily concerned with technical skills in developing instruction, evaluating programs, managing resource centers, producing films and television programs, etc. That we change our focus to grow towards the training of people who are more skilled in inquiring about problems and their solutions ... All student activities therefore that involve the actual development of instruction or production of films, etc. should be conducted in an atmosphere of *constant critical discussion of the usefulness of the concepts being acquired and the process being employed.* [emphasis added] (Ely, 1998, p. 59)

The theme of "constant critical discussion" could be said to be one of the hallmarks of Clark's career. He consistently exemplifies a questioning attitude, looking at fundamental problems and seeking evidence to reach a conclusion. This stance is neatly summarized in his article (Clark, 1984) responding to Heinich's propositions about the central concerns of instructional technology: "As responsible professionals, our only ethical choice is to ensure that we accept the evidence for the products we advocate" (p. 230).

That search for evidence led Clark into the center of the debate that prompted a hundred websites and became virtually synonymous with his name, the media-methods debate. The debate revolved around the issue of whether media in themselves affect learning. Throughout his graduate studies Clark had struggled with this question, unable to fully accept the intuitively obvious supposition that media, such as films and television programs, have a dramatic impact on audiences in ways that books and lectures cannot. It's probably fair to say that his insistent quest for proof of this supposition was found to be annoying to his colleagues, although tolerated and sometimes encouraged by his teachers.

A decade later Clark was still unsatisfied with the answers being proposed so he took a sabbatical leave in 1981 and devoted himself full-time to combing through every bit of the research literature related to media and learning. It was an intense and exhaustive effort. The result was his famous critique, "Reconsidering Research on Learning from Media," published in the prestigious *Review of Educational Research* (Clark, 1983), which has become the most frequently cited source in its field. In it he presented evidence for the hypothesis that instructional methods have been confounded with media and that methods are what influence learning. He offered the analogy that different media were similar to the different delivery systems developed by pharmacists to introduce medicine into the body. Tablets, liquid suspensions, suppositories, and injections are all different "media," but their effect is dependent on whatever the "active ingredient" is. Pepto-Bismol soothes traveler's dysentery whether it is taken in tablet or liquid suspension form. What matters is the active ingredient, bismuth. The "medium," of course, has an effect on the speed of the effect, the cost of the effect, and the convenience of the effect, but it does not *cause* the effect. That is, media selection ought to be based on logistical considerations—availability, expense, production requirements, and the like—because there is always more than one medium that has the capacity to provide the cognitive experience needed for effective learning.

This hypothesis was not new or original, as Clark went to pains to point out. It had been offered earlier by Mielke (1968) and by Schramm (1977) among others. The greater attention attracted by Clark's version may be attributed to the times, the venue, or, more likely, the strength of the claim made by Clark. He made the explicit and clear claim that there were *no* learning benefits possible and urged that researchers not continue to waste effort on the question until a "new theory" was developed.

This unpopular position was not one that Clark arrived at on purpose. He reports that he started out expecting to find evidence that media *did* make a difference:

> In 1980, when I began the two years of focused reading of media research which resulted in the original publication, I was taking a challenge from Bob Heinich (the former editor of *AV Communication Review*) to develop a specific taxonomy of media and learning outcomes. I was also working with Gabi Salomon on what became our *Handbook of Research on Teaching* review of media studies (Clark & Salomon, 1986). In those days before electronic mail, we were sending each other ten or more single-spaced letters of detail and argument as our manuscript developed. I began with the expectation that media were a significant element in any educational reform which sought achievement gains. The problem was that as I reviewed the evidence it seemed clear that it did not support my expectations or intuition. (Clark, 1991, p. 35)

A flurry of responses to Clark's 1983 article were published between the mid-1980s and 1990. Most of these attempted to suggest qualifications to the hypothesis or to define terms more precisely in order to explicate the constructs of media and method. It was not until 1991 that someone accepted the challenge to propose a "new theory." Robert Kozma's (1991) retort focused on the distinction between "learning *from* media" (Clark's phrase) and "learning *with* media" (Kozma's phrase). Kozma, Principal Scientist, Center for Technology in Learning, SRI International (at the time of the publication, Associate Professor, School of Education, University of Michigan) presented a new theoretical framework—basically the Constructivist one—that envisions the learner actively collaborating *with* the mediated message to construct meaning. His argument essentially was

> ...that capabilities of a particular medium, in conjunction with methods that take advantage of these capabilities, *interact with and influence the ways learners represent and process information* and may result in more or different learning when one medium is compared to another for certain learners and tasks. (p. 179, emphasis added)

This reframing of the issue stimulated even more debate, which raged in the pages of instructional technology journals and in panel discussions at professional conferences for several years, culminating in two special issues of *Educational Technology Research and Development* (42 #2 and 3, 1994) devoted exclusively to this debate. Clark's conclusion to this climactic debate is captured in the title of his contribution to the special issues,

"Media Will Never Influence Learning" (Clark, 1994). He contends that Kozma did not directly address the distinction between medium and method nor how the effects of these interacting variables might be separated; nor did he provide convincing evidence to support his theory. On the other side, Kozma has continued to espouse his viewpoint:

> But it seems to me that the interaction between medium and method (that is, the extent to which they "share" the variance) is the crux of the whole argument. The most powerful attribute of any medium is its ability to enable and constrain methods. The methods you can use with computers are very different than the methods you can use with video and this is because of the unique capabilities of the computer vis-à-vis video. (Kozma, 2000)

After 1994 Clark decided to move on from defending an essentially negative point back to his original quest to discover what *does* make a difference in instruction. His platform after 1978 has been as a tenured full professor in the School of Education at the University of Southern California (USC). From 1992 to 1996 he was head of the division of Educational Psychology and Technology. In response to invitations from institutions around the world he has traveled widely, with extensive immersion as teacher and consultant particularly in Ireland, Germany, the Netherlands, and Indonesia. In the early 1990s he took leave from USC to spend two years residing in Dublin, Ireland, creating and managing his own training consulting firm, Atlantic Training, Inc. He managed to out-compete some of the largest and most prestigious international consulting firms to win training contracts with the Irish Electricity Supply Board and the European Patent Office. These provided the opportunity to test his ideas about "what works" in training and education.

His focus in this latter period has been on the cognitive processes underlying teaching and learning, seeking instructional methods that facilitate the sorts of cognitive processes that lead to long-term retention and transfer to real life. Along the way he discovered the polar opposite of robust instructional methods, coining the term "mathemathantics" to refer to instructional methods that "kill" learning; that is, experimental treatments that turn out to be significantly *inferior* to the control treatment (Clark 1989).

This pursuit of powerful interventions has led to an increasing appreciation of the importance of motivation and the development of Clark's own model of motivation (Clark, 1999). This, in turn, opens the door to the world of interventions beyond instruction, leading to the domain of human performance technology. So his most recent research has been on the larger issue of what sorts of interventions in the whole working environment make a difference for human performance. His commitment to this larger issue led to the founding of a new doctoral program at USC in 1996,

Human Performance in the Workplace. This program has attracted national renown as the most prominent doctoral program devoted to human performance technology. Some fifty scholars have completed doctoral degrees in this program.

These vast and highly influential accomplishments have been spurred by a passionate conviction that one can accomplish great things by focusing attention on basic, urgent problems and then investing one's total effort on the pursuit of a solution. His advice to young researchers, "Believe in your vision, but follow the evidence!"

REFERENCES

Clark, R.E. (1983). Reconsidering research on learning from media. *Review of Educational Research, 53*(4), 445–459.

Clark, R.E. (1984). "Where's the beef?": A reply to Heinich. *Educational Communication and Technology Journal, 32*(4), 229–232.

Clark, R.E. (1989). When teaching kills learning: Research on mathemathantics. In H.N. Mandl, N. Bennett, E. de Corte, & H.F. Freidrich (Eds.) *Learning and instruction: European research in an international context* (Vol. II). London: Pergamon.

Clark, R.E. (1991, February). When researchers swim upstream: Reflections on an unpopular argument about learning from media. *Educational Technology,* pp. 34–40.

Clark, R.E. (1994). Media will never influence learning. *Educational Technology Research and Development, 42*(2), 21–29.

Clark, R.E. (1999). Motivation systems. In D. Langdon, K. Whitesides, & M. McKenna (Eds.) *Intervention resource guide: 50 performance technology tools.* Somerset, NJ: Jossey-Bass.

Ely, D. (1998) *An evolution of educational technology: Celebrating the Syracuse program at fifty.* Syracuse, NY: Instructional Design, Development and Evaluation, School of Education, Syracuse University.

Kozma, R.B. (1991). Learning with media. *Review of Educational Research, 61*(2), 179–211.

Kozma, R.B. (2000). *Bob Kozma's response on the great media debate.* Online document. http://hagar.up.ac.za/rbo/construct/kozma.html. Accessed January 24, 2001.

Mielke, K.W. (1968). Questioning the questions of ETV research. *Educational Broadcasting, 2,* 6–15.

Schramm, W. (1977). *Big media, little media.* Beverly Hills, CA: Sage.

INDEX